The Catholic Church In Peru, 1821-1985

A Social History

Jeffrey Klaiber, S.J.

The Catholic Church In Peru, 1821-1985

A Social History

The Catholic University of America Press
Washington, D.C.

This work is a translation, with a few revisions to bring it up to date, of the original work in Spanish, *La Iglesia en el Perú: su historia social desde la independencia* (Lima: Pontificia Universidad Católica del Perú, 1988).

Copyright © 1992
The Catholic University of America Press
All rights reserved
Printed in the United States of America

The paper used in this publication meets the minimum requirements of American National Standards for Information Science—Permanence of Paper for Printed Library materials, ANSI Z39.48-1984.
∞

Library of Congress Cataloging-in-Publication Data
Klaiber, Jeffrey L.
    [Iglesia en el Perú. English]
    The Catholic Church in Peru, 1821–1985 : a social history / by Jeffrey Klaiber.
       p. cm.
    Translation of: La Iglesia en el Perú.
    Includes bibliographical references and index.
    1. Catholic Church—Peru—History. 2. Peru—Church history.
    I. Title.
    BX1484.2K4213 1991
    282'.85'09034—dc20   90-29013
    ISBN 0-8132-0747-9 (alk. paper)

To the Little Kingdom of
San Cayetano, El Agustino, Lima

Contents

Preface	ix
1. A Panoramic View: The Nineteenth and Twentieth Centuries	1
2. A Church in Crisis: The Priest Shortage	38
3. The Militant Church, 1855–1930: Genesis and Development	59
4. The Resurgence of Religious Life: Pastors, Missionaries, and Nurses	102
5. The Resurgence of Religious Life: The Teaching Orders and Congregations	136
6. The Rural and Andean Church	172
7. The Militant Laity, 1930–1955	207
8. The Challenge of Modernization and the Social Question	245
9. The Church and the Military, 1968–1975	276
10. The Social-Pastoral Church, 1975–	300
Conclusion	359
Notes	365
Bibliography	393
Index	409

Preface

This general history of the church in Peru since independence is intended to fill a lacuna in contemporary studies of that Andean republic. The pastoral visit of Pope John Paul II in 1985, as well as his second visit in 1988, revealed the depth of religious sentiment of the vast majority of Peruvians. But it is not necessary to refer to a dramatic occasion such as a papal visit to demonstrate that religion is an important social phenomenon in Peru and in the rest of Latin America. To appreciate that fact, it is sufficient to observe the literally hundreds of religious manifestations that take place every year in every city, town, and village in Peru. The manifestations range from the great Lord of Miracles procession that takes place each October in Lima to the processions in honor of the patron saints in every little community in the Andes. There already exists a significant body of literature on the phenomenon known as "popular religiosity." In a previous book I studied the use of popular religious symbols in Indian uprisings and in modern political parties, especially in the Aprista Party.* Liberation theology is another theme that has attracted worldwide interest. The fact that thousands of Peruvians of the popular classes take theology seriously is another proof of the vitality of the newly renovated Catholic church in Peru and in the rest of Latin America. But in the midst of the many interesting studies on popular religiosity and theology there is a noticeable absence: a study of the church itself.

The five-volume *Historia de la Iglesia en el Perú* of the Jesuit historian Rubén Vargas Ugarte covers the colonial period and the nineteenth century. Many articles and several theses have been written on aspects of the church in the twentieth century, but there is no general history of the church covering both the nineteenth and the twentieth centuries. Although this work is limited to the postindependence period (which in Peru begins in 1821), I will give a brief overview of the salient features of the colonial church in the first chapter in order to show how those features influenced the course of later church history. My objective is to

---

Religion and Revolution in Peru, 1824–1976 (Notre Dame, 1977).

trace the evolution of the church from the end of the colonial period to John Paul II's visit in 1985. I also intend this to be a "social" history, that is, one that stresses the dynamic and fluid relationship between church and society. Furthermore, although this is a study of the "official" institutional church, which includes bishops, priests, religious, and men and women lay leaders, I aim to highlight especially the relationship between the church and the popular classes.

My basic point of reference is the church of the Second Vatican Council and the episcopal conferences of Medellín and Puebla. These watershed ecclesial encounters, which have so decisively shaped the course of events in the contemporary church, also offer key criteria for discerning which tendencies and movements of the past have been especially important for the evolution of the church. I have also had recourse to some insights into the Latin American church of other specialists such as the sociologist Ivan Vallier and the historian Enrique Dussel who is the president of CEHILA: Comisión para Escribir la Historia de la Iglesia en América Latina (Commission for Writing the History of the Church in Latin America), a project in which I have participated. My participation in CEHILA provided me the opportunity to learn much about the church in the rest of Latin America. It was also the beginning of many friendships with Latin American Catholics and Protestants who are committed to the same quest for justice and peace. I am also indebted to Father Antonine Tibesar, O.F.M., my doctoral dissertation adviser. His vast knowledge of the colonial Latin American church was certainly helpful to me in carrying out this present project. There are many other authors and friends that have influenced different parts of this work whom I will cite at the appropriate place. Naturally, the final synthesis, the chronology, and the different interpretations of each period are entirely my own.

Many different sources were used to write this work. I consulted the church archives of Lima, Cuzco, Trujillo, and Arequipa. The Rubén Vargas Ugarte collection in the main Jesuit residence in Lima was especially helpful. I visited the libraries of the Franciscans in Arequipa and in Rímac, Lima. I was also able to review practically all the Catholic newspapers of any importance in postindependent Peru, in Lima and in the provinces. *El Deber* (The Duty) of Arequipa and *El Amigo del Clero* (The Friend of the Clergy) in Lima were of exceptional value. In order to write the histories of the religious orders and congregations that went to Peru after 1821, I went directly to all their provincial or moth-

Preface

erhouses in Peru to consult their respective archives. Also, I interviewed at least forty representatives of those orders and congregations to fill in where the written materials left off. There are also certain documentation centers that greatly facilitate research on the church in Peru: in Lima, the Bartolomé de las Casas Center, the International Movement of Catholic Students (MIEC in Spanish), and the *Latin America Press* (which is published simultaneously in Spanish under the title *Noticias Aliadas*) of the Maryknoll Fathers; and in Cuzco, the Las Casas Center. Certain publications are especially helpful to follow events of the contemporary church: *Páginas* and the news bulletin, *Informativo quincenal*, both put out by Centro de Estudios y Publicaciones. I interviewed numerous eyewitnesses, who were also frequently the principal actors in the story itself, in order to write the history of the church for the past fifty years. I myself have been part of this historical process since I arrived in Peru in 1963.

Some parts of this work were published previously as articles: a section of the second chapter on the priest shortage was published in *Histórica* (the Catholic University of Peru); parts of chapters 3 and 4 were published in *The Americas* under the title "The Catholic Lay Movement in Peru" (see bibliography). I also wish to express gratitude to the Fathers of Maryknoll for a "Price-Walsh Fellowship" that helped me to carry out the initial stages of research.

Everywhere in Peru I have found a spirit of cooperation and hospitality, qualities of the Peruvian people in general but most of all of the committed Christians. I hope that this church history proves to be of use to them as well as to Latin Americanists in general who are rediscovering the importance of this very old but very young institution.

Lima, 1990   JEFFREY KLAIBER, S.J.

The Catholic Church In Peru, 1821-1985

A Social History

1
A Panoramic View
The Nineteenth and Twentieth Centuries

The Colonial Church: External Signs

Judging by certain external signs, it would seem that the church on the eve of independence (1821) was a solidly organized institution, with ample financial resources, apparently well prepared to face whatever crises might arise with relative ease. Thanks to some contemporary reports, complemented by recent studies, it is possible to gain a more or less exact idea of the social and economic reality of the colonial church.

Ten suffragan dioceses depended upon the archdiocese of Lima: Cuzco, Arequipa, Huamanga (Ayacucho), Trujillo, Mainas, Quito, Santiago de Chile, La Concepción, Cuenca, and Panama. Along with Lima the first five of these episcopal sees formed the basic structure of the Peruvian church after independence. In 1792 the Viceroyalty of Peru had about 1,818 priests belonging to the secular clergy and 1,891 priests and brothers belonging to religious life to serve a population of approximately 1,072,122 inhabitants.[1] Nor was this a "foreign" church because the vast majority of the secular clergy consisted of creoles, some of whom were bishops: Goyeneche in Arequipa, Moscoso y Peralta and Armendáriz in Cuzco.[2] In his report for the year 1822, Archbishop Las Heras noted that there were between seventy and eighty seminarians in the archdiocese of Lima.[3]

Economically, the church gave the impression of being a solidly established institution, though somewhat less wealthy than the church in New Spain. Of the 3,941 buildings in Lima in 1792, some 1,135 were churches, chapels, schools, hospitals, convents, and so on, that belonged to the church.[4] According to another testimony, in the viceregal capital there were some sixty-seven churches and chapels, nineteen convents for religious men, and fourteen monasteries for religious women.[5] The viceroy received an annual salary of 61,500 pesos and, according to some contemporary sources, the archbishop followed him closely with a salary of 60,000 pesos yearly. By the time of independence, however, this princely salary had been reduced to about 43,000 pesos a year.[6] The members of the cathedral chapter also received appreciable salaries, each member according to his rank, but the ordinary parish priests received considerably less. Nevertheless, even the lowliest missionary living in a far-flung point in the jungle was guaranteed a fixed salary. According to a report of Hipólito Rangel, the bishop of Mainas, a priest in an Indian parish in his diocese received 250 pesos yearly, a sum that placed him on the same level as a gentleman of a modest but respectable condition.[7] As a consequence of their expulsion in 1767, the Jesuits lost considerable properties throughout the entire viceroyalty.[8] But the other orders and the great monasteries and convents of Lima, Arequipa, Trujillo, Huamanga, and Cuzco continued to depend economically upon a great number of haciendas and agrarian properties.[9]

With the expulsion of the Society of Jesus, a vacuum was also created in the area of education, but to a large extent this was filled in by other orders or the secular clergy. In general, the schools, universities, and seminaries of the church were centers of the Enlightenment, and some of them even became focal points for the reformist ideas that gave rise to the independence movement. It was certainly not an "obscurantist" church, as some nineteenth-century authors claimed. On the contrary, the obscurantist minds that did exist were but a minority attempting to block the advance of a clergy that was increasingly liberal and creole.[10] The Inquisition, which today symbolizes all that was censurable in the colonial church, was in reality an institution increasingly looked down upon within the church itself, for it directed its efforts to investigate the intellectual activities not only of the laity, but especially of the clergy.

These external signs, however, do not say much about the internal reality of the church. For example, they clearly establish that the church was not a "missionary" or a "foreign" one, although many *peninsulares* (Spaniards) still held key posts in the convents and monasteries of the religious. Nevertheless, a century and a half after independence, the Peruvian church virtually had turned into a "missionary" church with a notable presence of foreigners in it. Obviously, there must have been some profound weaknesses in the church that these external signs hid. In time, these internal fissures became more evident, until they came to constitute a structural weakness in the entire edifice. We can appreciate the nature of this crisis by examining more closely, first, the social context in which the church functioned, and second, the ecclesial context.

The Social Context: Colonial Latin America

It is important to underline the fundamental idea that to a large extent the church in Peru, as in any other place in the Catholic world, was influenced, molded, and conditioned by the social milieu in which it existed. The church does not live an isolated existence within the society in which it functions. Although this may seem rather obvious, it is necessary to emphasize the fact that there is a relationship of mutual influence between church and society. Many of the problems the church faces today are the consequence, not necessarily of certain erroneous decisions made by the church, but rather of the type of society in which it exists. It should be evident, for example, that between the Catholic church in Europe, the United States, and Latin America there are profound differences. In the United States there arose a Catholicism that, at least until after Vatican II, was characterized by a high degree of regular observance on the part of the faithful. By way of contrast, relatively few baptized Catholics in Latin America practice their religion with any degree of regularity. These contrasts serve to highlight the fact that the Catholic church does not function in exactly the same way in all societies. It would be well, therefore, to examine those characteristics peculiar to Latin America in order to understand how they influenced the development of the church.

The "Distinct Tradition"

Colonial Latin American society reflected many of the same characteristics as those of medieval Europe: the organization of its members in hierarchically subordinate "corporations" under the monarch, the prevalence of a paternalistic vision of life that governed all relations among social classes, and the omnipresence of the church at all levels of society from top to bottom. But there also existed, to use the phrase of Howard Wiarda, a "distinct tradition" peculiar to Latin America.[11] Within a Catholic, Spanish, and medieval mold there arose a multiracial society that selectively assimilated certain elements and ways of being typical of the mother country and rejected others. It was not exactly a feudal or a capitalist society, although it possessed elements of both systems. Many authors have agreed upon using the convenient term "corporative" to describe this society: a theoretical model that has the advantage of including such nonmatching categories as "race," "caste," "class," and "status."

With this very apt phrase Lyle McAlister described Latin American colonial society: "There were Indians, castes, nobles, soldiers, priests, merchants, and lawyers, but there were no citizens."[12] In a corporative society the members were organized in "bodies" or "corporations" juridically recognized by the king or the state. Each corporation enjoyed its own privileges and rights granted by the king.

The model that inspired the relations between the monarch and the different corporations, as well as the relations within each corporation, was that of the family or the clan: the father, who is the natural leader, looks out for the common good of the entire family and for the good of each individual. Within each corporation there could coexist different hierarchies or grades. In the colonial church, which was the classic model of a corporation, there was a higher and a lower clergy. In the army there were officers, frequently with titles of nobility, and noncommissioned officers. The guild represented a professional corporation: the master assumed the role of "father" of the family with respect to the laborers and apprentices. The basic loyalty of a member of society was to his or her respective corporation and to the king and not to an abstract political entity, such as the "nation," above or apart from these two fundamental realities.

In Latin America the first and fundamental division of all inhabitants was between the "Republic of the Spanish" and the "Republic of the Indians." This was the juridical concept that justified the creation of the reductions and the missions in all of Latin America. Reductions were essentially towns for Indians, created with the aim of protecting the indigenous population from the Spanish and of facilitating the evangelization of the Indians. They also accelerated the process of Hispanization, which included learning Spanish and assimilating the Spanish mode of living in "civilization." Finally, the reorganization of the Indians in special towns also placed an abundant labor supply at the disposition of the Spanish to tap for work in the mines or for any other kind of task that required forced labor. Within this system of exploitation, however, each town maintained its traditional system of caciques (chieftains), who functioned under the supervision of the king's official and the priest, the two authorities most present in the lives of the Indians. The "Republic of the Indians" was in reality a fiction, because it did not place the Indians on an equal footing with creole-Spanish society. On the contrary, the former were subordinated to the latter. Nevertheless, even within the colonial Indian world, race, class, and status were all intermixed. As Emilio Harth Terré has observed, there were Indian caciques who had their own black slaves.[13]

Centralism and Paternalism

In colonial society there were no horizontal relations among the different groups. Rather, the relations were vertical, between each corporation and the king or his representatives: the viceroy, the *audiencia* (local governing board), the *corregidor* (the king's official directly in charge of the Indians), or the bishop. The linchpin that held all the different "kingdoms" and social groups together was the king. Government was essentially personalistic and paternalistic: the king was above the laws and other written norms. The very fragmentation of society into nonintegrated parts reinforced the need for a strong monarchy. To adopt the phrase used of Spain by Ortega y Gasset, Latin America was an invertebrate society: the parts functioned only when they were united to and subordinate to a central authority. When Spain lost its hold on America between 1808 and 1821, Hispanic America underwent a rapid process of regional fragmentation and social disintegration. Throughout the nineteenth century the liberals and the conservatives competed for power with the object of imposing order. But it was really the caudillo, with or without an ideological banner, who imposed order and unity on the different regions. Brazil alone escaped the worst effects of caudillism and regional dispersion, but that was due to a large extent to the fact that it enjoyed its own native monarchy, at least until 1889.

Colonial government was essentially paternalistic: the king and his delegates listened to the complaints of the subjects with the aim of resolving conflicts and of assuring the orderly functioning of society. For their part, the viceroy, the bishops, and other authorities sent reports to the king regarding the state of affairs in their respective jurisdictions. In general, they touched upon the same topics, each from his own perspective. Frequently, their juridical spheres crossed and intersected, a fact that gave rise to much infighting and disputes. This somewhat anarchical system, however, benefited the king, who assumed the different roles of "father," "patron," and "judge." The king stood alone above all others. It was his role to assuage the differences, punish those who upset the established order, and reward those who distinguished themselves for their loyalty and service to the crown. In this system the fundamental model was that of "patron" and "client": each authority in the chain of power was a "client" with respect to his superiors and a "patron" with respect to his inferiors. This was not a modern "rational" bureaucracy that applied the same norms democratically to each and all. Much to the contrary, the bureaucracy responded principally to the desires of the king and his delegates.

Needless to say, this type of personalistic and centralized government gave rise to many abuses of power. Each official or authority could use his position of power to maintain many "clients" in a state of dependency and to favor one group over another with the object of advancing his own status. Also, one gained favors within the bureaucracy by promising to return favors or by paying a bribe. In theory, colonial government was a benevolent paternalism; but in practice, it was a system that institutionalized favoritisms, bribes, the buying and selling of public offices, and other abuses. One practice that typified this relationship between abuses and dependency was the distribution of goods to the Indians. The *corregidor de indios* obtained goods to distribute among the Indians within his jurisdiction. They were then obliged to buy the goods at excessive prices, which caused them to fall into debt to the *corregidor*. In this way the *corregidor* used his political authority to create an economic monopoly over the Indians, who became dependent "clients." Very often the priests who worked among the Indians followed the same practice.[14]

Bourbon Absolutism

The model of a Catholic corporative state corresponded more properly to the era of the Spanish Hapsburgs. In the eighteenth century the Bourbons attempted to modernize the government of Spain, which had fallen economically way behind England, France, and other parts of Europe. Especially in the second half of the century they introduced many reforms in America to reactivate the economy, put new life into the local governments, and strengthen royal power in the face of rising creole demands. They also tried to eliminate many abuses committed against the Indians. The king, Charles III, and his officials saw in the revolution of Tupac Amaru in 1780, as well as the many uprisings of creole townsfolk, clear signs that the old system of government no longer worked. The reforms they proposed were designed to renovate the empire, but necessarily at the expense of some institutions that had sustained the empire for centuries, such as the church, and at the expense of some liberties that the creoles had accumulated. In Spain and in America, the Bourbons subordinated the church to the state and frequently intervened directly in the internal affairs of the religious orders in order to assure their control over the creoles. The expulsion of the Jesuits in 1767 fell within this general strategy. With the Bourbons in the latter part of the eighteenth century the age of benevolent paternalism ended, and the age of enlightened despotism began.

But these reforms came too late to change an entire process already in evolution. In many cases the reforms themselves accelerated the movement toward independence. With the collapse of royal power in America between 1808 and 1821, the creole leaders attempted to fill the vacuum by imposing democratic, constitutional governments in the various regions, often looking to the United States or England for models. But the social reality of Latin America did not favor these democratic experiments: society continued to be quite colonial in its composition and stratification. Furthermore, liberalism was the ideological banner of a very small intellectual elite made up of priests, lawyers, and middle-class landowners. These weak liberal governments were soon swept aside by the caudillos in the nineteenth century and by the military in the twentieth. These latter forces represented the other, and older, tradition of Latin America: authoritarianism and centralism.

The Permanence of the "Distinct Tradition"

The fundamental elements of the colonial Hispanic tradition—paternalism, personalism, the corporatist mentality—reasserted themselves in new and different ways throughout the republican period. The caudillos, whether they were civilians or uniformed soldiers, represented the reincarnation of personal power above laws and constitutions. Some caudillos, such as Ramón Castilla, stood out for their pragmatic idealism: they seized power in order to forge a nation from above. Others, less idealistic, sought mainly fame and riches.

In the twentieth century the populist regimes of the PRI (Party of the Institutionalized Revolution) in Mexico, Perón in Argentina, and Getulio Vargas in Brazil exhibited many of the characteristics of a corporatist state in a modern context. The government of Juan Velasco Alvarado in Peru also displayed many of the traits of a populist corporatism. Each one of these regimes was characterized by "organic statism," a mentality that presumes that all parts of society ought to function harmoniously together under the tutelage of the state in order to achieve a common ideal.[15] The state (or the armed forces) assumes the role of tutor, guide, and coordinator of the other parts: it organizes and directs the participation of the political parties, the labor unions, and the various social classes in order to minimize antagonisms and tensions. The corporate state may be of the right, and hence inclined to favor the middle classes, or it may be more to the left. In this case, it tends to "incorporate" certain sectors of the popular classes within organizations controlled by the state.

But it is not necessary to refer only to authoritarian regimes. The vestiges of the "distinct tradition" are to be found in democratic systems throughout Latin America as well. Under forms of democracy one can discover many ways of acting that are clearly throwbacks to colonial times, such as state bureaucracies that respond only to authoritarian commands issued from above or that operate only with the lubricants of bribes and favoritisms, the prevalence of a single party in society frequently dominated by a charismatic leader, and a suffocating centralism that inhibits local initiative. And if to all of these traits one adds the realities of illiteracy, racism, and the lack of a civic consciousness, then it is apparent that Latin America's colonial heritage is still very much alive.

The Ecclesial Context: A Nonreformed Church

Spain and Portugal were relatively unaffected by the two great revolutions that transformed the societies of northern Europe and the United States: the Protestant Reformation and the industrial revolution. Although Spain distinguished itself as a leader in the Counter-Reformation, it never had to contend with the threat of Protestantism on its own soil. In the words of Ortega y Gasset, "We do not have, nor have we ever had a real heterodoxy as a historical force. The Opposition, as Heterodoxy, has never amounted to more than a list of "outsiders."[16]

For this reason, the Council of Trent did not have the same impact everywhere in the Catholic world. The council (1545–63), which profoundly influenced the church for four centuries, imposed order and instilled discipline in the Catholic church in the face of the advance of the new Protestant religions. Although it clarified many doctrinal points, its principal fruit did not consist in the proclamation of new dogmas, but rather in the creation of a new spirit of militancy within the church. The two reforms, that of Luther and that of the church, had as their consequence the religious awakening of thousands of ordinary Christians who found themselves obliged to opt decisively in favor of one or the other of the two sides. In the Protestant world the Bible reached the masses, thanks to the Gutenberg press and the translations of Luther. In the Catholic world the catechism became the principal book in use among the faithful. Also, new religious orders (notably the Society of Jesus) arose to fortify the Catholic cause on many different levels: in the seminaries, in the universities, in the parishes, and in the countryside, where the concept of the popular mission took shape. For this reason the church historian Jean Delumeau proposed the thesis that in many ways the religious struggles of the sixteenth century, which witnessed intense proselytizing campaigns to win adherents, in fact signified the first real evangelization of many regions of Europe, especially in the countryside where popular Catholicism coexisted with an older paganism.[17]

But the new militancy did not have to be a response to Protestantism alone, as it was in the case of Catholics who lived within Protestant societies or in frontier areas. In Ireland, for example, adhesion to the old faith represented an important part of the rejection of English domination. In Spain the Catholic faith was perceived as an integral part of the upsurge of nationalism that accompanied the Reconquest. Whatever the particular nuances, the Council of Trent was not received in each instance as a list of new precepts to be obeyed, but rather as a revitalization of the faith in the face of an exterior threat. In this sense, though the Protestant Reform did not affect Spain directly, the Counter-Reformation served another function: that of reinforcing the spirit of militancy of the Reconquest.

The Counter-Reformation in America

In Luso-Hispanic America, however, there existed a situation entirely different from that of Europe. To be certain, the great church councils of Mexico and Lima faithfully incorporated the Tridentine legislation within their decrees.[18] Furthermore, the king sent over to the New World only those religious orders that had been reformed, such as the Franciscans, or totally new ones, such as the Jesuits, with the hope of avoiding many of the same problems that had produced the Reformation in Europe. Nevertheless, the principal task that confronted the councils and the missionary orders in the New World was not the need to reconquer European Christians, but rather the evangelization of thousands of Indians, with a mentality and culture profoundly different from that of Europe.

In the New World the missionaries encountered ancient indigenous religions, like those in the Andean regions, that consisted of local animistic cults with elements of pantheism and totemism. Those religions had no real point of comparison with the structure or the philosophical system of Catholicism. For this reason José Carlos Mariátegui expressed the opinion that there never was a real evangelization, precisely because the Indians did not resist the new religion; on the contrary, they accepted it with great docility, though not with great profundity.[19] No doubt this judgment is partially true, but it is also very simplistic. The messianic movement of Taki Onqoy clearly proves that there was some resistance.[20] But there are also many other signs that point to a profound acceptance of Christianity in the sixteenth century. Among others, one can point to the spontaneity with which thousands of Indians embraced devotion to Mary in all of Latin America.[21]

Perhaps the debate over whether the Indians were really evangelized in the sixteenth century will never be resolved to the satisfaction of all. On the one hand, those who hold the thesis that Christianity made only superficial inroads point to the campaigns to wipe out idolatrous practices or to the frequent warnings of the church councils against lapses into "ancient Gentile ways." Others, intent upon demonstrating that the neophyte Indians or blacks became real Christians while maintaining some of their older cultural ways, point to such popular manifestations of faith as the Lord of Miracles (in the case of the black slaves) or the Virgin of Guadalupe.[22] Whatever the outcome of this debate, one fact seems beyond discussion: once the church was established and the first stage of evangelization finished, there remained no other important religion in the entire continent to rival the Catholic faith.

The Lack of an Ecclesial Consciousness

The absence of any internal or external threat was one of the characteristic notes of the colonial Latin American church and is one that distinguishes it from the European or North American churches. There did not arise in the colonial period a single major organized force that competed with the Catholic church. Given this lack of authentically heterodox groups, such as Jews, Moors, or Protestants, the Inquisition expended its energies investigating lapses in public morality or the political activities of the creoles. Of course, the anti-idolatry campaigns of the sixteenth and seventeenth centuries represented a type of inquisition for the

A Panoramic View

Indians. But, in a formal sense, the Indians were not considered fit to be judged by the Inquisition proper.

Although all Latin Americans at the moment of independence professed the Catholic faith, that profession had never been tried by the experience of persecution or confronted by a rival religious system that questioned its basic premises. The biggest problem was an incipient liberalism that identified nationalism with a rejection of papal interference in the internal affairs of the new republics. But there was no rejection of Catholicism per se. This absence of a challenge to religion posed dangers for the future. During the colonial period and the first decades of the republican period, one did not distinguish between being a "Catholic" and a member of civil society. There did not exist an awareness that held loyalty to the church as an important element of faith. When different groups appeared that represented some kind of ideological or religious "competition" to the church because they preached new fundamental values in life, the church found that it did not have sufficient spiritual and psychological resources upon which to draw in order to mobilize the faithful in its defense. The church's general tendency was to defend itself by having recourse to the use of political power. By way of contrast, it rarely sought to help the faithful to develop a deeper or more critical understanding of their own religion.

For this reason, one of the most important tasks that the church began to assume in the second part of the nineteenth century was to forge a sense of its own identity. At the same time, it sought to inculcate in the faithful a sense of belonging to the church. This last task was especially difficult because three centuries of external conformity had given rise to a formal Catholicism with a weak ecclesial spirit, except in the case of certain extraordinary persons or groups. In this sense, the presence of some "opposition" groups has served to help the church gain a sense of its own identity and to react positively by forming the faithful to assume a more responsible role in practicing their religion.

The various groups of militant Catholics that arose in the nineteenth century, and in the twentieth century such organizations as Catholic Action, thus gave the church what it lacked in colonial times: a militant spirit and a sense of belonging. Later, in another historical context, the different base communities of committed Christians that have arisen since Vatican II, especially in the *pueblos jóvenes* (young towns) and in some dynamic parishes of the middle classes and in some rural dioceses (such as the southern Andean region) represent the continuation of this process. In these latter groups one can observe an enthusiastic participation in the liturgy and other parish activities as well as a continuous effort on the part of the ordinary Christians to deepen their faith on all levels, spiritually and intellectually. For them, the practice of religion and belonging to the church are values that have been consciously internalized. These groups, however, are still relatively small and scattered. Beyond them lies the great mass of believers whose Catholicism does not go beyond an imprecise religious sentiment and is not conducive to a deeper church commitment. For them, religion is usually limited to the reception of certain basic sacraments, such as baptism and marriage.

The Church and the Colonial Heritage

It would be well to point out the different ways in which the two contexts, the social and the ecclesial, have affected the Latin American church in its later development. These can be organized under five more or less related areas.

1. A Weak Institutional Life

In the sixteenth century the church was "imposed" from above. Although the Indians, blacks, and creoles were incorporated into the church, and one may speak correctly of a "Peruvian" church at the time of independence, the church continued to be highly dependent on political power until the end of the colony. As the patron of the church, the king named the bishops and other authorities, gave the *pase* (approval) for missionaries going to the New World, collected the tithes, and approved the statutes of the confraternities. The church was a corporation within society. The salaries of the bishops and priests were paid by the state. Clerics enjoyed certain privileges that went with their state, such as the ecclesiastical *fuero* (the right to be judged by church courts). In the second part of the eighteenth century the Bourbons sought to reform the church along with other institutions in society. What was a reform for them, however, turned out to be in reality the subordination of the church to the state. Examples of this increase in royal power over the church are numerous: the expulsion of the Jesuits, the *alternativa* (the obligation to replace creole superiors with Spaniards in the religious orders), the use of the Inquisition to investigate the activities of the creole clergy, and the naming of bishops who shared the same mentality as that of the Bourbons.

The image of a monolithic church, singularly efficient and all-powerful, is a myth, as Ivan Vallier has pointed out.[23] In reality, the colonial church functioned within great restrictions and limitations of all types: political, social, and geographical. The spinal cord that gave cohesion and unity to this church spread out over the immense New World territories was the king. Within the church there were men of notable character such as the two Spanish bishops, Chávez de la Rosa in Arequipa and Martínez de Compañón in Trujillo, and the creole bishop, Moscoso y Peralta in Cuzco. But these men were chosen not merely for their piety but also and especially because they fit the profile of a Bourbon functionary: they were intelligent, efficient, and loyal.

Furthermore, under the surface there were serious antagonisms that enervated the church's interior life. Toward the end of the seventeenth century, creole and peninsular religious vied openly with one another to run the convents and monasteries. This same rivalry also occurred between the creoles and Spaniards of the secular clergy over important posts in the diocesan chapters. Chávez de la Rosa himself failed in his efforts to reform the convent of Santa Catalina in Arequipa because of the opposition he faced from the nuns and their upper-class families.[24] Needless to say, the Inquisition, which investigated the activities of Toribio Rodríguez de Mendoza and other eminent creoles, served to divide the church even more.

Geographical dispersion was another factor that impeded the establishment of strong ties between the hierarchy and the faithful. The colonial bishops and those of the nineteenth century were barely able to visit the same town or doctrine (Indian parish) even once in their lifetimes. The church maintained real contact with thousands of peasants in the mountains through the doctrine priest, who was frequently absent. Apart from of this limited contact, Andean mountain dwellers had no other significant identification with the official church.

The independence movement served to reveal the internal weaknesses of the church. Bishops were expelled or resigned under pressure, liberal priests supported measures to control or reform the religious clergy, and various republican governments assumed the right of patronage, thus aborting whatever tendency might have existed in the church to assert autonomy from the state. The church failed to make use of the opportunity independence presented to claim that autonomy and to forge a clearer sense of self-identity. On the contrary, it accepted the new national patronage as a necessary condition for reorganizing itself and regaining its old privileges.

The church did, however, look to Rome as a counterweight in its efforts to establish some distance between itself and the state. Militant loyalty to the pope meant for many Catholics a way to strengthen the church in the face of an increasingly aggressive liberalism. But this strategy, no doubt necessary given that historical context, tended to reinforce external dependency. In one sense, the papacy became the "spinal cord" that the colonial church lacked. In spite of this effort, a widespread deep sense of commitment to the church did not develop. The basic unit of participation continued to be the local groups: the confraternities or the brotherhoods, not the parish. These pious associations revolved around an image or a particular devotion, but not around the "church" as such.

The bishops, priests, and religious who constituted the "official" church did not exercise dominion over a monolithic, compact, and uniform church. In reality, the church consisted of many small nuclei of the practicing faithful and, beyond them, of a great mass of Christians vaguely identified with Catholicism through certain external signs and pious practices. Nor can one really speak of a monolithic control within the "official" church. In rural areas and in the mountains the doctrine or Indian-parish priest in the postindependence period tended to be a solitary figure who was formally obedient, but in practice he lived his own life, which frequently included concubinage and other modes of behavior forbidden by the church. Many of the problems that confront the church even today are due not to a mere lack of obedience but, more fundamentally, to the low cultural level and at times the poor human quality of the clergy.

2. A Fragmented Church

The church is one of the few institutions that includes all races, social classes, and cultural groups. Nevertheless, even though it preaches unity and excludes no one, the same divisions that characterize Peruvian society in general manifest themselves in the church. The colonial church was a model on a smaller scale of the corporate society: there was an upper clergy and a lower clergy and there were creoles and Indians, rich and poor. The highest posts were reserved for the "peninsulars" (Spanish) and for trusted creoles. Very rarely was an Indian ordained to the priesthood, and the mestizos could ascend the ecclesiastical ladder only with difficulty. In the republic the church did not admit the existence of such divisions, but society imposed them anyway. For example, there have arisen in Peru two different types of clergy based purely on sociological criteria: on the one hand, a well-educated clergy usually from the middle and upper classes or from Europe and the United States, and on the other hand, a clergy from the popular classes or from the provinces, with less formation and therefore with less "prestige" than the former.

In general, the militant Catholics of the nineteenth and twentieth centuries were made up of groups from the middle and upper classes, while the rural peasants lived completely on the margin of this more "official" church. Since the Second World War in practically all the cities there have appeared three "churches," each one with its distinct social characteristics: in the downtown areas there is the more traditional church, in the middle- and upper-class neighborhoods there is the more "modern" church, and in the popular neighborhoods and in the country there is the more "popular" church. The so-called "popular" church is not only a theological concept but also a social reality: the Christians who belong to it are from the economically poorer strata of society. The projection of class and racial distinctions into the church does not correspond to any theological scheme nor does it represent the desires of the church. The distinctions are realities imposed by society, which limits and conditions the church's capacity to function.

3. The Relationship of "Patron-Client"

In the colonial church the priest assumed the role of "patron" with respect to his Indian parishioners, even to the extent of selling goods to them in order to supplement his salary. But the Mass, the sacraments, and other rites (blessings and funeral prayers) were also converted into "merchandise" to be sold: the priest demanded stipends and fees for his services as though they were commercial transactions. The rural priest who asked for exorbitant sums for the annual feast-day Mass established a relationship of "patron" vis à vis the peasants and community dwellers, who became his "clients." In some parishes and doctrines, the pastor treated the faithful as though they were petitioners asking for a favor from a civil bureaucrat.

In colonial society the priesthood was perceived more as a career than as a vocation. The churchman was seen as a professional who rendered certain services (as chaplains or parish priests) for which the public should pay. Given this widespread view, a problem that arose in colonial times was how to discern between a true vocation and purely economical and social motivations. In a study he did of the clergy in Lima between 1750 and

1820, Father Antonine Tibesar showed that religion was only one factor in a decision to enter the ecclesiastical state. According to the testimony of priests themselves, only ten out of fifty-seven claimed that they wanted to be priests in order to "serve" the people. Thirty-one of the rest stated that the priesthood for them meant ascending the social ladder and assuring a means of living.[25] In a similar way, in republican times the rectors of seminaries frequently expressed their concern over the fact that many families of the lower classes "pushed" their sons into the priesthood or the religious life with the aim of guaranteeing them a decent living. As a result of depending excessively on a system that assured its position in society, the church ran the risk of becoming a dependent bureaucracy in which the priest functioned as a career professional or as a patron with clients.

4. The Divorce between Church and Religion

In Latin America many men claim to be "Catholics," but few fulfill the minimal requirements (Sunday Mass, for example) of Catholicism. No doubt the low number of practicing Catholics is due to a phenomenon common to the whole Catholic world: secularization. Nevertheless, it should be noted that Spanish Catholicism especially fostered an individualistic religious practice, often disconnected from the official church. The official church, in contemporary Latin America as in colonial times, will sponsor "official" Masses attended by civil and ecclesiastical authorities and an undefined cross section of society. In many cases the occasion of the Mass will be a national feast day or a political anniversary. In contrast to this type of official celebration, the real practice of religion is found in the confraternities and the brotherhoods and in popular devotions. The colonial confraternity gathered people of the same social condition and profession. In the more private and exclusive world of the confraternity, one experienced a deeper sense of religion than in the more "official" celebrations.

The confraternity or the brotherhood reflected on a minor scale the reality of the colonial corporate society: there were confraternities for creoles of the upper classes (Our Lady of the O) and there were confraternities for the black slaves (the Lord of Miracles). Although the practitioners of popular religiosity did not always go to Sunday Mass regularly, they never failed to participate in the processions or devotions in honor of St. Martin de Porres (sometimes referred to in Spanish as "Porras"), the Cross of May, or Our Lady of Chapi. They are very religious persons, but not necessarily tied to the institutional church. At different moments in the republican period the church attempted to foster a more ecclesial piety, such as the devotion to the Sacred Heart. But a longer tradition of individualism posed a powerful obstacle to those attempts.

5. The Divorce between Ethics and Religion or between Public Norms and Real Practice

Colonial society imposed certain norms of conduct and ethics on its members. This external conformism was a necessity in an "invertebrate" society that had not been born organically from below. When the church obliged the Indians to attend Mass in the doctrines, it merely fulfilled the demands of political society that were approved and sanctioned by the rest of the population. The Inquisition, which was really more an instrument of the state than of the church, watched over the moral conduct of the priests and the ordinary faithful in order to protect social stability. One consequence of this rigid imposition of ethical norms was the tendency toward *criollismo* (creolism), the creole practice of looking for loopholes in the laws made by the Spanish. The widespread practice of bribery arose partially as a response to the arbitrary norms and the inefficiency of centralist and authoritarian bureaucracies. Pablo Macera noted the existence of this phenomenon in the sexual conduct of colonial times. Although everyone accepted the Catholic ideal of a stable marriage, at times the economic situation obliged a *hidalgo* (lower-scale gentleman) to marry for convenience while at the same time maintaining extramarital relations with the woman he really loved.[26] Even Viceroy Amat y Junient had his mistress, the "Perricholi."

Of course, the rigidity of the law was not the only cause of this "creole ethic," or lack of ethics. Promiscuity in the lower classes was also a product of economical instability, the lack of good upbringing, and, of course, *machismo*. Machismo is a generalized attitude in a society that looks down on poor women and overprotects women of the upper classes. The social morality of the church clashes with the values of a traditional society that fosters both machismo and marital instability. Finally, the dissociation between religion and ethics can be observed especially in the world of business, politics, and the state bureaucracy. In a society fragmented into particular groups, there is no strong consciousness of a "common good" or even of a "nation." In that kind of society, the only real ethical fault is failure to fulfill one's obligations to the family, to one's friends, or to the members of one's party. The same person is capable of practicing a double standard: one set of norms for one's private affairs and another for the public.

The colonial church was so closely identified with the status quo that its word lacked the moral power to influence the conduct of many persons who considered themselves to be Catholics. For these persons, a certain indifference toward the norms of the church was but an extension of their passive resistance to civil laws in general. Values not born within but imposed from the outside soon lose their capacity to influence the conduct of people, especially when the social controls that helped them live out those values cease to exist. On the positive side, the growth of a "sense of the church" in the current Christian communities is usually accompanied by a new sensibility toward personal and social moral questions.

Stages of Evolution, the Nineteenth and Twentieth Centuries

The church in the republican period was deeply influenced by the colonial experience. In order to understand the church's evolution during this period, it will be helpful to use a chronological outline inspired in part by a typology elaborated by Ivan Vallier for all of Latin America.[27] It should be noted that since this is an evolutionary process, many characteristics of a particular stage may continue to exist during the following stage; there are no radical breaks, but rather contextual changes in which a tendency that existed before becomes the dominant one during the following period. Somewhat arbitrarily we perceive the following stages in the church's evolution since independence:

1. Crisis and Restoration (1821–1855)

After independence, the church experienced a series of crises. In general, however, it did not lose its privileged status in society. The different republican governments claimed for themselves the right of patronage over the church, thereby provoking a crisis in the hierarchy: for a period of between fifteen to twenty years the majority of the dioceses were vacant. At the same time liberals tried to reform religious life by closing down many convents and monasteries and pressuring many religious to abandon the religious state and to enter the secular clergy. Economically, the church lost much of its wealth as a result of the war of independence.

A Panoramic View

In general, however, the liberal attack was relatively weak. The liberals of that period were doctrinaire regalists, but they were not anticlericals or antireligious. Their aim was to control the church in order to place it at the service of the new republic. They were opposed to the interference of the papacy in the internal affairs of the nation, but they did accept the pope as a symbol of unity for the faithful. Almost all of them approved the constitutional articles that established the church as the only religion to be protected and favored by the state. Tithing continued as before.

This stage of initial disorientation ended with the restoration of the bishops beginning in the decade of the thirties. The conservative caudillos such as Orbegoso (1833–36) and Echenique (1851–54), and one who was noted especially for his pragmatic flexibility, Ramón Castilla (1845–51, 1855–62), were positively interested in restoring the church as a stabilizing force in society. The call to order formulated by Bartolomé Herrera in his patriotic sermon of July 28, 1846, reflected the deepest desires of many Peruvians who were tired of the interminable wars between the caudillos but who were also disillusioned by the little progress brought about by the doctrinaire liberals.

The policy of the bishops and other church leaders in this period consisted in reorganizing the church and in attempting to regain for it the same privileged position that it had enjoyed in colonial society. The principal architects of this policy were Francisco Javier de Luna Pizarro (archbishop of Lima, 1845–55), José Sebastián de Goyeneche (bishop of Arequipa, 1818–60; archbishop of Lima, 1860–72), and Bartolomé Herrera (bishop of Arequipa, 1860–64). Under Luna Pizarro, the church managed to achieve some independence from the state, though within the limits imposed by the patronage. Santo Toribio Seminary was reopened and it was soon filled with candidates who aspired to the priesthood. At the same time, the liberal clergy that had aligned itself with the liberal politicians was gradually marginated within the church. Also, there was a resurgence of traditional religious piety in the decade of the forties. Twenty years after the separation from Spain, the church had been fully restored; it was more conservative but nevertheless intact.

Independence did not signify, therefore, an unsupportable crisis for the church. Liberalism, which was the doctrine of only a small elite, did not affect the lower classes. Nor were basic social realities or fundamental values put to the question. The church continued exercising great influence over all social classes. Although formally it had been obliged to accept a modus vivendi with the new national state, on a more informal level it continued to function within a colonial structure, especially in its relationship with the faithful. In the rural areas, far from the cities, the priests in Indian parishes continued to collect tithes, to call the people to Mass, and to influence daily life as though independence had never occurred.

2. The Militant Church (1855–1930)

About the middle of the fifties the liberals turned aggressively anticlerical. In the constitutional convention of 1855–56, they set out to eliminate some of the privileges the church still enjoyed, such as the tithes and the ecclesiastical *fuero*. They also proposed to separate state and church. This new attack provoked a wave of protest from the hierarchy, the clergy, and many of the faithful. Arequipa became the center of the antiliberal movement, which ended up forcing President Castilla to repudiate the more radical demands of the convention. In 1860 a new constitution, more conciliar in tone, which included both conservative and liberal measures, was written. Although Bartolomé Herrera, then president of the senate, refused to sign it because he considered it too liberal, the constitution of 1860 as a matter of fact constituted a victory for the church because it preserved its privileged status as the only religion protected by the state. Besides, the delicate problem of patronage had been resolved, at least for the moment, when Pope Pius IX published a bull in 1874 in which he recognized certain rights of the Peruvian state over the church, which in fact it had already been exercising since the reestablishment of the hierarchy. In 1880 Nicolás de Piérola gave the *exequatur* that signified official approval of the papal bull. Although a formal concordat was never celebrated between the Holy See and the Peruvian government, the bull of 1874 served the same purpose.

Although they did not achieve all their objectives, on other occasions the liberals managed to put into effect legislation that, though not directly anticlerical, was perceived as an incursion upon the church's sphere of competence. In 1867 the liberals tried to impose another constitution, of a more radical nature, but it lasted only a short time. They had more success with other laws and amendments: cemeteries were laicized in 1869, civil marriage for non-Catholics was recognized in 1897, freedom of worship for all confessions was established in 1915, and obligatory civil marriage for all and the right to divorce were upheld in 1930.[28]

But these liberal gains were not the cause by themselves of an increase in religious indifference and even hostility toward the church in the years after the war with Chile. Most of all, positivism, which arose as a reaction to a general state of pessimism, had a significant impact on the upper and middle classes. For them, the ideas of Comte and Spencer represented a solution to Peru's social and economic backwardness. In the University of San Marcos in 1894, Javier Prado delivered an academic lecture on the maladies that Peru had inherited from the colonial period. Among them, he underlined the "fanaticism" and the obscurantism of Spanish Catholicism. Also in this same period the Masons, now more numerous in Peru, displayed considerable strength. In many homes of the upper and middle classes attitudes toward religion became distinctly hardened. Frequently, religion became a barrier: husbands and sons became indifferent while wives and daughters continued to practice religion. Toward the end of the century, anarchists began to disseminate among workers the antireligious (to be more precise, anti-Catholic) criticism of Manuel González Prada.

Finally, Protestantism became more self-assured and began proselytizing in public. In 1890 the Uruguayan preacher Francisco Penzotti won celebrity when he was imprisoned for violating article 4 of the constitution, which forbade public worship by non-Catholics. Penzotti was acquitted, and many other missionaries soon arrived in the country. In the beginning of the century, the Adventists became the most important missionary group. They sent missionaries and educators to the southern highlands. The elimination of article 4 in 1915 provoked much opposition from the church.

In light of these tendencies of a more aggressive liberalism, antireligiosity among the upper and middle classes, and Protestant proselytizing, the church adopted a more "militant" posture. For the first time in Peru's history there were organized groups that advocated ideological and religious values openly competing with those held by the church. The cultural and religious unity of Peru had broken down, though these new tendencies affected only relatively small groups. In reaction, the bishops called upon the faithful to defend the church and to organize themselves politically with the aim of eliminating, or at least controlling, these new threats.

The church reacted in different ways and on different levels. First, ties with the papacy were strengthened. In colonial times the pope was an important person symbolically, but very distant. Now, he was converted into a symbol of the Catholic cause against liberalism. Second, the bishops and the faithful had recourse to political power to defend their interests. On different occasions, the church sponsored societies and even political parties that represented the Catholic cause in congress. Furthermore, it openly supported certain presidents (especially Nicolás de Piérola, José Pardo, and Augusto B. Leguía) who aided its works and respected its privileges. Third, the church invited many new congregations and religious orders to Peru to found schools or to staff abandoned parishes in the mountains. The founding of the Catholic University in 1917 represented an important part of this effort to provide for a Catholic education in the face of indifferentism and the antireligious tendencies of state schools. Fourth, priests and laypersons founded a Catholic press, which aimed to make the Catholic point of view known and to criticize liberalism. Finally, the church infused religious practice itself with a new militant spirit. By way of example, the devotion to the Sacred Heart of Jesus, spread especially by the Jesuits, symbolized the protest of the church against rationalism and indifferentism.

This display of activity by the church, however, also underlined some very profound weaknesses. Although the church managed to reorganize its external structure in the years after independence, it discovered that it lacked the internal spiritual resources to face a crisis of values or to "mobilize" Catholics on a grass-roots basis in its defense. There was no deep bond of identification with the church as a result of its having fought against an ideological or religious rival such as Protestantism, or of having been persecuted. The church sought to organize the campaign on the basis of alliances with power elites or with the government. In the face of Protestantism, for example, it did not reexamine its own religious message or the way in which it was presented. Rather, it pushed its cause in the political forum or by organizing protest marches in order to intimidate the newly arrived Protestants. Nevertheless, the church did manage to create a sense of solidarity between itself and certain small groups, which constituted the beginning of a lay movement. The concept of "Catholic Action," however, did not really take form until the 1930s.

In general, this was a period of retreat and reformation in the light of forces that the church perceived as hostile to itself. Lacking as it did a creative or original vision of society to offer, the church limited itself to the task of carving out a "Catholic" world made up of schools, associations, political parties, confraternities, and processions. Outside this tightly closed world of prominent families, there was the "secular" world of freethinkers, Masons, positivists, and a great mass of indifferent persons. Two different mentalities arose in the upper and middle classes: the liberal-positivistic and the Catholic-conservative mentality. In general, the women represented the latter.

Furthermore, in the same period the church displayed increasingly less intellectual vigor. This was the result in part of the priest shortage but also of the church's conservative attitude toward the problems of the day. The Catholic presence in the universities and intellectual circles was all but unnoticed. Although the social doctrine of the church was known since the publication of the encyclical *Rerum Novarum* (1891), the tendency in the church was to emphasize the defense of the church over the promotion of social change.

These new forces that threatened the church were relatively small and had little influence on the popular classes. Nevertheless, there were other factors that served to limit the church's influence on the peasants and the new working class, especially the removal of the social controls that characterized the colonial period, and the priest shortage. The first significant curb to the church's control over the population was the elimination of the tithes. At the same time, the church steadily lost its power of persuasion to summon the peasants, especially the Indian population living in the more remote areas, to attend Mass or to receive the other sacraments in the Indian parishes. The migrations from the mountains to the coast or toward the mines in the latter part of the nineteenth century accelerated this loss of control even more. Finally, during this period the crisis of the priest shortage became most acute: throughout the mountains and highlands numerous parishes were abandoned.

The culmination of this stage occurred during the eleven-year (1919–30) rule of Augusto Leguía, who most noticeably sought to tighten church-state ties. Archbishop Emilio Lisson returned the gesture and lost no opportunity to strengthen those ties. The attempt to consecrate Peru to the Sacred Heart in 1923, which ended in a total fiasco, symbolized better than any other example the strength and the weakness of the "militant church." On the one hand, the church had the capacity to galvanize a great number of faithful but, on the other, it was incapable of serving as a symbol of national unity on account of its excessive dependence on political power and its overidentification with certain groups in society. It was a church that aggressively organized campaigns against its rivals but yet was fixed in certain traditional molds that no longer attracted many people, especially men of a more modern mentality who criticized the established order.

3. The Militant Laity (1930–1955)

During this period, in the midst of great social tension provoked in part by the new forces of *Aprismo* (the ideology of the Aprista Party) and Marxism, the church reacted by giving far more importance to the laity as defenders of the church. Although the lay movement had its roots in the nineteenth century, those first groups lacked internal discipline and soon turned into social clubs for upper-class gentlemen and ladies. The eleven-year period of Leguía marked the end of a stage in Peru's political life and the end of the traditional militant church. The bishops who stand out the most in this new period, Mariano Holguín of Arequipa and Pedro Pascual Farfán of Lima, gave full support to the initiative to get the lay movement going again. The Eucharistic Congress of 1935 was the high point of the new militancy. Thousands of men and women walked in procession in the streets of Lima to make a public profession of their faith. And it was in this congress that Catholic Action in Peru was born. Catholic Action instilled new life in the lay movement and inculcated in middle-class Catholics a sense of ecclesial participation that had been lacking before. The two paladins of the Catholic cause were Víctor Andrés Belaunde and José de la Riva-Agüero.

Perhaps the principal achievement of Catholic Action was the creation of an awareness among many Catholics of the social teachings of the church. In the face of Marxism and *Aprismo*, Catholics acquired a political and social consciousness based on their own social message. The Catholic University, founded in 1917, became a center of the lay movement and gave impetus to the intellectual formation of a new generation of Catholics. Also in this period there was a change in the attitude toward the secular world from closed hostility toward an effort to understand it. A "missionary" mentality, as Ivan Vallier termed it, was born: a perspective that gave priority to studying a political or religious rival in order to combat it and to recapture members who might have crossed over to the other side.

Nevertheless, the church's reaction only partially solved its problems. Catholic Action was the work of very small groups that failed to reach the lower classes steeped in the atmosphere of popular religiosity. Furthermore, Peru had become polarized between two hostile bands: APRA (the acronym for the Aprista Party) and anti-Apristas. Politically, the groups within Catholic Action accepted the need for social reform in principle, but they had no clearly identifiable political space of their own. APRA, with its laicist and welfare-state mentality, had a monopoly over many reformist groups of the middle classes, and the oligarchic political right, supported by the military, dominated the upper classes. Social Christianity did not have its own channel of expression outside the church.

Catholic Action itself came to experience an identity crisis between being "shock troops" in defense of the church or an instrument to bring about real social change, between being a passive instrument at the beck and call of the bishops or a free agent with a mandate to make its own decisions. On a deeper level, the militants of Catholic Action were not adequately prepared for their new role. Their movement was not grounded in a biblical and theological understanding of the world. Most of all, there was no attempt to engender a new experience of faith. On the contrary, traditional piety and uncritical loyalty to the church were maintained but without fostering a new sense of lay participation in the liturgy or in the pastoral planning of parishes. On the positive side, however, one can see in Catholic Action and in the earlier lay movements the equivalent of the Counter-Reformation for Latin America and Peru: a movement that instilled in the faithful a spirit of militancy in the face of an external threat. Catholic Action emphasized the use of visible signs, slogans, and hymns intended to foster a sense of esprit de corps in the militants and to heighten the lines of division between them and lapsed or indifferent Catholics. In this sense, the militants of Catholic Action, though they lacked a deeper understanding of the theology or the liturgy, attended Mass and received the sacraments as a sign of faith and of loyalty to the church.

This was also a period of intellectual awakening. Besides studying the social encyclicals, the militants delved into St. Augustine and St. Thomas Aquinas and contemporary Catholic European authors such as Jacques Maritain and Gilbert Keith Chesterton. In general, however, the tendency was to read for apologetical purposes, not to "dialogue" with the opposition, which would be an attitude more appropriate to the church of Vatican II. Finally, the pro-Indian stance of the left was combated by the pro-Spanish posture of many Catholics. This *hispanismo* (Hispanism) frequently manifested itself in an admiration for the colonial past and for Francisco Franco's Spain. The most important representative of this tendency was José de la Riva-Agüero.

Perhaps the most important aspect of Catholic Action and other similar groups was the break they made with a colonial mentality that presumed that all members of society are Catholics. It fostered a new mentality that called upon laypersons to assume responsibility for their own religion in a pluralistic world that at times would be hostile to their basic values. Most of all, it encouraged the laity to question their conduct in the light of the social teachings of the church.

4. The Modern Church (1955–1968)

In 1955 the bishops of Latin America held the first continental general meeting of the episcopacy. They thus broke the bonds of isolation that separated them and gave impetus to the creation of a real Latin American church. That same year, militant Catholics in Peru broke their own bonds of isolation and stepped into the world of politics by giving rise to the Christian Democratic Party. These and other phenomena symbolized the beginning of the stage of "modernization," that is, a confrontation between the church and the "modern" world, which in this context is defined as the western world, especially the more advanced nations of Europe and the United States, that set the pace for the nonsocialist world ever since the end of World War II. The "new" values that now reigned were political democracy, economic development, cultural and religious pluralism, and anticommunism. In Western Europe and the United States there was an increase of dialogue between more open-minded Catholics and Protestants.

The theologians of modernity—Ives Congar, Karl Rahner, Henri de Lubac, Jean Daniélou, Edward Schillebeeckx, and others—underlined the importance of intensifying biblical studies, of creating a more humanistic theology open to the non-Catholic world, and of returning to the sources of the primitive church in order to bring about a profound reform within the church of the twentieth century. Specialized centers that carried out experimental liturgies and emphasized lay participation had already sprung up in different places. In 1959 Pope John XXIII convoked the Second Vatican Council, which was destined to mark the end of the period of the "militant" church and to set in motion a new period that would be as decisive for the church in the twentieth century as the Council of Trent had been in the sixteenth century.

The council signified most of all a change in attitude toward the secular world. Where Trent had attended principally to the task of reordering the church and instilling discipline in its own house, Vatican II sought to open the doors of that house to the outside world. For this reason, the central themes of the council were expressed in certain words that became widely popularized in the Catholic world, such as "aggiornamento," "dialogue," and "pluralism." The fathers of the council described the church as a "light of all nations," "the people of God," or as a "pilgrim," biblical metaphors that emphasized its mission toward the non-Catholic world. In the postconciliar period, distinct theologies of the "secular" flourished. These theologies exalted the values of commitment, maturity, and responsibility. Protestant theologians such as Jürgen Moltmann and Harvey Cox, and the Catholic theologian Johannes Metz, proposed a secular person as a model for Christians. A secular person is characterized by dominion over self and the surrounding world, a sense of mission in history, and optimism concerning the possibility of forging a more just and freer world. Liturgical reform and the use of the vernacular reinforced the call for the laity to participate more actively in the sacramental life of the church.

The period of modernization coincided in Latin America with the nadir of the vocation crisis. First Pope Pius XII and later John XXIII exhorted North American and European Catholics to send personnel to Latin America. In Peru missionaries from the English-speaking world had already set up residence—the Maryknoll (since 1943) and the Columban Fathers, for example. In the sixties and seventies there was a considerable increase in the number of priests, brothers, and women religious from the United States, Canada, and Ireland. Perhaps the group that best symbolized the new missionary wave was the Maryknollers: North American priests, brothers, and sisters who created "modern" parishes in Lima and Arequipa and who concentrated their efforts in the southern highlands (in Puno, Juli, and other areas). They founded cooperatives, installed radio networks, and used new methods for promoting development. The use of the clerical suit (until then priests wore cassocks in public), a more open pastoral style, and direct contact with the North American culture represented some of the facets of "modernization."

This was also a time of construction and expansion. In Lima the primate of the church, Juan Landázuri Ricketts, who succeeded Cardinal Guevara in 1955, began an ambitious program of building new parishes to keep up with the geometric rate of urban growth. At the same time, Cardinal Cushing of Boston helped make possible the construction of several seminaries and other works throughout the country. Many teaching congregations moved their schools from the center of Lima to new sites in the suburbs of the capital. Everywhere new and modernistic church buildings sprang up.

Modernization worked in a double direction: on the one hand, it signified a change in the church's image, and on the other, an increase in social consciousness. Following the guidelines of the council many parishes renovated their catechetical programs and reformed their liturgies. New movements oriented especially toward the laity sprang up: the Christian Family Movement and the *cursillos de Cristiandad* (short courses in Christianity). The former emphasized the renewal of family life and the latter aimed to motivate especially men to become more involved in the church. At the same time, the new parishes in the *barriadas* (the squatter villages that were springing up around the cities), as well as the priests, religious women, and catechists who went to help in these parishes, became more interested in social and political problems. During this period Cáritas (an international relief service of the church) sent food and clothes to be distributed among the *barriada* dwellers.

On another front, many lay members of Catholic Action, inspired by the social encyclicals that emphasized the relationship between faith and society and influenced by the thought of such intellectuals as Father Louis-Joseph Lebret, went into politics. The Christian Democratic Party represented the response of many laypersons to the challenge of underdevelopment, poverty, illiteracy, and foreign economic exploitation of natural resources in Latin America. It also arose as a reaction to the advance of communism and other movements of a laicist or totalitarian tendency. "Social Christianity," as it was called, reached maturity in these years and enjoyed considerable prestige in intellectual circles. The fusion of the terms "social" and "Christianity," the fruit of many years of labor, gained widespread acceptance.

The official church organized a forum in which these modernizing influences could come together and reach a new synthesis: the First Social Week, held in 1959. During that week priests and laypersons, many of whom came from the ranks of Catholic Action, discussed Peru's social problems in light of Catholic social doctrine. Bishop José Dammert Bellido and other speakers underlined the responsibilities of Christians in the modern world. A few year later, in 1963, the bishops published a pastoral letter in which they called upon Christians to take greater responsibility in politics in order to bring about more social change.

The fifties and sixties represented a springtime of new movements and directions: Christian Democratic parties flourished throughout Latin America, liturgies became more attractive, lay movements that touched the deepest values in life sprang up, and new churches and seminaries were built. Soon, however, the church discovered that modernization was but a transitional stage leading to a new period of crisis. The momentum of political and social forces that arose in the fifties and the full impact of the council's reforms combined to undermine the foundations of security upon which the preconciliar church rested. When the council did away with the façade of the "militant church" it invited the laity to develop a more critical and pluralistic mentality and to assume a more responsible role in the church and in the world. But many laypersons were not prepared to act with such liberty or to use their own judgement. Furthermore, many bishops and priests did not understand the spirit of the council: they imposed liturgical reform while discouraging any real lay participation. During this period, a significant number of priests and religious women left their respective calling in order to marry. Modernization either as a psychological reality or as a theological postulate created a dilemma for many religious personnel. On the one hand, the older values of celibacy, the consecrated way of life, and unquestioned obedience were still held in esteem, but the newer and more "modern" values of integral personal development in married life, social and political commitment, and having a critical and mature conscience were emphasized more.

In the middle of the crisis that the council generated, the social crisis loomed as well. The decade of the sixties was above all else a time of rising expectations. The Cuban revolution, the Alliance for Progress, and the reformist promises of Fernando Belaúnde created a psychological climate for rapid social change. The growth of the *barriadas*, an outbreak of guerrilla warfare in 1965, the death of Camilo Torres and "Che" Guevara, as well as many other events, produced a note of tension in the middle of the decade. Increasingly, daily discussion revolved around the question of reform or revolution.

The accentuation of the social question put to the test many of the premises upon which modernization rested. For many committed Catholics a mere change in the church's image was not sufficient. The foreign clergy who watched over the construction of the new parishes in the *barriadas* began to understand the need to carry out structural changes in society itself. In the face of massive poverty in the countryside and in the *barriadas*, the need arose to rethink pastoral action in new terms; in addition to administering the sacraments and doing other spiritual works, "pastoral" began to mean fostering local development, raising the level of health care, or providing for basic education. This new social sensitivity soon led to a reevaluation of many political premises.

In short, the period of modernization signified a change of direction: from the church toward the world. In the period of the "militant church," Catholics did think about the "world," but they did it with the aim of fighting it in order to convert it. After the council, the new militants saw the world as a stage full of promise and hope upon which they were called to act in order to come to maturity as Christians.

5. The Social-Political Church (1968–1975)

In 1968 two events occurred that profoundly influenced the Peruvian church: the episcopal conference of Medellín in August and September and a military revolution in October. The first general conference of the Latin American bishops had been held in Río de Janeiro in 1955. The bishops in Río directed their efforts principally toward the task of self-organization. The second major conference of the bishops, in Medellín, reflected the many changes that had occurred in the church since the first, and it turned out to be a dramatic watershed. During that conference the bishops took a strong public stand in favor of social justice in solidarity with the marginated classes of the entire continent.

This official stand, taken in such a solemn context, symbolized the end of the period of the "modern" church, which in reality had limited itself to following the guidelines of the Second Vatican Council. By way of contrast, the Medellín conference not only assimilated the positive aspects of the council but went considerably beyond the council in its effort to forge a Latin American identity for the church. The spirit of Medellín had repercussions in all the local churches of Latin America, most noticeably in the more progressive groups.

The military regime that came to power in October of that year gave a special impetus to the process of change. In reality, the Peruvian church during the military revolution, carried out under General Juan Velasco Alvarado (1968–75), constituted a unique situation in the Latin American church. In the rest of Latin America during that period, the church had to face rightist military regimes (in Brazil, Argentina, Bolivia, and Chile), whereas in Peru alone the military turned out to be reformist. Furthermore, unlike the revolutionary experiences of Mexico or Cuba that produced governments hostile to the church, the Peruvian military openly sought the support of the church. There were other phenomena of a more social nature that also favored rapid change in the church, such as a growth of the *barriadas* or *pueblos jóvenes* (young towns, as the military came to term them) around Peru's major cities.

During this period the dominant tendency was concern for social change. Furthermore, in the very experience of supporting the government's reforms, through the church advisers who participated in the making of the reforms or as a result of the consultations carried on within the church over the reforms, the church acquired a far greater political awareness than it ever had before. During most of the republican period the church had entered the political forum privately or publicly, usually to defend its own interests by supporting or rejecting certain laws. In the Velasco years the church took on a much more universal role as promoter or legitimizer of laws and reforms that affected all groups in society: farmers, educators, and workers. Although the church had always been "political" in one sense, it had never participated so directly in the making of so many decisions in so many areas at once.

The participation of the Peruvian church in the revolutionary (or "reformist" in the vocabulary of some) process was so visible in those years that it was considered one of the most progressive in all of Latin America. In reality, things were more complex. The church did not formally legitimize the military regime. It limited itself to supporting some of the government's reforms, the very ones that it probably would have supported under a democratic government. Furthermore, there was not a total uniformity of criteria among church people as one would be led to believe by reading the documents published by the church in that period. The velocity of the changes in society and in the church distracted the public from noticing the deep divisions that were appearing within the church. During these years, the progressive sector stood out the most. The progressives consisted of priests and others who sympathized with liberation theology or who were connected with ONIS (the National Office of Social Information, a radical priests' group). At the other extreme were to be found the more conservative clergy, which included priests of Opus Dei and many native Peruvians belonging to the secular clergy, usually in the provinces. In the middle were the "moderates": priests, religious women, and pastoral agents who sympathized in general with the military's reforms and the changes in the church but who maintained a critical distance from both the government and the more advanced clergy. Furthermore, within the so-called "progressive" clergy, a few distinctions are in order. For example, those groups most identified with "liberation theology" did not in general participate in the government, preferring instead to promote change from below.

The intellectual current that most inspired the religious personnel who worked among the popular classes was liberation theology, closely associated with Gustavo Gutiérrez, a priest of the secular clergy from Lima. The book that Father Gutiérrez published, bearing the title *A Theology of Liberation*, came out in 1971, although the basic ideas had been aired much earlier. Also, the ideas of the Brazilian educator, Paulo Freire, on "conscientization" and liberating education influenced avant-garde Christian groups considerably in those years. The concepts of "liberation" and "conscientization" point out most sharply the differences between the "social-political church" and the "modern church." The social encyclicals had already taken a clear stand in favor of a more just society, but they did not state with much precision, apart from condemning violent means and praising democracy, how that goal was to be achieved. Grounding themselves in biblical concepts, the liberation-theology thinkers conceived of the process, especially in the third world, as one of "liberation" from unjust structures, whether they be national or worldwide. However, they did not propose a mere change of structures as the solution. Most of all, they called for "conscienticizing" the oppressed so that they might assume control of their own destinies and bring about the necessary changes themselves.

These ideas had important pastoral implications. First, the model of a Christian that was proposed was that of the "committed" Christian, one who actively takes a role, as pastoral agent, community organizer, or basic militant, in the struggle to achieve a more just society. At the same time, the concept of the passive, noncommitted Christian was severely criticized. According to the theologians of the new line, if "peace" is the result of an unjust order (and that would be the case in most of Latin America), then to favor "peace" is virtually to legitimize that order. What is more in consonance with the Bible is to promote justice as the only guarantee of a truly lasting peace. Second, the committed Christian should identify himself or herself as much as possible with the oppressed in order to conscienticize them, that is, to teach them their rights and to help them come to have a sense of their own dignity. Third, conflict and political tension therefore become a necessary consequence of this decision to support the oppressed within society. Fourth, the fundamental distinction to be drawn in the world is no longer between "Catholics" and "non-Catholics" but between persons of good will who fight for justice and others who, for different reasons, choose not to commit themselves to the struggle.

This new interpretation of pastoral action as the sum of attitudes and steps that in some way or other promote social justice had immediate consequences. On several occasions priests, sisters, and pastoral agents participated in protest marches organized by workers, teachers, and *barriada* dwellers. Quite naturally, this new perspective produced confusion in the minds of many over the distinction between what is "pastoral" and what is "political." In the famous case in which the Minister of the Interior, Armando Artola, arrested Bishop Luis Bambarén in 1971 for celebrating Mass for a group of squatters who seized private property, what was "pastoral" for the bishop was perceived as an aggressive "political" action by the minister. There were consequences for the laity, too. In light of the pluralism fostered by Vatican II, many Christians, eschewing the old guidelines of Catholic Action that called for the creation of "Catholic" parties or unions, began to enter different political parties hitherto held in question by the church, particularly on the left. For them, the new theological currents that emphasized the concepts of "commitment" and "justice" fully justified venturing into this previously forbidden political world.

The great majority of religious orders and congregations continued to fulfill the same tasks as before in schools, hospitals, and other works. Nevertheless, during this period many of them questioned their entire pastoral approach. Some opted for abandoning traditional charitable assistance in favor of offering human development in a wider sense. Cáritas and other social-assistance organizations changed many of their methods in order to rid themselves of the image of being paternalistic. For example, instead of giving out clothes or food in the *pueblos jóvenes* directly, these groups now favored distributing goods in mothers' clubs, parishes, or schools that also included a program of human formation for the poor. Some of the hospital congregations, beset by the population explosion and the impersonal bureaucracies imposed by the government, withdrew from the large state institutions in order to work directly with the poor in the *pueblos jóvenes*, in the rural areas, and in the jungle. The crisis of those years was especially sharp for the educators: some religious schools maintained their traditional upper-class character; others opened themselves up to the new social and theological currents. Finally, there was a considerable increase of church-run schools among the popular classes.

The "First Phase" (the term given to the Velasco years) meant, most of all, a fundamental change of mentality for the church with respect to society. Never before had the word "pastoral" been so closely identified with social or political change. In parishes, schools, and religious orders the military's reforms became a subject of daily debate and in many cases a source of division and discord. In general, however, there reigned an atmosphere of optimism about the possibility of bringing about rapid social change without violence. This was the period in which the "progressive" church came to fruition. Perhaps the most important characteristic of this period was the accent on being "committed": an attitude that affected lay militants, not just from the middle classes but especially from the popular classes.

6. The Social-Pastoral Church (1975–   )

The end of the "First Phase" of General Velasco's government also signified a change within the church. In various formal and informal ways the government presided over by General Francisco Morales Bermúdez put a halt to the reformist process, maintaining some reforms and scuttling others. In 1978 a Constitutional Assembly was called as a first step toward holding general presidential elections in 1980. Although both church and state avoided a direct confrontation, the relations between the two cooled considerably. The church, which had supported many of the reforms of the Velasco government, did not agree with the dismantling of those reforms under the new regime.

This period signified the end of the illusion of rapid social change. In light of the end of the reformist experiment of Velasco and its own withdrawal (in some cases the church's advisers in the ministries were "nudged" out) as a direct participant in the government, the church looked within itself and reexamined its relationship with society in general. As a consequence, the church adopted a more "pastoral" stance, partially because the recourse to direct politics as an instrument of change was no longer possible. But the word "pastoral" had also acquired newer and broader meanings since the council and Medellín. Traditionally, it meant to attend to the faithful in parishes, administer sacraments, visit the sick, run youth clubs, and so forth. By the beginning of the sixties, it acquired a more social and even a political sense: to help the popular classes economically, to raise their educational level, and to support their struggle to win political rights. In these years also, church leaders began to emphasize what had previously been a nuance: to "accompany" the people, that is, to become identified with their real situation and, without imposing formulae or dictating methods from above, to construct a church from below.

In the time of Velasco a certain triumphalistic or messianic attitude affected many priests and pastoral agents who came close to identifying the advance of Christianity with the imminent creation of a new and just social order, and quite possibly a socialist one. After the "First Phase," however, many Christians who worked among the popular classes accepted the necessity to think in more long-range terms. In many subtle ways their role became transformed from that of "leader" to that of "companion" or "guide." Although these Christians continue to be concerned about social change as before, they now emphasize more the necessary prior steps to bringing about lasting change in the future. They stress the need to form and to educate the people humanly, socially, and spiritually. The "social-pastoral church" can be defined as a period of patient waiting during which the new values underlined in the council and Medellín can be more deeply assimilated and internalized.

The "social-pastoral church" is in general more mature, pluralistic, and universal in its thinking than in previous periods. In this period the divisions between progressives and conservatives also have become more pronounced. In 1978 the bishops convoked the third major episcopal conference, which was held in Puebla, Mexico. There were sharp divisions evident between conservatives and progressives at the conference. Nevertheless, the document the conference wrote represented a conciliatory consensus between the two sides. Unlike the Medellín document, which addressed itself principally to the social reality of Latin America, the Puebla document emphasized much more the theological dimensions of the social commitment of Christians. It was more "pastoral" because it aimed at integrating the spiritual and the social dimensions of men and women more harmoniously. In Peru the conservative groups organized themselves to slow down the advance of the new church born in Medellín. But the hierarchy in general avoided imposing any particular orientation on the church: traditionalist, conservative, or liberationist. Instead, it chose to highlight the positive values in each of those positions.

On another level, parish life was greatly dynamized, especially through the application of pastoral methods that incorporated the new spiritual and psychological advances of the Vatican II era. Catholic Action, with its more intellectual approach and preconciliar piety, no longer responded to the needs of the renovated church of the sixties. In its place new pastoral movements that respond directly to the needs of families and the youth have arisen. Marriage Encounter and the youth movements that are its derivatives, such as "Choice," emphasize the strengthening of family ties through dialogue and mutual understanding. Furthermore, these movements tend to strengthen the ties of the family with the parish. Other movements, which highlight the affective and communitarian elements in the liturgy, such as the restored catechumenate (known also as the rite of Christian initiation) and the charismatic movement, have also had a significant impact. In another historical context, these movements would have been criticized as "alienating," given their emphasis on personal relationships and their lack of emphasis on social problems. However, in many cases persons who have experienced a renewal in the affective dimension of their lives also acquire a deeper sense of "church" as a result of the experience, and through that experience a deeper social sense as well. The effort to integrate the new social and political consciousness with the affective and spiritual experience is one of the outstanding features of the "social-pastoral church."

The "pastoralist" tendency has generated certain tensions within the church. In the previous period, confrontations between "progressives" and "conservatives" were frequent. In the current period the conflicts that occur are frequently between "pastors" and "politicians" and "traditionalists": that is, between those who, without diminishing the social message of the church, seek a more pluralistic church open to new pastoral experiences, and those who, trapped psychologically in fixed mindsets, have become sectarian in their treatment of others or who habitually reduce religion to politics.

Within the "progressives" one can observe certain changes of viewpoint since the previous stage. In the beginning the promoters of liberation theology constituted a small group of priests, religious women, and laypersons with a level of formation far superior to that of the great mass of ordinary Christians. Within a short period of time, however, what was initially a bit of an elitist movement has become much more of a grass-roots movement. Furthermore, in the beginning many critics considered liberation theology as a type of "theology of protest" intended to justify protest marches of the poor. In contrast to that original image, after many years of work in the *pueblos jóvenes* and the rural areas, the pastoral agents who sympathize with liberation theology now give a much wider meaning to the word "liberation," which for them means human development, daily support to communitarian projects, the fostering of popular education, and the spiritual formation of both adults and youth. Finally, there has been an intellectual rediscovery of popular religiosity among the "liberationists" who previously dismissed many popular practices as "alienating." Also, more critical studies of national problems have helped to free Peruvian intellectuals from their dependency on the mechanical application of theories born in the European or North American contexts.

The new constitution of 1980 put an end to the system of national patronage. This was a merely symbolic gesture, because for quite some time the church and the state already acted as though they were separate. In many ways the stage of the "social-pastoral church" represented the overcoming of many defects that characterized the church from colonial times on. For one thing, the church has managed to forge a greater freedom and autonomy with respect to outside pressures and, as a result, it has become a more coherent and inner-directed organization. One can observe the existence of many groups of laypersons who feel themselves quite identified with the church on every important level of their lives: the intellectual, the spiritual, and the affective. In these laypeople one can note the integration of the concepts of "church" and "world." They are more ecclesial in their mentality and more universal in their vision of the world than previous generations. They fuse the social, the political, the religious, and the ethical in a personal synthesis that would have been difficult to achieve in another period. In this sense it may be stated that each period or stage, the postindependence period, the "militant church," the "militant laity," the "modern church" and the "social-political church," have all signified stages of maturation in the formation of the contemporary church.

Nevertheless, it is evident that many problems that go back to the colonial past still have not been overcome, such as the scarcity of native vocations and the dependence on foreign religious personnel, the prevalence of a popular religiosity that is incompatible with a more ecclesial piety, and the existence of an upper-class church alongside a more popular church. It would be well, therefore, to look at the origins of these and other problems in order to understand the long crisis through which the church has gone since the colonial period up to the present moment.

2

A Church in Crisis
The Priest Shortage

After independence the Peruvian church, like that in most of the rest of Latin America, began to undergo a long and profound institutional crisis. This crisis manifested itself most of all in two symptoms: a certain intellectual and pastoral atrophy and a shortage of vocations to the priesthood and the religious life that became increasingly pronounced beginning in the second half of the last century. Only in recent years has the second problem been seriously faced. With the changes of emphasis that came with Vatican II, the priest shortage is no longer considered the most urgent crisis in the church. Nevertheless, the rapid decline of vocations was, and still is, a clear symptom that the body is suffering from some general sickness. In order to analyze this general crisis more in depth, we shall trace the history of one of its principal symptoms, the decline in vocations to the priesthood.

In 1820, on the eve of independence, there were about three thousand priests in the Viceroyalty of Peru for a population of two million inhabitants.[1] But in 1984, in the same approximate area, Peru had about 2,265 priests for a population of eighteen million.[2] This widening disproportion can be observed in the case of the archdiocese of Lima that had approximately one priest of the secular clergy for every 510 inhabitants in 1810, and in 1973 one priest of either the secular or religious clergy for every 3,841 inhabitants.[3] In reality, the crisis is graver than what these statistics imply, because the native Peruvian clergy has been declining in number since independence, while the foreign clergy, which came to fill the vacuum, has been increasing. In 1901, for example, 82 percent of the clergy in Peru was native-born, but in 1973 only 38.8 percent of the clergy was Peruvian; the other 61.5 percent was foreign born.[4]

It is important to indicate more precisely when this shortage began to manifest itself in order not to arrive at "easy" conclusions. As will be shown later, there was no shortage of priests during the first few decades after independence, except in the central mountain region and the jungle. In 1948 Father Rubén Vargas Ugarte, S.J., published a short book entitled *Un gravísimo problema nacional* (A Most Grave National Problem) in which he sounded the alarm with respect to the sharp drop in the numbers of native clergymen. According to Father Vargas, the diocese of Puno had seventy-four priests in 1865, in contrast to the fifty-eight that it had when he wrote, although the population of that department had increased considerably.[5] This same phenomenon can be observed in almost all other areas of Peru. It is sufficient to cite the case of Arequipa to confirm this general truth.

In the department of Arequipa in 1847, with a population of 50,045 inhabitants, there were about 109 secular priests and eighty-two religious priests. Almost all the religious were concentrated in the large monasteries in the center of the city of Arequipa, while the secular clergy staffed the parishes in the city and in the small towns in the country. The proportion of priests to inhabitants in the entire department during that period was approximately one to every six hundred. Obviously, this statistic does not reflect the real pastoral situation because it does not take into account the dispersion of the people and the concentration of religious priests in the city of Arequipa itself, which had a population of about 15,176. It would therefore be more realistic to cite the proportion of priests to inhabitants in the little towns around Arequipa (Miraflores, Cayma, Tiabaya, Characato, etc.), where there was approximately one priest for every eight hundred to one thousand inhabitants.[6]

Another important indicator was the situation in the seminaries. After a period of abandonment following the wars of independence and the social instability and economic impoverishment that ensued, in the middle of the century the bishops managed to restore the seminaries. The most notable example was Santo Toribio in Lima, restored by Archbishop Luna Pizarro in 1847. Luna Pizarro and the other heads of the church in Lima who succeeded him all sought to name rectors and professors of good intellectual and moral quality. Among them one can mention the names of Juan Ambrosio Huerta, Manuel Teodoro Bandini, Manuel Tovar, and Pedro Manuel García. All of them became bishops of considerable prestige later on. According to Father Vargas, the years between 1847 and 1861 constituted one of the best periods in the history of the seminary. In 1864 there were forty-five students in the major seminary.[7] By way of contrast, in 1942 there were only fourteen students.[8]

From all of this it may deduced that it was not independence in itself that caused the shortage, as is frequently stated, but rather other factors inherent in the social and political reality of the nineteenth century. Furthermore, it is important to stress again the positive image the church projected during and after independence. Recent studies have clearly established that the great majority of the secular clergy in the last decades of the colonial period consisted of creoles.[9] Although the "peninsulars" continued to predominate in the most important jobs, the creoles had come to occupy many important posts in the ecclesiastical chapters, and at one time two of the six bishops were creoles. More important than their numerical presence, however, was the level of intellectual and moral quality of these secular clergymen as well as their notable enthusiasm for the independence movement. Among the creole priests who supported independence, and who later played a significant role in the formation of the new republican state, were Francisco Javier de Luna Pizarro, president of the first constitutional assembly and later archbishop of Lima; Toribio Rodríguez de Mendoza, venerable precursor of independence who taught many of the first liberals who graduated from San Carlos; and Francisco de Paula González Vigil, a deputy to congress from Tacna and Arica and a staunch defender of liberty of conscience. By reason of its formation and its articulate liberalism, this creole clergy constituted one of the most progressive elites in the nineteenth century.

In short, a church that at the moment of independence had an abundance of native priests turned into a mission church one century later. In that same period of time the church, which was characterized by its creative contributions to culture and thought, became transformed into a rather conservative institution opposed to political and social change.

To begin our analysis of the vocation crisis, it is well to make an important distinction between the secular or diocesan clergy and the "regular" or religious clergy. In contrast to the secular clergy, which enjoyed considerable social prestige and seemed to be in the best of health at mid-century, the religious clergy was in a state of decline well before independence. Furthermore, unlike the secular clergy, which was made up principally of creoles, the religious clergy, which included numerous "peninsulars," was seriously affected by independence and particularly by the coming of liberalism. In order to distinguish more clearly between the two types of clergies, we shall first examine the case of the religious.

The Religious Clergy

The decline in religious life can be illustrated with statistics. According to a reliable source, in 1790 there were 711 religious priests in Lima, but in 1857 that number had dropped to 155.[10] Even taking into account the fact that many Spanish religious had to leave Peru after independence, this decrease is still quite noticeable. And the crisis continued during the second part of the century. Although the total number of religious—priests and brothers—increased toward the end of the century as a result of the growing number of foreign missionaries, the number of Peruvians in religious life continued to decrease. Of the 271 priests and nonpriests who belonged to religious orders in Lima in 1908, only 130 were Peruvian born.[11]

The causes of this crisis in religious life were multiple and complex. One key factor was the image the religious orders projected toward the end of the colonial period. Increasingly, for many liberals, and liberal priests as well, the orders symbolized all that was wrong in colonial times. Somewhat similarly to medieval Europe, the great religious convents and monasteries had become refuges for the "number two" son or daughter who could not find a place in the secular world, or, especially in the case of women, religious life offered a decent way out for the daughters of wealthy families who failed to arrange a satisfactory marriage for their offspring to advance their interests. Many families saw the church as an extension of their own economic and social aims.

This phenomenon affected the secular clergy as well, but it was more noticeable among the religious. The critics of religious life were scandalized not only by the number of the religious but also by the number and size of their convents and monasteries, which frequently covered entire city blocks in the center of every major city. Most of all, they questioned the reason for the existence of those "monastery villages" because they could not see what social or public function they fulfilled. While the secular clergy preached and instructed the people, the religious lived sheltered from the world. Their monasteries were, claimed Manuel Lorenzo de Vidaurre, "asylums for the lazy and the ignorant" in the very middle of Lima.[12] The decadence in religious life was therefore partially the result of the very medieval character of colonial Peru.

Another factor was the constant interference of the crown in the internal affairs of the religious in order to "reform" them. In reality, the reformist measures usually tended to speed up the process of decadence. One example was the *alternativa* (the alternative), which consisted in an arrangement imposed by the king by which every other superior of a province or a monastery had to be a Spaniard. Evidently the "alternative" was not perceived as a "reform" in America because it touched off several scandalous battles between creole and peninsular friars in the seventeenth and eighteenth centuries.[13] But the prime example of the interference of the Bourbons in religious life was the expulsion of the Jesuits from Spanish America in 1767. These and other measures (the *recurso de fuerza*, for example, which permitted religious to file legal complaints against their religious superiors) interjected politics into the heart of religious life, a fact that served to demoralize the members of religious orders even more.

Furthermore, partially as a result of this royal interference, certain orders and establishments of the religious acquired a distinct Spanish image. The secular clergy, made up principally of creoles, identified itself with the liberal cause that overthrew Spanish power, while the religious clergy became identified in the public's mind with the old regime. At the time of independence many religious were expelled or executed because they were Spanish or supported Spain. In 1824 Bolívar closed the great missionary center of Santa Rosa de Ocopa and deported the Franciscan missionaries who used the monastery as their base of operations to evangelize the central mountains and the jungle. The nineteenth-century liberal historian Mariano Paz Soldán offered as an explanation the fact that Ocopa was "a purely Spanish establishment."[14]

Later on, in 1836, Ocopa was restored and new missionaries, almost all Spanish, arrived to take charge of their old missionary center. Although their arrival provoked much criticism from the liberals, who claimed that the missionaries would spread antiliberal ideas among the faithful, the Franciscans who returned to Ocopa gave themselves over to the task with zeal. But they were not nearly so numerous as before, and they were barely able to cover a small part of the vast central mountain and jungle region to which their predecessors, deported in 1824, and the Jesuits, expelled in 1767, had attended. The priest shortage was therefore felt in these areas long before it was noticed in other parts.

Finally, the Peruvian liberals, who had been greatly influenced by the doctrines of regalism and Gallicanism, made the religious way of life a special target of their reformist plans. The most notable example was the "Reform of the Regulars," decreed in 1826. Among other articles the decree declared that there could only be one house of each religious order in any given city or town. Only the Franciscans and certain other special groups were exempt from this rule. As a result, some thirty-nine houses for religious men were suppressed (the feminine orders were exempt).[15] It is not known exactly what happened to the religious who were affected by this and other measures. The government offered to facilitate the process of transferring from religious life to the secular clergy for those who wished to make the change. In Lima alone some 231 religious men were secularized between 1826 and 1830.[16] The impact of the decree was devastating. In 1845 Archbishop Luna Pizarro gave this bleak testimony of its consequences in his archdiocese:

> "In the course of the twenty-four years since that fateful decree of the first protectorate only five Dominicans, one Franciscan, two Augustinians, four Mercedarians, and not a single religious of the Recollection Fathers have been ordained. One deacon of the Good Death Fathers was ordained. But in the same lapse of time more than 160 religious have disappeared in Santo Domingo, and almost the same number in San Francisco, and the same loss is true of the other orders. Many of the religious who died were men of great sanctity and wisdom. But very few remain and there are few to take their place."[17]

The convents and monasteries of women religious were not touched; in general, there were fewer criticisms directed at the women than the men. Of course, the same irregularities existed among the women. Chávez de la Rosa failed in his plan to reform Santa Catalina in Arequipa. In 1831 a nun from Arequipa, Dominga Gutiérrez, provoked a public scandal when she fled from her convent after leaving a cadaver in her bed.[18] In spite of such examples, however, there are other testimonies that offer a different view of the women religious. William Bennet Stevenson, an English Protestant who lived for twenty years in Latin America, referred to a visit he made to Lima between 1804 and 1805. Stevenson, who had held the positions of secretary to the president of the captaincy general of Quito and secretary to Lord Cochrane, stated that, although he had had many conversations with nuns, he had never found an unhappy one.[19] Without doubt, the fact that the great majority of religious women were Peruvian also helped their overall image. Nevertheless, the women did not entirely escape the liberals' attack. As a result of the different liberal laws of the nineteenth century, they lost many of their properties and their income was greatly reduced.[20] This impoverishment of the convents and monasteries, coupled with the liberals' constant criticism of the usefulness of the religious way of life, hurt the general image of the religious. In this sense, the decline in the number of professed women religious from the colonial period to the middle of the century is worth noting: in Lima in 1790 there were 434, but in 1857 that number had fallen to 211.[21]

Thus the crisis in religious life, which began in the colonial period, became even more acute after independence. With the reopening of Ocopa and the arrival of many foreign religious in the second part of the nineteenth century, religious life experienced a noticeable revitalization.

The Secular Clergy

In spite of the problems that affected the religious clergy, it would have been difficult at mid-century to predict a dark future for the secular clery. There was no scarcity of priests of the secular clergy in the cities and towns, their intellectual and moral level was relatively high, and the seminaries were full of promising young men. Nevertheless, this positive picture changed radically in the space of some thirty to forty years. Without doubt there were many factors at work that caused this phenomenon. We can single out four that seemed especially important: first, the "romanization" of the church as a result of the struggle of the Holy See to establish its control over the church in Latin America after the long period of royal patronage; second, the different liberal reforms of the nineteenth century that undermined the colonial supports upon which the church rested, especially the economic aid that came from the tithes; third, certain social factors, such as the cultural and educational abyss that separated the lower classes and especially the Indians from the westernized middle classes, as well as the lack of a stable family life among the popular classes, and finally, the progressive dechristianization of the upper and middle classes, the result in part of campaigns carried out by liberals, positivists, and Marxists, and in part of a general secularization that manifested itself in a growing indifference toward religion and at times an open hostility toward the church. In chronological order, the first of these factors was what some have termed the "romanization" of the Peruvian church.

The "Romanization" of the Church

As a consequence of independence, almost all the bishops were forced to abandon their dioceses. Bolívar and his immediate successors attempted to assume the right of patronage over the church and to name new bishops to fill in the vacant dioceses. Rome rejected these attempts to create a national patronage and ignored the petitions in the hope of gaining control over the church. Since neither side gave in, Peru found itself with vacant dioceses for long periods: Lima, 1821–35; Trujillo, 1820–36; Huamanga (Ayacucho), 1821–43; Cuzco, 1826–43; and Mainas (later on Chachapoyas), 1821–36. The only diocese not affected was Arequipa, where José Sebastián de Goyeneche, bishop since 1818, managed to defy the pressures to replace him. He continued to be the head of his diocese until 1860, when he was named archbishop of Lima.[22]

In a study of this subject, Father Antonine Tibesar showed how the Holy See managed to impose its will on the church in Peru.[23] In face of the demands of the Peruvian state, Rome conceded to the government the right to name candidates to fill the episcopal vacancies, but only on one very important condition: the candidate named had to be a man acceptable to the Holy See. Two of the key criteria for approving or disapproving a candidate were his attitude on the question of papal supremacy in the church and his feelings toward liberalism in general. In reality, the battle between Rome and Lima over national patronage was but an extension of a bitter ideological conflict in full process in Europe. The church in Europe, which had already suffered the impact of violent anticlericalism in France and faced other liberals and their allies, such as the Masons, who threatened to unleash similar persecutions in Spain, Portugal, and Italy, did not look with sympathy on the appearance of liberal ideas in any part of the world. For that reason, even though all the first bishops named by the government in Lima and confirmed in Rome were Peruvians of unquestionable patriotism and priests of excellent qualities, they were also ultramontanists and political conservatives. Agustín Guillermo Charún, bishop of Trujillo (1835–57) and a critic of the ideas of Bartolomé Herrera, was an exception to this rule.[24]

At the same time, the new bishops set about reorganizing the church, beginning with the seminaries, which soon felt the impact of the new orientation. Furthermore, the church invited to Peru the first foreign missionaries since independence in order to evangelize the central mountain region and the jungle. This explains why the Franciscans were able to return to reopen Ocopa in 1836. Given their antiliberal mentality (most of all of Pedro Gual, who became the Commissary General of the order), they helped to strengthen Rome's position in the areas where they worked. Finally, the outstanding architect of ultramontanism in Peru and therefore of the "romanization" of the church was Bartolomé Herrera. These were the principal means, concluded Father Tibesar, by which the Holy See established its presence in Peru and at the same time transformed the church into its own image.

This reform had ambiguous consequences for the church. The liberal-minded priests such as Luna Pizarro, González Vigil, and Juan Gualberto Valdivia were forced to choose between their liberalism and their loyalty to Rome. Each had to face the dilemma in his own way. Luna Pizarro renounced the liberalism of his youth and years later rose to become a conservative archbishop of Lima, 1843–55. González Vigil did not accept the new orientation and in 1851 was excommunicated by Pope Pius IX. In another notable case, the national convention of 1856 elected Juan Gualberto Valdivia, a distinguished liberal in the postindependence period, to be bishop of Cuzco. Although Valdivia had already retracted many of his advanced ideas, including a plea in favor of a married clergy, this was not sufficient and Rome rejected his nomination. The liberalism of these clergymen was not the only factor in Rome's decisions. Vigil had ceased to practice his priesthood long before, and Valdivia, who participated in many of the rebellions that characterized Arequipa's history, was known for his quick temper.[25]

In this manner a generation of liberal priests began to disappear from the ranks of the clergy. However, it would be an exaggeration to say that this "romanization" process was the only, or even the principal, factor in the vocation crisis. First, the clergy that came to predominate in the church were in general more conservative, but not less capable or educated. And second, the full restoration of the church was achieved under this ultramontanist clergy. Under the leadership of such outstanding prelates as Bartolomé Herrera (Arequipa), Ambrosio Huerta (Puno and Arequipa), and Teodoro del Valle (Huánuco), seminaries flourished, the Catholic press prospered, and priests continued to enjoy the public's esteem.

Nevertheless, in the middle of this brief religious rebirth, one phenomenon stands out: the increasingly uniform character of the church in its mentality, in the formation of the clergy, and in the social composition of the faithful. The pluralism that had characterized the church during and after independence (there were royalists, liberals, and moderates among the clergy) was extinguished and replaced by an intellectual uniformity with respect to religion, politics, and society. When the church broke off the dialogue with liberalism, it also closed the doors to important groups within the middle and upper classes. By mid-century people began to associate the terms "Catholic" with "conservative," and "anticlerical" with "liberal."

The new coastal capitalist class that emerged in this period tended to identify with liberalism and later on with positivism. In contrast, the petite bourgeoisie, the lower middle classes of the provinces, and the older established families of the upper classes that were not tied to the coastal oligarchy, tended to identify with Catholicism. One may defend the posture adopted by Rome in the eighteenth and nineteenth centuries as a necessary reaction against unreasonable liberals, who quite frequently contradicted their own liberalism by assuming very intolerant attitudes, especially toward the church. Yet Rome's own intransigence did not seem to produce positive results for the church. Everywhere in Latin America the church became more exclusive and even sectarian, and in so doing closed off possibilities of attracting candidates to the priesthood from certain social classes.

Economic Factors

There have been no studies to date of the impact on the church of the elimination of the tithes and other sources of income that it received in colonial times. What we aim to establish here is the probable relation between the church's loss of revenue and the drop in vocations. The church had already begun to experience economic stress with the expulsion of the Jesuits and the wars of independence. All during the nineteenth century the church steadily lost properties and other sources of revenue. In 1833 the wealth of the suppressed monasteries and other religious houses was nationalized. In 1865 the wealth belonging to the confraternities was transferred to municipal charitable works. In 1911 another law caused the church to lose many urban properties.[26]

But the biggest blow of all was the abolition of tithes in May 1859. President Castilla, in order to ease the blow, proposed a formula that was incorporated into all future church-state agreements. According to the formula, the state promised to pay the salaries of all prelates (and other church dignataries) and to help support seminaries and church-administered hospitals. The state also agreed to pay the salaries of the clergy, taking as a base what the clergy received in 1852 and 1853, until such time as the clergy could be self-supporting. This additional aid was reduced in 1887 and eliminated soon afterwards.[27] Much later, under Sánchez Cerro, the practice of subsidizing parishes in the border areas was established.[28] Therefore, the suppression of the tithes did not mean a total reduction of state aid to the church.

Nevertheless, as a consequence of the abolition of the tithes and the loss of other forms of income that it normally received since colonial times, the church was forced to rely upon the offerings of the faithful and stipends for Masses, the sacraments, and burials. It is therefore not surprising that the bishops became increasingly concerned over the precarious economic state of the church after the elimination of the tithes. Among other topics, the prelates complained that the state either reduced the official contribution that it promised the church or simply failed to comply with its promise.

Barely a decade after the abolition of the tithes, the impact was already noticeable, especially in the mountains. In 1868 Ambrosio Huerta, the bishop of the new diocese of Puno, raised his voice in protest over a proposed law that would drastically reduce stipends for marriages and funerals. According to Huerta, the income received from these sources should not be lost because it "represents compensation for the tithes."[29] Even more eloquent is the testimony of the bishop of Ayacucho, José Ezequiel Moreyra, in 1867. In a letter to Archbishop Goyeneche, Moreyra complained about the ridiculous rent of "480 soles monthly" that the state paid to priests in the more important parishes. That sum, said the prelate, was the same that "a doorkeeper at a state ministry received." Even worse, in some cases the state simply defaulted on its payments. In his letter, Moreyra singled out the situation of certain members of the cathedral choir who had not received their salary "for the space of seventeen months," and that of the chaplain of La Merced who had not received his salary "in twenty months."[30] Finally, in a collective pastoral letter in 1891 the bishops of the entire country referred to the abolition of the tithes and other laws that reduced the church's revenues. According to the bishops, as a result of those measures the clergy, "which ordinarily had very few resources experienced a notable decline in their income."[31]

It is evident that the church found itself in difficult economic straits. It remains now to establish a more direct link between this fact and vocations. In his letter of 1867, Bishop Moreyra warned that if the economic situation of the clergy did not improve, there would soon be a general abandonment of parishes, especially in the rural areas. Declared Moreyra, "Not even a bishop can oblige someone to die of hunger."[32]

This prophecy of the bishop of Ayacucho was fulfilled. Toward the end of the nineteenth century and at the beginning of this one, the general picture the bishops and other witnesses painted of the church was very somber. Everywhere, but especially in the rural areas, parishes and doctrines were in a state of abandonment. In 1903 an ecclesiastical visitor, Esteban Pérez, who was a Spanish missionary, informed Archbishop Tovar about the pastoral situation in Yauyos, to the southeast of Lima. In his report, Pérez noted that the shortage of priests had reached such an extreme that some parishes had not seen a pastor in four years.[33] Furthermore, the local priests had become increasingly destitute. Not only did they not receive any aid from the state, observed the visitor, but the state even demanded from them a tax for all the sacraments they administered or the marriages and funerals they conducted. The faithful themselves, noted Pérez, are quite poor, and even "haggle over the church stipends" and at times carry out clandestine burials so as to avoid paying the fees due the church.[34]

In 1912 the bishop of Puno, Valentín Ampuero, described the precarious situation of his clergy in a report to the central government. The prelate from Puno noted that the priests in his diocese lived mainly off the fees and stipends they received from the marriages they performed and the Masses they celebrated for the village feast days. But what they received was so insufficient that many of them were obliged to "seek their livelihood by other means, generally licit, but completely foreign to their ministry."[35] Ampuero concluded his report by stating that if the government did not remedy this situation, within a few years there would no longer exist a "single civilizing influence" among the peasants. In 1904 a "priest from Cuzco" wrote about the "sad spectacle of the abandonment of many parishes" in the country, although this anonymous author noted with critical sharpness that this was due not to the shortage of priests but rather to the fact that no one wanted to work in "poor and far away Indian parishes."[36]

The impact of the economic crisis was felt in the seminaries as well. Although they received a subsidy from the state, this never covered more than a few general expenses. In 1880 the rector of Santo Toribio in Lima, Manuel Tovar, presented a study on the state of the seminary. Tovar, later to be archbishop of Lima, warned that, given the pressing economic situation of the times, it would be necessary to reduce the number of scholarships to the seminary to "the thirty-one permanent openings, but to none beyond that number. . . ."[37] Tovar added that the state paid for six of those scholarships.

The documentation on the seminary of San Carlos y San Marcelo in Trujillo is especially illustrative. In an extensive chronicle he wrote on the seminary, the rector, Conrad Oquillas (1919–25), also saw a direct relationship between the drop in the number of seminarians and the seminary's financial problems. As a point of reference, Oquillas cited the year 1849 when twenty-one candidates presented themselves for sacred orders.[38] By way of contrast, between 1883 and 1891 the total number of young men ordained had fallen to eighteen.[39] According to Oquillas, one of the principal obstacles in the way of attracting students to San Carlos was economic. The number of students rose and fell according to the number of scholarships available. In 1846 San Carlos offered thirty-six full scholarships. But toward the end of the century the seminary offered far fewer scholarships: twelve in 1898, eleven in 1899, and seven in 1900.[40]

Although the number of scholarships increased to around twelve in the next few years, the number of seminarians continued to fall drastically. In 1892 there were fourteen in the major seminary and fifty-eight in the minor seminary. But by 1918 the total number of students in the "ecclesiastical section" had dropped to six.[41] There were, however, other factors that influenced this sharp decline. In 1908 the diocese of Cajamarca, which sent seminarians to Trujillo, founded its own seminary, and in 1911 a central seminary for the entire country was created in Lima. But these latter phenomena cannot by themselves explain the decline in candidates for the priesthood in Trujillo.

It is revealing to see why there was a dramatic increase in the number of candidates in the following years. In attempting to solve the crisis in San Carlos, the directors started a campaign to attract more youth to the seminary. An important part of that campaign consisted in searching for funds and asking for contributions from the parishes in the diocese. As a result of the campaign, in the years 1923 and 1924 the number of students who presented themselves for an ecclesiastical career jumped sharply to thirty-four. According to Father Oquillas, almost all of these students "enjoyed full scholarships." Furthermore, there were very few paying students left. In 1906 there were fifteen paying students, but in the years 1907 and 1908 there were none. Oquillas, who had organized the entire campaign, was highly satisfied.

He wrote: "The organization of the ecclesiastical section and its maintenance required many economic sacrifices, but they were well worth it, because they have enabled us to solve the crisis of many small towns that were suffering morally as a result of the shortage of priests . . . ."[42]

Notwithstanding these bright hopes expressed by Father Oquillas in the decade of the twenties, the number of young men who came to be ordained in the following years was far less than expected. Between 1930 and 1963 some fifty-four priests were ordained for the archdiocese of Trujillo (the diocese was elevated to that rank in 1943), that is, an average of one or two each year, a very insufficient number if one takes into account the fact that the city of Trujillo grew seven times in size during this same period. In 1984 the archdiocese of Trujillo had thirty-four priests of the secular clergy born in Peru, a number hardly superior to the twenty-six it had in 1890.[43]

In reality, the economic crisis that affected the church was not the only factor to explain this drop in the number of students for the priesthood or the high number of those who left the seminary before ordination. During this same period (1850–1930), Peru underwent a process of transformation from a colonial to a modern, capitalistic society, especially on the coast. With this change, public education became more available. At the same time, higher education became modernized and the number of new careers increased in response to the needs of the times: engineering, agronomy, commerce, and teaching were added to the list of possibilities. Teaching especially became attractive as the number of public schools increased. Unlike the colonial period, when the priesthood was one of the few "prestige" careers that a creole could follow, the new capitalistic society of the late nineteenth and early twentieth centuries offered a much more expanded horizon of possibilities for a young man from the middle and the upper classes. Given this fact, the seminary continued to be a means of social mobility, but not necessarily for an ecclesiastical career. Bishop José Dammert of Cajamarca reported that in the major seminary in his diocese, which normally had thirty to forty students, in a period of forty years (1911–60), only forty reached the priesthood. "The rest," observed Dammert, "went to work in commerce, became teachers, took up the liberal professions, or went into the Civil Guard (the national police)."[44] The following petition in 1919 for a scholarship to San Carlos, typical of many others, raised certain doubts in the mind of the bishop about the purity of motivation that lay behind it:

Your Excellency:

I am José J. Sánchez, master of the chapel and a neighbor of Pueblo Nuevo de Cobán. I wish respectfully to present the following petition to you. My son Wilfredo feels a vocation toward the ecclesiastical state, but given my lack of resources I cannot provide for him the necessary basic studies . . . .[45]

In this case the bishop, no doubt a bit skeptical, granted a scholarship "for the academic year of 1919." Needless to say, one cannot establish a precise relationship between economic factors and the shortage of vocations; there are other social, psychological, and religious factors that influence the decision of a person to pursue an ecclesiastical career. Nevertheless, in general it may be affirmed that after the suppression of the tithes, a priestly career in Peru meant entering a lower economic scale and living a life of far greater insecurity than in previous periods.

Social and Cultural Factors

In Latin America and Peru it is important to examine the theme of priestly vocations in relation to that of the popular classes. Although the categories of "class" and "race" are not entirely adequate to describe colonial realities, it can be said that in general the secular clergy at the time of independence came largely from the equivalent of the middle class, neither poor nor rich. Racially, the majority were creoles. Mestizos and Indians played a far lesser role in the official church. For different historical reasons, from the sixteenth century on the crown and the church adopted a policy of not ordaining Indians to the priesthood, and mestizos only if they fulfilled certain rigid norms, such as "purity of blood," not being a "natural son" (born out of wedlock), and having "good manners."[46] In the seventeenth century the crown softened this policy, and in several royal cédulas (decrees) it ordered the seminaries to offer a certain number of scholarships to mestizos and Indians. In general, however, this reform was not heeded and very few mestizos were actually ordained, and even fewer Indians.[47]

This social and racial reality did not change radically with independence, and until very late in the nineteenth century the great majority of the members of the secular clergy came from the middle classes in the cities or the towns in the provinces. Toward the end of the century, however, one can note a change in the social composition of the clergy, which came increasingly from the popular classes. Many testimonies from that period underline this

The Priest Shortage

change from a middle-class clergy to one largely from the lower classes. Very rarely did a vocation come from the upper classes. At the same time the bishops and rectors of the seminaries expressed their concern over the decline in the level of the formation of the clergy.

Bishop José Ezequiel Moreyra, to whom we referred above, revealed his fear that with the elimination of fixed means of income, the level of quality of the clergy would also fall. "Priests used to come from the best families," wrote the prelate from Ayacucho, but given an uncertain future economically, the priestly career no longer attracted the sons of those families. "And so it will happen," he continued, "that ignorant men with a bad education who are unable to pursue a career will begin to enter the service of the church . . . ."[48]

Although it is not necessary to agree with the pejorative judgment that Bishop Moreyra expressed concerning the character and motivation of candidates from the popular classes, one can say that this prophecy was fulfilled in a way, too. In his report written in 1912, Bishop Ampuero of Puno complained that the clergy of his diocese was not up to their mission, "either because they do not have an adequate formation or because of the bad social conditions in which they work . . . ."[49] The anonymous author of Cuzco (1904) claimed that a general decadence had set in among the clergy of the diocese, a phenomenon he attributed to the fact that "every day they ordain priests in the seminary without the necessary formation."[50]

In 1907 the bishop of Huánuco, Pedro Pablo Drinot y Piérola, gave a fuller explanation for this lack of "able pastors." Drinot blamed first the general state of ignorance regarding religion. But even more important than this was the mistaken image that the people had of the priesthood. Very frequently, he claimed, families "pushed" their sons toward the priesthood because they saw it as "one of many professions, but easier, less costly, but still lucrative." Finally, Drinot emphasized the lack of adequate means for forming the clergy as another important cause.[51] It is worth noting that when this Andean bishop described the priestly career as "lucrative," he was referring to lower-class families for whom the priesthood would be a step up the social and economic ladder.

Another important testimony is that given by Father Vargas Ugarte himself years later. The work by Father Vargas on this subject, published in 1948 and reedited and revised in 1967, repeats many of the same concepts and judgments expressed by the churchmen who first felt the effects of the crisis. Father Vargas complained of a "notable weakening of the Christian spirit" in Peru, which was due most of all to a "shortage of good and zealous priests."[52] At the same time, he attributed the shortage of priests principally to the loss of quality of the clergy, which came increasingly from the popular classes. For this reason, the national clergy lacked a level of formation worthy of their state. According to Father Vargas, "All this has reduced the credibility and the social influence that our clergy used to have, and it explains why there are few priests from the upper and middle classes."[53]

On the other hand, the Jesuit historian did not oppose the idea of young men from the popular classes entering the seminary. The problem for him was that those social classes lacked the necessary level of formation to enter the seminaries, and some, especially from the "Indian race," lacked the necessary moral energy to practice the self-discipline that the priestly career demanded. Father Vargas's solution was to apply more severe standards in admitting candidates to the seminaries and to raise the level of formation once the candidates were admitted.

This analysis by Father Vargas helps us to appreciate the complexity of the problem and to understand the church's dilemma. In colonial times, the church was under pressure to ordain only a very limited number of mestizos or Indians. As a result, it necessarily had to depend upon small cultural elites to fill the ranks of the clergy: Spaniards, creoles, and mestizos of a certain category in colonial society and, in postindependence times, the white middle classes. However, when the double crisis of the "romanization" of the church and the elimination of tithes arose, and to this a third crisis may be added—the increase of secularization and religious indifference—the middle classes no longer found the priesthood a very attractive career to follow. For young men who tended to be liberals, the church itself symbolized Peru's colonial past. But for more tradition-oriented families, the priestly career meant entering a lower economic scale. And for other families who had drifted away from religious practice, the priesthood no longer held the attraction of prestige or social status that it once had.

In the light of these considerations, the church had to face more seriously the need to foster vocations for the priesthood from among young men of the popular classes. In theory this did not pose too much of a challenge since the church from the sixteenth century on had always incorporated these classes into its institutional framework. Within the hierarchical world of colonial Catholicism, the Indians and mestizos performed a multitude of functions: catechists, deputies, and assistants to priests in Indian parishes, cantors, sacristans, lay brothers (St. Martin de Porres), etc. In some exceptional cases, an Indian or mestizo reached the priesthood, but with little prospect of advancing beyond that state up the ecclesiastical ladder. In 1766 the University of San Marcos granted the titles of licentiate and doctorate in theology to José Joaquín de Avalo Chauca, an Indian priest who described himself as a "legitimate descendent of the first Catholic *cacique* (chieftain) of the town of Lurín . . . ." And a year later the new doctor was named professor of theology at San Marcos.[54] This extraordinary Indian priest was the exception that proved the rule, but the example also underlines the fact that the church did not place any theological or other obstacle of an intrinsic nature in the way of the ordination of Indians or mestizos.

Nor did the church impose class or economic barriers. Throughout the last century the bishops and rectors of seminaries made a great effort to offer scholarships to those in need. Manuel Tovar, the rector who complained in 1880 that he was forced to reduce the number of scholarships because of hard times, had himself studied in the seminary on a scholarship.[55] And many years before him Bartolomé Herrera had also gone to the seminary on a scholarship. But these two men represented the white middle class that had come down the scale economically, not the "popular" classes.

The fundamental problem was the very nature of Peruvian society, which included human groups separated by enormous social and cultural barriers. Until the middle of the twentieth century the great majority of Peruvians were illiterate or had very little formal education. For them, higher education was simply an unattainable goal. But the seminaries continued to be what they had been in colonial times, the ecclesiastical equivalents of the universities that formed the political and economic elites. And very frequently the seminaries performed the same function: Santo Toribio in Lima and San Carlos y San Marcelo in Trujillo educated the sons of the best families, some of whom became priests and others political leaders. Priests in Peru, before and after independence, came from the middle classes that represented only a small percentage of the population. But there was another important impediment that affected the Indians especially: the prevalence of western cultural ways in the seminaries, not only in Peru but in the entire Catholic world. Only in recent times has the type of formation offered in Catholic seminaries been questioned. In a report he made in 1971, Bishop Dammert of Cajamarca underlined this disparity between the cultural world of the seminary and the cultural milieu of the students who attended them:

> In the major seminaries of Latin America the candidates were formed with programs, methods, and books appropriate for forming rural priests in Italy, France, or Spain; upon leaving the seminary the young priest assigned to care for the people of a parish in a remote part of the Andes discovered that 90 percent of what he had learned in the seminary was useless, but unfortunately, sometimes in throwing out that which was useless, he also disregarded that which was useful.[56]

Furthermore, within the same country the great cultural differences from one region to another can also create difficulties of adaptation for many youths who lack the necessary preparation or capacity of assimilation to study in a milieu different from the one in which they were raised. In a letter written in 1901, Bishop Puirredón of Trujillo invited the Franciscans to establish a minor seminary in Cajamarca. In his letter he explained that it was not convenient for the youth of that mountain city to come to Trujillo on the coast because "the climate, the habits, and customs of the coast are completely strange and harmful to the health of the inhabitants of the mountains."[57] In a more recent example, in 1969 the Maryknoll Fathers closed their minor seminary in Puno because very few of their students reached the priesthood. Among other reasons, life in the seminary was so different from that to which the people of the highlands were accustomed that Quechua- or Aymara-speaking youths actually suffered a cultural shock in the seminary. And of course the Peruvian church, which is subject to the norms of the universal church, was not free to experiment or change the system of formation.

Besides this obvious cultural problem, there was another, even greater, and almost insoluble one: the human and moral breakdown of many families, especially among the popular classes, as a result of being socially marginated and economically exploited since the sixteenth century. It is not necessary to cite all the abundant literature that attests to the widespread incidence of promiscuity and marital instability among lower-class groups in colonial times: blacks, mulattos, Indians, and mestizos. It is sufficient to cite a few testimonies from republican times to show that these problems not only did not go away, but that they have probably increased as a result of many new factors, including the migrations of the Indians to the coast, the impact of western culture upon traditional Andean cultures, and the lack of economic stability. In 1858 Manuel A. Fuentes, an assiduous compiler of statistics, noted that 56 percent of all births in Lima were illegitimate.[58] The authors of the census book on Lima in 1908 stated quite clearly what was the nature of the problem. According to the declarations of the women in the census: "Less than 15 percent of all white women have had children born out of wedlock, but about 40 percent of all Indian and mestizo women have had illegitimate births, and black women have an even higher percentage."[59]

Finally, the census of 1981 revealed the fact that approximately 29 percent of all homes in Peru were made up of "incomplete families," that is, either the father or the mother was absent. In the great majority of these cases the woman ran the household.[60]

Given this discouraging picture, it should be evident that one of the causes of the lack of good candidates to the priesthood or the religious life is not merely the cultural disparity between social classes, but more basically the deficient human upbringing that a significant portion of the population has received. In the sixteenth century Viceroy Toledo pointed to the need to teach the Indians to be "men" before baptizing them.[61] In the nineteenth and twentieth centuries the church has had to face a similar problem with respect to the admission of youths from the popular classes to the priesthood or the religious life. The gesture of giving out scholarships or conditioning studies to meet the level of the students does not resolve this deeper problem: the lack of certain human qualities that reflect a general breakdown in family life. In this sense, the crisis of vocations is a reflection of a crisis in the very heart of Peruvian society.

Finally, to all of these factors one should add the growing indifference and, in some cases, open hostility toward religion, a phenomenon that became more and more evident in the second part of the last century. We shall explore this theme more extensively in the next chapter. It is sufficient for now to cite a survey carried out in 1967 on the occasion of the Conciliar Mission of Lima to appreciate the extent of this religious indifferentism. According to the survey, only 25 percent of all Catholics regularly attended Sunday Mass, and the majority of these were women.[62] On the other hand, the great majority of Peruvians do practice some kind of popular religiosity. But popular religiosity is not, by its nature, very ecclesial, that is, it does not awaken in the individual a desire to serve the church as a priest, brother, consecrated woman, or committed layperson.

By the middle of the twentieth century the Peruvian church found itself in the middle of a prolonged and deep crisis, with few Peruvian priests, and many of them without an adequate level of formation or education, at least according to the norms of western culture. In response, the church began to depend increasingly on foreign clergy. For a while the presence of the foreign clergy alleviated the crisis, but it also encouraged the tendency to put off the day of reckoning with the question of why there were so few native vocations. In a famous article on this theme, "The Seamy Side of Charity" (1967), Iván Illich outlined the dilemma: the more foreigners among the clergy, the less the need to analyze the real underlying problems of the church.[63]

With the great renovation that the church in all Latin America began to experience after Vatican II, the problem of the vocation shortage has become, ironically, less urgent. Among other reasons, the vocation crisis and a greater awareness of the importance of the laity led the church to reorder its priorities and to elaborate a more original and dynamic pastoral plan. For many church persons the vocation problem has been relegated to the status of a second-class priority in favor of other, more urgent tasks, such as forming lay adults to became more conscious of their own Christianity or educating parents to raise their children as better Christians.

Paradoxically, the creation of a church "from below" was exactly what the sixteenth century missionaries intended from the beginning. But given its excessive dependence on political power and power elites, the church did not finish that process. In this sense, the crisis of the priest shortage served to reveal this fundamental weakness of the church, and it also forced the church to question the image that it projected to the world outside itself. In the years since the council the dilemma has become even more acute: as long as the church does not change its pastoral methods and its relationship with society in general, it will not attract the persons it desires to the priesthood or the religious life. It would be well now to examine more in depth the context in which this crisis arose: the long period beginning in the middle of the last century during which the church reacted against the attacks of liberal-positivistic society. It was during this period that the postcolonial church emerged as the "Militant Church."

3

The Militant Church, 1855-1930
Genesis and Development

The times are very difficult . . . the storm that has been unleashed on the church is severe. The waves of error threaten to drown revealed truth, and the corruption of customs produced by error does not cease to assault the boat of Peter.

TEODORO DEL VALLE, 1879

With these words[1] the bishop of Huánuco expressed the generalized pessimism of the church toward a society that was increasingly influenced by liberalism and religious indifference. At the same time he revealed what was the dominant note of the church in all of Latin America from the middle of the nineteenth century until the middle of the twentieth: the adoption of a defensive mentality, at times very closed, in the face of all groups and currents it perceived as hostile to its existence. Among these enemies were to be found liberals, positivists, Masons, Protestants, anarchists, and socialists. To contain the growing influence of these groups the church set itself up as a bulwark of traditional values. In the struggle to defend those values, as well as not a few of her own interests and privileges, the church mobilized the faithful and converted them into "militants" called upon to participate in a great cause that was both religious and political. The concept of a Catholic as a "militant" soldier of a cause was something radically new in the history of the Peruvian church and constituted a decisive dividing line between the colonial church and the first decades of the republic, on the one hand, and all subsequent history on the other.

The church did not react to its critics or to its own internal problems, such as the shortage of priests, in a way that was always coherent and systematic. Nevertheless, a certain uniformity can be discerned in the different ways in which it did react to the crisis. The principal objective was to forge a model of society and church opposed to that of liberal-positivistic society. The principal methods to attain that end were first to fortify the ties with Rome; second, to strengthen the church's place in society, especially by winning official protection; and third, to form laypersons of the upper and middle classes to be Catholics conscious of their faith and prepared to assume the mission of defending the church.

The specific means to carry out these objectives were to make the Catholic position well known by whatever means of communication possible—sermons, newspapers, pamphlets; to invite missionaries from Europe to fill certain areas of great need, especially the area of education; to form groups of laypersons in each region in order to heighten their awareness of the need to defend the church, including in politics; and to foster public acts of piety to fortify the faithful in their resolve to fulfill their new mission.

The adoption of this militant attitude had ambiguous consequences for the church. On the one hand, in the process of reorganizing itself, the church inculcated in the faithful a deeper sense of "church." On the other hand, it also engendered a unidimensional and at times closed mentality. During this period the word "Catholic" come to signify "conservative" or "traditionalist." Of course, from the Catholics' point of view, the liberals and positivists operated on intellectual visions that were highly biased against religion and the church. Nonetheless, the loss of a Christian presence in intellectual circles and universities in the second half of the last century was also due to the prevalence of a closed mentality on the part of the clergy and many laypersons with respect to new intellectual currents. The following declaration made in 1915 by Fidel Olivas Escudero, the bishop of Ayacucho, sums up the Catholic stand toward liberalism: ". . . It is sufficient to remind you, dear children in the Lord, that nobody can be a Catholic and a liberal at the same time. These are mutually exclusive terms, such as truth and error, good and evil, or light and darkness."[2]

The Liberals and the Church

Although the caudillos dominated national politics during the first decades after independence, it was the liberals who elaborated the ideological foundations upon which the republic rested. The ideal of the liberals was the creation of a democratic, egalitarian society solidly based upon respect for the law. On the other hand, the liberals had a very limited concept of social change and very little contact with the popular classes. For this reason, their idealism and their emphasis on the law above all other considerations constituted their greatest weakness.

Nevertheless, somewhat conscious of their distance from the popular classes, the liberals recognized the importance of the church as the only national institution truly present in all social classes. The church exercised considerable moral and cultural influence over the Indians in their parishes and over the middle and upper classes in the high schools, seminaries, and universities it ran. And, of course, through public worship it touched practically every Peruvian in some way or other, whatever his or her social station. This is why for the liberals and the caudillos the first important task of the new republican state was to win control over the church. Without the moral legitimization of the church, the task of laying the foundations of the republic would be very difficult. The necessity of winning the loyalty of the church formed the background of the crisis that arose over the naming of bishops as well as many other conflicts between the church and the state throughout the nineteenth century.

However, it is well to point out that the first liberals were not properly speaking "anticlericals," nor were they antireligious. Their aim was to control the church, not destroy it. Among the first liberals were many priests who believed that religion, and Catholicism specifically, was the only solid social foundation that could guarantee an orderly and civilized society. This was the mind-set that led the first liberals to establish Catholicism as the only religion favored and protected by the state in the first constitution of Peru, promulgated in 1823. Although some liberals in the beginning favored religious toleration for non-Catholics, there was none who defended the right to be an atheist, which was considered a form of deviant behavior. Manuel Lorenzo de Vidaurre, the first president of the supreme court, declared: "I fear the atheist more than a beast in the middle of the mountains. I cannot think of a crime of which one who denies the power of a Supreme Being would not be capable."[3]

With this attitude, the liberals revealed themselves to be heirs of a very colonial mentality and, more precisely, of three hundred years of royal patronage by which the king governed the church and watched over the smallest details of its daily life. In this sense, the Peruvian liberals did not draw their inspiration so much from the rationalist doctrines of the French revolution as from Spain's royalist tradition in America. Just as the king had used the church as an instrument of ideological domination in colonial times, so now the liberals hoped to use the church as an instrument at the service of the republic and liberalism.

True anticlericalism appeared in the middle of the nineteenth century in most of Latin America. In Peru the liberals who criticized what they believed to be the excessive influence of the church in society belonged to the new capitalist class enamored of the ideal of social progress. Finally, the really antireligious attack came toward the end of the century in the person of Manuel González Prada (1848–1918), for whom religion was a form of superstition used to justify clerical exploitation of the Indians.

From this point of view, the liberal attack corresponded to the stages of Peru's development. With political emancipation, the doctrinaire liberals limited themselves to claiming what had belonged to the king: the right of patronage. By the decade of the fifties the liberals sought to reduce or eliminate the church's social and economic privileges. It is not a coincidence that the abolition of the tithes (1859) and ecclesiastical exemption from civil proceedings (1856) corresponded to the beginnings of modern capitalism in Peru. And González Prada's radical criticism reflected the positivism of the oligarchies in all of Latin America. Although González Prada himself attacked the oligarchy, he shared with the defenders of the oligarchy in the academic world the same positivistic mentality in regard to the church. For both, the church represented an obstacle in the way of social change.

The Liberal Clergy

Priests of a liberal tendency such as Luna Pizarro, Francisco de Paula González Vigil, Mariano José de Arce, and Juan Gualberto Valdivia found themselves caught between two pressures: the Holy See that condemned liberalism, and the increasingly anticlerical attitudes of many of their coliberals. Furthermore, the social anarchy of the first decades after independence made many liberal priests yearn for a more conservative social and political order. Each faced the dilemma in his own way. Luna Pizarro, after having pursued a very distinguished political career (as deputy in congress and president of that body several times), retired from public life and reappeared much later as archbishop of Lima (1843–55). However, between these two periods he abandoned many of the liberal positions of his youth.

In contrast to Luna Pizarro, Francisco de Paúla González Vigil never renounced his liberalism. Originally from Tacna, Vigil was

The Militant Church, 1855–1930

elected to congress several times. He won fame for a speech in which he denounced the dictator, Agustín Gamarra (1832). Like Luna Pizarro, he too withdrew from politics and later on was named director of the National Library (1836–40; 1845–75). During the years of his directorship he devoted his energies to his favorite cause, writing on the need to create a national church free of interference from Rome and linked to the Holy See only by fraternal ties. In 1848 he published his major work in which he elaborated his message, "Defense of the Authority of Governments and Bishops against the Pretensions of the Roman Curia."[4] Gallicanism and regalism found their best expression in Peru in Vigil.

Obviously, liberals like Vigil could not remain for long in the Catholic church at a time when the papacy was engaged in a full-scale battle against liberalism throughout the entire Catholic world. In 1851 Pius IX condemned Vigil's work and Vigil himself was excommunicated. This condemnation, however, only served to encourage Vigil to continue his personal crusade in favor of a national church. Ironically, the brief of excommunication was published by his ex-seminary professor and erstwhile liberal colleague, Francisco Javier de Luna Pizarro, the conservative archbishop of Lima. And so a generation of liberal clergy began disappearing from the ranks of the church. In the light of their disappearance one can appreciate the exclamation in 1869 of Francisco Javier Mariátegui, close friend of Vigil and founder of the Masons in Peru, "What the men of Peru would not give so that the clergy of today could be like the clergy of 1820 in wisdom, patriotism, and virtue!"[5]

The Militant Church Is Born, 1855–1879

Goyeneche and the Convention of 1855–1856

Although there is no particular date on which the Catholic reaction began, one can single out the campaign directed by the bishops against the liberal convention of 1855–56 as the beginning of the "militant church." The measures adopted by the anticlerical parliamentarians provoked much antagonism in Catholic circles. During the sessions, several upper-class women went to the congress building and interrupted speeches by the liberals.[6] Perhaps the sharpest voice raised in protest raised was that of José Sebastián Goyeneche, bishop of Arequipa since 1818. A glance at the letters exchanged between Goyeneche and President Castilla reveals the birth of a Catholic movement throughout the country and especially in Arequipa. Even before the constitutional convention was seated, the Catholics of the "White City" (Arequipa's adopted name) had sent a statement of protest against the liberal tendencies of Castilla's government. The statement contained ten thousand signatures.[7] Although Castilla informed Goyeneche that he personally was not in agreement with his own convention, this was not sufficient to placate the bishop from the south: Goyeneche wrote in reply that the bishops and priests of Peru could not in conscience swear loyalty to the new constitution.[8] This act of defiance by the clergy was the most serious act of disobedience of the church to the state in all of Peru's history. The focal point of this antiliberal sentiment was Arequipa, which rose up in rebellion in November 1855 under General Manuel Ignacio Vivanco. Castilla found himself forced to lay siege to Arequipa for eight months to regain control of the situation. This mobilization of the church's followers to protest against the convention was but the first of a series of actions that signaled the beginning of the "Catholic cause" in Peru.

The Conservative Clergy

The clergy that came to predominate in the church in the middle of the century was ultramontane and politically more conservative than the clergy that fought for independence. Notwithstanding the observation made by Mariátegui cited above, this clergy was also notably cultured. Among their precursors one may mention José Ignacio Moreno, born in Guayaquil, who was vice rector of San Marcos, member of the Cathedral chapter in Lima, and a zealous defender of orthodox causes. His best-known work, "Essay on Papal Supremacy" (1831), went through six different editions. Goyeneche himself symbolized continuity with the past. He was bishop of Arequipa for forty years and then went on to become archbishop of Lima from 1860 to 1872. Luna Pizarro himself, after his conversion from liberalism, continued to be one of the country's leading intellectuals as archbishop of Lima. One of his most important acts was to reopen and reorganize Santo Toribio Seminary in 1847. Less well known is Agustín Guillermo Charún, who served as deputy to congress and minister of state, rector of San Carlos, and finally bishop of Trujillo (1853–57). Charún in particular does not fit into simple categories because he was ultramontane like all other bishops of the period, but he also opposed the political conservativism of Bartolomé Herrera.

The Militant Church, 1855–1930   65

Other bishops who stood out for their intellectual qualities were Teodoro del Valle and Juan Ambrosio Huerta. Del Valle was the first bishop of the diocese of Huánuco, which was separated from the archdiocese of Lima in 1865. In 1867 he founded the Peruvian Catholic Society, one of the first groups dedicated to the cause of the defense of the church against the attacks by the liberals. Ambrosio Huerta was a professor at Santo Toribio Seminary, for a time rector of the seminary, the first bishop of Puno (1865–74), a delegate at the First Vatican Council, and finally bishop of Arequipa (1880–87). He was known as one of the best speakers and thinkers among the nineteenth-century clergy. These clergymen graduated from the best educational centers of the later colonial period: San Carlos, San Marcos, or the seminaries of Santo Toribio, San Jerónimo in Arequipa, or San Antonio Abad in Cuzco. With their formation and intellectual gifts they ranked among the best minds, liberal or conservative, of last-century Peru. In the case of Luna Pizarro, president of the first constitutional assembly in 1822, or Agustín Guillermo Charún, president of the congress of Huancayo of 1839, or Bartolomé Herrera, president of the constitutional congress of 1860, their contribution to Peru's political life was equally as important as their spiritual leadership. The one who probably best typified the mid-century reformed clergy was Bartolomé Herrera.

Bartolomé Herrera and Conservative Thought

The church did not possess a clearly defined social or political doctrine in colonial times or during the first few decades after independence. The same theory that sustained secular society also served the church. The church, which was hierarchical, authoritarian, corporativist, and paternalistic, bore the same marks as colonial secular society. But with the collapse of colonial society the church found itself exposed to attacks from civil society. This fact forced churchmen to grope for a new theory to redefine the relationship between church and society. The liberals, and later on the positivists, forced the church to take a more defensive attitude toward society and to work out a more original view of the church's role in society.

An organic and systematic theory did not appear in Peru until the thirties of this century. Nevertheless, certain basic elements of the theory were worked out by Bartolomé Herrera (1808–64). Although Herrera came to be the best-known conservative thinker in the first decades of the republican period, he by no means represented a moneyed class or an aristocratic clergy. Quite to the contrary, he was of humble origins and was orphaned at the age of five. With the help of a scholarship he studied at San Carlos, where he later became a professor of philosophy. During his studies he discovered his vocation to the priesthood and was ordained in 1829. Among his experiences as a priest he worked as a pastor in the Indian parish of Cajacay, near Huaraz, and later on in Lurín, near Lima. In both parishes he came to know the Indians very well. In 1842 he was named rector of San Carlos. As rector he reformed the college and gave it a very definite conservative and ultramontane orientation. As in colonial days, San Carlos once again became a prestigious center of learning. An entire generation of public figures was educated at the reformed San Carlos: Manuel Pardo, president of the Republic; Pedro Gálvez, the noted liberal; and Manuel Bandini, an archbishop of Lima.

Herrera's fame was due not only to his reforms at San Carlos but also to two sermons of national significance. In 1842 he delivered the funeral oration on the occasion of the death of President Agustín Gamarra, who had fallen in a frustrated attempt to invade Bolivia. Of greater importance, given its ideological message, was the patriotic sermon he delivered in the cathedral on independence day, July 28, 1846, in the presence of President Ramón Castilla and other dignitaries. His sermon contained the first important criticism of liberalism in republican Peru and at the same time constituted the first affirmation of "Hispanism" in Peruvian history.

In his sermon Herrera exalted the values of order and respect for authority that he singled out in contrast to the anarchy wrought by the caudillos and the illusory ideas of the liberals. Most of all, he rejected the concept of popular sovereignty, claiming that Peru had progressed more when it was governed by authoritarian elites, such as the Incas or the Spanish. Herrera pointed out that he meant governing elites based on intelligence and moral integrity. Furthermore, it was not his intention to return to the past, but rather to call his fellow Peruvians to practice the older virtues that Spain had cultivated in Peru. Most of all, he emphasized the Christian faith and the deep respect for legitimate authority that the faith instilled in believers.

President Rufino Echenique (1851–55) named Herrera minister of justice and government, and later on minister of foreign relations. In 1852 he sent Herrera to Rome as a special ambassador to the Vatican to propose a concordat with the Holy See. Herrera failed to achieve his objective, however, mainly because of bureaucratic delays in Rome, but also because of the intransigence of liberals back home. Nevertheless, the Peruvian churchman was well received in Rome, a fact that enhanced Herrera's role as defender of the papacy in Peru. When he returned in 1853 he founded *El Católico*, a weekly newspaper dedicated to combating liberalism.

In 1860 he presided over the constitutional congress that convened that year. Herrera presented his own constitutional plan in which he reorganized society into "associations" and "bodies." Furthermore, he insisted on restoring the privileges that the convention of 1855 had eliminated: the right to have church courts and the collecting of tithes. This was the first explicit program calling for a Catholic corporativist state in Peru. The plan was rejected by the moderates, however, who saw the wisdom of conserving some of the liberals' reforms.

Deflated by this rejection of his proposal, Herrera withdrew from politics. But he continued to play a prominent role in society because he was named bishop of Arequipa, a post he held until his death in 1864. Although the conservative ideas of Herrera held little attraction for later generations more enamored of democratic doctrines, it is important to note that Herrera did not speak for any economic interest group. He had intimate knowledge of Peru's Indians and adopted his conservative position precisely with that knowledge in mind. The best example of the compatibility between his politics and his concern for the Indians was the celebrated debate he held with Pedro Gálvez in congress in 1849. The liberals had proposed a law by which Indians and mestizos were exempted from the requirement of being able to read or write in order to vote. Gálvez, though a former student of Herrera, was a doctrinaire liberal who defended the motion. Herrera opposed the measure because, in his opinion, conceding the right to vote to illiterates would not give rise to a real democracy in Peru. What Peru needs, said Herrera, is to abolish illiteracy itself:

> I also love the Indians; I have lived among them for years; I have heard their cries; I have locked their pained whispers in my heart and in daily life I have mixed my tears with theirs.... Let a substantial portion of public money be spent on schools. Instruct and educate the Indian and his condition will improve.... Education, education, gentlemen, for the Indians; and as far as rights, let us recognize the fact that we cannot do more than declare that they exist when they exist and that God alone can create them.[9]

With these words Herrera summed up the attitude of the past-century church toward the popular classes: elitism, paternalism, but also concern for their social well-being. In this case, Herrera rejected universal suffrage because he did not believe that it would really better the condition of the Indians. While the liberals proposed reforms without knowing the real situation of the Indians, the conservative clergy, which lived close to the Indians, rejected those reforms. By proposing popular education instead of universal suffrage, Herrera showed that he had a more critical social consciousness than the liberals. But, given his skepticism of liberalism in general and his defense of the church's privileges, he also showed himself to be a representative of the conservative tendencies in the clergy.

Stronger Ties with Rome

With the restoration of the church under Luna Pizarro, Bartolomé Herrera, and others, Peruvian bishops gave top priority to the strengthening of ties with Rome as well as becoming part of the universal church in general. There is no doubt that in one important sense this tightening of relations with the papacy was beneficial to the Peruvian church. First, the newly restored episcopate, made up now of Peruvians, no longer obeyed the state in such a servile way as did the colonial church. Second, under Goyeneche, Herrera, and others, internal order was restored to the church after the rather anarchical postindependence period. These bishops felt secure in their leadership most of all because they believed that they had the full support of the distant but powerful personalities of Pius IX and Leo XIII.

Nevertheless, compared with the missionary church of the sixteenth century or the renovated church of the Second Vatican Council, the church of the period of Pius IX lacked creative openness. In its reaching out to Rome, the Latin American church lost something of its own identity. The themes that pervade the pastoral documents of the episcopacy were the very ones that most concerned Rome: liberalism, rationalism, Protestantism, and secularism. Furthermore, the different councils and synods of the church devoted themselves to such questions as how best to incorporate decrees promulgated in Rome into local legislation. By way of contrast, in the nineteenth century and well into the twentieth, these documents make scant reference to the Indians of Latin America, certainly far less than during the great Lima councils of the sixteenth and seventeenth centuries.

On two different occasions the Peruvian bishops established

The Militant Church, 1855–1930

direct contact with the Holy See. In 1852 Bartolomé Herrera, then only a priest, visited Rome to propose a concordat between Peru and the Holy See. In 1869 three prelates, José Ezequiel Moreyra, Ambrosio Huerta, and Teodoro del Valle set off to attend the First Vatican Council. Goyeneche, the archbishop of Lima, was too old for the trip and so he sent Pedro Gual as his representative. Gual, a Franciscan missionary, was one of the restorers of Ocopa and at that moment was the Commissary General of the Franciscans in all Latin America. Later, in 1899, four bishops attended the Latin American Plenary Council: Manuel Tovar, the archbishop of Lima; Ismael Puirredón of Puno; Juan Antonio Falcón of Cuzco; and Manuel Ballón of Arequipa.

The Catholic Press: First Period

The church used different literary arms to spread its cause: pastoral letters of the bishops, polemical pamphlets written by priests and laymen, catechisms, and newspapers. Of all these arms, the newspapers were the most important. On different occasions priests and laymen worked together to bring the Catholic cause to homes everywhere. In 1845 Archbishop Luna Pizarro patronized the publication of *El Redactor Eclesiástico*, which came out in 1845 and 1846. Bartolomé Herrera returned from Europe with a new printing press that he installed at the seminary. He and José Huerta, the brother of the rector, Juan Ambrosio Huerta, published *El Católico* (with the subtitle "A religious, philosophical, historical and literary bimonthly") between 1855 and 1860. In 1860 the government arrested the two priest-editors, José Jesús Ayllón and Francisco Solano de los Heros, for their opposition to the new liberal constitution. With the demise of *El Católico* they published *El Progreso Católico*, using the same printing press at the seminary. The person mainly responsible was Ambrosio Huerta, who counted among his supporters José Antonio Roca y Boloña, a priest, and Nicolás de Piérola, an ex-seminarian and future president of the country. This newspaper suffered the same fate at the hands of the liberals and was closed in 1862. Piérola went on to found two other newspapers, *El Tiempo* and *La Patria* (which appeared from 1867 to 1879). In 1867 *El Perú Católico*, published by another priest, Manuel González de la Rosa, came out. Of a polemical nature, it suspended publication in 1868. González had also published another newspaper, *El Bien Público* (1865), but shortly afterwards he turned the direction over to José Antonio Roca, who in turn was succeeded by Manuel Tovar. In 1870 González took over the direction of *La Sociedad*, a daily that came out until 1879.

In Arequipa, Primitivo Sanmartí published *La Revista Católica* between the years 1877 and 1879. After the war with Chile, Sanmartí refounded the same magazine in 1884, this time in Lima, where it continued to appear until 1906. It was the best Catholic publication of this first period.

The Peruvian-Catholic Society

In 1867 the bishop of Huánuco, Teodoro del Valle, conceived the idea of founding the "Peruvian Catholic Society." The first session of the new association was held in Lima that year, and affiliated groups soon sprang up elsewhere in the country, in Huánuco, Arequipa, Puno, and Cuzco. The society also established a women's section. In the Mass that he celebrated in the church of San Francisco to inaugurate the society, Del Valle spoke of the idea that had inspired him: "I am convinced of something else, that outside of this temple there are many good Catholics; but we must distinguish between those who are simply Catholics and those who are Catholic soldiers."[10]

The prelate of Huánuco pointed out the enemies of the "Catholic soldier": Protestantism, rationalism, positivism, and pantheism. In the same inaugural session another speaker, Manuel Cisneros, denounced liberalism and the various efforts of the state to change people. The real solution to society's problems lay in the individual, said Cisneros, not in society.[11]

Who belonged to the new society? The statutes admitted only laypersons. Furthermore, the annals of the society describe those who attended the first sessions as "our cultured class." A report on the first meeting of the society in Puno stated that "the most distinguished part of society of both sexes" was present.[12] Del Valle himself in his writings referred to the example of England where the nobility had formed a similar society with the aim of propagating the Catholic religion.[13] Very clearly, Del Valle and his sympathizers hoped to gather in society's elite. For all its solemn beginnings, however, the society languished and soon ceased to exist. In any case, the war with Chile in 1879 would have put an end to any activity of that sort.

The Battle Is Renewed, 1884–1930

Positivists and Oligarchs

The war of 1879 left Peru with a psychological wound from which it never fully recovered, not even a century later. The gen-

The Militant Church, 1855–1930

eration of intellectuals who arose after the defeat expressed their bitterness and frustration in the universities and in other public fora. Manuel González Prada was the main exponent in the nonacademic fora. In the University of San Marcos, Javier Prado y Ugarteche placed the blame for Peru's slow progress on its colonial past. He singled out especially the factors of race, climate, and religion. Although Prado recognized the healthy effects of Christian morality, he nevertheless took Spanish Catholicism severely to task because, in his opinion, that form of religiosity represented a step backwards: "It is certainly true, although it may be painful to admit it, that the clergy, instead of giving example, actually contributed to the moral depravation of many in Peru with their scandalous conduct."[14]

This rather caustic and unobjective judgment of Prado revealed an undercurrent of generalized pessimism with respect to all of Peru's history, traditions, and indeed the people themselves. The criticism of the positivists was inspired by the rationalistic mind-set of the eighteenth century and by a few pseudoscientific theories of such nineteenth century authors as Gustave LeBon, who wrote on the racial inequalities of mankind. In this vein Prado expressed his concern over the "pernicious influence that the inferior races have exercised in Peru. . . ." For remedies to these evils he proposed teaching the lower classes the virtues of hard work and fostering the immigration of "superior races" to Peru.[15]

It is within this context of defeat, pessimism, and disdain for the colonial past that one can appreciate the aggressive antireligiosity of the period. For the generation of the nineties, the church, church bells, *beatas* (pious laywomen), processions, and antiliberal priests all symbolized the colonial heritage that weighed heavily upon the present. The historian Jorge Basadre used the term "apostate" to describe Manuel González Prada (1848–1918), who was the principal critic of religion. According to Basadre, González Prada typified the frustration and disorientation of the middle classes that emerged after the war with Chile. They severely criticized the past and the present but had no clear vision of the future. González Prada was an "apostate" because he rejected the religion of his fathers but did not discover a new one to replace the old.[16] His mission was to be a prophet in the desert: to construct by denouncing, leaving to others the task of designing the new order to be built. What González really rejected was not a system of beliefs but the memories of his youth. In a humorous vein, but not entirely free of bitterness, he once explained to his wife, Adriana, why he was anticlerical. In his family there reigned an atmosphere of "Spanish fanaticism" that dominated the women, who were transformed into mere "cleaning cloths" to be used. "In my house," he observed, "I ate monks for breakfast, I ate monks for dinner, I breathed monks, and their will alone prevailed. . . ."[17].

Needless to say, the grand master of anticlericalism found sufficient grounds for his criticism, especially in the clerical exploitation of the Indians in the mountains and in the intellectual narrowness of many priests. Yet in the middle of these concrete accusations, one discovers an exaggeration that points to a more underlying problem. González Prada is also known for his call for reform for the Indians. But his protest was never more than a romantic literary gesture aimed at the ruling elite. González Prada himself harbored racist attitudes toward the popular classes, the same attitudes shared by many other middle- and upper-class Peruvians.[18]

In this sense, González Prada was not very distant from the positivists of the academic world who expressed the sentiments of the upper classes. Both racism and antireligiosity were fashionable sentiments among thinkers, politicians, and oligarchs. According to a widespread belief, the church and the oligarchies of Latin America have enjoyed a mutual attraction. But in reality their relationship was more complex. Some older aristocratic families, such as the López de Romaña in Arequipa or the Pardos, were sincere Catholics and maintained a close relationship with the church. In general, however, the great landed oligarchy and the upper-class entrepreneurs were practical men who judged the church according to their interests. If the church helped to maintain the established order, it deserved to be supported. But if the church stood in the way of "social progress," then it deserved to be criticized. Although they were never aggressively antireligious, the great oligarchs did not go out of their way to favor the church.

Furthermore, many of the sons of these families who studied in San Marcos University, as Luis Alberto Sánchez observed, made a show of being "elegant skeptics."[19] Both José de la Riva-Agüero and Víctor Andrés Belaunde adopted positivistic attitudes toward religion in their university days. This "liberalism of convenience"—in favor of or against the church according to one's interests—is particularly noticeable in *El Comercio*, the principal daily newspaper of Lima, which followed a liberal-rationalist line throughout most of its history. On a number of occasions it criticized the church for its obscurantism and intolerance. An example of this is the support it lent Haya de la Torre in 1923 in favor of his protest against the consecration of Peru to the Sacred Heart.[20]

The Masons

The group that most fostered anticlericalism in the postwar period were the Masons. There were Masonic lodges in Peru since the time of independence, and among the illustrious founders of Freemasonry in Peru was Francisco Javier Mariátegui, who along with Vigil was a proponent of a national patronage to exercise greater control over the church. In 1830 the various lodges consolidated to become a single federation, the Great Peruvian Orient. But in 1859 a few dissident lodges broke off to found their own federation, the Supreme Council, with some 680 members throughout Peru. In 1881 the Great Orient was reorganized under the name The Great Lodge of Peru, with five member lodges and some three hundred members.[21] Both federations followed the Scottish rite. The differences between the two was more a question of style than of substance; they were both anticlerical. In general, the Masons tended to be professionals or merchants belonging to the middle classes. Besides Mariátegui, other notable Masons were Christian Dam and Carlos G. Amézaga.[22] Their most important publication was the magazine *La Ilustración Popular*. González Prada himself never became a Mason because, he said, with their rites and ceremonies they seemed like "pseudopriests."[23]

Ideologically, the Masons represented the same line of thought as liberalism. But their use of symbols and rites lent an aura of religiosity to their beliefs. González Prada was not far from the truth when he caricaturized Masonry as a sort of pseudo-Catholicism. It was the Masons of Lima who precipitated the first major crisis between the church and liberalism after the war with Chile. In general, until the appearance of the Aprista Party in 1930, the Masonic lodges constituted the principle bastions of anticlericalism in Peru.

Profile of a Model Layman: Nicolás de Piérola

The Catholics who answered the call of the church to come out in its defense against the liberal-positivist attack shared certain social characteristics. In general, lay leaders of the nineteenth and twentieth centuries came from older families or from certain sectors of the middle classes. Arequipa in particular stands out for the number of prominent persons identified with the "Catholic cause." In the nineteenth century ecclesiastics such as Mariano José de Arce, Juan Gualberto Valdivia, Francisco Javier de Luna Pizarro, and José Sebastián Goyeneche all played an important role in the history of the "White City." But there is an equal number of prominent laymen who have played important roles as politicians or diplomats: Nicolás de Piérola, Víctor Andrés and Rafael Belaunde, José Luis Bustamante, and others. Besides their regional ties and explicit Catholicism, these lay leaders also distinguished themselves for their opposition to authoritarian rulers and the liberal oligarchy. Piérola especially exhibited all these qualities.

He was born in 1839 in Arequipa of a family of Spanish background. The family moved to Lima when Piérola's father was named director of the Museum of Natural History, and later on minister of finance under President Echenique. His father sent him to Santo Toribio Seminary (1853–60), where he distinguished himself as a student. It is not clear if Piérola really felt a vocation to the priesthood. Whatever the case, when he left the seminary and married, he always practiced his Catholicism and kept close ties with the church. Several of his companions at the seminary went on to hold important posts in the church, such as José Antonio Roca, a founder of the Catholic press, and Manuel Tovar, archbishop of Lima during Piérola's second period. Three of his younger brothers also studied at the seminary but only one of them, Felipe Amadeo, reached the priesthood. Felipe Amadeo also served as rector of the new seminary of Puno under Bishop Ambrosio Huerta, who had been rector of Santo Toribio when the Piérola brothers were seminarians. In 1860 Nicolás de Piérola collaborated in *El Progreso Católico* founded by Huerta.

In the style of a layperson of the nineteenth century, Piérola was characterized by his unquestioning loyalty to the church. In 1870 he signed a statement protesting the invasion of the papal states.[24] When he assumed power in 1880 as dictator, he gave the *exequatur* (permission) to publish the papal bull *Praeclara inter beneficia*, which constituted a sort of concordat with the Holy See. During his second period as president (1895–99) his wife, Jesús Itúrbide, who was a benefactress of many charitable works of the church, was elected honorary president of the section for the Catholic Union of Women in the Catholic Congress of 1896. In 1913, when the aged former caudillo was dying, as a sign of recognition for his support to the church the dean of the cathedral marched in solemn procession to his home to administer the last rites of the church.

Politically, Piérola does not fit twentieth-century definitions easily. He was a civilian caudillo who represented at the same time a populist antimilitary and antioligarchy sentiment and a desire for order and peace. He was a living incarnation of the lower middle classes and older traditional families that did not trust the nouveau-riche values of the civilist oligarchy.[25] Piérola and González Prada represent two social types in contrast. Both had studied together in Santo Toribio Seminary: one left to become the spokesman for the newly emerging middle classes, and the other for the traditional upper and the lower middle classes. For these latter classes the values most esteemed were family stability, religion, and respect for property. The radicalism of González Prada led him to reject Peru's Spanish past and Catholicism, while exalting the values of "science" and "social progress."

Piérola was not, of course, a philosopher. He was above all else a man of action. Nevertheless, one can perceive a definite harmony between his personal values and his political action. The conservative government over which he presided toward the end of the century (1895–99) did not contradict the populist instincts that inspired his followers. For him the most important values in life—personal honesty, fiscal responsibility, loyalty to one's friends, discipline in one's work—were precisely the civic virtues that he believed most necessary for the good of the republic. And these were the values most esteemed by the "decent folk" of the middle classes—professionals, teachers, farmers, and merchants—who took up arms on Piérola's side in the civil war of 1894–95.[26]

Women as Militants

According to a widely spread stereotype, the Latin American church is made up largely of women. This characterization, though exaggerated, does have a basis in history. With the advance of liberalism, the church grew more conservative and many men began to associate the practice of religion with what were presumably feminine qualities: a love for tradition, sentimentalism, and passive submission to authority. In so doing, liberalism acquired certain *machista* nuances that became part of its ideological program. For the nineteenth century liberal, who prided himself on his freedom and capacity to reason, it was out of keeping with his manhood to submit humbly to the authority of the church or to express religious faith in public by receiving the sacraments like a small child on his or her First Communion day. Whatever other psychological nuances may be hidden in this phenomenon, one fact remains clear: everywhere in Latin America in the nineteenth century, men, even those of upper-class conservative families, drifted away from the practice of religion, which for them was deemed a custom more appropriate to women and children.

By way of contrast, women in general of all social classes continued to be religious. Indeed, women became the bulwark of the Catholic cause in the nineteenth and early twentieth centuries. It was with certain admiration that Manuel A. Fuentes, a lawyer of liberal tendencies, underlined this fact when he described the piety of Lima in 1861: "The women of Lima are very devout; they never fail, unless for some grave reason, to attend Mass on all feast days; and in many homes they keep the custom of praying the rosary at night."[27]

Some years later, in 1873, the Jesuit Francisco Javier Hernáez also pointed to the singular importance of women in the church: "There is no altar, no matter how hidden, that is not cared for by the women, who adorn it with their own hands and at their own expense. They found congregations, they organize novenas, and they are the ones who foster the many pious works."[28]

Although González Prada termed women "the slaves of the church" because in their ignorance they allowed themselves to be dominated by the priests, there are many reasons to describe this judgment as a mere caricature. In the first place, even though they were still excluded from the university, most women of the upper and middle classes received a very ample education in their homes and in their own schools. On several occasions women seized the initiative with greater decisiveness than men in defending the church, and in so doing they also displayed an independence of spirit. In 1855–56 groups of women organized protest meetings in the congress building during the speeches of the anticlericals. In 1886 they initiated the movement to defend the Jesuits against imminent expulsion. The Catholic Union of Women was notably more active than the corresponding association for men. Finally, their critical independence can be seen especially in the case of certain women who, in spite of being the sisters or wives of leading anticlericals, took a public position to the contrary. Juana Rosa de Amézaga, sister of Mariano Amézaga, a liberal professor of the Guadalupe *colegio* who attacked the very basis of Christianity in his writings, wrote an essay on the "social, religious and domestic aspects of Christian virtues."[29]

Similarly, Carolina García Robledo de Bambarén, whose husband, Celso Bambarén was famous for his antireligious polemics, composed religious poetry and was the director of "Peter's Pence."[30] In 1914 she was also elected president of the Catholic Union of Women in Trujillo.[31]

From these and other examples, one can conclude that religion not only divided social classes but also divided families, at times creating a barrier between husbands and wives and brothers and sisters. Perhaps what some freethinkers termed "ignorance" or "submission" in these Catholic women was in reality a display of feminine independence against *their* authority.

The Catholic Union

The Expulsion of the Society of Jesus, 1886

The spark that ignited passions and touched off a small war between liberals and the church after the war with Chile was the publication of a compendium of Peruvian history by Ricardo Cappa, a Jesuit who taught at La Inmaculada *colegio* (grade school and high school). The Jesuits had returned to Peru in 1871 and, although the liberals knew of their presence, they chose not to make an issue of it until the appearance of Father Cappa's book. The history book published by the Spanish Jesuit in 1886 exalted the heritage of Spain in Latin America and disparaged the efforts of the Peruvians in the independence movement. Ricardo Palma, the noted literary figure, reacted by satirizing the Jesuits with his pen. The Masons and others organized meetings in Callao, and in the Politeama Theater they demanded that the Society of Jesus be expelled from the country. As a result of this campaign, the congress passed a law that removed recognition of the Society's right to exist as a religious order. The law also abolished an earlier resolution that recognized the creation of the Jesuit high school in Lima. Finally, in October, a majority in Parliament voted to expel the Jesuits from Peru. The Jesuits packed up, closed their *colegio* in Lima, and left the country; but they returned a year later when the storm had subsided.[32]

The expulsion of the Society of Jesus was the catalyst that reactivated the "Catholic cause." The militant Catholics reawoke better organized and more determined than in the first period before the war with Chile. It was the torment provoked by the expuslsion of the Jesuits that gave rise to the Catholic Union, which would be the most important lay organization in the church until the thirties of this century. In face of liberal aggressiveness, Catholics held meetings throughout the country that led to the creation of the Catholic Union. In July a group of women, headed by Mariana Barreda de Pardo, widow of the assassinated ex-president, Manuel Pardo (1872–76), presented a plea to President Andrés Cáceres in favor of the Jesuits. Finally, on October 10, 1886, the Central Council of the "Catholic Union" convoked the first public assembly in Lima of the new organization, in the Politeama Theater. The president, Evaristo Gómez Sánchez, opened the session to a packed house. Other members of the council included Federico Panico, Primitivo Sanmartí, Agustín Escudero, Francisco Moreira y Riglos, Tomás Salazar, Alejandro J. Puente, and Lizardo Velasco. Many ladies of upper-class families were also present, such as Emilia González du Bois, Manuela Orbegoso de Panizo, and Mercedes Vigil de Rospigliosi. The meeting was interrupted at times by loud noises coming from, according to one witness, "Italians and other foreigners."[33]

Foundation and Expansion

It is not clear exactly when the union was born. During the inauguration of the Central Council in 1888 the new president, Carlos M. Elías, noted that the initiative to found the union had come from Arequipa. The union of the "White City" sent Mariano Belaunde and Manuel Bustamante y Barreda to Lima to create a national organization. As a result of their visit a "Founding Committee," made up of the priest Francisco de Sales Soto and the laymen Primitivo Sanmartí and Luis Jorge Tola, was formed to write the statutes.[34] In Lima the union had especially close ties to the Society of Jesus. Some of the leaders, such as Carlos Elías and Felipe Varela y Valle, were also members of the Congregation of Our Lady of the O, based in the Jesuit church of San Pedro. In 1886, after an absence of a century, the Jesuits returned to take charge of that colonial confraternity.[35] Furthermore, several members of the Union had their sons in the new *colegio* founded by the Jesuits. In 1889, when the Jesuits had already returned from their exile, some seventy "gentlemen" of the Catholic Union consecrated themselves to the Sacred Heart of Jesus in San Pedro's.[36]

In Arequipa the ties with the Jesuits were more indirect: Juan Manuel López de Romaña, the first president of the union, sent his two sons, Eduardo and Alejandro, to study with the Jesuits at Stonyhurst, England, and later on the López de Romaña family, the Belaundes, and other leading families would be instrumental

The Militant Church, 1855–1930 79

in bringing the Jesuits to Arequipa.³⁷ The union of the "White City" displayed a dynamism that was maintained for years. In the first year of its existence, it created chapters in all the surrounding towns: Characato, Sabandía, Sachaca, and Socabaya.³⁸ For a short while it published its own newspaper, *El Amigo del Pueblo* (the Friend of the People, 1908–09), right in its main office in the Plaza San Francisco. Men and women of the most distinguished families belonged to the union. Among the names in the declaration of support for the Society of Jesus (October 1886) are those of Enrique Marcó del Pont, who was the second president after Juan Manuel López de Romaña, José de la Fuente, Evaristo Vargas, Alejandro L. de Romaña, Mariano Belaunde, Manuel T. Marina, and Abraham de Vintea.³⁹ There were some ten thousand signatures on the declaration. In a later generation new members would be incorporated into the union. The central committee for the year 1910 was made up of Justo Muñoz Nájar (the president), José María Bustamante y Rada, Gustavo Llosa, Manuel Soto Loayza, José Luis Bustamante y Rivero (the future president of Peru), and Manuel E. de Piérola.⁴⁰

In the old Inca capital of Cuzco, another chapter of the union was created. The principal force for years was the cathedral canon and priest Fernando Pacheco, who was also Prior of the Third Order of St. Dominic. The union of Cuzco was a model of organization. It divided its members into *centurias*, and each *centuria* was subdivided into *decurias*. The acts of the Cuzco union reveal the social background of the members. Typical among the professions that appear are "merchant," "professor," "carpenter," "tailor," and "shoemaker." But the most frequent of all was that of "merchant."⁴¹ From this it can be concluded that the union in general was predominantly of middle-class origin. A comparison with the membership lists of other cities confirms this. In 1916 Lambayeque, a northern coastal city in the diocese of Trujillo, the list includes (besides most of the local authorities) judges, medical doctors, farmers, notaries, secretaries, and "merchants."⁴²

The Catholic Union for Ladies

The women's section of the union deserves special mention since it seemed to have had more life than the corresponding section for men. Furthermore, the Catholic Union for Ladies was for years the most prestigious women's organization for the middle and upper classes. A study of this select society is a key to entering the women's world in general. Although Limanian women played a very important role in the campaign in favor of the Jesuits in 1886, the union for women was not founded officially until June of 1888. Under the guidance of Bishop Francisco de Sales Soto, the union for women undertook an impressive number of works, including the Propagation of the Faith in the Peruvian Orient (founded during the Catholic Congress of 1896), the Work of Saint Francis Regis, Sunday Schools, Peter's Pence, the Collection for the Poor, the Workshop of St. Jeanne Francis Chantal, and scholarships for the seminaries. The presidents of the union in Lima included Catalina Mendoza de la Guarda, Emilia González Orbegozo du Bois, María González de Heudebert, Jesús Beltrán de Elías, Augusta Espantoso de Elías, Clotilde Porras de Osma, Isabel del Valle y Osma, Constanza Puente de Valega, Luisa Paz Soldán de Moreyra, and Eugenia Rosas de Porras.[43]

In Arequipa, according to the *Revista Católica* of 1887, "[t]he most distinguished ladies . . . belong to the union. . . ."[44] In the list of officials for 1892, for example, one can find the names of María Josefa Cornejo de C. Quezada, María Nieves y Bustamante, Candelaria López de Romaña, Emilia Llosa y Llosa, Isabel Marcó del Pont de Romaña, and Mercedes Diez Canseco y Belaunde.[45] They were virtually all wives or daughters of the leaders of the Union for Gentlemen. In 1919 the Union for Ladies was reorganized under a new moderator, the Jesuit priest Luis Menéndez. The officials who were elected that year included Mercedes V. de Ricketts, Raquel Romaña V. de Belaunde, and Zoila Romaña de Stafford. That year there were some sixty-one members in all.[46]

In Cuzco the women's union, founded in 1891 by Fernando Pacheco, was the most active lay organization in the diocese. It was known by the name "The Catholic Union of Ladies of San Blas," a prominent parish in the city. In 1917 it had a total of 104 members. Their surnames sum up a good deal of Cuzco's history: Farfán, Angulo, Yábar, etc.[47]

In Trujillo and in most of the north, chapters of the union were founded everywhere. A list in 1906 in Trujillo is virtually the equivalent of a list of the most distinguished families: Adela Orbegoso de González Orbegoso (the president), Josefina Pinillos de Larco, Elicia Chopitea de Ganoza, Manuela Rosa G. de Ganoza, Manuela Cabrera de Pinillos, Micaela la Cox de Mink, Ana Hoyle de Loyer, and Zoila Victoria de la Torre de Haya.[48] In 1911 Señora de la Torre de Haya, the mother of Víctor Raúl Haya de la Torre, was elected president of the union in Trujillo, a post she held for years. In a letter she sent the bishop in 1912, she informed him that there were eighty-six members of the Union. And she added, "As far as our meeting place, although my house is modest, it is always open for the sessions of the Catholic Union."[49]

The Union flourished in all the smaller cities and towns of the diocese. In Piura in the far north the list of officials for 1916 included Amelia Reuche, Antonia Eguiguren, Genara Seminario de Rodríguez, Vicente Seminario, and Mica María de Seminario.[50] In Lambayeque in 1898 the president was Carmen Salcedo de Leguía, the mother of the future president of Peru, Augusto B. Leguía.[51] In Chiclayo (northern coast) the union was founded in 1916 with some 135 members. Even the small town of Cartacaos (near Piura) had eighty-nine members in 1926. The influence of the Catholic Union for Ladies was so noticeable that Bishop Irigoyen of Trujillo rendered it effusive praise: "In Chiclayo, as in Trujillo and all other places where the clouds of revolutionary impiety have darkened the sky, the Catholic Union for Ladies is an organization of the lay apostolate of the highest quality and that which produces the most fruit."[52]

By way of contrast, the Union for Gentlemen, after an enthusiastic beginning, lost impetus in later years. In 1910 the president of the union in Trujillo, Pedro Martínez de Pinillos, in a letter to Bishop Irigoyen, complained about the "permanent absences" of many members at the meetings.[53] That same year Irigoyen tried to found a new newspaper, *La Voz de Trujillo* (The Voice of Trujillo), that would be under the direction of the Union of Gentlemen. But the project failed for lack of money and determination. The decline of the union for men was noticeable in its publications. The official organ of the union was *El Bien Social* (The Common Good), which came out from 1896 to 1912. Among the editors were José María de la Jara y Ureta, Pedro José Rada y Gamio, Rodrigo Herrera, Ismael Portal, and Carlos Arenas y Loayza. When publication was suspended, probably for the same reason as in the case of the newspaper in Trujillo, another one, *La Unión*, was founded in its place. But its life was even shorter: 1913–15. In the twenties the Catholic Union for Gentlemen continued to exist, but it increasingly seemed like a club for retired gentlemen, with little dynamism or plans for the future.

Catholics and the Social Question

Rerum Novarum, *1891*

The encyclical *Rerum Novarum* was published in its entirety in the pages of the *Revista Católica* in August 1891.[54] From that moment on, the "social question" made itself increasingly felt in the Peruvian church. The encyclical coincided with the beginning of the indigenist and workers' movements. These two topics, the "Indians" and the "workers," began to receive greater attention in the pastoral letters of the bishops and in the statements of synods and other church assemblies. Nevertheless, one should not exaggerate; in this period the social question was strictly subordinate to the defense of the rights of the church. As Jorge Basadre noted, "The influence of the central ideas of *Rerum Novarum* in our country is not very visible."[55]

In spite of the limited concept that most militant Catholics had of social change, the new social message of the church helped to give form and shape to a clearer Catholic social thought in Peru. Leo XIII's encyclical represented a third position with respect to capitalism and communism. This "third way" would be a constant in practically all papal pronouncements from then on. It also corresponded basically to the social and ideological outlook of Catholic militants in Peru; they belonged neither to the great capitalist oligarchy nor to the radical elements of the middle class that looked to González Prada as their mentor. In general, the militant Catholics of the period drew together two groups: first, some older families of the upper class that did not wish to be associated with the new coastal oligarchy, which they perceived as a nouveau-riche class, without values or a social conscience; and second, members of the small middle classes from Lima and especially the provinces. These groups were not attracted to the radicalism of González Prada because his brand of liberal anticlericalism meant a rejection of traditional values in favor of a vague "scientific progress." An intermediate position therefore drew these Catholic groups together: social concern for Indians and workers, without violent changes and within the context of a Catholic society sustained by a basic respect for the family, small private property, and of course the practice of religion. The two major themes on the agenda for militant Catholics were, in order of priority, defense of the church, and a mild social reformism that aimed to create an orderly society free of class or racial antagonisms.

The Catholic Congress of 1896

In November 1896, the Catholic Union organized the first Catholic Congress in Peru. Judging from external signs, the congress was a complete success. More than three hundred men and women delegates, representing all the Catholic organizations and

The Militant Church, 1855–1930 83

all the dioceses, filled the Franciscan church in downtown Lima for an entire week. Archbishop Manuel Bandini was elected honorary president, but it was the auxiliary bishop, Manuel Tovar, who was the moving force in organizing the congress. But more important than the many clerics present was the lay leadership of the Catholic Union. The president of the congress, José Jorge Loayza, and the vice president, Felipe Varela y Valle, belonged to the Congregation of Our Lady of the O. The delegation from Arequipa was headed by Mariano Belaunde and Pedro José Rada y Gamio. The representative from Huaraz was Alejandrino Maguiña, who several years later would conduct a parliamentary investigation into the abuses committed against the Indians in the southern Andean region. The congress was supposed to meet in 1894 but, given the political and social unrest that resulted from the civil war between President Cáceres and Nicolas de Piérola, it had to be postponed. Under President Piérola, who won the war, conditions were more favorable for the congress. Piérola's wife, Jesús Itúrbide, was elected honorary president of the section for the Catholic Union of Ladies, and his sister, Eva María de Piérola, became the principal promoter of the Work for Propagating the Faith in the Peruvian Orient, which was created during the congress.

In the inaugural speech, Carlos Elías, president of the Catholic Union, touched upon the call to militancy: "While it cannot be said that there has existed in Peru an open and declared war on Catholicism, nevertheless there has existed a tenacious and unrelenting guerrilla war against the country's institutions and principles...."[56]

Elías called upon the delegates to study ways and means to bring the Catholic point of view to the attention of municipal governments and of the national congress.[57] The congress adopted resolutions to support a campaign to combat Protestant and Masonic propaganda. It declared itself firmly in support of the pope in the conflict between the Holy See and the new Italian state. In these and other conclusions one can see the influence of *Rerum Novarum*. The congress also exhorted industrialists as well as hacienda and mine owners to look out for the "moral and material interests" of employees and mine workers.[58] Attention was given to the Indians in a chapter entitled, "Ways of Bettering the Conditions of the Indians." The authors of that chapter proposed certain concrete measures, such as establishing schools for the Indians to be run by the Salesians or the Christian Brothers, and fostering the teaching of Quechua and Aymara in the Seminary of Puno.[59] Nevertheless, the congress stopped short of analyzing the underlying social causes of Peru's problems. It attributed the sufferings of the Indians to the lack of "paternal charity" on the part of hacienda owners and government authorities.[60]

Carried away by enthusiasm, the delegates proposed many projects they could hardly carry out. As a result, many of the resolutions became a dead letter. Still, the congress had an overall positive influence in strengthening the Catholic cause. It was the first time numerous Catholics from all over the country had come together to discuss common issues. In this sense, the Catholic Union and the congress of 1896 signaled the beginning of a real lay movement in Peru. The most important result of the congress was a new degree of awareness on the part of Peru's militant Catholics. Following the suggestion of its president, Carlos Elías, they began to take concrete steps to bring their cause to the public arena. One of their resolutions was to hold another congress in Arequipa in 1898. However, that turned out to be one of the many resolutions never carried out.

Holguín and the Circles for Catholic Workers

In 1896 Mariano Holguín, superior of the Franciscans of the Recollection in Arequipa, founded the Circle for Catholic Workers. Later, as bishop (1906–45) he was also the principal promoter of his own organization. In his inaugural speech on March 19, although he did not refer specifically to *Rerum Novarum*, he did cite the ideas of Leo XIII about workers. The sixty-four members of the new organization were almost all artisans.[61] In a photo taken in 1921, one can observe the mestizo and lower middle-class features of the members, dressed formally in suits and ties.[62] During the first twenty-five years of its history, the circle had on an average some three hundred members. In the night school that the circle ran there were approximately 150 students.

Following the guidelines in *Rerum Novarum*, the circle became a combination of a mutual-aid society, a savings cooperative, and a center for cultural formation. But it was not a union in the proper sense because it did not approve of strikes or any other type of pressure to advance the cause of workers. In an editorial in *El Deber* on the occasion of the twenty-third anniversary of the circle, the author condemned a general strike in Lima and rejected socialism. "The social question for workers does not exist in Peru," he concluded, because there were few workers and little industry. What Peru needs now, he added, is to foster a national industry by having recourse to both foreign and national capital.⁶³ In order that there might be no doubts about its conservative stance, the circle in Arequipa conferred an honorary membership on Augusto B. Leguía.⁶⁴ In March 1919, Father Francisco Cabré founded *La Colmena*, which until it ceased to be published in 1940 was the official voice of the circle. Cabré was the main moderator of the group after Holguin.

Although the circle in Arequipa was the most active and best organized, it was not the only one. In 1899 the Circle for Catholic Workers was founded in Cuzco, which, like its counterpart in Arequipa, was made up mainly of artisans. When Haya de la Torre led a march against the consecration of Peru to the Sacred Heart in 1923, the "Union of Artisans" of Urubamba (near Cuzco) sent a declaration to the bishop of Cuzco in which they supported the church and denounced the anticlerical actions of the workers who supported Haya de la Torre.⁶⁵ Presumably this group had connections with the circle in Cuzco. In any case, the conservative orientation of all of these groups is patent. In Lima, a Center for Catholic Workers was founded in September 1913. The editor of the newspaper that the center put out, *El Obrero Ideal* (The Ideal Worker) was Father Jorge Dintilhac.⁶⁶ There are scattered references to other workers' circles in Trujillo, Puno, Ayacucho, and Huanta.

It can be said in general that these groups of Catholic workers sprang up on the fringe of the main trade-union movements that emerged in the decade of the twenties. Their existence does demonstrate the fact that there was a social conciousness in the church, though somewhat limited and conservative, in the very first years after the publication of *Rerum Novarum*.

Catholic Political Parties

Although Catholics intervened in politics since independence by way of petitions sent to congress, protest marches, or the application of episcopal pressure on the central government, they had never organized themselves into a political party as such. The various pious associations had no direct political orientation. The Catholic Union officially limited itself to the task of convoking Catholics to meet on pressing issues or of disseminating Catholic opinion in the press, in pamphlets, and in public meetings. Occasionally it organized protest marches against proposals for legislation or to counteract Protestant propaganda. But it did not intervene formally in partisan politics. For this reason the leaders of the Catholic movement thought it worthwhile to create their own political parties with the aim of sending representatives to municipal councils and the national congress. There already existed several different regional Catholic centers that could serve as platforms for creating these parties. Indeed, almost all these parties were founded and directed by the various Catholic centers of the Catholic Union itself. It was quite common for a militant Catholic of this period to belong to three different organizations at the same time: a pious association or a confraternity, the Catholic Union, and one or other of the Catholic political parties that sprang up at that time.

Furthermore, this new political activism of the laity corresponded to a period in which the clergy participated less and less in direct partisan politics. In 1823 there were twenty-three clergymen among the seventy members of congress; but toward the end of the century there were only eight clergymen in congress, which by then consisted of 150 deputies and senators.[67] In reality, there was no explicit rule in the church against clergy participation in politics. But given the increasingly lower level of formation for the clergy and, on the other hand, the higher level of culture that many laypersons possessed, it was only natural that the laity should assume the role of direct political participation. And of course the number of clergy had began to diminish rapidly toward the end of the century. Already in 1901, 17 percent of the clergy was foreign born.

Notwithstanding the essentially lay character of these parties, however, the hierarchy and the clergy played a very important role as promoters, moderators, and propagandists of the parties. These parties can properly be defined as "Catholic," not only because their main objective was to defend the church, but also because of their close ties to the hierarchy. Mariano Holguín in Arequipa and Pedro Pascual Farfán in Cuzco especially took a very active part in the founding and the running of the Catholics parties in their respective dioceses.

The Conservative Party of Cuzco, 1896

On November 22, 1896, in the convent of San Francisco in Cuzco, the first of these "Catholic" parties was born. Founded by the Conservative Center, it announced that its principal objective was to "[w]ork for the intellectual, moral, and material life of the people, and seek to place representatives in congress and in places of local leadership who are exemplary models of Catholicity, patriotism, and honesty. . . ."[68]

Data about this and the other parties are very scarce. On the occasion of Haya de la Torre's protest march of May 1923, the party was reorganized and renamed the Catholic Conservative Party. There was no ambiguity about the ties between the party and the hierarchy and clergy. The bishop himself presided over the installation of the directing committee of the party, and the invitations to attend important party meetings bore the letterhead of the bishop's office. In the manifesto announcing its reorganization in 1923, the provisional committee called upon Catholics to take an active part in future elections so as to insure that "out-and-out Catholics are elected to power." The manifesto also declared that "all the ecclesiastics of the diocese... will take a special oath to obey the decisions of the party...."[69]

The Catholic Party of Arequipa, 1913

In October 1913, the groundwork for founding the Catholic party of Arequipa was laid. In November of that year the president of the Catholic Union, Manuel Marina, informed the bishop of Cuzco that the union had resolved to found a political party because it was not "really efficient to send written declarations to the public authorities."[70] As a consequence it was announced that the new party would be independent of the Catholic Union. The first president elected was Dr. E. Lorenzo Montoya. As in the case of Cuzco, the bishop had a direct role in founding the party. In 1917 Bishop Mariano Holguin sent a note of thanks to the ecclesiastical chapter for defending him against the attacks of the liberal press "on account of my activities in the political work of the Catholic party of this diocese."[71] The founding of these two parties, in Cuzco and Arequipa, inspired the Catholics of other dioceses to study the possibilities of creating a nationwide party. In November 1913, Bishop Fidel Olivas Escudero of Ayacucho wrote to the Catholic Union of Arequipa to inform them that he had founded in his diocese a Center for Catholic Youth, which followed the same ideals as the new party in Arequipa.[72] In Cajamarca, the *Boletín Eclesiástico* expressed its "joy" over the creation of the parties and announced that "in a short time all Catholics of Peru will support this movement."[73] In 1915 *La Unión* in Lima, with a touch of envy, pointed to the centers in Cuzco and Arequipa as models for Catholics in the capital.[74]

In spite of this initial enthusiasm, however, no such national movement sprang up. These various Catholic parties never became anything more than regional movements with little impact on the national scene. In Bishop Olivas Escudero's letter cited above, the prelate from Ayacucho expressed his skepticism about the possibility of creating such centers or parties in all the provinces, especially given the "shortage of apt personnel." This concern was well founded, as one can judge by a report made by the pastor of San Jerónimo parish for the bishop of Cuzco, who had inquired about the possibilities of establishing a section of the Catholic party in that district. The pastor's report, a faithful reflection of the social reality of the provinces, is not without a bit of ingenuous humor. From a list of fifteen leading townsfolk the pastor had to eliminate almost all as possible candidates to found the party in his district: one because he was "given over to liquor"; another because he "goes frequently to dances"; and another because "he doesn't want to get involved in anything." With some pessimism the pastor concluded, "One cannot count on them for anything because for a drink of liquor they will stand firmly for Christianity one day and the next for the Moors."[75] Evidently, not all of the obstacles in the way of attracting people to the new parties were ideological in origin. These parties did not prosper mainly because their outlook was too limited or regional and their programs too narrow in scope for them to become serious national parties.

The Catholic Press: Second Period

The Catholic press was reborn after the war of the Pacific. The *Revista Católica*, originally published in Arequipa, was refounded by Primitivo Sanmartí in Lima in 1884. It continued to come out until 1906. The only other publication that reached the same level of prestige in Lima was *El Bien Público* (The Public Good), organ of the Catholic Union, which came out between 1896 and 1912. When it ceased to be published, *La Unión* (1913–15), edited by Emilio Huidobro and Gonzalo Herrera, was founded in its place. It was reorganized by J. Vitaliano Berroa, but it lasted only for a short time. Its successor was *La Nueva Unión*, which circulated until the first years of the twenties. In 1918 *La Tradición* was founded under the guiding inspiration of Archbishop Lissón. It led a precarious existence until it was closed down in the middle of the *Oncenio*, as the eleven-year rule of Augusto Leguía was called. In general, these last three publications, *La Unión*, *La Nueva Unión*, and *La Tradición*, each of which consisted of about four pages, represented a decline in Catholic journalism.

In 1891 *El Amigo del Clero* (The Friend of the Clergy), the official voice of the archdiocese of Lima, was founded. Right to the last number in 1968 it was one of the most important monthly news sources for the church in Lima. In the same period many other magazines, of varying quality, also appeared: *La Rosa del Perú* (the Rose of Peru), 1886–1967, published by the Dominicans; *Los Principios* (Principles) 1900–1902, a publication of the Catholic youth of Peru; the *Hogar Cristiano* (Christian Home), which came out between 1908 and 1910; *Revista mensual de los Sagrados Corazones* (The Monthly Review of the Sacred Hearts), 1907–?; *Las Florecillas* (The Little Flowers) of the Franciscans, 1911–78. But the Catholic magazine that enjoyed the greatest prestige was undoubtedly *El Mercurio Peruano* (the title was taken from a late colonial publication, The Peruvian Mercury), founded by Víctor Andrés Belaunde in 1918. It was the most important expression of Catholic thought in Peru until it ceased to be published in 1978.

In the provinces, the other dioceses also had their own publications: in 1900 *El Estandarte Católico* (The Catholic Standard) was founded in Ayacucho; in 1923 *El Heraldo* (The Herald) of Puno was founded, and in 1919 *El Diaro* (The Daily) of Cuzco was founded and directed for many years by the canon Hernando Vega Centeno. In Arequipa the organ of the Catholic Workers' circle, *La Colmena* (The Beehive), came out between 1920 and 1940. None of these publications could compare, however, with *El Deber* (The Duty) of Arequipa for its quality and longevity and for the special place it occupied in regional journalism. Founded in 1890 by the priest José María Carpenter, who later became auxiliary bishop of Lima, with the help of Mariano Belaunde, and Eduardo and Alejandro López de Romaña, it counted among its directors Adolfo Chávez, Abraham de Vinatea, F. Ruben Berroa, Juan Gualberto Guevara, the future cardinal of Lima, and Bishop Erasmo Hinojosa. It bore the proud subtitle, "Dean of the Southern Press." Along with *El Pueblo* (The People), founded in 1905, it was one of the two most important dailies in Arequipa in the twentieth century. With rising costs and competition from the Lima dailies flown in by airplane, it declined and was finally closed down in 1958.

Popular and Official Religiosity

The anticlerical press would frequently accuse the church of fostering idolatry and superstition among the popular classes, especially the Indians in the country. There was some truth to this accusation because the many feast day Masses, the Masses for the dead, and the sacraments in general were steady sources of income for the priests in rural and mountain areas. Nevertheless, this subject is more complex than what the anticlericals claimed.

First, not only did the official church not display much sympathy toward certain more or less superstitious expressions of popular religiosity, but it condemned them openly and repeatedly in various assemblies and in pastoral letters. Indeed, on some occasions the criticism of the church was more harsh than that of the liberals themselves. In 1907 the bishop of Huánuco, Pedro Pablo Drinot y Piérola, denounced categorically what he called the "sinful customs" of the Indians in their feasts, because these customs were "shot through with superstitions."[76] The hierarchy also condemned the complicity of priests who fostered superstitions or who demanded exorbitant stipends for feast-day Masses. In various synods the bishops laid down the official stipends for Masses and sacraments. Furthermore, the church complained about the practice among the Indians of burdening the *mayordomos* or the *alféreces* (those in charge of the feast) with all the expenses of the feast day. These decrees stand in contrast to the real situation: there were priests who normally collected excessive stipends, either because the Indians were unaware of the official rates, or simply because they accepted as completely legitimate the right of the priest to collect what he wanted.

Second, the church did take the initiative to weed out certain practices and unorthodox elements in popular religiosity and to foster more orthodox practices. For this reason, from the sixteenth century on two kinds of religiosity emerged in Peru and in the rest of Latin America: one that is more closely associated with the popular classes but also less "orthodox" and ecclesial and therefore less under the control of the official church, and one that is more orthodox and ecclesial, that is, more expressive of official church mentality.

Popular Religisosity

In the world of Peruvian popular religiosity there exists a multitude of devotions, processions, and customs that vary from place to place and from one subculture to the next. In 1928 Emilio Romero published a book entitled *3 Ciudades* (Three Cities), in which he analyzed the great differences that existed between the religiosity of the three principal cities of the southern Andean region: Arequipa, Puno, and Cuzco. According to the author, Arequipa is a classically colonial city in which Spanish traditions predominate in all their strength and purity. On the other hand, Puno, located in the middle of the bleak southern highlands, is an example of Indian religiosity, characterized by its melancholy songs produced by the *quena* (a typical Indian flute), multicolored apparel, interminable dances, and last but not least, bouts of drunkenness. Finally, Cuzco is above all else a *mestiza* city in which the two cultures, the Hispanic and the indigenous, have become fused. This juxtaposition of cultures can be seen in the racial composition of the inhabitants, in the architecture, and in the religious manifestations of the people.[77] By way of contrast, the prevalent religiosity on the coast is "creole," which is distinct from Spanish, *mestiza*, or indigenous religiosity because it expresses the sentiments of an urban working class.

In Cuzco the great annual procession is that of Our Lord of Tremors. But not very far from the old Inca capital there is another procession of a mixed *mestizo*-Indian nature called "Quollur Rit'i," which is centered on an image of Christ in the middle of snowcapped peaks. In Arequipa the great annual procession occurs during Holy Week, but there is another procession that takes place in the middle of the desert in honor of Our Lady of Chapi, which attracts thousands, especially from the lower classes. On the coast the major processions include those of The Lord of Luren, in Otuzco, Our Lady of the Door, and in Lima, Our Lord of Miracles. In Ancash the great annual procession is that of The Lord of Solitude, in the Callejón de Huaylas.

These popular devotions frequently center on a single person, such as St. Rose of Lima or St. Martin de Porres. But beyond these more "official" saints there are noncanonized figures who are also objects of veneration, such as Father Urraca and the "Beatita de Humay" (Little Blessed One of Humay). In the decade of the forties of this century, Sarita Colonia in the port city of Callao began to occupy an especially important place in the pantheon of popular devotions. Both St. Martin de Porres and Sarita de Colonia were characterized by their humble origins and by their simplicity and sheer goodness that came close to being naïve; but these very qualities make them very attractive to the lower classes.

Without doubt the most important popular religious manifestation in Peru is the great procession of Our Lord of Miracles, which takes place three times during the month of October in Lima. The procession, which began as a private devotion of the black slaves in seventeenth-century Lima, soon grew to become the favorite devotion of all the popular classes in the viceregal capital. In the nineteenth century the white middle classes also adopted the procession as their own; and in the twentieth century the upper classes, especially the women, discovered certain values in the procession for themselves. According to José Carlos Mariátegui, the devotees of the upper classes felt a nostalgia for colonial Lima that they relived in the procession.[78]

Nevertheless, the procession never lost its essentially popular character. From colonial times to the present, street vendors follow the procession selling *chica morada* (a purple brew made from corn), sweet cakes, and other specialties of the month of October. But the really distinctive note of the procession is the use of a purple penitential garb. The faithful who accompany the "Purple Lord" form an immense purple sea that flows through the streets of Lima. The brothers who belong to the confraternity of the Lord of Miracles, blacks, mestizos, and mulattos, carry the heavy platform bearing the image of the crucified Christ. The Brotherhood of the Bearers of the Lord of Miracles had three hundred members in the twenties; by the eighties the membership had reached some four thousand. In 1878 a mutual self-help association was founded by the brotherhood to offer aid to sick members and to cover funeral costs.[79]

Official Religiosity

The church has always looked on these popular manifestations with different degrees of favor. Those that seemed to be "pagan," especially in the highlands, were condemned. But those that seemed more compatible with Catholicism were tolerated. The church initially censured the Lord of Miracles procession; later it tolerated it and finally approved it. The elections and the naming of officials for the confraternity are approved by the archbishop of Lima and the procession begins and ends each year with official liturgical acts at the church of the Nazarenes. But there are other devotions and processions that have enjoyed a more official status because they were founded or promoted by the church itself and because they express more clearly the church's thinking.

An example of an "official" type of devotion par excellence is the devotion to the Sacred Heart. Although this devotion antedates the eighteenth and nineteenth centuries, it was especially in those centuries that it became an officially propagated devotion of the universal church. The church saw in the suffering Christ an image of itself: a victim of indifference, hate, and anticlerical repression. The religious order that most spread the devotion was the Society of Jesus. Given this background, the devotion in Peru became a symbol of the militant church struggling against liberal society, and news of the devotion began to appear about the same time as the return of the Jesuits. In 1881 Ambrosio Huerta consecrated Arequipa to the Sacred Hearts of Jesus and Mary, and that same year the superior of the College of Missionaries of the Recollection informed the bishop that he had fostered the devotion "for several years."[80] In 1889 the Gentlemen of the Catholic Union in Lima consecrated themselves to the Sacred Heart in the Jesuit church of St. Peter's. In 1898 The Brotherhood of the Sacred Heart of Jesus was founded in the Parish of San Ildefonso in Pueblo Nuevo in the diocese of Trujillo.[81] In 1916 the Society of the Gentlemen of the Sacred Heart of Jesus was created in the parish of San Lázaro in Lima.[82]

The culminating moment of the devotion each year occurs in the month of June. The procession in honor of the Sacred Heart became the most important religious expression of the official (and especially the "militant") church. The men and women of the Catholic Union and, years later, of Catholic Action, participated in the procession as a sign of their loyalty to the church and as a protest against liberal society. In well-ordered lines they marched: Jesuits, the mothers of the Sacred Heart, and other Catholic militants, most of whom came from the white middle and lower middle classes. Given the conservative orientation of the church, the procession also acquired a certain socio-political air. This phenomenon also occurred, on a lesser scale, in the "official" processions of The Lord of Tremors in Cuzco and of Holy Week in Arequipa. In this period the association known as the Daughters of Mary, which paralleled the Catholic Union for Ladies, was also founded in many parishes.

Protestant Activity

Until 1890 Protestantism in Peru was not a major concern of the Catholic church. The first Protestant missionaries in Peru worked mainly with the English colony and other foreigners, most of whom lived in Lima and Callao. In general, these first groups did not carry out proselytizing activities. The most important person in the early history of Protestantism was James Thomson, a Scottish minister who implanted the Lancasterian system of teaching in schools.[83] In 1849 the first Protestant church—Anglican—was formally set up. In 1877 the first Methodist missionary, from the United States, arrived. But the real initiator of modern Protestantism in Peru was Francisco Penzotti, a Uruguayan citizen born in Italy. Penzotti came to Peru in 1888 as a representative of the American Bible Society, and he zealously set about preaching beyond the narrow confines of the foreign colonies. In 1889 he was arrested in Arequipa as a consequence of his proselytizing, and a year later he was imprisoned in the Real Felipe (a colonial fortress) in Callao for the same reason. His detention provoked a public scandal that led to his being freed. But this incident had a more important consequence: it created a climate that favored the nonapplication of article 4 of the constitution, which prohibited the practice in public of non-Catholic cults or religions. After Penzotti's victory, many other Protestant missionaries began arriving in Peru.

The two groups that made most use of the new freedom of activity were the Methodists and the Seventh Day Adventists. Under the leadership of Dr. Thomas Wood and his daughter Elsie, the Methodist church carried on the work begun by Penzotti. Already in 1900 the Methodists had founded four schools in Callao and one in Lima.[84] But even more impressive was the work of the Adventists, who beginning in 1898 and 1899 began to concentrate their efforts in the highlands by Lake Titicaca. By 1916 they had established some nineteen schools for Indians in the region around the lake, and by 1926 the number of schools reached eighty, with a total of 3,892 students.[85] They also founded numerous medical clinics in which the Indians learned the basic rules of health and hygiene. The educational and health efforts of the Adventists drew praise from many *indigenistas* (pro-Indian writers) such as Luis Valcárcel in *Tempestad en los Andes* (Storm in the Andes); and even the old anticlerical war-horse, Manuel González Prada, rendered them praise.[86]

But this rapid expansion also provoked the hostility of the Catholic church. In 1895 two English missionaries founded the East London Institute in Cuzco. This led the Ladies of the Catholic Union to send a letter of protest to the president of the republic in 1899. The women declared: "The Protestant sect is a seedbed of unending errors, a source of political anarchy, of corruption for the people, and of divisions in families: in a word, it is unconstitutional, antisocial, antipolitical, and anti-Catholic."[87]

In 1913 the Adventists founded a school for Indians in a town called Platería, not far from the city of Puno. Shortly afterwards the bishop, Valentín Ampuero, organized an expedition to threaten the mission. Fortunately, no one was killed during the attack, but several years later, in another town in the province of Azángaro, several Indians who had converted to Adventism were massacred.[88] The attack in Platería set off another national controversy that contributed much to congress's decision in 1915 to eliminate the restriction against the practice of non-Catholic religions. In spite of this official modification, however, the Catholic church did not change its attitude of hostility to the founding of opposing religions in Peru. In some cases the Catholic church and the *gamonales* (small but tyrannical landowners) in the southern Andean region associated Protestantism with communism because both created social discontent. That was the general sense of this accusation a priest made in 1924: "Máximo Salas, pastor of Urcos, denounces the presence of Adventists in his doctrine (parish) and accuses the Indian Gavino Yupanqui of being a propagandist of the Protestant cult and of the idea that the Indians should be the only owners of the land that has been usurped by the *viracochas* (white lords)."[89]

The best-known Protestant of that period was Dr. John Mackay, a Scotsman by birth and a missionary of the Presbyterian church. Mackay, who had studied Spanish literature in Madrid before going to Peru, enrolled in San Marcos University in 1917 and wrote his doctoral thesis on Miguel de Unamuno. He founded the Anglo-Peruvian School, later renamed Saint Andrew's. Among the notable teachers in Mackay's school were Haya de la Torre, Luis Alberto Sánchez, Raúl Porras Barrenechea, and Jorge Guillermo Leguía. This was the basis of Mackay's special relationship with the founder of the Aprista Party. In 1923 Haya de la Torre sought refuge in Mackay's house in Miraflores (a suburb of Lima) shortly before being deported. Mackay was the author of several works that provide eyewitness testimony to the political and religious life of Latin America in those years, especially *The Other Spanish Christ* (1932) and *Christianity on the Frontier* (1950). After sixteen years in Latin America as a missionary, educator, and circuit speaker for the YMCA, Mackay went to the United States, where he taught as a professor at Princeton Theological Seminary. He also served as president of the seminary for a number of years.[90] In spite of his rather open spirit, however, he did not escape being criticized by Archbishop Lissón, who in 1926 referred to him as "the Protestant propagandist, Mr. John A. Mackay, at San Marcos University."[91] In 1919 Lissón forbade Catholics to belong to the YMCA, officially founded in Lima in 1920, given its ties with Protestantism.[92]

In spite of this crusading zeal that gave new life to Protestantism, its progress was rather modest. In 1928 the total number of Protestant pastors and ministers, counting both foreigners and Peruvians, was 339, and, according to one estimate, there were approximately 14,933 Protestants in Peru in 1930.[93]

The Evangelization of the Asiatics

Between 1840 and 1879 more than ninety thousand Chinese were brought over to Peru as contract laborers. The great majority were sent to work on the sugar haciendas on the coast. Between 1898 and 1923 some 18,258 Japanese arrived in similar conditions.[94] The wide-scale importation of Asiatics drew protests from Peruvians, some for humanitarian reasons and others for reasons of racism. In the years following the conflict with Chile, Manuel Tovar expressed his indignation over this type of trafficking in human beings: "The speculation in Chinese labor, which is really slave labor in another form, cannot be good for our country. This repugnant trafficking in human flesh is a cancer that should be cut out at the roots."[95]

Very little is known about the initial evangelization of these immigrants from the Orient. Chinese names appear in parish records at a very early date. A list from a doctrine (parish) in Chancay in 1840 refers to a certain "Juan Cortés, a free Chinese," and to a "creole Chinawoman"[96] However, there was no officially organized effort by the Catholic church to evangelize the Asiatics. In general, this mission was assumed by certain pious individuals who went out of their way to reach the newcomers. In *El Deber* of Arequipa in 1919 there is an article about a Señorita Carmen Rosa Polar, who was a godmother in the baptism of two Japanese that she herself had converted to Catholicism.[97] Frequently, the newly converted took the initiative and outdid the efforts of Peruvians or the foreign missionaries. In the jungle department of Madre de Dios Father Zubieta, the superior of the Dominicans, marveled over a neophyte Japanese whom he had baptized in 1915. This zealous convert returned a year later with five new candidates to be baptized.[98] In 1941 in Huaral, on the northern coast, a Japanese school teacher prepared 174 children from fifty-eight familes for a mass baptism.[99]

The migration of these two groups to Lima and other urban centers accelerated the process very much. In Lima, a pious woman, Dominga Gazcón, spent years until her death in 1879 working among the Chinese. She centered her efforts in the church of San Pedro and in the Santa Rosa retreat house.[100] Partly for this reason San Pedro became a center of attention for the Chinese colony, just as it would be for the Japanese colony in the sixties of this century. Dominga Gazcón's work was continued by Juan Chávez, a Chinese-Peruvian who was ordained a priest in 1876. His successor was the Jesuit priest, José Pineda, who until his death in 1940 managed to baptize hundreds of Chinese and Japanese.

Another person who stood out for her work among the Japanese was Mother Françoise Gros, a French Daughter of Charity. In Dos de Mayo Hospital where she worked as a nurse from 1906 until 1936, she was responsible for the conversion of more than a thousand Japanese, most of whom were indigent workers from the haciendas.[101] It was not until 1936, however, that a permanent apostolate to the Japanese colony was established. Through the efforts of the papal nuncio, Cayetano Cicognani, Father Calixte Gelinas Yonekawa of the Canadian Franciscans, with twenty-four years of service in Japan as a missionary, arrived to set up the new apostolate. In 1938 he was joined by Father Urbain-Marie Yonekawa, and between the two of them the Japanese colony was systematically brought into the Catholic religion.

Relations with the State

A Modus Vivendi Amid Tensions

Following the bitter feuds between the church and the liberals, which culminated in the liberal victories in the years 1855–57, the constitution of 1860 established a modus vivendi between state and church. The relationship between the two was characterized by a double level of interaction: on one level, purely formal and juridical, the state assumed the right of partonage over the church with the obligation to protect it and to offer it economic assistance; but on another and more informal level, the state in fact tended to subordinate the church to its interests. What is more, it frequently put obstacles in the way of the church's work. The modus vivendi was not a contract between equals: the state demanded more than it gave. For example, in return for the legitimization that the state received from its close relationship with the church, it offered in return rather paltry sums by way of economic support. When the tithes were suppressed, Castilla made a special arrangement whereby the state would support bishops, seminaries, and hospitals. The constitution of 1860 ratified this arrangement. But the state never really fulfilled its offer. It did not pay the salaries in relation to the cost of living in the same way in which it did with respect to other groups that depended on the state. In 1962 the monthly "wage" of the archbishop of Lima was only five thousand soles, roughly the equivalent of 180 dollars.[102] The amount reserved for seminaries suffered the same fate. In

1941 the seminary in Lima received two hundred soles a month from the government. "With this amount," wrote Father Vargas Ugarte, "one couldn't pay a doorkeeper."[103]

Among the rights the state fought to retain, none was so important as the naming of bishops. Between 1860 and 1940 congress elected the candidates to be bishops. Only in exceptional cases of "conscience" did Rome reject these nominees. But not all members of congress were practicing Catholics; there were also anticlericals, Masons, and indifferent nonpracticing Catholics. Given this anomalous situation of a state and a congress that were formally "Catholic" but in practice regalist and at times openly anticlerical, there was a lot of room for ambiguities and tensions. A notable case in point was the "interdict of Lampa." In 1864 the *Diario de Debates* (Parliamentary Debates) reported on the election of Ambrosio Huerta as the first bishop of Puno: "The selection of a bishop for the diocese of Puno was made and, from the votes cast eighty-five were for Dr. Juan A. Huerta, thirty-one for Dr. Barranco . . . ."(104)

Huerta took possession of his diocese in 1866 and convoked the first synod in its history. But as he prepared to leave in 1869 to attend the First Vatican Council, he found himself in serious difficulties with the attorney general, José Gregorio Paz Soldán. Huerta had committed two errors that were unpardonable in the minds of the liberals: he did not ask for the *pase* (official seal of approbation) to convoke the synod and publish the results, and he did not ask for authorization to leave his diocese to go to Rome. The affair soon turned into a storm when Huerta placed the district of Lampa under interdict because some of the citizens rejected the conclusions of the synod. Under pressure, and to avoid further grief for his diocese, Huerta resigned as bishop in 1874. This case shows clearly that the state did not merely select bishops; it also reserved the right to censure them if they went beyond certain bounds. The incongruity of having bishops named by men who were openly hostile toward the church is further illustrated by the words of a deputy to congress from Callao who asked in 1915 why it was necessary even to vote for a new bishop for the diocese of Puno. In his opinion, the election would serve only to "put a monk in a position to barbarize, alcoholize, humiliate, and ruin a people under the pretext of having religious feasts."[105]

Furthermore, the election of bishops in congress unnecessarily introduced political and regional interests into church questions. For example, in 1933 congress members from Arequipa and from Cuzco proposed their own candidates for archbishop of Lima. Mariano Holguín, bishop of Arequipa, was acting at the time as apostolic administrator of Lima, and he seemed to be an appropiate candidate to become archbishop. But he was also the preferred candidate of Víctor Andrés Belaunde, a fellow Arequipanian. According to a contemporary witness, the candidacy of Pedro Pascual Farfán, bishop of Cuzco, was promoted in order to "give a blow" to Belaunde's plans.[106] To avoid these kinds of abuses, in 1940 the election of bishops was taken out of congress's hands. From that time on the president of the republic alone presented the candidates to be confirmed by the Holy See.

Another sensitive area was the growing number of foreign clergy. On different occasions congress members accused the foreign missionaries of enriching themselves at the expense of the people or of spreading antiliberal ideas. In 1910 several deputies proposed a law prohibiting the entrance of priests who had been expelled from Spain and Portugal as a consequence of anticlerical purges carried out there.[107] In 1915 *El Comercio* published the complaints of several members of congress who accused the foreign priests of carrying off to Europe the wealth of Peruvian monasteries and convents.[108] This animosity toward the foreign clergy became a constant sore point, especially among politicians of a laic mentality.

Given this aggressiveness, the church sought to support public figures who might defend its interests. Three different presidents, Nicolás de Piérola, José Pardo, and Augusto B. Leguía, were especially disposed to assume that role. In the case of Piérola, the ties with the church were both personal and ideological. The same could be said of Pardo, whose brother was a Jesuit priest. But these two, although conservative, practiced democracy. The church's ties with Leguía, a dictator, however, were to prove quite harmful for the church.

The Oncenio

The union between church and state was never so visible in modern times, or had such negative consequences for the church, as during the eleven-year rule (the *Oncenio*) of Augusto B. Leguía, 1919–30. Leguía signified the beginning of the end of the traditional oligarchy and the rise of the emergent middle classes. He was not quite a "conservative" or a "liberal" but rather a "modernizer" who dreamed of lifting Peru out of its underdevelopment by injecting large quantities of foreign investments into the economy and by fostering the rapid expansion of modern capitalism.

Leguía was not a philosopher given over to mere speculation. Most of all, he was a practical man and, in the opinion of many, a dangerously astute man.

Of ordinary background, Leguía rose rapidly in the world of business and finance. In 1903 he became minister of finance and in 1908 he was elected president of the country. When he left power in 1912, his enemies forced him to leave in exile. He stayed in England until his return in 1919. He returned as a candidate for the presidency in the middle of great expectations, promising to create a "new fatherland." Elected for the second time as president, he soon disillusioned many when he assumed dictatorial powers. He deported his enemies, closed down San Marcos University, and silenced the press. But the founder of the "new fatherland" was careful not to alienate the church. He went out of his way to create the image of perfect harmony between state and church, and he never failed to show up at official ceremonies of the church.

The churchman who fostered this special alliance with the state was Emilio Lissón, who was archbishop of Lima during the entire *Oncenio*, 1918–31. Born in Arequipa, he entered the congregation of St. Vincent de Paul. He studied and was ordained in Paris. In 1909 he was consecrated bishop of Chachapoyas. When he became head of the church in Lima, he was known for his zeal and energy. As archbishop of the capital city he built several minor seminaries, gave new life to Santo Toribio Seminary, and organized and presided over several episcopal assemblies, one diocesan synod (1926), and a provincial council (1927). He also fostered the creation of Catholic Action. He was considered by all, even by his critics, as a man of exemplary piety.

Like most churchmen of that period, he believed that in order to strengthen the church it was necessary to procure state protection. With this in mind, he always invited the head of the state to be present at all church ceremonies in order to underline the president's role as "patron" of the church. The culmination of this effort came in February 1929 when the papal nuncio, Bishop Cayetano Cicognani, named Leguía a Gentleman of the Supreme Military Order of Christ. The entire hierarchy, presided over by Lissón, surrounded President Leguía during the ceremony.[109] But the majority of Peruvians best remember another, more famous date, May 23, 1923, when Lissón attempted to consecrate Peru to the Sacred Heart of Jesus. Before the consecration ceremony he had invited Leguía to be present as the representative of the state. The ceremony was never held, however, because Víctor

The Militant Church, 1855–1930

Raúl Haya de la Torre and the workers of the popular universities that he founded, along with students from San Marcos, organized a protest march. Although the protest was directed primarily against Leguía, it was also directed against the church that legitimized the dictator's government.

From that moment on, the fate of the two figures was tightly bound together. When Leguía fell from power in 1930, overthrown by Colonel Luis Miguel Sánchez Cerro, Leguía's enemies, including some priests, campaigned for Lissón to resign as archbishop. In December 1930 Lissón left quietly for Rome and shortly afterwards submitted his resignation, which was accepted. Another shadow hovered over the former archbishop: he had contracted a large debt for the archdiocese with an American construction company.[110] In his defense his friends pointed out that Lissón not only did not intervene in politics but on a number of occasions opposed the idea of having Catholic political parties.[111] This notwithstanding, in the opinion of the majority of Peruvians, practicing Catholics or not, the archbishop did intervene in politics by way of the effusive praise he showered upon the former dictator on innumerable occasions and by his silence when the dictator suppressed liberty of expression and deported his critics. Lissón spent the rest of his life, until his death in Spain in 1961, compiling documents on Peruvian church history.

The end of the *Oncenio* signaled the end of the first stage of the militant church. Although a considerable amount of time separated Bartolomé Herrera and Emilio Lissón, there was a central linking theme: a profound concern about the secular world that had grown increasingly hostile toward the church. This concern gave rise to a spirit of militancy and combat. The fundamental strategy of the bishops, priests, and laity of this period was the same: to unite forces, defend the church, and fight to protect the church's position in society. But given the shortage of priests, and the lack of well-formed laypersons, that task was very difficult. Among the different means the church chose for regenerating itself, none was so important as the revitalization of religious life. With the arrival of numerous new orders and congregations in the second part of the last century, and with the reform of some of the older groups already in Peru, many new works of charity and public assistance were founded. Moreover, with the schools these new groups founded the church was able to produce the militant laity that it needed for its survival.

4
The Resurgence of Religious Life
Pastors, Missionaries, and Nurses

Perhaps the most important phenomenon in the life of the Peruvian church in the nineteenth and early twentieth centuries, which changed its face substantially, was the resurgence of religious life. This revitalization of what was the weakest link in the church at the time of independence was due principally to three factors: a vigorous reform carried out in the older orders toward the end of the nineteenth century, the birth of new congregations in Peru that displayed a zeal characteristic of missionaries orders, and the arrival of numerous men and women religious from Europe and later on from the United States.

The foreign religious personnel in general, both religious in the strict sense as well as the secular clergy, came for different reasons: some in response to an invitation proffered by the government or by the various benevolent societies to attend to works of charity; others because they were invited by certain families to educate their sons and daughters; and others, impelled by the missionary spirit that touched thousands of men and women in Europe in the nineteenth century, to carry out such specific tasks as the evangelization of the jungle, the formation of seminarians, or the administration of abandoned parishes.

By the middle of the twentieth century, religious men had come to assume an increasingly predominant role in the church. In 1940, for example, there were 637 religious priests in Peru as compared to 655 secular priests.[1] But by 1984, though the total number of priests had grown (to a total of 2,265), the disproportion between the two clergies had also grown: there were 984 secular priests as compared to 1,251 religious priests.[2] Equally significant is the fact that of the fifty-four bishops in Peru in 1976, only twelve were from the secular clergy; the majority of the rest came from the ranks of the religious, a few from secular institutes or missionary associations.[3]

Pastors, Missionaries, and Nurses   103

In this sense, the second part of the nineteenth century and the greater part of the twentieth seem somewhat like the sixteenth century, which was the golden age of the great missionary orders. In that century, Franciscans, Dominicans, Augustinians, Mercedarians, and Jesuits evangelized the Indians and black slaves and laid the foundations of the church in the New World. Perhaps the distinction between the religious clergy and the secular clergy seems somewhat academic and of little importance, but it does have real and practical consequences for the church. For example, the secular clergy generally run parishes in areas where Christianity is already well established. Bishops are generally chosen from the ranks of that clergy. By way of contrast, religious clergy, who take the three vows and live some type of community life, assume such special tasks as teaching, pastoral care in hospitals, or missionary work among non-Christians. In the sixteenth century, the religious predominated because Peru was obviously a mission land. The orders had certain advantages over the secular clergy in this respect: the organization of their members into apostolic communities that could be dispatched to other parts of the world with relative ease; the capacity, typical of any large institution, to accumulate capital and goods and to use them in an efficient way to support certain projects; and greater possibilities of training their members for specialized mission tasks.

But, most of all, the sixteenth century religious possessed a zeal that led them to risk their lives and to undertake creative and imaginative works such as the Jesuit missions in Juli or Paraguay. There were, of course, priests of the secular clergy who displayed this same missionary spirit, such as Toribio de Mogrovejo or "Tato" Vasco de Quiroga in New Spain. In general, however, the secular clergy were characterized by their vocation to be pastors in the "civilized" world of the Spaniards and the creoles. In time, tensions arose between the two clergies regarding their respective privileges and jurisdictions. A main source of friction was the concept each had of the correct way to evangelize and civilize the Indians. The religious in general were inclined to evangelize without imposing Spanish culture. But the secular clergy tended to identify evangelization with "Hispanization." The political authorities naturally viewed the secular clergy with greater sympathy. In order to resolve these conflicts, the Crown adopted toward the end of the sixteenth century a policy of sending the religious to more rural and distant regions and of leaving the cities and parishes close to urban areas in the hands of the secular clergy.

The religious, of course, were allowed to retain their great monasteries and houses in the city centers.

Largely because of the priest shortage, the religious once again toward the end of the nineteenth century and the beginning of the twentieth began to take on parishes and other works normally administered by the secular clergy. The prevalence of religious in the church, and especially among the hierarchy, is a sign that a local church is, or has gone back to being, a "missionary" church. Today there are no open antagonisms between the two clergies as there were in colonial times. Nonetheless, the present situation is not normal. A bishop, who is the supreme authority in his diocese, cannot interfere in the internal affairs of a congregation or an order, nor can he transfer the members of a religious community as though they were his own diocesan clergy. He must always consult with the respective superiors of the religious orders in his diocese in order to make any changes affecting them. As a result, in some dioceses in Peru where the religious make up half or more of the clergy, the bishop is in the peculiar position of not being able to govern directly a large part of the religious personnel within his jurisdiction.

Given this extraordinary situation in the Peruvian church, similar to that of many other countries of Latin America, it is important to study with special attention the role that the religious congregations and orders have played in the life of the church and not subordinate that topic simply to a review of the various dioceses. We will limit this panoramic view to the period between independence (1821) and the Second World War, because by that time, especially taking the first national eucharistic congress (1935) as a key dividing date, the Peruvian church was well on its way out of the deep crisis that began in the nineteenth century. We will return to the story of the religious in the postwar years in later chapters. Finally, strictly for reasons of convenience, we will divide this subject into two chapters: one for those orders and congregations that work principally in the areas of charity, missions, the formation of the clergy and parishes, and another for those religious groups that have distinguished themselves principally by their educational work. Needless to say, many orders and congregations have worked in all these areas at the same time.

The Reform of Religious Life

As indicated in the second chapter, religious life had fallen into a state of disorder, if not outright decay, during and after the wars of independence. This situation would not be remedied until the end of the century. In 1861 the archbishop of Lima, José Sebastián Goyeneche, referred to the "bad state in which the religious of this archdiocese find themselves." He proceeded to promulgate a new "Reform of Regulars" by virtue of his title, conferred upon him by Pius IX, of "Apostolic Visitor of the Religious" of the archdiocese (1860). The reform was similar to earlier ones proposed during colonial times. It called for a complete reordering of religious life and for all religious to have a "useful" occupation, and it forbade religious to engage in "lucrative businesses." Most of all, it insisted upon the importance of community life.[4] But ten years later, Goyeneche himself admitted that this attempt at reform had failed. In 1870 he removed the superior of the Mercedarians in Lima from office because he had not even tried to put the reform into effect in his community.[5] In November of 1871 the apostolic delegate to Peru, Bishop Serafín Vennutelli, promulgated another reform, but this also had little success.

The problem in essence resided in the fact that many religious had lost the habit of regular observance of their vows and the spirit of religious discipline. In 1879 Pedro Gual informed the Apostolic Delegate that in the Beaterio (home for pious laywomen) of Saint Rose of Viterbo the religious did not even have a rule because they had "lost" it a long time ago![6] Given this state of affairs, the mere multiplication of rules and decrees would not be sufficient to bring about a radical change in religious life. It would be necessary to inject new life from the outside. In the case of the older colonial orders, reform was brought about by means of visits and the naming of superiors of recognized capacity and strength of character, almost all from Europe. This was the role Pedro Gual himself performed among the Franciscans. In 1894 Eustacio Estéban arrived from Spain to reform the Augustinians.[7] In 1878 Father Vincent Nardini, also from Spain, initiated a reform of the Dominicans in Bolivia and Peru.

These visitors were very successful. One testimony of the period speaks laudably of the changes brought about in the convent of the Dominicans in Lima: ". . . The constant efforts of Father Nardini . . . , carried out for three straight years, have completely transformed the Dominican community, which has grown in numbers and observes community life, etc."[8] In other cases, the renovation was brought about principally by sending reinforcements from the outside. This happened with the Franciscans, who underwent a revitalizing reform long before the other traditional orders. For this reason they were the most important missionary order in the Peru in the beginning of the nineteenth century.

The Franciscans

Ocopa and the Mission Colleges

With the closing of Ocopa in 1824 and the expulsion of numerous Spanish friars, the Franciscans underwent a profound crisis. Furthermore, the "national" (Peruvian) Franciscans had to submit to the interference of the central government in their internal affairs, and their direct contact with Rome and other groups of Franciscans was cut off. As late as 1884 Pope Leo XIII named a Peruvian visitor, Friar José María Gago, to reorganize their houses in Peru and Bolivia. During his visit in 1898, Father Gago limited himself to Peru and to houses of the Peruvian province of the Franciscans.[9] In 1907, as we shall see, the Peruvian province of the Franciscans was formally constituted as an entity distinct from the Spanish province.

In 1838 President Orbegoso decreed the reopening of Ocopa, and shortly afterwards a group of nineteen Franciscans arrived to start missionary work in the central mountain and jungle region once again. Other groups soon followed. By 1860 some forty-three priests and fifty-nine students for the priesthood had gone through the mission college of Lima (the Discalced Franciscans) and that of Ocopa.[10] The reason behind the government's change of attitude toward the existence of Ocopa was the growing realization that it was only through the missionaries that the Peruvian nation could maintain a visible presence in the vast Amazon jungle that touched the borders of Peru's neighbors, Ecuador, Colombia, Brazil, and Bolivia. In parliamentary debates, some deputies of liberal persuasion emphasized the Spanish origins of the missionaries and warned that they would spread antiliberal ideas. But other deputies stressed the need to support the missionaries because they constituted the most efficacious means of carrying civilization and the Peruvian flag to many remote Indian tribes. This geopolitical view of evangelization, in reality as old as the Catholic kings, was aptly put by a deputy from Jauja, a city near Ocopa:

> Given the fact that civilizing and evangelizing are twin themes, to the degree to which the many savage tribes are catechized they will also pick up elements of culture, and they will therefore be-

come more closely associated with us. Think of the relatively little cost involved in extending our frontier all the way to Brazil—and that means civilizing the savage tribes that block the path of progress—compared to the great wealth that could come out of that region.[11]

Some of the missionaries had been expelled from Spain in 1835 as a result of anticlerical uprisings. They sought refuge in the papal states. The most famous of these exiled religious was Pedro Gual, who would come to be at different times superior of Ocopa, Commissary General of Peru, Ecuador, Colombia, Venezuela, and Chile, and representative of the Peruvian church at the First Vatican Council. He was also the author of numerous polemical tracts. The Franciscans at Ocopa preached popular missions throughout the entire central mountain region in Huánuco, Tarma, Ayacucho, Cerro de Pasco, and Jauja. On various occasions local politicians and their friends in Lima placed obstacles in the way of the friars, accusing them of spreading "subversive doctrines." On one occasion, the missionaries were charged with having provoked an uprising in Jauja. But upon closer examination Archbishop Luna Pizarro of Lima discovered that in reality the "uprising" consisted of a public parade in support of the friars.[12]

In 1852 Gual founded in the monastery of the Discalced in Lima another mission college, which was elevated to the rank of an apostolic college a year later. The purpose of the new college was to train missionaries for work in the Andes and the jungle. Later on, other colleges were founded in Cuzco, Arequipa, Cajamarca, Ica, Quito, Guayaquil, and Loja.[13] The Apostolic College of Moquegua, which had been in operation since 1825, did not reopen.[14] Four of these colleges, in Lima, Ocopa, Arequipa, and Cuzco, became the principal bases of operation for the reevangelization of entire regions of Peru. Ocopa included within its sphere of operation practically the entire Peruvian jungle from Ecuador and Colombia to the Ucayali river and practically the entire central Andes. The college in Arequipa took charge of the southern departments of Arequipa, Moquegua, Tacna, and Puno.

The college that functioned within the Recollection monastery of Arequipa is a good example of the rebirth of a house. Before the new arrivals, there were only three priests, three students, one brother, and a "few consecrated laypersons."[15] In 1869 a small group of Franciscans from Lima, under the leadership of Father José María Masiá, later to be bishop of Loja, preached a mission in the "White City." The mission created a very favorable reaction, and soon the people urged the friars to stay. As a result, that same year the Apostolic College of the Recollection in Arequipa was founded with fifteen religious, priests, and students. In 1898 the college welcomed twenty-six new young students, all from Spain. One of the principal benefactors was Mariano López de Romaña, who aided the new foundation economically. The Recollection Franciscans preached missions in Arequipa itself and in the outlying towns of Tiabaya, Paucarpata, Majes, and Aplao as well as in the big haciendas of Chucarapi, Pampa Blanca, and elsewhere. As a rule, each mission team remained a month in each place.

The missionaries soon began venturing outside the department of Arequipa, traveling by mule to the other departments in the south. In 1873, for example, a group of twenty-five missionaries covered the entire department of Puno, beginning with the city of Puno, and including Lampa, Azángaro, Juli, and other cities. In Puno they met a cold reception; the Freemasons there organized a campaign against them. By way of contrast, in July some eight thousand Indians came in from the country to participate in the mission.[16] Given the immensity of the territories they tried to cover, the missionaries managed to visit each town only every eight or nine years. However, to maintain the spirit of the mission, the missionaries founded a third order for laypersons in each town.

One of the best-known missionaries of that period was Father José Ramón Rojas, "Father Guatemala." Born in Guatemala and exiled by anticlericals in 1831, he became very popular in Lima as a preacher. After four years in the capital, where he spread the devotion to the Virgin of Guadalupe, he established himself in Ica, on the coast to the south of Lima, and set about preaching missions, founding chapels, visiting convents, and carrying out many other apostolic activities until his death in 1839.[17] In each city where they worked, the Franciscans fulfilled a key role in the religious rebirth of Peruvian society after independence. In Lima in 1852 the Discalced Franciscans reorganized the retreat house of Saint Francis Solano, thereby filling a vacuum left by the Jesuits. Gual himself was the director of the house for a period of thirty years.

The missionaries used two basic instruments to carry out their work, the popular mission and the third order. The object of the mission was to revitalize the faith in each place visited; the residents were invited to come to confession and receive the sacraments. In a manual he wrote on how to preach a mission, Gual, who relied upon the teachings of Alphonsus Liguori, the founder of the Redemptorists, gave this advice to students and future missionaries:

> The mission sermons should be simple and free of heavy Latin references. Some young missionaries fill their talks with quotations from Scripture and long Latin texts of the fathers of the church. But of what use are all those quotations for the poor who don't understand them? . . . During the mission we should express ourselves in a simple and ordinary way so that the people understand what we preach and are moved by it.[18]

This advice summed up the success of the Franciscans: the use of a simple, direct, and humble style. On the other hand, the weakness of this type of evangelization is also evident: the lack of intellectual depth.

The Third Order

The third order (the first is that of the Friars Minor and the second is that of the women, the Poor Clares), consists of laypersons who wish to live the spirit of Saint Francis of Assisi but who are not called to be religious. Other orders, such as the Dominicans and the Augustinians, also have a third order or the equivalent.

Structurally, the third order seems like a confraternity or a brotherhood. The person in charge is a "minister." The Third Order of Saint Francis, founded everywhere in Peru by the missionaries from Ocopa, Lima, Arequipa, and Cuzco, gave great impulse to Christian life in hundreds of little towns where there were no priests in permanent residence. It was probably the most important religious organization among the popular classes throughout most of the postindependence period. In 1936 the first national congress of third order members affiliated with the Province of Saint Francis Solano was held in Ocopa. A second congress was held in Lima in 1945. In both of these congresses thousands of persons of the lower classes participated, including Indians dressed in native costumes. On both occasions it was estimated that there were about four hundred different brotherhoods of the third order in the entire country, with a total of thirty thousand men and women members. In the area around Ocopa alone there were fifty-four brotherhoods with 3,700 members.[19] A few members of the upper classes also wore the habit of the third order, such as Víctor Andrés Belaunde and José de la Riva-Agüero.

The third order fulfilled many of the same functions as a confraternity. In a report made during a visit to the northern town of Catacaos, the capitular vicar of Trujillo stated in 1898 that he had placed the responsibility for all religious practices in the town in the hands of "the Third Order of Saint Francis, as well as the fostering of pious devotions such as the Way of the Cross . . . ."[20]

The Division into Two Provinces

In 1907, following the recommendations of the Visitor General, José Bottaro, the Franciscans in Peru created two distinct provinces: the Province of the Twelve Apostles, made up principally of Peruvians, and the Province of Saint Francis Solano, with a majority of Spaniards. The division was not made solely out of nationalistic considerations but principally because the so-called "Spanish" province was essentially a missionary one, created for work in the mountains and in the jungle, whereas the "Peruvian" or "national" province devoted itself principally to traditional pastoral work in parishes.[21] The two provinces divided all the Franciscan houses between them, though they did not arrive at a final arrangement until 1916. According to that agreement, Saint Francis Solano (Spanish) would have the Discalced monasteries in Lima and Ocopa, the Recollection in Arequipa, and the houses in Ayacucho, Ica, Cuzco, Cajamarca, and Trujillo. The Province of the Twelve Apostles (Peruvian) kept the great colonial church of Saint Francis in Lima and houses in Cuzco, Juliaca, Arequipa, Piura, Huancayo, and Mollendo. In Arequipa they ran a school for postulants and another for laypersons.[22] And, of course, wherever the two provinces had houses, brotherhoods of the third order sprang up.

Although the Province of Saint Francis Solano (whose members are known as the "Discalced") has a majority of Spaniards, it has never been exclusively Spanish. Even before the division of the provinces there were Peruvians in the mission colleges. In 1890, for example, of a total of forty-nine religious in the mission college in Lima (Rímac), there were twenty-nine Spaniards, fourteen Peruvians, and five from other Latin American nations.[23] That same year there was one Peruvian priest and fifteen Spaniards at Ocopa.[24] Among notable Peruvians who belonged to the "Spanish" province are the two retired archbishops, Juan Landázuri Ricketts of Lima and Leonardo Rodríguez Ballón of Arequipa.

Notwithstanding the missionarary charcter of the "Spanish" province, both provinces have undertaken very similar works, including preached missions, retreats, charitable works, catechism in schools, and the publication of religious literature with a general appeal. *Las Florecillas de San Antonio* (The Little Flowers of Saint Anthony), founded in Cajamarca in 1911 by Father Pablo Ascondo of the Province of Saint Francis Solano, had at its zenith thirteen thousand subscribers. It ceased to be published in 1978. The Peruvian province published *La Revista franciscana* (The Franciscan Review), which was published between 1916 and 1965. Wherever they had houses, the Franciscans also administered works of mercy for the needy. In Arequipa in the thirties the "Pious Union of Saint Anthony of Padua" was founded. The Union sponsored a work called "The Bread of the Poor," which, to cite one single year, 1935, gave out more than 1,500 packages of food and clothes.[25] Two Franciscans of the Recollection in Arequipa who displayed singular zeal were Mariano Holguín and Francisco Cabré. Holguín, superior of the mission college since 1891, founded the "Circle of Catholic Workers" in 1896, and Cabré founded the newspaper, *La Colmena* (1920–1942), and for many years was the principal promoter of Catholic Action. Father Bernardino González in Lima, noted for his work with the poor, cofounded with Mother Ermelinda Carrera the Saint Thomas Prison for Women in 1892.

The majority of religious among the hierarchy have been or are Franciscans. To mention a few: Hipólito Sánchez Rangel, first bishop of Mainas (1805–24); Francisco de Sales Arrieta, archbishop of Lima (1841–43); Juan de La Cruz Calienes, bishop of Arequipa (1865); Juan Estévanes y Seminario (1880); Alfonso María Sardinas, bishop of Huánuco (1890–1902); Francisco Solano Risco, bishop of Chachapoyas (1865–1903); Santiago Irala, bishop of Chachapoyas (1904–8); Mariano Holguín, bishop of Huaraz (1904–06), bishop of Arequipa (1906–45); Francisco Irazola, vicar apostolic of Ucayali (1925–40); Buenaventura Uriarte, vicar apostolic of Ucayali and of San Ramón (1940–45); Leonardo Rodríguez Ballón, auxiliary bishop of Lima (1943–45), bishop of Huancayo (1945), archbishop of Arequipa (1946–80); Juan Landázuri Ricketts, coadjutor archbishop of Lima, (1952–55), archbishop of Lima and primate of Peru (1955–90); Luis V. Arroyo, vicar apostolic of Requena (1957–72); Luis M. Maestu, vicar apostolic of San Ramón (1971–83); Odorico Saíz, vicar apostolic of Requena (1974–87); Víctor de la Peña Perez, vicar apostolic of Requena (1987–   ); Héctor Miguel Cabrejos, auxiliary of Lima (1988–   ).[26]

In general, the bishops in the apostolic vicariates are Spanish-born, though almost all came to Peru as young seminarians. Two bishops named from among the Peruvian Franciscans are Salvador Herrera, bishop of Puno (1933–48), and Federico Richter Prada, auxiliary bishop of Piura (1973–76), archbishop of Ayacucho (1976–1991).

This listing of Franciscan bishops underlines a salient trait of the Peruvian church, the predominance of religious among the hierarchy. Although a religious who has been named a bishop is no longer strictly under his religious superior, he continues to be a member of his own religious family. In the jungle where the majority of the clergy belong to a single order, the bishops generally reside in houses or communities of their own order.

The influence of the Franciscans in the entire republican period was surely as great as during colonial times, even though religious life was submitted to far greater pressures in the postindependence period. In spite of the low esteem in which the religious were held, and the attacks of the liberals, the Franciscans once again brought organized religion to hundreds of small villages and towns throughout the Andes and in the jungle. Nevertheless, the missionaries of the republican era were far fewer in number than in colonial times and as a result they could barely cover a minimum of the territory under their care. In the year 1791, when Ocopa was at the height of its prosperity, there were eighty-five religious in the monastery; but in 1890, a century later, there were only thirty-five.[27]

The Hospital and Charitable Congregations

From 1858, the year in which the Daughters of Charity arrived, until shortly after the Second World War, the great majority of hospitals in Peru, as well as clinics and other social works for the sick and poor, were administered by religious congregations. The presence of the hospital or social assistance congregations was a response to the need to fill the vacuum created by the reduction in numbers of religious or, in some cases, by the total disappearance of the hospital orders of colonial times. The three principal colonial hospital orders were the Bethlemites, the Religious of Saint John of God, and the Camillians or Fathers of a Good Death (known today as Ministers of the Sick). These three groups all suffered greatly as a result of independence since most of their members were Spanish. In Lima in 1826, the year of the Reform of Religious, the Religious of Saint John of God had three priests and twenty-seven brothers, the Fathers of a Good Death had fourteen priests, two students and two brothers, and the Bethlemites, fifteen lay brothers.[28] But in 1833 the Saint John of God religious had only twelve members, the Bethlemites, eight, and the Fathers of a Good Death, eighteen.[29] In 1858 there were still scattered references to the Saint John of God religious, but by that date the Bethlemites had simply ceased to exist.[30]

The impact of the crisis in religious life was felt especially in the hospitals. In the first years of the republic there were only three hospitals in Lima as compared to ten in colonial times.[31] Even before the reform of 1826 the central government attempted to resolve the crisis by creating the first benevolent society in 1825. It was modeled after the philanthropic and humanitarian societies that arose in Europe in the eighteenth and nineteenth centuries and that incarnated the liberal ideal of total citizen participation in public affairs. But enlightened despots also fostered this type of participation. The best examples in the Hispanic world were the "Friends of the Country" societies. The benevolent society in each city was made up of ladies and gentlemen of the upper class who assumed the mission of attending to the welfare of hospitals, asylums, orphanages, and cemeteries.[32]

However, the first benevolent societies did not function well because of poor organization and lack of funds. In 1848 the government reorganized the benevolent societies in the entire country. This reform was somewhat successful. The Chilean writer, José Victorino Lastarria, who visited Lima in 1850, noted that "the hospitals are perfectly well attended to."[33] The compiler of statistics, Manuel A. Fuentes, reported in his guide to Lima for the year 1858 that the principal hospitals were "orderly and clean."[34] Yet this same author also observed that the books in Saint Anne's and Saint Andrew's hospitals were "kept by inept persons."[35]

This last observation underlines the nature of the problem. The benevolent society limited its function to the administering of funds for the external or material care of the buildings under its responsibility, but it did not involve itself in the internal administration of the centers. A glance at the list of employees drawn up by Manuel Fuentes in 1858 will reveal a noticeable lacuna in the hospitals; there were doctors, doorkeepers, cooks, pharmacists, and dishwashers, but there were no nurses.[36] In fact, the nursing profession was an entirely new concept in nineteenth-century Peru. It is helpful to observe the functioning of a modern hospital anywhere in the world to realize that the key personnel who attend to the patients on a twenty-four-hour basis are the nurses. For this reason, in spite of Lastarria's and Fuente's optimistic reports, the hospitals did not really function well at all. Not only was there a lack of hospitals and other humanitarian social assistance centers, but there were no qualified persons to run them and to attend to the patients or the needy in an efficient and humane way.

The Daughters of Charity

The first hospital congregation to arrive after independence was the Daughters of Charity, sometimes called the Vincentians in honor of Saint Vincent de Paul. In view of the lack of hospitals and of competent persons to run them, the government itself extended an invitation to the Daughters and later on to other similar congregations. By coincidence, the daughter of the director of the Benevolent Society of Lima, Virginia Carassa, wished to join the Daughters of Charity; they had already won worldwide fame, but her father did not want her to spend the rest of her life in France. The solomonic solution to the dilemma consisted in bringing the Daughters to Peru. In May 1857, the director, Francisco Carassa, authorized Peru's minister in France, Francisco Rivero, to draw up a written agreement with the Daughters of Charity, and in 1858 the first group of forty-five sisters of Charity, all French, arrived at the port city of Callao. Two priests and a brother of the congregation of Saint Vincent de Paul accompanied the sisters. According to tradition, the sisters, though they are an independent congregation, always have recourse to the Vincentian Fathers for spiritual guidance. The first Peruvian woman to enter the Daughters of Charity in Peru was Virginia Carassa.[37]

The sisters soon took charge of a great number of charitable and public service works: the Hospital of Saint Anne in the Plazuela Italia, the Hospital of Saint Andrew for men in the center of Lima, and the military hospital of the capital city. These three hospitals all went back to colonial times; Archbishop Loayza had founded Saint Anne's for Indians and Saint Bartholomew's (the military hospital) for black slaves. The sisters also took over the direction of many other health centers: Guadalupe Hospital in Callao in 1865, Saint Toribio de Mogrovejo Hospital in Lima in 1869, Larco Herrera Mental Hospital in 1859, Bellavista Hospital for Women in 1870, and between 1929 and 1936 the Children's Hospital in Lima. In 1875 Saint Andrew's was moved to a new location and renamed Dos de Mayo, and in 1925 Saint Anne's was moved to Alfonso Ugarte Avenue and renamed Archbishop Loayza.

In the twentieth century many other changes followed. In 1918 the sisters withdrew from Larco Herrera. In 1940 an earthquake destroyed Guadalupe Hospital in Callao and the sisters and nurses moved to Carrión Hospital. In 1948, for lack of personnel, they withdrew from Bellavista Hospital. For the same reason they withdrew from other hospitals, from the Children's Hospital in 1952, the Military Hospital in 1956, and Loayza Hospital in 1972. In 1967, however, they took over the direction of Saint Vincent de Paul Asylum for the old and indigent.

In response to an invitation of the benevolent society, the sisters also took charge of many schools and other works that involved the care of children. In 1858 they assumed the direction of the School for Orphans and Abandoned Children (known in colonial times as Santa Cruz de Atoche). In 1930 this school was moved to its current location with the new name of Puericultorio Pérez Aranibar. In 1978 the sisters withdrew from that institution. In 1859 they also took charge of Santa Teresa School for little children. This was moved after the earthquake of 1940 and renamed Colegio Sor Rosa Larrabure. One of their schools, Saint Vincent de Paul, was expropriated by the government in 1952 in order to make way for a new housing project, Manzanilla. Another school, Virgo Potens, founded in 1955 by combining three other schools, still functions today.

The work of the sisters in the provinces was as intense as it was in Lima. The Daughters worked in the following hospitals at different moments: San Ramón Hospital in Tacna after the war with Chile; San Juan de Dios Hospital in Puno between 1875 and 1953; Belén Hospital in Cajamarca until 1968; Belén Hospital in Trujillo, 1875–1967; San Juan de Dios Hospital in Moquegua, 1893–1967; San Vicente de Paul Hospital in Tarma, 1900–67; Lourdes Hospital in Jauja, 1904–64, and finally Goyeneche Hospital in Arequipa from 1907 until the present. The sisters also ran schools throughout the provinces. They still administer schools today in Tarma, Mollendo, Pisco, and Trujillo. They also run an orphanage in Puno, a school for working girls in Magdalena (Lima), centers for peasants in Aquia and in Cajamarca, and several social works in the young towns of Arequipa.

It should be evident from this panoramic sketch that the Daughters of Charity were by far the most important hospital congregation in Peru's modern history. What is not so evident from this list of statistics is their inner history, the attention and care that the sisters showered on the hundreds of patients who spent time in these hospitals. In the more than 130 years that they have been in Peru, the Daughters have cared for thousands of Peruvians of all social classes: the rich, the poor, workers, peasants, children, and the aged. Among the more famous of the sisters was Sor Francisca Gros from Lyons. During the many years that she worked at Dos de Mayo Hospital in Lima, she devoted her energies especially to the evangelization of the Japanese (see chapter 3).[38]

But the best-known Daughter of Charity was Sor Rosa Larrabure y Correa (1880–1961), superior and administrator of Loayza Hospital for thirty-six years and director of the hospital's School of Nursing for the same length of time. From a distinguished family in Lima, she studied first with the French sisters of Saint Joseph of Cluny and later on with the sisters of the Sacred Heart at San Pedro's parish. She entered the Daughters in 1904 and, after working for a period in the Chávez de la Rosa Institute in Arequipa and the Orphanage "de Lactantes" in Lima, she was named superior of Santa Ana Hospital in 1924 and a year later superior of Loayza. She soon became the most visible symbol of the Daughters of Charity in Peru. In 1935 she was honored by the Red Cross with the Florence Nightingale medal for excellence, and President Benavides conferred upon her the Order of the Sun, the highest civilian decoration in Peru. The School of Nursing she directed, raised to the category of a national school for nursing in 1928, trained hundreds of nurses who carried on the work of the sisters in the many hospitals they ran long after the sisters withdrew from them.[39]

In the years after Vatican II the sisters made many fundamental decisions that affected all their works. The decision to withdraw from some of their hospitals, for example, was prompted in part by their desire to maintain the original charism of their congregation. As a result of the population explosion, especially in Lima, the number of patients increased so much that the sisters more and more became administrators and had no time left to be nurses. They decided to limit their presence to fewer centers and thereby fulfill better the special call of their nursing vocation. Furthermore, one important influence of Vatican II was the reduced emphasis on large institutions. Accordingly, the sisters have turned their energies to work in small medical posts for the poor in the young towns of the big cities or in the mountains and jungle. The Daughters, who numbered 152 in 1983, are almost all Peruvians by birth.

Saint Joseph of Cluny, 1870

The second hospital congregation that came to nineteenth-century Peru was that of Saint Joseph of Cluny, in 1870. The sisters of this congregation came for a reason somewhat different from that of the Daughters of Charity: they responded to an invitation made by the benevolent society of the French colony. In 1860 the members of the French colony had founded a benevolent society to attend to their own. In 1867 they laid the cornerstone for the Maison de Santé Clinic, which was formally opened in 1870. The congregation of Saint Joseph of Cluny was founded in 1807 by Anne Marie Javouhey in order to send missionaries to France's overseas missions. The sisters had already founded houses in the Antilles to work with freed slaves by the time they came to Peru. They began in Peru with only four members. One of them, Ferminie Renault, the director of the new clinic (known also as the French Hospital) from 1912 until 1940, was decorated by the French government for her services in Peru.[40] The sisters of Saint Joseph of Cluny also founded several schools since their arrival more than a century ago.

Good Shepherd, 1871

In 1871 one of the most important of the social service congregations arrived in Peru: the Sisters of the Good Shepherd, founded by Rose Virginie Pelletier (1796–1868), who took the name in religious life of Maria of St. Euphrasia. The Good Shepherd nuns had already established houses in other parts of the New World when the government invited them to work in Peru. In 1869 a group of ladies, associated with the Daughters of Charity, presented a petition to the government explaining the need for sisters who could "take charge of women who had repented of a wild life, and who could protect young and needy women from corruption. . . ."[41]

With the government's consent and in the name of Archbishop Goyeneche, Monsignor José Antonio Roca y Boloña wrote to the Mother General in France. She in turn ordered seven sisters from French Canada to go to Peru, and later that year four more set out for South America. During the first few weeks after their arrival President Balta himself looked after the new arrivals. Balta was assassinated in 1872 during the rebellion of the Gutiérrez brothers, but the mother of the new president, Petronila Lavalle de Pardo, assumed the responsibility of looking after the sisters. In their first year in Peru they founded their first work, the Colegio del Buen Pastor, in the part of old Lima known as El Cercado. In 1873 they opened a small boardinghouse that later on became the Asylum of the Good Shepherd for the rehabilitation of repentant women. As a consequence of their work a sort of subbranch grew up called the Magdalenes: young women in the Asylum who aspired to follow the religious way of life. In 1888 the sisters opened a house in downtown Lima that was donated by the mayor of Lima, César Canevaro, who laid down one condition, that the sisters also open a vocational school for poor girls. Thus the third work of the sisters was founded in 1889: Santa Rosa vocational school for girls, near San Pedro's church in the center of Lima. It began with ten students. That same year the sisters also founded Santa Eufrasia Colegio, also near San Pedro's. The vocational school received state aid. Finally, in 1898 the sisters took over the direction of the Sevilla Institute, previously in the hands of the Salesians, for the formation of domestic servants. These were the basic works of the congregation until the decade of the forties of this century when it expanded and took on new tasks.

The congregation received support from the government and also from many private benefactors of the upper classes and from businesses. The list of contributors for the year 1878 for the Asylum of the Good Shepherd includes the Supreme Government, the Bank of Peru, the Bank of La Providencia, and Dreyfus Brothers and Co.[42]

During the presidency of Manuel Pardo (1872–76) the sisters also took charge of a school in Tingo just outside of Arequipa. The school had two sections, one for "normal" students and the other for children of broken homes. The sisters also assumed the administration of similar works, generally for the reeducation of young women: the Gelicich Institute in Huancayo, the Rosa María Checa Institute in Chiclayo, and Santa Eufrasia Home in Trujillo. For a while they directed a teachers normal school in Tacna until the advent of Velasco (1968). In 1971 they founded another school with the name Santa Eufrasia in Lima. Wherever the sisters have houses in Peru they give special attention to the rehabilitation of young women. There were more than one hundred members of the congregation in Peru in 1984, almost all Peruvians.

The Daughters of Saint Anne, 1887

Founded in Genova by Rosa Gattorno, who named her congregation Saint Anne to honor that saint, the Daughters of Saint Anne had already established themselves in Bolivia (1878) when they were invited in 1887 by the Benevolent Society of Cuzco to administer the Central Hospital there.[43] They had some differences with the society, however, and soon withdrew. In 1893 they founded Santa Anna Colegio in Cuzco. In 1888 they began working in San Ramón Hospital in Tacna, where they continued until 1980. In 1895 the Italian Benevolent Society invited them to run the Italian Hospital in Lima. Unlike the case of the sisters of Saint Joseph of Cluny who were warmly received by the French colony, certain anticlericals in the Italian colony opposed the invitation. Notwithstanding this opposition, the sisters began administering the hospital, and no further complaints were heard.

The Italian Hospital was razed to the ground in 1959, and its successor was the Italian Clinic where the sisters continued to work until 1979 when they withdrew for lack of personnel. Their second most important work was Antonio Raimondi Colegio (initially named in honor of the king, Umberto I), where they taught from 1902 until 1969. In 1920 the sisters founded their own novitiate on a piece of land in San Miguel, Lima, donated by a former patient. They also founded a free school for poor children in the neighborhood. In 1932 the sisters also took charge of Santa Ana Colegio of Tacna, and for a while they administered the Faustino Figueroa Hospital in Huánuco (1943–67). Like many other congregations, they began diversifying their works after Vatican II in order to recapture their original charism. In the late eighties there were forty-six sisters in Peru.

Saint Joseph of Tarbes, 1892

This congregation, founded by the bishop of Tarbes in southern France in 1842, emphasized contemplation and mission work. In 1887 some of the sisters of the congregation visited Lourdes where they met, purely by coincidence, the Jesuit bishop of Guayaquil, who in turn invited them to work in his diocese. The sisters had hardly begun to work in Guayaquil when a conflict arose between the bishop and the ladies in charge of the local benevolent society. At the same time, a senator of the Peruvian congress from Piura in northern Peru, who was also the president of the benevolent society of that city, invited the sisters to take charge of Belén Hospital, formerly run by the Bethlemites. In 1892 the sisters established themselves in Piura.[44] In 1897 they founded Lourdes Colegio for the daughters of the upper class. In 1902 they also founded a school in the hospital itself for poor children. In 1971 the hospital was converted into the state-run Regional Hospital, and the sisters withdrew. In 1918 they also took charge of Las Mercedes Hospital in Chiclayo. In the fifties they created many new works, including a residence for university students and missions posts in the prelature of Chulucanas.

The Camillians, 1897

The order of Saint Camillus, officially called the Clerks Regulars Ministers of the Sick, or the Fathers of a Good Death, was established in Lima in 1709, but as indicated above, it had practically ceased to exist as a result of the war of independence and the liberal attacks that followed. In 1897 Father Pablo Serna initiated a reform and requested that the Peruvian province be incorporated into the original province in Italy. In 1900 Father Angel Ferroni arrived as Visitor General along with Father Luis Tezza, founder of the Daughters of Saint Camillus (1892). Soon German priests of the same order also arrived to take up work as chaplains in different hospitals in Lima. In 1953 the Fathers of Saint Camillus founded a free clinic in Barrios Altos (Lima) near their old colonial monastery, and in 1964 they also founded Saint Camillus Clinic. The Daughters of Saint Camillus arrived in Peru in 1960 and took over the administration of the clinic named in honor of its founder, Father Tezza, who died in 1923. In 1975 the Monastery of a Good Death came under the jurisdiction of the Province of Lombardo-Veneta in Italy. [45]

The Little Sisters of the Aged, 1898

President Nicolás de Piérola himself invited the sisters of this congregation, founded in Spain in 1873, to come to Peru, and he paid all their travel expenses. The first ten religious arrived in January of 1898 and founded an asylum that bears their name. It was first located in Barrios Altos (Lima) but later moved to its current location in Breña. Since Piérola had invited them in his own name, they did not have official government support when he left power in 1899. Nevertheless, by donations alone the sisters were able to maintain the asylum and to open up nine other houses, with asylums and schools, throughout the rest of the country. In spite of their exceptionally difficult work, or perhaps because of it, the sisters of this congregation grew rapidly. In 1984 they had 139 members and a large number of novices.

The Augustinian Daughters of the Most Holy Savior, 1895

The Third Order of Augustinians of the Most Holy Savior was founded in Lima in 1895. The foundress was Rafaela Veintemilla, the sister of General Ignacio Veintemilla, president of the Republic of Ecuador between 1878 and 1882. As a result of political unrest, her brother was overthrown and the entire family was forced to seek asylum in Peru in 1883.[46] In 1894 Father Eustacio Estéban arrived with the title of "Visitor General" with a mandate to reform the Augustinians in Peru. Under his spiritual direction Rafaela Veintemilla, who had felt an attraction toward the religious life since her youth, along with several other women began to take in poverty-stricken or abandoned girls. In 1896 her newly founded group was recommended to the Catholic Congress, though it did not receive canonical approbation until 1927. The foundress died in 1918. In 1931 the congregation founded a house in Chosica (outside of Lima) for poor girls, which became Colegio Nuestra Señora del Rosario in 1942. In 1960 the sisters founded another school, Nuestra Señora de la Consolación in Rímac (Lima). They also founded several baby-care and youth centers. In 1983 their congregation had forty-eight members in Peru.

The Servants of Mary For the Care of the Sick, 1922

This congregation was founded in Spain in 1851 to care for the sick, especially by visiting homes. A professor of medicine at San Marcos University, Pablo Sixto Mimbela, was impressed by their work and prepared the way for their coming to Peru. The Servants founded two houses, one in Lima and one in Arequipa. In the early eighties they had twenty-eight members.

The Missionary Mercedarians, 1927

Through contact with the Mercedarian Fathers, Bishop Farfán in Cuzco invited the Missionary Mercedarians, founded in Barcelona in 1860, to take charge of the orphanage of his diocese. The Missionaries accepted and in 1927 began directing the orphanage, which is currently called Casa de Hogar San Pedro (Saint Peter's Home). In 1936 the sisters united with the Cloistered Mercedarian nuns in Barrios Altos (Lima), who had only six members. The sisters also founded homes and schools in Arequipa and Chimbote and do mission work among the Campas Indians in the jungle. In the short time in which they have been in Peru, this congregation has rapidly become a Peruvian one: in 1984 there were 127 sisters, of whom only nine were foreign-born.

The Missionary Carmelites, 1936

The Missionary Carmelites, founded in Barcelona in 1860, came to Peru at the request of the minister of health and several medical doctors to administer the Hospital del Niño (Children's

Hospital). The sisters also directed the school of nursing at the hospital. They also ran a sanatorium for children in Collique (Lima) until 1970; this was turned into a government-run regional hospital. Since 1960 the sisters have also been working as the directors of the Regional Hospital of Arequipa. In 1963 they founded Colegio Carmelo in Lima. In the years after Vatican II the sisters have increasingly stressed the social call of their vocation. Some of the sisters work as teachers in the schools of Fe y Alegría and others as pastoral agents at Lurigancho Prison. Of the seventy-four religious in Peru in 1984, fifty-three were Peruvian.

The Franciscans of the Immaculate Conception (Valencia), 1936

Aware of their work for the deaf in Chile, a delegation of Peruvian families went to Santiago in 1935 and invited the sisters of this congregation, founded in Valencia in 1883, to establish a similar mission in Peru. Under the sponsorship of President Benavides's wife, four sisters of the congregation founded a school for deaf children in 1936, the first school of its kind in Peru. The minister of education, General Ernesto Montagne, was so impressed by their work that he persuaded the sisters to take blind children under their care as well. In 1980 a special center, San Fransico de Asís in Surco (Lima), was founded for blind children. Two religious of this group, Mother Milagro Grotons and Mother María de la Pasión Castelló, received special awards in 1963 from the government for their teaching services. Besides their center in Barranco (Lima), the sisters also founded a school for deaf children in Piura, a school in Arequipa, a mission house in Satipo (in the jungle), and a teachers normal school in Huancayo.[47]

The Missionaries of the Sacred Heart of Jesus, 1938

In 1938 six German sisters, invited by President Benavides and his wife, arrived to run the new hospitals under construction for workers and a recreation camp in Ancón (near Lima) for poor children. The first house founded by the sisters themselves, in 1950, was the Stella Maris Clinic. The sisters of this congregation are both nurses and missionaries. They were founded in 1899 as a women's branch of the Missionaries of the Sacred Heart (men), which had been founded in 1854 by Father Jules Chevalier to work in Oceania. As with the Vincentians, the men's and women's branches of this congregation frequently work together. When the sisters arrived in Peru in 1938, they were accompanied by the first men missionaries of the Sacred Heart in the country.

Pastors and Missionaries

The Lazarists or Vincentians, 1858

The congregation founded by Saint Vincent de Paul in 1625 has been known by different names: the Vincentians, the Paulists, the Lazarists, and the Congregation of the Mission. They are called Lazarists because Saint Vincent founded his congregation in the monastery of Saint Lazarus in Paris. The congregation was founded in order to teach catechism to the poor and to preach missions. A modern-day version of their apostolate is the Saint Vincent de Paul Society that functions in Catholic parishes throughout the world. Very soon, however, Saint Vincent and his companions realized the importance of imparting a better formation to the secular clergy in order to multiply their own efforts. For this reason the congregation also took up the work of running seminaries and forming future priests, first in France and later in other parts of Europe.

The first Vincentians arrived in Peru in 1858 with the Daughters of Charity, two priests and a brother. They worked as chaplains to the sisters but soon initiated their own works. In 1864 the French Vincentian, Juan Marcelo Touvier, took over the direction of the seminary in Cuzco, but his reforms produced such opposition that he was forced to resign in 1866. The Vincentians were more successful, however, in running the seminaries in Trujillo, where they worked from 1883 to 1911, in Arequipa (1900–11 and 1916–23), and in Cuzco (1917–18). They also ran a minor seminary in Cajamarca between the years 1925 and 1958. In 1914 Vincentians from Barcelona began arriving, and soon the Spanish replaced the French. Father Hipólito Duhamel, who arrived in Arequipa in 1880, became one of the best-known religious in the history of the "White City." The seminary and school that he founded educated many of the sons of the middle and upper classes. One of his students was Víctor Andrés Belaunde. Duhamel was also the rector of San Jerónimo Seminary from 1899 to 1905.

Several Vincentians became bishops: Emilio Lissón (Chachapoyas, 1909–18; archbishop of Lima, 1918–31); Valentín Ampuero (Puno, 1909–14); Juan José Guillén (Cajamarca, 1934–37) and Federico Pérez Silva (auxiliary of Lima, 1946–52; bishop of Piura, 1953–57; archbishop of Trujillo, 1957–65). One of the best-known Vincentians was Amelio Placencia, pastor of the church in Miraflores, Lima, and a founder of Catholic Action. Of the fifty-nine priests and five brothers in 1984, nine were Peruvians.

The Redemptorists, 1884

The Redemptorists had already established themselves in Ecuador and Chile when they visited Arequipa in 1881 to study the possibilities of working in Peru. Founded in 1732 by Alphonsus Liguori, the Redemptorists devote themselves especially to preached missions. In 1884 they took over the parish of Our Lady of Perpetual Help in Rímac, Lima. Soon afterwards, they founded houses in the central mountain region of Ayacucho, Junín, Huancavelica, and Apurímac. The two principal bases of their missionary work were Huanta and Coracora. In Huanta they founded a school to train carpenters and masons. The missions they preached attracted hundreds of Indians. The Redemptorists soon became experts in the Quechua language. One of them, Pedro Perroud, of Swiss-French background, wrote several works on the Inca empire and the Quechua language. In 1905 other Redemptorists, expelled by the Eloy Alfraro regime in Ecuador, arrived in Peru. They founded a parish and other works in Piura. Three Redemptorists became bishops: Carlos María Jurgens (bishop of Cuzco, 1956–65; archbishop of Trujillo, 1965–77), Luis Baldo (auxiliary of Trujillo, 1969–78; bishop of Chuquibambilla, 1978–83), and Florencio Coronado Romaní (Huancavelica, 1956–82).

The Canons Regulars, 1905

Approved in 1887, the congregation of the Canons Regular of the Immaculate Conception was founded in France by Dom Adrien Gréa with the objective of restoring the community of canons of the primitive church. He sent missionaries to Canada, and in 1905, in response to the Holy See's call for missionaries for the Peruvian jungle, a group of five canons founded a community in Chachapoyas.[48] The Canons established themselves in Lima in 1908 and took charge of the San Simón and San Judas parishes, and in Ica they founded a school and a retreat house. Father Cipriano Casimir was a spiritual director of Teresa de la Cruz Candamo, who named her own congregation the Canonesses in his honor. The Canons have not flourished in Peru and their work has been limited to a few parishes. Their main house is located at Santa Teresa parish in Lima.

The Claretians, 1910

The Sons of the Immaculate Heart of Mary left Europe in 1909 at the invitation of Archbishop García Naranjo to run Santo Toribio Seminary.⁴⁹ Founded in 1849 by Antonio María Claret, the congregation devoted itself especially to teaching poor children, preaching missions, and training seminarians. In Europe they took charge of many seminaries. In this sense they are very much like the Vincentians. The archbishop of Lima hoped to reform the seminary, which had lost many of its best professors. He asked the Jesuits first, who declined for lack of personnel. He discovered the Claretians by contacting the cardinal primate of Spain, who recommended them.

In 1910 the first Claretians, six priests, began their work in the seminary. A year later they converted Lima's seminary into the central seminary for all major seminarians in Peru. They remained in the seminary until 1921 when the bishops decided to return to the old system of regional seminaries. In 1922 the Claretians withdrew from Santo Toribio Seminary and turned it over to the secular clergy.

Their stay at San Carlos y San Marcelo Seminary in Trujillo, however, was considerably longer. At the request of Bishop Carlos García Irigoyen, the Claretians took charge of that seminary in 1914, formerly run by the Vincentians. When they arrived, they discovered that the seminary and adjoining school had fallen into a state of disorganization. In fact, there was not a single seminarian left in the seminary. The Claretians reorganized the seminary and separated the ecclesiastical section from the regular school for laymen. Under the direction of Conrado Oquillas, the seminary made a fresh start. Indeed, the school attached to the seminary became, as it had been in colonial times, the most prestigious school for young men in Trujillo. In 1914 the school had eighty-six students. But in 1949, when it celebrated its hundredth anniversary, it had nine hundred students. In 1927 the Claretians also accepted responsibility for the seminary in Cuzco. There were only nine candidates for the priesthood that year. In 1960, when they turned the Cuzco seminary over to the secular clergy, there were only four candidates for the priesthood.

The Claretians founded schools and parishes everywhere. Their most important school, built in 1933, was in Magdalena del Mar in Lima. After the war they founded schools in Arequipa, Huancayo, and Trujillo, and a second one in Lima. Archbishop García Naranjo also entrusted the parishes of Cocharcas in Barrios Altos, Lima, and Huacho to the Claretians. They also ran parishes in Arequipa and Trujillo. Like the Vincentians, they continue to be a predominately Spanish group. Of the thirty-nine priests of the congregation in Peru in 1984, only ten were Peruvians.

The Discalced Carmelites, 1911

The order of the Discalced Brothers of the Blessed Virgin Mary of Mount Carmel went to Peru in 1911 at the invitation of Bishop García Irigoyen to attend to the spiritual needs of the Discalced Carmelite nuns in Trujillo. The nuns had been in Peru since 1643. The Carmelites had actually passed through Lima briefly in the seventeenth century, and two Carmelites from Navarre, Spain, founded houses in Cuzco and Arequipa, but these houses did not last long.

Soon the Discalced Carmelites founded houses in many parts of Peru, but only a few became permanent: Trujillo (founded in 1911), the old Jesuit parish of El Cercado in Lima (1921) and San José Parish in Jesús María, Lima (1943), and the Shrine of Our Lord of Luren in Ica (1951). The thirty-eight members of this branch of the Carmelites maintain fraternal ties with other members of the Carmelite family in Peru, such as the North American Carmelites from Chicago.

The Canonesses of the Cross, 1919

The foundress of this Peruvian congregation was Teresa de la Cruz Candamo, daughter of Teresa Alvarez Calderón and Manuel Candamo, president of the republic in the years 1903–4. She had known the Daughters of Charity in her youth and studied for four years in Sagrado Corazón Colegio in San Pedro. After the sudden death of her father in 1904, she traveled to Europe and there discovered her vocation. In Peru in 1907 she devoted herself to the teaching of catechism in the cathedral parish in Lima. Following the advice of her spiritual director, Father Cipriano Casimiro of the Canons Regular, she decided to found a congregation similar to that of the Canons, fundamentally oriented toward parish work. With the aid of her sister Mary, who was president of the Work of Nazareth and a member of the central committee of the Catholic Union for Women, she brought together several women who helped her teach catechism. She was also aided by Father Tezza of the Camillian Fathers. Her first petitions to found a new congregation, however, were rebuffed by the papal nuncio. Finally, a new nuncio, Lorenzo Lauri, gave the necessary approbation.[50] In 1922 the Canonesses (Las Canonesas) began to work in parishes in the center of Lima and Callao and to make home visits. They also organized classes on religion for housewives and began teaching in state schools. In the forties and fifties they founded other houses in the provinces, in Chiclayo, Piura, Huaraz, Chimbote, and Yurimaguas. Their house in Chaclacayo (outside of Lima) functions as a retreat house and a center house. The concept of doing pastoral work outside church buildings, such as home visits or teaching in state schools, was a novelty that anticipated by many years changes that would be common only after Vatican II.

The Handmaids of the Sacred Heart, 1922

Known in Spanish as the Esclavas del Sagrado Corazón or the Esclavitas (Slaves), the Handmaids came to Peru in 1922, first to Arequipa and later to Lima. Several persons were responsible for their coming: Benito Jaro, a Jesuit priest, Señora Benjamina Heudebert de Prevost, and the Marquise of Goyeneche among others. The foundress of the congregation was Rafaela María Porras (1850), who wished to foster devotion to the Blessed Sacrament and to teach the poor. The Handmaids founded a school for poor girls in Arequipa and another one in Lima. The school in Arequipa continues to function, but the Lima school closed in 1968 because it lost its original character as a result of an increase of wealthy students. The Handmaids began work in Lima in a house in the center, but in 1940 they moved to their present location on Avenida Wilson. Since the sixties they have diversified their work considerably. In 1961 they took charge of two state teachers schools, Regina Mundi in Arequipa and another in Chota. The school in Arequipa closed when other teachers schools were founded in the same area a few years later. The Handmaids also began founding vocational schools for working girls, and at the same time they engaged in social work in the "young towns" of Lima and in the mountains. They also work in the Fe y Alegría school in Piura. In all of these places they give special emphasis to the advancement of women from the lower classes. In 1984 there were fifty-eight Handmaids in Peru, the great majority of whom were Peruvians.

The Daughters of Immaculate Mary, 1929

This congregation was founded in Madrid in 1876 by Mother María Vicente López y Vicuña under the spiritual guidance of the Jesuits in order to attend to the cultural and religious formation of domestic servants. In 1929 they were invited by the Jesuits in Peru and they founded their first work for domestic servants in the old Hospital of San Andrés. The work consisted of a home and a day and night school. In the beginning the benevolent society helped maintain the work, but later on the sisters had to support themselves, usually by selling clothes and other products made by their students. In 1974 the sisters founded a new center in Monterrico, Lima.

The Parish Missionaries of the Infant of Prague

The foundress, Angélica Recharte (1873–1957), was the daughter of Colonel Andrés Recharte, notorious for his campaign against the pro-Indian fighter, Juan Bustamante, in 1867–68. Señorita Recharte began her adult life as a school teacher and was for a while director of the school in San Mateo, a town outside of Lima, and also of the school in Chorrillos, Lima. She worked for the parish in Chorrillos teaching catechism. In 1930, along with other women, she founded her own apostolic work, which consisted in carrying out "missionary" activities within the parish: preparing parishoners to receive the sacraments, visiting homes, and educating the youth. Her congregation soon expanded its original concept to include the founding of charitable works for the poor, schools, and many other pastoral activities to help parishes in Tacna, Tarma, and the vicariate of San José. In 1984 there were sixty-two members of this Peruvian congregation.

The Missionaries of the Sacred Heart, 1938

In June 1938 two priests of this congregation left Germany in order to become spiritual directors of the sisters who belong to the women's branch of the same congregation. But there was another, politically inspired reason: fear of the imminent confiscation of their houses by the Nazi regime. The newly arrived priests attended to the German colony in Lima, and in 1939 they founded their first parish, in Surco, at that time a sparsely settled suburb of Lima. In 1940, with the help of new members from Germany, they also began to work in Ica, and in 1941 they laid the foundations for the parish of San Felipe in San Isidro (Lima), which would be their main house. They also did pastoral work in the outlying districts of Lima. The founder of this congregation was the same as that for the sisters, Jules Chevalier, who aimed to send missionaries to Oceania and the Far East. When their missions in China were closed down, some of the displaced missionaries came to Peru in 1948. In 1951 they began to administer parishes in Huaraz, and in 1957 they also sent personnel to the newly created prelature of Caravelí under the prelate *nullius*, Federico Kaiser.[51] Their first Peruvian vocation was Germán Schmitz, who became auxiliary bishop of Lima in 1970. The Missionaries of the Sacred Heart were practically the first group of foreigners to work as missionaries, not in the jungle, but in the mountains and in the outlying districts around Lima, later to be known as "young towns."

The Jungle

Until 1900 virtually the only missionaries in the Peruvian jungle were the Franciscans. That year the Holy See created three apostolic prefectures: one, under the Augustinians, that covered the entire department of Loreto; another, under the Franciscans, in the central jungle region around the Ucayali and Huallaga rivers; and a third one, to the south, under the Dominicans, near the Urubamba and Madre de Dios rivers. The creation of these new ecclesiastical jurisdictions grew out of the general missionary enthusiasm that affected both Europe and Peru. In 1894 Leo XIII wrote to the Peruvian bishops about the need to evangelize the jungle. The Catholic Congress of 1896 supported the papal call by creating the "Work for the Propagation of the Faith in the Peruvian Orient," under the responsibility of the Catholic Union for Women. The first president of the work was Eva María de Piérola, the sister of President Piérola. Father Francisco de Sales Soto of the Sacred Hearts Fathers was chosen as the official church promotor of the work. The general plan for the three prefectures was drawn up in 1898.

The Augustinians, 1900

The Augustinians, who had accepted responsibility for the prefecture of San León de Amazonas, saw the need to ask for the help of foreign missionaries. In 1905 the Province of the Holy Name of Jesus of the Philippines, based in Spain, began sending missionaries to the Peruvian jungle. The first four missionaries of that province arrived in Callao in 1900 and set off for the jungle a year later.[52] From that moment on, two provinces of Augustinians arose in Peru, that of the Spanish missionaries in the jungle and that of the "national" Augustinians. Later on, other groups of Augustinians arrived, the Spanish Recollection Augustinians in 1939 and the Chicago Augustinians in 1964.

The Franciscans

The area assigned to the Franciscans was placed under the jurisdiction of the Province of San Francisco Solano (the Discalced). For a short time (1912–18) there were English Franciscans working along the Putumayo River, but they left. Given the immense territory under their care, the Franciscans asked for help from Franciscan women religious. But as an exception, in 1916 a group of Salesian sisters went to work in La Merced to take charge of a primary school for women and a hospital.[53]

The first group of Franciscan women religious were the Franciscan Missionaries of Mary, founded in India in 1877 by Hélène Chappotin de Neuville, a French religious who founded her congregation exclusively for the foreign missions. For this reason, the sisters of this congregation, almost all French in the beginning, went directly to the jungle. They founded a school in Iquitos in 1921 and thereby became the first women school teachers in that eastern jungle city. In 1932 they took over the direction of Santa Rosa Hospital in Iquitos and founded houses in Yurimaguas, Requena, Chanchamayo, and other places in the jungle. In 1918 they founded a house in Barranco, Lima, and soon they began taking charge of many other works that were not strictly missionary in character: the Youth Camp at Ancón, schools in Barranco, Cuzco and Arequipa, and hospitals in Moquegua and Cartavio. This taking on of works not originally foreseen came to be typical of many other missionary orders who went to Peru. Although the Franciscan Missionary sisters originally went to work in the jungle, they soon saw the need to have works in the rest of the country. One motive for founding schools, for example, was to cultivate vocations among Peruvian girls. Currently there are nearly two hundred sisters of this congregation in Peru, half of whom are Peruvian.[54]

Beginning in 1930 German Franciscans established themselves in Villarica, and in 1934 the Franciscan sisters of Bamberg settled in Oxapampa. These two groups came in response to petitions of the German colonists in Oxapampa, who were descendants of the first German settlement in Peru in Pozuzo, founded in the middle of last century. The sisters took charge of the hospital in Oxapampa and shortly afterwards they also began running a school for girls. In 1953, when there was less need for German-speaking religious, the male missionaries withdrew and sought work in Bolivia, and the sisters were replaced by the Missionary Franciscans of the Mother of the Divine Pastor, of Spanish origin. When the mayor of the district of La Victoria in Lima learned that the sisters of Bamberg were looking for a new apostolate, he invited them to found a school, which became Colegio Santa María Goretti. The sisters also took charge of the Health Resort of Ñaña (outside of Lima) from 1950 to 1975 and later on an orphanage in Huánuco as well. For years they have also worked with the German Comboni Fathers to help maintain their seminary in Tarma.[55]

The Franciscan Sisters of the Immaculate Heart, called the "national" Franciscans because they were founded in Peru, also went to work in the jungle, in Puerto Ocopa in 1922. The Missionary Franciscans of the Infant Jesus, founded in Italy in 1879, began doing missionary work in the upper Ucayali region in 1935, in Satipo in 1947, and later on in Pucallpa and Requena. They also founded schools in Lima and Huancavelica.

The Dominicans

In 1898 the Dominicans were invited to send missionaries to the jungle, but like the Augustinians they decided to ask for help from foreign missionaries within the Dominican family. They also appealed to the Dominican province in the Philippines. The key man in founding the new mission was Ramón Zubieta, from Navarre, who had worked for years in the Philippines. In 1902 he arrived in Peru with two companions, and soon afterwards many other Dominican volunteers went to work in the jungle.[56] Zubieta established the first "mission house" in Chirumbia, in Madre de Dios. Soon the Dominicans founded many mission schools among the tribes in their area: the Machiguengas, the Huarayos, the Piros, the Campas, and the Mashcos. In 1912 the government turned over to the Spanish Dominicans the care of the Sanctuary of Saint Rose in Lima, which became their main house. That same year the department of Madre de Dios was created, and a year later the prelature was elevated to the rank of vicariate apostolic. In 1916 Zubieta was named vicar general and the vicariate became independent of the Philippine province.

In 1912 Zubieta returned from one of his frequent visits to Spain, this time with five Dominican women religious. In 1915 the sisters opened Santa Rosa de Maldonado, the first school for girls in the entire Peruvian jungle. In 1918 the sisters constituted themselves an independent congregation and called themselves the Missionary Dominicans of the Rosary. That same year they founded their own house and a school in Lima. The school, Colegio Jesús, operated in front of San Marcelo church in the center of Lima until 1956 when it was moved to its current location on Avenida Brazil. The sisters also opened two novitiates, one in Huacho (northern coast) and another in Pamplona, Spain. Besides the large school in Lima and those in the jungle, others were founded in Arequipa (Ascención Nicol, in honor of the first superior in Peru), Talara, Piura, Lambayeque, Huacho, San Ignacio,

Ica, Cuzco, and Calca. The congregation came to be one of the most numerous in Peru before Vatican II with more than three hundred members. They divided Peru into two provinces, Santa Rosa in the north and Santo Tomás in the south. The Missionary Dominicans are an example of the missionary groups that went to Peru originally to work in the jungle but ended up creating a multitude of other works. In this case, the sisters went as missionaries but soon turned into a teaching congregation as well.

The Passionists

In 1911 the bishop of Chachapoyas, Emilio Lissón, visited the Curia of the Passionists in Rome and asked for missionaries for his diocese, which at that time had only twenty-two priests. In 1913 the first group of Passionists arrived, with six priests and six brothers, all Spanish, to work in Eastern Peru.[57] The missionaries came with the understanding that they would work with a certain amount of autonomy and that they would depend directly on the pope but not the bishop. The bishop would not agree to this and the Passionists withdrew from his diocese in 1918. But in 1921 Lissón himself, then archbishop of Lima, advocated the creation of the apostolic prefecture of San Gabriel del Marañón, to be under the care of the Passionists based in Yurimaguas. The first prefect was Atanasio Jáuregui. In 1936 the prefecture was elevated to the rank of vicariate apostolic and Jáuregui became the first bishop. In 1926 the congregation also began to take on parishes in Lima with the expectation that they would be places of rest for the men in the jungle. For a while the Passionists administered the parish of Sullana (1935–52). Their principal house is the parish of Virgen del Pilar in San Isidro, Lima. In 1948 the *prefectura nullius* of Moyobamba was created and separated from the diocese of Chachapoyas. The new prefecture was also given over to the Passionists. The first prefect and since 1954 the first bishop was Martín Elorza. In 1984 there were forty Passionist priests in Peru, all foreign-born.[58]

The Second World War marked the end of the first stage of this missionary impulse that began with the creation of the three apostolic prefectures in 1900. During this period the Franciscans, Augustinians, Dominicans, Passionists, and related women's congregations laid the foundations for the reevangelization of the jungle. But the missionaries were still very few in number. According to Father Villarejo, in the area covered by the Augustinians, "Until 1943 the average number of missionaries in such an extensive region was never more than seven. . . ." [59] In the postwar years new prefectures and vicariates were created and many new works were established. Many new groups also came: the Jesuits in 1944, the Canadian Franciscans in 1947, the Augustinians from Chicago in 1964, and others.

Before going on to the teaching orders and congregations, it may be well to make a few general observations about the groups we have seen so far. In the first place, almost all of them came to Peru in response to a specific social or ecclesiastical need; but almost all soon diversified their work and assumed many new tasks. The Daughters of Charity, the Sisters of Saint Joseph of Tarbes, and the Sisters of Saint Joseph of Cluny, for example, originally came to attend to hospitals and clinics; but within a short period of time they all turned into teaching congregations as well. At the same time, the missionary groups in the jungle founded houses, parishes, and schools in Lima and other cities. These houses and parishes served as links with Europe as well as places of rest, while the schools provided vocations.

The congregations that have grown the fastest and that have become more visibly Peruvian have been the women's ones. The Daughters of Charity, for example, began in 1858 as an exclusively French group. But one century later the great majority of the Daughters were Peruvians by birth. By way of contrast, the Vincentian Fathers have not had the same good fortune: the great majority of their personnel continues to be Spanish. In almost all of the religious orders of men, including the Camillians, the Redemptorists, the Carmelites, and the Claretians, the foreign-born predominate. And the missionaries in the jungle, the Franciscans, Augustinians, Passionists, and Dominicans, all retain their predominately foreign character. The women religious have therefore become "Peruvianized" to a far greater extent than the men. About half of the Franciscan Missionaries of Mary and about one-third of the Missionary Dominicans are Peruvians.

In order to explain this phenomenon several historical, cultural, and psychological factors should be taken into account. In the first place, the foreign religious, men and women, began arriving just at the time when vocations to the priesthood began to decline. Everywhere the role of the priest in society was submitted to harsh scrutiny, especially by the liberals. On the other hand, the role of the women religious was never submitted to the same severe questioning, in part because the women fulfilled social tasks in great demand as nurses, educators, and directors of orphanages. For many young women of the middle class, to wear the habit of the Daughters of Charity or that of the Sisters of the Good Shepherd brought some well-deserved social esteem. To this consideration other more subtle factors should be added. Within the context of the culture of Latin America, the foreign religious men usually had more education than the women, but this actually tended to create a barrier between them and the youth of the popular classes, who could not easily identify with them. By way of contrast, the kind of work that many of the women religious performed, such as nursing or caring for orphans, made them much more attractive to girls of the lower classes. One notable example is the case of the Little Sisters of the Aged, who began in 1898 with ten sisters, all Spanish; in 1984 they had 139 sisters, of whom sixty-two were Peruvians.

The degree of insertion into the cultural reality of Peru cannot, of course, be reduced to the question of the number of Peruvians in any given religious order or congregation. The Redemptorists who preached popular missions in the mountains or the Franciscans who walked up and down the Andes and through the jungle came to have a far greater knowledge of those parts of Peru than the majority of Peruvians who lived on the coast. The missionaries in the jungle retained their foreign character, not out of desire, but as a consequence of the fact that the great majority of the inhabitants of the jungle simply did not have the necessary human or cultural qualities to be considered candidates to enter religious life. Only recently, in the decade of the sixties, after years of work, did the first native vocations of real promise in the jungle come forth.

Finally, all the foreign missionaries came to Peru with the hopes of establishing roots in the new land. In spite of the criticisms of the liberals, the Spanish Franciscans did devote themselves to carrying out development projects. Ramón Zubieta, the superior of the Dominicans in the jungle, sent numerous reports to the central government on the jungle, and on one occasion he established a telegraph line with materials the government sent him.[60] The missionaries were very conscious of the fact that evangelization also meant civilization. Everywhere, in the jungle, in the mountains, or on the coast, the religious justified their presence in the country by founding schools, hospitals, orphanages, and other works. For the religious of this period there did not exist any incompatibility between compliance with the government and their own mission. In general, they openly sought the support of the government to carry out their works. For this reason Peruvian society looked benevolently upon the religious who came to offer a social service. The work of the teaching orders and congregations, however, met with considerably more criticism, for reasons we shall see.

5
The Resurgence of Religious Life
The Teaching Orders and Congregations

What does Lima seem like? A dead sea in which churches and monasteries appear like islands without water or vegetation. Wherever a new street is being planned, there a Jesuit school shoots up. Wherever a new avenue is laid out, a Salesian school juts up. National convents that for lack of personnel should be closed down arise from their ruins and, as though obeying some command, turn into schools.[1]

This acid observation of González Prada, written at the turn of the century, reflected a very real phenomenon: the creation of new religious schools everywhere in Peru, almost all administered by foreign orders and congregations. The founding of these schools responded basically to a double exigency: one on the part of the church, which saw in religious education a sure defense for Catholics against the advance of liberal society, and another on the part of Peruvian families, who desired a quality and religious education for their children.

When the wars of independence ended, education in Peru was in a state of chaos. But under the government of President Ramón Castilla it received a new impetus, thanks in part to the new prosperity created by the "guano boom." During this period many national schools were reorganized, such as the school of science for young men and the school for women (known as Educandas) in Cuzco, both founded by Bolívar in the first years of the republic. At the same time new ones were created. Although both presidents Ramón Castilla (1845–51, 1855–62) and José Rufino Echenique (1851–55) personally favored religious education and at times sought the counsel of Bartolomé Herrera, the doctrinaire liberals also had spokesmen in positions of power. The most notable among them was José Gregorio Paz Soldán, a fierce defender of national patronage over the church and a strong advocate of placing religious schools under the control of national schools.²

In practice, however, the ideological orientation of each school depended on the director or the teachers. Given the advance of liberal ideas in the schools, many Catholic families began to see the importance of creating their own educational system, which necessarily would be private in character. Some of these families sent their sons to Europe; thus Juan Manuel López de Romaña entrusted the Jesuits at Stonyhurst in England with the education of his two sons, Alejandro and Eduardo. But these families also saw that there existed another way to resolve the problem by bringing the European educators over to Peru. For their part, European religious, and in the twentieth century Americans and Canadians, influenced by a resurgence of missionary zeal in the church, were entirely disposed to accept the proposal. Finally, the government itself acted as the inviting host on a number of occasions for several of the teaching orders that came to Peru.

In reality, history does not always follow such logical lines. Some groups, such as the Sisters of the Sacred Hearts who founded Colegio³ Belén, came by accident. The Jesuits returned to Peru after their colonial exile somewhat furtively in order to teach in the seminary of Huánuco, and the idea of founding a school occurred only later. Whatever the real explanation in each case was, there is no doubt about one striking fact: everywhere the schools founded by the religious orders and congregations turned out to be the most prestigious. Many of the leading men and women in politics, commerce, law, banking, or the church itself came from these schools. Two schools especially rivaled each other for the number of public leaders that they formed: La Recoleta of the Sacred Hearts Fathers and La Inmaculada of the Jesuits in Lima. Famous graduates of La Recoleta include José de la Riva-Agüero, Luis Alberto Sánchez, and Raúl Porras Barrenechea. Graduates of La Inmaculada include two presidents of the republic, Manuel Prado and General Francisco Morales Bermúdez. The Jesuit school of Arequipa educated Víctor Andrés Belaunde and José Luis Bustamante y Rivero, president of Peru in the years 1945–48. Víctor Raúl Haya de la Torre, founder of the Aprista Party, was educated at the seminary school of San Carlos and San Marcelo in Trujillo, run by the Vincentian Fathers.

Although Catholic education in Peru comprised only 7 to 8 percent of the entire student body in the twentieth century, its schools nevertheless have enjoyed the prestige of being considered the best in the country.⁴ But for this very reason religious education posed a dilemma for the liberals. On the one hand, these spokesmen for a society free of excessive religious influence could hardly be complacent over the spread of Catholic education in the country. That is clearly the attitude of González Prada, whose biting words we cited at the beginning of this chapter. In truth, the liberals were justified in some of their fears; the school of San Carlos under Bartolomé Herrera became a center for the spread of conservative and ultramontane ideas. Herrera formed an entire generation of leaders steeped in what he considered a more coherent view of the world than that of the liberals. But more than the influence of one man, the liberals feared the influence of a religious order that seemed to be the incarnation of antiliberal values, the Society of Jesus.

In 1900 González Prada directed a particularly caustic attack against the work of the Jesuit Fathers who taught at Colegio La Inmaculada since its foundation in 1871:

> Without doubt the Jesuits prefer action to contemplation; they do not foster exaggerations in asceticism and they even seem to relegate to secondary importance routine and practices born out of habit. But their educational system is essentially oppressive for human dignity. With their doctrine of passive obedience they form men without real will or character. They are despots when they give orders and humble even to being obsequious when they obey.[5]

Nevertheless, in spite of all their prejudices, the liberals found themselves in an ambiguous position with respect to Catholic education. It was undeniable that the religious in general offered a quality education, of great utility for a nation with scant resources. Furthermore, some of the newer congregations, such as the Salesians or the Sisters of the Good Shepherd, devoted themselves to educating the poor or youth with family problems. The service these groups offered to society was too evident to deny. Furthermore, many of the new religious groups, such as the priests at La Recoleta, the Salesians, and the sisters at Belén, came from non-Spanish Europe and did not form a part of Peru's colonial experience.

The French religious most of all were considered to be more cultured than the Spanish. In his memoirs Luis Alberto Sánchez relates that his father sent him to La Recoleta because the French priests in that school "enjoyed the prestige of having given rise to a democratic cultural movement." But his father did not want him to go to La Inmaculada run by Spanish Jesuits who were considered to be antiliberal.[6] González Prada himself was scandalized

The Teaching Orders and Congregations 139

by the fact that many liberals were hypocrites; while they denounced religion in public, they sent their children to religious schools: "What should we do? Masons and liberals contribute to the founding of dioceses, decree subsidies to religious communities, act as financial overseers for monasteries or as patrons for the inauguration of altars, and what is worse, they educate their sons and daughters with the Sacred Hearts Fathers, the sisters of Saint Joseph of Cluny, the Dominicans, the Augustinians, or the Jesuits."[7]

The teaching orders, like the religious who worked in hospitals, did not suffer the stigma of being "antisocial" or unproductive, traits the liberals associated with monastic life. This was the liberals' dilemma: to allow the religious schools to exist with the quality education they offered or to impose a secular-lay education on the entire country without regard for the benefits the church schools brought to society.[8]

In the light of the Second Vatican Council and especially the episcopal conferences of Medellín (1968) and Puebla (1979) that stressed the call to "opt preferentially for the poor," many Catholics in Latin America criticized their own educational system for being classist and elitist. In many cases this questioning led to a positive change of attitude. Some congregations even arrived at the conclusion that their schools, instead of forming students to be agents of change, actually inculcated an elitist mentality in the students, thus making them guardians of the status quo.

Nevertheless, even though this critical questioning represents a healthy and positive reaction, it has sometimes gone to extremes and been overly severe in its judgment of the past. First, Catholic education in Peru was never exclusively elitist. The Salesian brothers and sisters or the religious of the Good Shepherd, for example, came to Peru to work with the lower classes. Second, even the congregations that taught the rich usually maintained parallel schools for the poor.

This policy of maintaining schools for the rich and for the poor at the same time no doubt seems "paternalistic" in the light of more contemporary standards. Nevertheless, there were circumstances that made that policy more justifiable. Unlike the great colonial orders that had numerous estates and other properties, the new groups had only their schools to support them. Furthermore, the concept of state aid for those schools did not exist. The only exception to that rule were the centers administered by the Good Shepherd religious for working mothers and their schools for youth from broken homes. In general, however, the teaching congregations had to depend on the middle and upper classes to maintain their schools for the poor. These are some of the realities that limited their flexibility and freedom of action.

An overview of the history of the various teaching orders and congregations in Peru's republican history will help bring to light the somewhat complex and ambiguous nature of Catholic education in that country. We will end this overview with the Second World War because by that time almost all of the more prestigious Catholic schools had been founded.

San Carlos and the First Schools

During the first decades after independence, Catholic education was offered in three types of centers: schools that functioned within convents or the colonial monasteries (Augustinians, Dominicans, Franciscans, or Mercedarians); schools founded by priests of the secular clergy, generally connected with parishes; and finally, the seminary schools.

The government itself, desirous of creating a national system of education for the poor, took the initiative by promulgating a decree (February 23, 1823) in which it ordered all convents and monasteries to open free schools. Few actually complied with the order. But an interesting exception was Father José Francisco Navarrete, pastor of San Lázaro Parish (Lima), who collaborated actively with James Thomson, a Presbyterian minister who had been designated by General San Martín to implant the Lancasterian method of education in Peru. In 1826 Navarrete also founded the first free grade school for girls in independent Peru. At the same time he gave lessons to girls from the upper classes at Santa Rosa Retreat House. In 1840 three of these convent schools were functioning in Lima.[9]

In Arequipa, aside from the seminary school of San Jerónimo, there were two religious schools that functioned during this early period: San Francisco, founded in 1833, and the Mercedarian school of San Pedro Pascual, founded in 1832, but which closed in 1869 and was finally reorganized in 1898. In the second part of the century Hipólito Duhamel, a French Vincentian, founded the seminary school of San Vincente de Paúl that, along with the Jesuit school of San José, was considered one of the best in the city. Víctor Andrés Belaunde was a student in both schools.[10]

But the most famous school of this period was San Carlos in Lima, especially during the years it was governed by Bartolomé Herrera (1842–52). Founded in the old novitiate of the Society of

Jesus when the Jesuits were expelled, San Carlos drew its student body from two of the Jesuits schools that were forced to close with the expulsion. Under Toribio Rodríguez de Mendoza, San Carlos formed an entire generation of enlightened thinkers and precursors of Peru's independence. After independence, however, it suffered an economic crisis and barely survived from one year to the next. In 1842 Bartolomé Herrera was named rector and he soon reorganized the entire curriculum and code of discipline. Under Herrera, San Carlos flourished once again, though this time the guiding philosophy was openly conservative and ultramontane.

Herrera dreamed of putting an end to the anarchy caused by the caudillos by forming an intellectual and moral elite that would be capable of governing the nation. A glance at some of the graduates who studied under Herrera would seem to indicate that he was very successful: the two brothers, José and Pedro Gálvez, Evaristo Gómez Sánchez, Luciano Benjamín Cisneros, Manuel Bandini, Manuel Pardo, etc. Under Herrera, San Carlos came to have nearly two hundred boarding students. The only other school that rivaled San Carlos was Nuestra Señora de Guadalupe, founded in 1840 by Domingo Elías and Nicolás Rodrigo. But the teachers at Guadalupe were liberals, most notably the historian, Sebastián Lorente, and their aim was to check the influence of San Carlos. Years later, when José Gálvez became rector of San Carlos (1855), the school adopted a liberal line and in 1860 it was incorporated into San Marcos University, thus virtually ceasing to exist.[11]

The Seminary Schools

In the modern Catholic church, seminaries exist to train young men for the priesthood. But, in nineteenth-century Peru and elsewhere in the Catholic world, the seminaries began admitting lay students or opening up special sections for them. This was done largely at the request of many families who wanted their sons to receive a good moral and intellectual education and, given the scarcity of schools after independence, saw the seminaries as a solution. The seminaries for their part needed the income that came from accepting lay students. Finally, many young men were sent in the hopes that they would "discover" a priestly vocation by going to a seminary. But in the end this practice of mixing lay with ecclesiastical students did not produce positive results and the experiment had to be called off. Nevertheless, during the entire nineteenth and a good part of the twentieth century the seminaries were also considered among the best schools in the country, even for laymen.

Santo Toribio

Santo Toribio Seminary, as pointed out in the second chapter, fell into a state of abandonment after independence. It was restored under Archbishop Luna Pizarro in 1847, and at the same time it opened its doors to lay students.[12] It was not always easy to distinguish between the lay students and the seminarians, principally because during the first few years the seminaries themselves did not make a clear distinction between them. The real dividing line was between the colegio, which included the equivalent in the United States of grade and high schools, and the major seminary, which would be the equivalent of a university. Only upon entering the major seminary did a seminarian begin to receive the first orders of the Catholic church and thus officially become a "cleric," though not yet a priest.

The concept of a "minor seminary" did not exist until the twenties of this century when Emilio Lissón was archbishop. Before that, the premajor seminary was simply called "primary and secondary instruction," although the students were called seminarians. It was understood that in some way or other all the students at that level had indicated a desire to go on to the priesthood. Very few, however, actually did so. In 1864, for example, the entire Seminary of Santo Toribio, including the primary and secondary levels and the major seminary, had some 1,242 students. But of that total only forty-five were in the major seminary.[13] This meant that the vast majority of students had no real intention of pursuing an ecclesiastical career. There is a further distinction to be made. In Trujillo, Arequipa, and Cuzco there were seminary schools for students who explicitly did not intend to become priests. In these schools, the seminarians studied in what was termed the "ecclesiastical section," only for them.

The relationship between the preparatory levels and the major seminary at Santo Toribio was always ambiguous. In 1880 in a speech he delivered on the annual day for presenting prizes and honors, the rector, Manuel Tovar, complained about the fact that the seminary formed many men for society but not for the church:

> Some thirty-three years have gone by since the restoration of this seminary and already its graduates occupy some of the most

important posts in government and in all the professions. . . . I do not wish to diminish in the slightest the glory that this means for the seminary that has made such a significant contribution to the regeneration of society; but, gentlemen, we should be sad because we see so few priests at the altars today.[14]

After the war of the Pacific the primary and secondary levels of instruction were suppressed, and the seminary once again acquired its strictly ecclesiastical character. In 1902, however, an "external" seminary school was opened to prepare students better who intended to go on to the seminary. In 1905 the rector, Alejandro Aramburú, stated in his annual message that this new arrangement was necessary because "many boys go to the seminary without a real vocation and they leave after one or two years. . . ."[15] In 1924 Archbishop Lissón gave the Santo Toribio External School the official designation of minor seminary. Lissón rather ambitiously created five minor seminaries within the archdiocese of Lima, including the External School. By 1928 there were 544 students in these seminaries.[16]

San Jerónimo

Unlike Santo Toribio, San Jerónimo in Arequipa had a tradition of educating laymen since colonial times. Founded in 1616 and reformed by Bishop Chávez de la Rosa, the seminary educated the entire generation of precursors of the independence movement in Arequipa: Mariano Melgar, Mariano José de Arce, Francisco de Paula González Vigil, Benito Lazo, Francisco Quiroz, and others.[17] In this sense San Jerónimo was really the Arequipanian equivalent of San Carlos in Lima. During the entire nineteenth century it continued to be one of the leading schools, though it too went through periods of uncertainty. In 1899, with Father Duhamel as rector, the Vincentian Fathers began administering the seminary; but in 1927 the diocesan clergy took charge once again. During all these changes the seminary always admitted lay students, though the latter were also urged to consider the priestly vocation. When the Jesuit school closed its doors in 1935 (it was reopened in 1948) the number of "seminarians" suddenly jumped to a new high at San Jerónimo.[18] In 1968 the seminary moved to its current location in Umacollo, a suburb of the "White City."

San Carlos and San Marcelo

For the first few decades after independence San Carlos y San Marcelo in Trujillo, founded in 1625, was the only school of higher education in the entire north of Peru. Among its more distinguished graduates are José Faustino Sánchez Carrión, Fernando Casós, and Víctor Raúl Haya de la Torre. San Carlos y San Marcelo also provides an example of the many conflicts that arose as a result of the attempt to mix seminarians with nonseminarians. On numerous occasions during the nineteenth century, rectors complained about the disorder, the lack of discipline, and the secular spirit that pervaded the halls of the seminary as a consequence of having lay students. In 1853 the lack of discipline was so grave that all the lay students had to be expelled.[19] Nevertheless, given the scarcity of vocations, succeeding rectors once again attempted to run a school for nonseminarians within the seminary. The disproportion between seminarians and lay students reached the absolute extreme in 1914, the year in which the Claretians took charge. That year there were many lay students but not one single seminarian![20]

In 1967 the seminary moved to a new site outside Trujillo. The Claretian Fathers decided not to maintain the school along with the seminary. Instead, they founded another school, Colegio Claretiano, that filled the vacuum.

The Schools of the Colonial Orders

The Mercedarians

The Reform of Regulars of 1826 constituted a severe blow for this order that went back to the sixteenth century. It lost many of its convents and schools and never really recuperated from the liberal attack. Already before the reform the Mercedarians were forced to turn over one of their schools in Lima, San Pedro Nolasco, to the government.[21] Nevertheless, for most of the nineteenth century a small primary school continued to function within the large Mercedarian monastery in Lima. In 1917 the order founded a new school, Nuestra Señora de la Merced, as a continuation of the primary school. In Arequipa the Colegio of La Inmaculada Concepción, founded in 1765, closed during the independence period but reopened in 1832. In 1869 it closed again but reopened in 1898 with the new name of San Pedro Pascual. Their *colegio* in Cuzco, San Pedro Nolasco, also a colonial foundation, lasted for most of the nineteenth century. The Mercedarians also ran small schools at different times in the last century in Huacho, Abancay, Caraz, and Puno. In general, the intellectual level in these schools was only slightly higher than that in the national schools.

The Dominicans and Santo Tomás, 1892

The Peruvian province of the Dominicans founded Colegio Santo Tomás de Aquino in 1892 as part of the reorganization set in motion by the visitor, Vicente Nardini. It functioned as an extension of the old colonial monastery of the Dominicans in the center of Lima and for quite a while was considered one of the best boys' schools in the capital. Among its distinguished graduates are the two men of letters, Arturo and José Jiménez and General Ricardo Pérez Godoy, president of the military junta of 1962–63. But the school eventually succumbed to the impact of Lima's urban problems in the mid-sixties. By 1984 there were 1,500 students, mostly from the lower middle class, but only eleven Dominicans. The Peruvian Dominican province, which has few members, is basically a pastoral order and is not equipped to maintain a large presence in the area of education (see chapter 4).

The Augustinians and Colegio San Agustín, 1903

The province of the Augustinians was restored by Eustacio Esteban, who came from Spain in 1894 as the Commissary Provincial. Esteban was also the principal promoter of San Agustín colegio, which began in 1903 within the walls of the Augustinian monastery.[22] Within a few years it was considered one of the best young men's schools in Lima. In 1955 it moved to its current location on Avenida Javier Prado and became at the same time one of the important middle- to upper-class schools in the capital. The Augustinians also founded schools in Chosica (1911), Pacasmayo, and a seminary school in Chiclayo (1965). The Peruvian province of Augustinians (there are three distinct groups of Augustinians in Peru: Peruvians, Spaniards, and Americans) is relatively small. In fact, the majority of its members are Spaniards by birth.

New Orders and Congregations

The Religious of the Sacred Hearts, 1848

The first foreign teaching congregation that went to Peru in the postindependence period were the religious women of the Sacred Hearts (in honor of Christ and Mary), founded in France in 1797 by Henriette Aymer de la Chevalerie. For a while the congregation of priests that bears the same name, founded in 1800 by Marie Joseph Coudrín, was part of the same congregation as the women. Although the men's and women's branches separated to form two distinct congregations, they continue to maintain a close relationship. These congregations, which bear the name Sacred Heart, are inspired by an ancient devotion that goes back at least to the thirteenth century, but that received its great impetus in the mystical encounters between Christ and Margaret Mary Alacoque in the seventeenth century. The spiritual director of the saint was a Jesuit. After a period of skepticism toward the devotion, the Society of Jesus finally began promoting it. There is therefore a historical tie between the devotion and the Jesuits.

Most of these congregations arose in response to Jansenism, the philosophical rationalism of the eighteenth century, and the fierce antireligiosity of the French revolution. Almost all of them adopted as their object reparation to the Sacred Heart of Jesus for the destruction wrought by the anticlericals. But they also experienced a strong missionary impulse. Marie Joseph Coudrín founded his congregation, for example, to give popular missions in the French countryside, and later on he sent his followers to France's overseas colonies, especially to those in Oceania. The foundation of these new congregations can also be understood as a reaction of both the lower classes and the old aristocracy in France toward the open persecution wrought by the liberals and anticlerical intellectuals who disdained Catholic values.

Between 1826 and 1834 different groups of the Sacred Hearts Fathers passed through Valparaíso, Chile, and the port of Callao on their way to Oceania. In 1835, at the request of a Franciscan, one of the missionaries stayed in Valparaíso, and soon others remained as well. In this purely circumstantial way Valparaíso became a center for the congregation's missionary activities in Latin America. In 1838 the first group of women religious of the congregation of the same name also arrived in the New World. The sisters founded a boarding school for young women of the upper classes and another school, entirely free, for the daughters of workers. That same year the archbishop of Lima, Francisco de Sales Arrieta, sent a representative to invite the sisters to go to Peru. The War of the Peruvian-Bolivian Confederation (1836–39) frustrated this first initiative. A few years later the president of Bolivia, José Ballivián (1841–47), also extended an invitation to the sisters to go to Bolivia, which they accepted. But upon arriving at the port of Valparaíso they met face to face, to their astonishment, with President Ballivián himself, who informed the sisters that he had just been overthrown. The sister in charge of the small group, Cleonisa du Dormier, decided to continue the trip, but instead of going to Bolivia, she chose Peru. When the group arrived unannounced in Callao, port authorities accused them of being "agents of the Jesuits" and denied them permission to land. Fortunately for the religious, the minister of foreign affairs, Felipe Pardo y Aliaga, heard of their plight and offered them a safe conduct to land. The archbishop of Lima, Luna Pizarro, also offered them his protection, and soon President Ramón Castilla formally invited them to stay in Peru.

Impressed by reports he heard of their work in Chile, President Castilla asked the sisters to take charge of Espíritu Santo School, which was supported by the government. In March, 1849, they opened up a free school and shortly afterwards a residence for young ladies. In 1851 they moved their school to the site of a former monastery of the Mercedarians, Nuestra Señora de Belén. Their school was henceforth known as Colegio Belén. In the meantime other members of the congregation began arriving from France and some from Valparaíso. Within a few years many upper-class mothers were sending their daughters to the new school, which was also the first educational center in Peru where French, the symbol of culture and humanism in Latin American since the eighteenth century, could be learned.

But the anticlerical liberals were not pleased with this intrusion in Peru. When Castilla left power in 1862, the liberals in congress accused Bartolomé Herrera, who had also helped the sisters become established, of bringing foreign nuns to Peru. The new president, Juan Antonio Pezet (1863–65), received a resolution from the minister of education calling for the expulsion of the religious. Under pressure from the French colony in Lima, however, he withheld his signature.

In spite of these crises, Belén soon achieved fame as the best school for young women in Lima. It was, in the words of one of its graduates, "the first modern educational institution" in Peru. In 1878 the congregation founded another school in Arequipa and it soon enjoyed the same level of prestige in the White City as in the capital. One of the most famous of the sisters of the congregation was Hermasia Paget. As superior of the congregation, in 1881 she went out to meet Admiral Bergasse du Petit Thouars, the commander of the French fleet in the Pacific, to ask him to protect Lima against total destruction during the Chilean invasion. The admiral complied and Lima was eternally grateful to this intrepid religious.

The school educated many women who achieved distinction in

Peruvian society: María Wiese, a writer; Beatriz Cisneros, director of the national school Rosa de Santa María; Matilde Pérez Palacios, founder of the school of journalism at the Catholic University; and many leaders of Catholc Action for Women, such as Caty Cassinelli, Rosa Stiglich, and Teresa Cantuarias. Many daughters of presidents and state ministers went to Belén. When it celebrated its golden anniversary in 1948, President Bustamante and his wife, María Jesús, a graduate of the Sacred Hearts school in Arequipa, attended.[23] By that date Belén was a well-established institution in Peruvian society. During all these years the sisters operated a free school for the poor alongside their famous school. In 1962 Belén moved to a new site in San Isidro, Lima.

The Jesuits, 1871

"The reestablishment of the Society of Jesus is not permitted in Peruvian territory" (Law of November 23, 1855). This succinct declaration, promulgated by the National Convention of 1855–56, underlined the nearly paranoiac hostility toward the Jesuits shared by liberals, Masons, and others. The prohibition of 1855 is especially curious if it is kept in mind that the Jesuits had been expelled in 1767 and not a single Jesuit was to be found in Peru at that time. As a matter of fact, in 1852 a small group of Jesuits who had been expelled from Ecuador did touch Peruvian soil. After a few months in Piura in the north, they left for Guatemala.[24]

It was Bishop Teodoro del Valle of Huánuco, while in Rome during the First Vatican Council, who took the initiative of bringing the Jesuits to Peru. After meeting with the general of the Society, Pieter Beckx, he received permission to invite a few Jesuits to teach in his diocesan seminary. In September 1871 four Jesuits arrived in Lima. Shortly afterwards three more arrived from Ecuador. One member of this latter group was Father Francisco Javier Hernáez, who was named superior of the newly restored Society of Jesus in Peru. Although the Jesuits were not violating any law because the prohibition of 1855 had not been incorporated into the new constitution of 1860, Bishop del Valle nevertheless took the precaution of requesting permission from President Balta for the Jesuits to return. The minister of cult, Manuel Pardo y Lavalle, gave his assent. But the liberals took note of their presence. In 1874 the attorney general, José Gregorio Paz Soldán, sent a message of protest to the minister of cult.

The Jesuits divided themselves into two groups: one group

The Teaching Orders and Congregations 149

went to work in Huánuco and another decided to remain in Lima. A certain Christian gentleman, Melchor García, invited the Jesuits in Lima to teach in a national school he directed. At the same time, on the occasion of a visit to the new teachers normal school run by the Sisters of the Sacred Heart, President Mariano Ignacio Prado expressed his admiration for the work of the sisters and at the same time complained that there was no one to do the same for men. Upon learning that there were Jesuits in the country, the president immediately fostered the passage of a law (May 18, 1878) that established the Normal School for Men, under the direction of the Jesuits. The "new" school was in reality Melchor García's school transformed and refurbished. This was the origin of Colegio de la Inmaculada, which began with three Jesuits and 101 students.[25] In 1879 seven new Jesuits arrived from Europe, and in 1880 the nine Jesuits who were working in Huánuco decided to leave that work and went to Lima. The church of San Pedro, which was the Society's great colonial church, was not returned to the Jesuits until the end of the war with Chile. When it was returned, it soon became the center of many apostolic activities that the Society traditionally carried out: devotion to the Sacred Heart, the Marian congregation (also known as the sodality) and the Pious Association of Our Lady of the O.

During the war of the Pacific, the Jesuit Fathers served as chaplains while the brothers worked as nurses. The school was turned into a hospital. In one dramatic episode, Colonel Andrés Cáceres, later to be president of the republic, hid from the Chileans in the superior's bedroom at San Pedro's church while he recuperated from wounds sustained in battle.

In 1886, as a consequence of a history book written by Father Ricardo Cappa (see chapter 3) the Jesuits were expelled from Peru for the second time. The move to expel them provoked many stormy debates in parliament and in other public forums. The Masons held meetings to further the cause of expulsion, and Catholics organized countermeetings. Finally, in October 1886, parliament voted 65–18 in favor of expulsion. Although President Cáceres, whom the Jesuits had hidden during the Chilean invasion, vetoed the measure, he nevertheless counseled the Jesuits to leave the country at least temporarily. Some of the Jesuits went to Bolivia, others to Europe. Their school, of course, had to close, at least for a while. Only one incident occurred when a group of Jesuits in Arequipa delayed leaving. The army escorted them to the train station. Slightly more than a year later, in 1888, the Jesuits returned when the storm had blown over.

No new major dramatic episodes occurred and the Jesuit school in Lima soon established its place as one of the most prestigious boys' schools, along with La Recoleta of the Sacred Hearts Fathers. In 1902 the school moved to a new site on "La Colmena," in the center of Lima, and then in 1966 it moved again to Monterrico, a suburb. The list of graduates who distinguished themselves in their careers is impressive. Among them are Manuel Prado y Ugarteche, president of the republic (1939–45; 1956–62); General Francisco Morales Bermúdez, president of the military government of the "Second Phase" (1975–80); Aurelio Miró Quesada, director of *El Comercio*; Luis Alayza y Paz Soldán, writer; Arturo García Salazar, diplomat; Armando Revoredo Iglesias, a celebrated pilot; Javier Prado y Ugarteche, professor and rector of San Marcos University; Augusto Tamayo Vargas, man of letters; Luis Antonio Eguiguren, magistrate; Alberto Tauro del Pino, historian; Rubén Vargas Ugarte, Jesuit historian; and Manuel Ulloa Elías, politician.

In 1898 a second school was founded, San José of Arequipa. Two of its famous graduates were Víctor Andrés Belaunde and José Luis Bustamante y Rivero. The school enjoyed the same prestige in Arequipa as La Inmaculada did in Lima. But because of a shortage of Jesuits, it was forced to close in 1935. President Bustamante, a graduate, helped the school reopen in 1948. In 1955 it moved to its current location near the town of Tingo. For many years the Peruvian Jesuits belonged to the Spanish province of Toledo. In 1938 a novitiate was founded in Miraflores, Lima. In 1943 the vice province of Peru was entrusted with the mission of San Francisco Javier by the Marañón River in the northern department of Cajamarca. Some of the missionaries there, notably José María Guallart, specialized in working with the Aguaruna Indians. In the fifties new schools were founded in Piura and Tacna. Beginning in 1959 American Jesuits began arriving. In the sixties and seventies the province set up schools for adult education among workers and peasants in Urcos, Ilo, Huancayo, and Piura. In all these places parishes were also founded. One of the most important popular educational works of the Society in Peru is the Fe y Alegría (Faith and Joy) schools, founded in 1965. By 1987 there were thirty-four of these schools, with over thirty-four thousand students.

Of the 254 Jesuits in Peru in 1984, counting priests, brothers, and students, some eighty-six were Peruvian by birth. The great majority of the rest are Spanish, almost all nationalized Peruvian citizens. The first Peruvian provincial was Father Felipe Mac-

The Teaching Orders and Congregations 151

Gregor, who was also rector of the Catholic University for many years (1963–77). In 1966 Ricardo Durand Florez was named the first Jesuit bishop in Peruvian history. After serving as archbishop of Cuzco, he became bishop of Callao. This was a tradition-breaking move, since Jesuits usually accept appointments as bishops only in mission lands. Since then, however, several others have been named bishops: Luis Bambarén, auxiliary bishop of Lima and later bishop of Chimbote; Manuel Prado, bishop of Chachapoyas and later archbishop of Trujillo; Fernando Vargas Ruiz de Somocurcio, bishop of Huaraz, then of Piura, and in 1980 archbishop of Arequipa; Augusto Vargas, bishop of Jaén, later secretary of the bishop's conference and finally archbishop of Lima (1990–); and Alfredo Noriega, auxiliary bishop of Lima. All of these are Peruvians. Antonio Hornedo, Spanish by birth, after serving as apostolic prefect of the Jesuit mission territory by the Marañón River, was named bishop of Chachapoyas.

The Society of Jesus, partly because of its numbers but also because of the exceptionally long period of training its members receive, has exercised considerable influence on the Peruvian church. By means of the Spiritual Exercises of St. Ignatius, the Jesuits have been among the principal promoters of a spiritual renewal among university youth and professionals. It is also one of the few orders that maintains an intellectual presence as university teachers and writers in Peru. Other Jesuits work as advisers to special groups. An example of the latter was Romeo Luna Victoria (1921–84), a popular and charismatic speaker who gave retreats to teachers. He served in the Velasco regime as one of the advisers for the educational reform. Unlike other Jesuit provinces throughout the world, however, the Peruvian province is eminently pastoral and devotes little of its energy to higher education.

The Religious of the Sacred Heart, 1876

Founded in 1800 in France by Madeleine Sophie Barat in circumstances very similar to the founding of the congregation of the Sacred Hearts, this new group gave high priority to reparation and education as means of rechristianizing France in the face of the advance of rationalism and liberalism. It established schools for the upper classes and for the lower classes. The congregation came to Peru in response to an invitation by President Manuel Pardo of the Civilista Party, which sought to foster public education.

In 1871 the Peruvian government sent the first of several invitations to the congregation through the Dreyfus Company in Paris. On three other occasions President Pardo repeated the invitation: in 1874, through José Antonio Lavalle, in 1875 through Aurelio García y García, and finally in 1876. The third and decisive invitation was presented in a letter written by the president's mother in a very personal tone: "For some time in Lima we have felt the urgent need of a convent of the Sacred Heart to raise the cultural level of our daughters. The leading families of this country would be extremely pleased the day they could count on having such an institution worthy of respect."[26]

In May 1876 the first three religious of the Sacred Heart, which ran a school for girls and a teachers normal school in Santiago, left Valparaíso for Peru. On July 27 of that year President Pardo created by decree the Teachers Normal School for Women, which began functioning in 1878 in the building where the old colonial Colegio de San Pablo of the Jesuits once existed. The school was also known as the "Normal of San Pedro," since it functioned right next to the Jesuit church of that name. Soon the sisters founded a residence for young ladies of the middle and upper classes and a free school for poor girls, which served as a school for practice teaching. The residence was the original nucleus for the future schools of Sophianum and the Chalet.

The Women Teachers Normal

Without doubt the Teachers Normal School for Women was one of the most important educational works in the history of Peru. For the first fifty years of its existence, it was the only center in Peru for training women teachers. In the beginning it formed only teachers for the primary level, but in 1927 it changed its name to the National Pedagogical Institute and began training its students to teach on the secondary level as well.

The new teachers normal signified an enormous advance for women in Peru. Throughout most of the nineteenth century, schools prepared women to be housewives and mothers. The women's normal of San Pedro broke with that tradition; it educated women to work and to offer a service to society. It also represented a means of social mobility for middle- and lower-class families; a teaching post meant financial security in life. The law that created the school expressly stipulated that the applicant should be a "legitimate daughter of poor but honorable parents. . . ." It was understood that this referred to daughters of government employees, military personnel, or professionals. In the first years almost all the students, who came from all of Peru's

The Teaching Orders and Congregations   153

departments, had scholarships. The beginnings were also modest. In 1899 only twenty-eight new students matriculated. This was in marked contrast to the 160 students who entered in 1981.[27]

The agreement worked out by the state and the congregation was a model of church-state cooperation, free of the friction over other questions such as tithes, tolerance for non-Catholics, or civil marriages. The school was really a state school run by religious; the government provided scholarships and the sisters administered and taught in the school. Many liberals expressed their concern over the influence the sisters would have on their students. In 1904 some members of congress went so far as to propose closing the school.[28] In general, however, the public was very favorable toward the work of the religious. On several occasions San Marcos professors, some of whom were known for their criticism of the church, such as Javier Prado, Alejandro Deustua, Mariano Cornejo, and Carlos Wiese gave talks at the teachers normal.

In the beginning the religious represented different nationalities, including Spanish, French, English, and Italian. By the beginning of the century the first Peruvians, usually graduates of the schools run by the sisters, began to join the congregation. The wide cultural background and high educational level of the sisters also served to attract many daughters of some of the more distinguished upper-class families in Lima, the Heudeberts, De Lavalle, Barreda, Pardo, Echenique, Balta, Alvarez, and Valle-Riestra, and some presidents of the republic.

In 1953 the school moved to the Chalet (a summer residence for the sisters) in Chorrillos and in 1958 it moved again to its current location in Monterrico, a suburb of Lima. In the postwar years many other congregations founded normal schools for teachers. Nevertheless, the National Pedagogical Institute of Monterrico—its current name—continues to be one of the most important centers for training teachers in all Peru.

Primary and Secondary Schools

In 1909 the sisters founded a residence for young women that soon turned into a school. Known in the beginning as León Andrade, it changed its name to Sophianum, an allusion to the foundress, when it moved to its current site on Salaverry Avenue in 1942. Earlier, in 1903, the sisters founded a school in Chorrillos near the Chalet. These two schools, along with Belén of the Sacred Hearts sisters, became the most sought-after schools for girls of the upper classes in Lima. The daughters of Presidents Manuel Pardo, Andrés Cáceres, and Manuel Candamo went to these schools. In 1947 the congregation founded another school in Arequipa, but in 1978 the sisters withdrew from it. In 1962 they founded the Women's University of the Sacred Heart in Lima. Of the 120 members of the congregation in 1983, the great majority were Peruvians.

The "National" Franciscans, 1883

During this period several new congregations for women were founded in Peru itself. One of these were the Franciscans of the Immaculate Conception, popularly known as the "national" Franciscan Sisters. Their foundation is an example of cooperation between men and women religious. In this case, a Franciscan missionary who worked in Huánuco, Alfonso María de la Cruz Sardinas, served as spiritual adviser to a school teacher in Callao, Carmen Alvarez Salas, who dreamed of founding her own congregation. She had previously attempted to enter religious life at Santa Clara Monastery, but she lacked the necessary dowry. She and her sister, moved by the plight of hundreds of poor children with no educational opportunities in the years following the war with Chile, opened Immaculate Conception School. That same year she founded her own religious congregation.

The new congregation grew very fast; many novices entered and several of the lay third orders of the Franciscans joined as groups. In 1911, for example, the women belonging to the Third Order of Santa Rosa de Viterbo, founded in 1670, joined as a group. In 1914 the women of the Third Order of the Pure Heart of Mary, founded near Ocopa in 1894, joined. In 1922 the women of the Third Order of Santa Rosa de Viterbo in Huaraz, founded by Bishop Fidel Olivas Escudero in 1886, all entered the new congregation. Also, in 1916 the Institute of Sisters of Charity (an association of pious women who were not officially religious sisters), founded in 1892 by Ermelinda Carrera del Valle to administer the Central Penitentiary for Women, was incorporated into the "national" Franciscans. The pious works created by these third-order women also passed into the hands of the congregation. The third order founded in Ocopa, for example, administered schools in Ocopa, Huánuco, Huancayo, Jauja, and Cerro de Pasco. It also ran the public hospital of Huancayo.[29]

The congregation founded by Sister Carmen Alvarez soon grew to be one of the most numerous in Peru. In 1980 it had some twenty-two houses in the country and 188 members of the congregation. Its principal school in Lima, La Inmaculada Concepción, moved to Monterrico in 1967.

The Salesians, 1891

The educational work founded by St. John Bosco (1815–88) for poor boys in Italy, which Bosco chose to name in honor of Saint Francis de Sales, became known worldwide even during the life of its founder. In 1890 the Benevolent Society of Lima, with the full support of the government, signed a contract with the Salesians, both with the men's branch and with the women's branch that had been founded in 1872. Their coming to Peru was part of the church's response to the incipient industrialization in Peru and the emergence of a working class. Both groups arrived in 1891. The Vincentian Fathers and the Daughters of Charity, who shared common apostolic concerns with the Salesians, housed the newcomers in the beginning.

In 1891, according to the contract, the Salesian sisters took charge of the Sevilla Institute for the education of working women. But when the contract expired, the sisters, desirous of having a center fashioned according to their own ideas, turned the Institute over to the Good Shepherd sisters.

For their part, the priests and brothers inaugurated the first of their "oratories" in Rímac (Lima) in 1891 and opened a School of Arts and Manual Work for workers. The government was so impressed by their work that in 1896 Congress passed a law to foster the creation of similar schools for men and women workers everywhere in Peru, all to be run by the Salesians. The proposal was far too ambitious for a group that was still very small; there were only two priests and nine brothers. But the Salesians grew very fast. In 1897 the sisters founded a second house in Callao and in the following year the men founded their own school, also in Callao. In 1896 they were reinforced by Salesians who had been expelled by the anticlerical government of Eloy Alfaro in Ecuador.[30]

With the help of the inheritance that Bishop Manuel Teodoro del Valle left them in 1898, the Salesians founded their principal school in Lima, in the neighborhood known as Breña. In 1902 the sisters also founded a school next to the school for boys. The two schools together educated thousands of lower-middle-class students, and even today they form an enormous educational complex not far from the center of Lima. The Salesian fathers and brothers also founded schools in practically every major city of Peru: Arequipa (in 1905), Cuzco, Ayacucho, Chiclayo, Huancayo, and Piura. The sisters did the same in Arequipa, Ayacucho, Cuzco, Huancayo, and Huánuco.

156   *The Teaching Orders and Congregations*

Besides their schools, the Salesians devoted themselves especially to the formation of youth destined to be workers. Their School of Arts and Manual Work received financial support for years from the Catholic Union of Women. Later they changed the name to the Polytechnical School. Alongside each of their works the Salesians also run what they call an "oratory," which is a sort of social club where neighborhood youth can play sports and receive a general humanistic, albeit nonacademic, formation. Their oratories in Lima attract hundreds of youth.

In the decade of the twenties, at the invitation of the different "Patrons of the Indians," the Salesians founded two farm schools, one in Yucay in 1924, and another in Puno (Salcedo) in 1929. These rural educational centers aimed to offer a technical and humanistic formation to peasants in that region. In 1931 the Salesian Farm School and Indian Center of Yucay had fifty-eight boarding and 123 day students.[31] Years later the Farm School of Puno was converted into the Saint John Bosco Regional Teachers Normal School and in 1964 the Farm School of Yucay was turned over to the French Dominicans.

The work carried out by the Salesians symbolized the presence of the church among the urban lower middle class and, to a lesser extent, among the peasantry. With the passage of time, however, some of the Salesians' schools turned into middle- and even upper-class schools, especially in the provinces. The Salesians also administered parishes and seminaries at different times (in Ayacucho and Piura). Currently the Salesians are among the largest groups in Peru, with 113 priests and thirteen brothers in 1983. Nearly 60 percent of them are Peruvians by birth.[32]

The Sacred Hearts Fathers and La Recoleta, 1893

The congregation of the Fathers of the Sacred Hearts (sometimes called "Picpus," a reference to the street in Paris where the congregation had its first house) was founded in 1800 in France to preach popular missions and to send missionaries to France's colonies. It first established itself in Latin America in Chile in 1834. Archbishop Luna Pizarro offered them the direction of the recently reorganized Seminary of Santo Toribio, and the provincial of the congregation in Chile even came to Lima in 1846 to discuss the offer. Nevertheless, the plan was frustrated because the civilian authorities believed that they were really Jesuits in disguise.[33] Strong support for their coming, however, sprang up among many families who wanted a Catholic school for their sons. The Association of the Sacred Hearts was founded in 1838 by the religious sisters in Belén to promote the idea of having the congregation invited to Peru. In 1870 a priest of the congregation arrived in Peru to serve as chaplain to the sisters. Another important promoter of the cause was Father Francisco de Sales Soto, the director of the Propagation of the Faith in Peru and future bishop of Huaraz, who also served as a chaplain to the sisters at Belén. In 1884 Sales received permission and acquired the necessary funds from the Benevolent Society of Lima to begin reconstruction of the church of the old suppressed convent of the Recollection Dominicans. That same year other Sacred Hearts priests arrived from Chile to take charge of the church and to found the new school.

The church was finished in 1886 and the school opened in 1893 with twenty-two students. Among them were Francisco García Calderón, Ventura García Calderón, and José de la Riva-Agüero. Other famous graduates from the first generation of the school were Javier Correa Elías, Raúl Porras Barrenechea, Luis Alberto Sánchez, Ricardo Bentín, and Luis Aspíllaga Anderson. For a brief period Fernando Belaúnde Terry, future president of the country, studied at La Recoleta. La Recoleta quickly established itself as one of the two best schools for young men in Lima, along with La Inmaculada of the Jesuits. In 1900 it had 125 students. By 1943, the year of its golden anniversary, it had 620 students. Many prominent Peruvians who graduated from the school were present for the celebration, including Riva-Agüero, Ismael Aspíllaga and Ismael Bielich, Raúl Ferrero, Alfonso Benavides, and three future ministers of President Bustamante y Rivero.[34]

La Recoleta and La Inmaculada became important centers in Lima for the creation of a lay movement at the beginning of the century. Furthermore, La Recoleta was also the basic nucleus from which the Catholic University arose in 1917. Until the decade of the fifties, the school was practically the only work of the congregation. In 1960 the school moved to a new location near Monterrico and La Molina.

The Sisters of the Reparation, 1896

This strictly Peruvian congregation was founded by Rosa Mercedes de Castañeda y Coello, who had been a boarder with the sisters at Belén and at one time a candidate for the Poor Clares. Her confessor for a while was Father Gual. She was sent to France by her parents to dissuade her from thinking about entering religious life. Not to be so easily dissuaded, however, she sought the advice of a Jesuit, who urged her to enter a religious institute, which she did. When her mother visited her in 1880 she was forced to leave the institute, but she then accompanied her mother to Rome where they were received in audience by the pope. She returned to Paris and entered religious life again. In 1895 she went back to Rome and requested a private audience with Pope Leo XIII, who gave his blessing to her plan to found her own congregation.[35]

She returned to Peru that year with her constitutions already written, but with no members as yet for the congregation. She set up residence along the Alameda de los Descalzos (Rímac) in 1896 and, with the approval of Archbishop Bandini, recruited other pious women to help her visit homes and attend to the sick. In 1903 she founded a school in the center of Lima and another one in Miraflores in 1916, which soon became one of the principal schools in that fashionable Lima suburb. The religious of her congregation later on founded schools in Callao and Piura and social works for the poor in Huaraz and Huánuco.

The Teaching Dominicans, 1898

In 1898, at the request of the departmental government in Trujillo (northern coast), the Third Order Dominican Sisters of the Immaculate Conception, later to be known simply as the "Teaching Dominicans," opened up Santa Rosa National School for girls. In reality, the congregation had been founded in France in 1866 for a more specific purpose: to educate blind children, especially girls. For this reason, in 1912 the sisters also opened in Lima the Institute for Blind Girls.

The religious of this congregation divided their efforts between teaching and social work. In the beginning they taught almost exclusively in state schools, but later they began to take over the direction of private religious schools, such as Santa Rosa in Lima and in 1980 Colegio Belén. Their social works include a boarding school for those who suffer Parkinson's disease and two homes for the aged in Chaclacayo, one of which is for priests. In 1983 there were 123 members of the congregation in Peru, the majority of whom were Peruvians who graduated from the congregation's own schools.[36]

The Marists, 1909

In the first decades of the new century, two congregations arrived in Peru that are known worldwide for their educational work: the Brothers of Mary, or Marists, and the Brothers of La

The Teaching Orders and Congregations 159

Salle. Many people frequently confuse the two because they share several common traits, their French origin, their educational work, and the fact that they are nonclerical religious. The idealism of the two founders was also similar: Jean Baptiste de la Salle (1651–1717) founded the Brothers of the Christian Schools to combat the influence of Jansenism and religious indifference in general, and Marcellin Champagnat (1789–1840) founded the Marists (1817) in order to rechristianize French youth in the wake of the revolution. Champagnat himself was a priest, and a branch of Marist priests did arise. But it was the brothers who created the impressive educational system for which they are famous.

The two groups also came to Peru for practically the same reasons, to stem the influence of Protestantism and to strengthen Catholic education for boys in general. In 1907 the Catholic Center of Lima, especially at the initiative of Carlos Arenas and the Jesuit priest, Francisco Javier Lecocq, founded the English Commercial School of Callao. Its purpose was to be a Catholic alternative to the different commercial schools the Protestants had founded. The center had first invited the Jesuits, who declined for lack of personnel, then had recourse to the Marists. In 1908 four French brothers, under Carlos María Constantín who acted as superior, left their central house in Italy. They spent a few months in New York to learn English and in 1909 opened their new school in Peru. One member of the original group, Brother Plácido Luis, would become the best-known Marist in Peru. In 1913 the school in Callao changed its name to Saint Joseph College but later on changed it again to the Spanish form, Colegio San José. The school was also the base for Labor Center, the first Catholic Action group in Callao.

Once established in Peru, the Marists rapidly expanded everywhere. In 1923 they founded San Luis School of Barranco; in 1927, Champagnat School in Miraflores; in 1932, San José in Huacho; in 1934, the Marist School of San Isidro (Lima); in 1939, Santa Rosa in Sullana (extreme north); and in 1953, a school in Cajamarca. They also founded teachers normal schools in Cajamarca (1954) and Tacna (1959). For a period the brothers also administered Augusto Pérez Aranibar home for poor boys (1937–58) and San Vicente Orphanage. In 1967 they had ten schools in Peru, of which three were teachers normals. They also founded houses specifically for the formation of the students of their own congregation, such as Villa Marista in Chosica. Famous Peruvians have also graduated from their schools, including Armando Villanueva del Campo (an Aprista political leader), Javier

Arias Stella (a leader of Acción Popular Party), Felipe MacGregor (the Jesuit rector of the Catholic University), and "Chachi" Dibós, a popular mayor of Lima.[37]

Before Vatican II the Marists were one of the largest congregations in Peru, with 120 members. But by 1981 they had dropped to eighty-one members, the majority of whom were Spanish.

La Salle, 1922

In 1872 President Pardo formally invited the Brothers of La Salle to Peru, and in 1908 the Catholic Center of Lima repeated the invitation. In 1920 Archbishop Lissón used his ties with France and Belgium (he was a Vincentian) in order to establish contact with the Brothers of La Salle. Finally, in 1922, a group of brothers arrived in Peru from Ecuador. Lissón offered them the direction of the minor seminary of Santo Toribio. In 1926 the brothers founded their own school in Lima and another one in 1931 in Arequipa. In 1926 they also took charge of a teachers normal school in Arequipa at the request of President Leguía, who was impressed by their work. Near their school in Arequipa they founded another one, Colegio Muñoz Nájar, for poor boys. They founded another school in Cuzco (1939) and several teachers normals: in 1942 in Cajamarca (since closed), in 1964 in Abancay, and in 1965 in Urubamba. They also directed the teachers normal school of the Catholic University between 1935 and 1969.

Their schools began rather modestly (La Salle in Lima had forty-five students in 1926 and their school in Arequipa had 460 in 1931). But a few decades later they had turned into large and influential educational complexes; the Lima school had 1,862 students in 1976 and the one in Arequipa, 1,200 students in 1981.[38] The brothers also ran a reformatory for boys in Surco (Lima) for a time. In 1982 there were sixty members of the congregation in Peru, of whom forty-five were Peruvians.[39]

The Immaculate Heart of Mary, 1922

Augusto B. Leguía's coming to power in 1919 signaled an abrupt change of focus in government and society from Europe to the United States. This reality also affected the church. In fact, the founding of the Marists' school in Callao for the teaching of English already symbolized the change in times. Archbishop Lissón requested the archbishop of Philadelphia to aid him in founding a Catholic school in Lima that would specialize in teaching English. In 1922 the first three Immaculate Heart of Mary sisters arrived in Lima. The "I.H.M.'s," as they are popularly known in the United States, were founded in 1845 to teach in the new Catholic educational system. In 1923 they founded Villa María Academy in Miraflores, Lima, and in 1928 a few of the sisters also began offering classes to youth from the lower classes in Callao. Until 1944 Villa María was coeducational. That year the Marianists, who had founded their own school for boys in 1939, reached an agreement with the sisters by which Villa María would be for girls only, but the sisters would assume the direction of the primary school for boys run by the Marianists. Also, since 1944 the Marianists and the sisters have worked together in San Antonio School in Callao. For a time the sisters also taught in the parish school of the Carmelites of San Antonio, Lima.[40]

Villa María soon became known as one of the best schools in Lima, and when it ceased to be coeducational, it became, along with Belén and the Sophianum, one of the most important upper-class schools for young women. It responded to the desire of the middle and upper classes to learn English and to receive a "modern", that is, American, education, a fact that also reflected the growing American influence in all of Latin America in those years. The religious of the Immaculate Heart of Mary were the first American congregation in Peru, anticipating by many years the arrival of other American groups. In the decade of the sixties the sisters offered accelerated courses in English to other religious who wished to attract students to their own schools, especially in the light of increased competition from Protestant schools. In 1955 Villa María moved to a new site in La Planicie, outside Lima. In the years following Vatican II there were nearly sixty members of the congregation in Peru. By 1983 that number had dropped to forty, of whom slightly more than half were Peruvian.[41]

The Ursulines, 1936

Three different groups of religious went to Peru on account of the Nazi persecution of the church: the Missionaries of the Sacred Heart, the Dominicans of Saint Mary Magdalene, and the Ursulines. The anti-Christian nationalism of the Nazi regime increasingly threatened to confiscate Catholic schools and other religious works. At the same time Archbishop Farfán extended an invitation to the Ursulines to open a school in Lima that would emphasize the teaching of German. In 1936 the first two religious arrived, both from a centuries-old convent of Fritzlar, Cáritas Knickenberg and Gertrudis Neugebauer. In April of that year they opened up Colegio Santa Ursula in a private home, and in

August three new religious and a postulant arrived from Germany. In 1941 their fears were confirmed: the German government expropriated the convent of Fritzlar and turned it into a hospital during the war. Another group of Ursulans, from Erfurt, also arrived and founded a school in Sullana near Ecuador.

The idea of a German Catholic school was well received in Lima. Many upper-class families esteemed German culture and education in the same way in which others admired the French, British, or American cultures. These families formed an association to build the school. The leaders who took the initiative were Alberto Ulloa, Francisco Alvarez Calderón, Fritz Bauer, Guillermo Cornejo, and Cristóbal de Losada y Puga.[42] President Benavides himself, who admired German order and discipline, sent his daughter to the new school. In 1941 the school began functioning in the new building in San Isidro, Lima. Sister Cáritas, who went back to Germany to face the crisis there, returned to Peru in 1950 as superior of the congregation. Father Pedro Vankann, a German-born missionary of the Camillian Fathers, helped the sisters in the beginning and acted as an intermediary between them and Archbishop Farfán.

In 1955, at the behest of the Holy See, the Ursulines in Lima joined the Roman Union of Saint Ursula, which governed 180 Ursuline houses throughout the world. Later on, the Ursulines in Sullana turned their school over to the Carmelites of Charity and joined the Ursulines in Lima. Among the Sullana Ursulines was Sister Loyola Weinart, who came to be a living symbol of the Ursuline presence in Peru among the Ursulines and their students. Colegio Santa Ursula very soon took its place among the best upper-class Catholic girls' schools in Lima.

The Dominicans of Saint Mary Magdalene, 1938

This congregation, which goes back to the thirteenth century, also had a long teaching tradition and, like the Ursulans, suffered from Nazi persecution. In 1938 the municipality of Speyer declared, "The teaching principles in Catholic educational centers are not in harmony with those of the state." With that as a justification, the city closed down many Catholic schools. But even before that crisis, the Dominicans of Saint Mary Magdalene explored the possibilities of coming to South America, especially Brazil and Peru. In 1937 two groups came to Brazil, and in 1938 three different groups came to Peru at the invitation of Bishop Salvador Herrera of Puno. A fourth group arrived in 1939. Altogether, forty Dominican sisters left Speyer for Peru in those years.

In February 1938 they founded a convent and a school, Elena de Santa María, in Juliaca. In July they assumed the direction of Santa Rosa National School for girls in Abancay. In March 1939 they founded another convent and another school, Beata Imelda, in Chosica, not far inland from Lima. These were founded principally to serve as points of contact with Lima. The school in Chosica also became a German-Peruvian educational center. In each of the three places, Juliaca, Abancay, and Chosica, the sisters carried out a great variety of tasks, including the teaching of catechism and short courses for women, and visiting prisoners (Juliaca). Many of their former students entered the congregation, and currently one-half of the members are Peruvians.[43]

The Marianists, 1939

With the arrival of the Marianists in 1939 the desire of many families to have a Catholic school for boys modeled on American education became a reality. The school founded by the Marianists complemented the school founded by the Immaculate Heart of Mary sisters. The Marianist congregation was founded (1817) in circumstances very similar to those of other French-born congregations. The founder, Guillaume Joseph Chaminade, hoped to restore the Christian faith in a land that had grown hostile toward religion. Different Limanian families, especially that of Carlos Alvarez Calderón, took the initiative to invite the Marianists to Peru and formed an association to help support them economically. The first group of Marianists, which included both brothers and priests, arrived in 1939. They belonged to the St. Louis Province of the United States.

Santa María Colegio began to function on Avenida Arequipa in 1939, but in 1941 it moved to María Reina parish in San Isidro. In 1959 it moved again to its current location in Chacarilla del Estanque (an upper-class suburb of Lima), and at the same time an English-speaking parish school, run by Franciscan sisters from Wisconsin, took its place at María Reina. In 1944 the Marianists took charge of the section for boys at Colegio San Antonio in Callao. In 1957 they also founded Colegio San José Obrero in Trujillo. In 1961 Father William Morris founded Santa María Catholic University of Arequipa, a work that in reality involved only a few Marianists. In the decade of the sixties there were nearly sixty priests and brothers in Peru, the majority Americans. By 1983, however, the Peruvian province of the Marianists had dropped to twenty-eight members, of whom half were Peruvian by birth.[44]

The Theresian Institute, 1943

Founded as a pious union for laywomen by Father Pedro Poveda in Spain in 1911, the Theresian Institute became a secular institute in 1947. The members of the institute are not formally religious but rather committed laywomen who devote their lives to bringing Christian attitudes to the world of business, education, and modern mass communication. The first Theresians (they took their name from Saint Theresa of Avila) arrived in Peru in 1943 at the invitation of the bishop of Huaraz to administer a newly founded teachers normal school. When the school closed in 1947 they went to Lima, where they founded a residence for female university students and also began teaching at the teachers normal school of the Catholic University. In 1952 they took over the direction of the normal school of the university, which then changed its name to The Urban Teachers College of the Theresian Institute. In 1977 the normal school ceased to exist and was incorporated into the education program of the university. The Theresians continue to teach in that and other programs at the university. In 1952 they also founded their own school, Isabel Flores de Oliva, in Lima. Between 1960 and 1982 they taught at the school on the Hacienda San Jacinto near Chimbote. In 1970 they also began working by the Napo River in the Amazon jungle, where they specialized in training bilingual teachers. In 1983 they took charge of a teachers normal school in Chimbote. Along with the Congregation of the Sacred Heart sisters, the Theresian Institute is one of the few women's groups that work on the university level in Peru. Of the fifty members in 1986, thirty-eight were Peruvians by birth.

An Overall Assessment

Their Positive Contribution

With the founding of Santa María, the last of the great traditional colegios was built. La Inmaculada, La Recoleta, San Agustín, Santo Tomás de Aquino, the schools of the Salesians, the Marists, and La Salle offered a wide range of choice of Catholic education for boys. And Belén, Sagrado Corazón (Sophianum), the teachers normal of San Pedro, the school of the Reparation sisters in Miraflores, the Salesian sisters, the Teaching Domini-

The Teaching Orders and Congregations   165

cans, the "national" Franciscans, the I.H.M.'s (Villa María), and others offered the same wide selection for girls. In 1949 there were fifty-one colegios (the full ten years that include both primary and secondary education) run by men's religious orders or congregations, with some 18,834 students, and 111 colegios run by religious women, with 34,471 students.[45] In the postwar years, with the arrival of many new congregations and in response to the enormous increase in the number of school-age children, the number of schools run by religious also increased considerably. In 1982 there were approximately 397,347 students in 639 different educational centers administered in some way by the church.[46] We will cover this later period in more detail in chapter 10.

Between the foundation of Colegio Belén in 1848 and the founding of Santa María in 1939, nearly a century had gone by. During that century numerous new orders and congregations that either were founded in Peru or came from abroad slowly but surely changed the face of the Peruvian church. The hospitals, schools, parishes, and other works they founded projected an image of vitality and public service the church lacked after independence. In spite of the liberals' complaints, the church did respond to society's needs through the creation of these works. Whereas the modern mind looked askance at the contemplative orders, it could not fail to admire the achievements of the missionaries in the Amazon jungle with their medical posts, schools, and civilizing efforts. The schools founded by the religious attracted the sons and daughters of the leading families of the country. In contrast to the stereotype drawn by the liberals, who cast the church in the role of defender of medieval ideas, the new religious schools projected an image of order and progress. They represented the best of western culture and civilization. The French religious at La Recoleta, the American nuns at Villa María, or the German sisters at Santa Ursula, among many other examples, offered Peruvians the opportunity of vital access to the cultural and educational achievements of the leading nations of the world. The anticlericals could no longer make blanket generalizations about an obscurantist church.

The new orders and congregations also reflected the changing times in Peru and in the world. In the first years after independence, religious schools were founded to fill a vacuum left by the independence movement and especially by the nearly total absence of educational centers for young women. Belén of the Sacred Hearts sisters and the teachers normal of the Sacred Heart sisters helped fill that vacuum. But as liberalism grew more belligerent, many families saw the need for schools specifically for their sons. La Recoleta, La Inmaculada, the schools of the Augustinians and the Dominicans, and others responded to that need. Toward the end of the century, the church began to worry more about Protestantism. The founding of the Marist school of Callao and Villa María of the I.H.M. sisters represented a response to that concern.

At the same time, the schools and social works of the religious reflected changes on the international scene. In last-century Latin America the most esteemed culture was the French. The French sisters at Belén and San José de Cluny and the French priests at La Recoleta offered access to that culture. In the second part of the century Latin Americans were increasingly attracted to English culture, which rivaled the French in elitist circles. The positivists, who admired the scientific advances and commercial practicality of the Anglo-Saxon world, first England and then the United States, saw the English language as a key to progress. The founding of Saint Joseph College in Callao in 1909 and Villa María in 1923 clearly show that the church also recognized these realities. In the thirties many families were attracted to the German culture while others were attracted to modern American education, different tendencies that helped give rise to Santa Ursula and Santa María.

Although many different nationalities were represented, the majority of religious personnel who came to Peru after independence were in fact Spanish. And they came for the obvious reason that there were still historical, cultural, and linguistic ties between Spain and Latin America. Spanish continued to be the principle common language in countries with multiple Indian groups. But the religious did not come to America merely because of a cultural affinity; many went to perform a specific task for which they were especially prepared. The Vincentians and the Claretians were known in Europe as good seminary teachers. The Salesians were known for their work among the popular classes in Italy. The first Jesuits came to teach in the seminary of Huánuco.

But it is also important to take into account another factor, the resurgence of a missionary mystique that influenced Catholics especially in countries such as France, Spain, and Italy that were experiencing antireligious persecutions. The priests and sisters of the Sacred Hearts came to America originally on their way to Oceania. They stayed at the invitation of Catholics in Chile and Peru, who presented them with their own local needs. Other religious went expressly to work in the Amazon jungle, first the Franciscans, and later on the Augustinians, the Dominicans, and the Passionists. Almost all of these latter groups founded houses and parishes in Lima as places of rest and points of contact with Europe. In some cases, religious schools were founded to meet a need that arose after the congregation had already established itself in Peru. The sisters of Saint Joseph of Cluny and the Daughters of Saint Anne went to Lima at the invitation of the French and Italian colonies to run hospitals, but they both ended up administering schools for those colonies as well.

The Upper-Class Schools

The severest criticism that has been made of the religious schools was and is their upper-class and elitist character. The Jesuits, the Sacred Hearts priests, the Augustinians, and later the Marianists all offered an education for the middle and upper classes of Lima and some cities in the provinces. The sisters of Belén, the Sophianum, Villa María, and Santa Ursula did the same for the daughters of the families of those same classes. By way of contrast, the schools run by the Salesians, the Marists, and the brothers of La Salle were oriented more toward the lower middle classes. With the passage of time some of these latter schools also moved up the social scale. At the same time there were educational centers such as those of the Good Shepherd sisters or the farm schools of the Salesians that directly benefited the working class or the peasants.

Furthermore, some of these congregations, even those that maintained schools for the rich, ran schools for the poor alongside the latter. The sisters at Belén maintained a school for poor girls from the very beginning. The brothers of La Salle ran Colegio Muñoz Nájar for the lower class next to their school for the middle and upper class in Arequipa. The school for practice teaching at the teachers normal of San Pedro (Sacred Heart) was really a school for the lower class. These examples underline the fact that many congregations, even though their schools for the wealthy were more famous, did educate the poor. Furthermore, the great majority of the religious themselves who taught in these schools came from the middle and even the lower classes of Europe and the United States. And, of course, the congregations, lacking any other source of revenue, had no choice in the beginning but to run schools for the wealthy.

All of these mitigating factors notwithstanding, the great traditional schools of the teaching congregations projected an undeniable image of elitism. A description of the colegio of the Sagrado Corazón in 1927 presented it as "one of the most aristocratic schools for young ladies in Lima." The description also included a piece of advice for parents who sent their daughters there: "Given the strict vigilance that is observed, the directors recommend that the girls be accompanied daily by family servants."[47]

In the religious schools, as in any well-run private school, there reigned an atmosphere of peace, order, discipline, and study. Furthermore, the experience and happy memories of the years spent at these schools left a deep imprint on the students, with their friendships, excursions, games, special devotions, and favorite teachers. Almost all students recall with nostalgia their primary and high school days. In his memoirs Luis Alayza y Paz Soldán describes a day in the life of the students at La Inmaculada in the beginning of the century. "The colegio of the Jesuits," wrote Alayza, "was the best in Lima." It was also small, with approximately two hundred students. The day began with Mass at 8:30, followed by classes and then lunch at one o'clock. Afternoon classes began at 2:35 and ended at 5:30 after the common recitation of the rosary. The girl students at Sacred Heart, located across the street, left at 5:00 so as not to meet the boys when they finished school.[48]

Luis Alberto Sánchez remembers with affection the education he received at La Recoleta, where, unlike at the Jesuit school, there did not exist any "narrow-minded dogmatism," but rather an "authentic democratic spirit."[49] Víctor Andrés Belaunde recalls with nostalgia the years he spent at Father Duhamel's school and with the Jesuits in Arequipa. The generalization frequently made that these schools did not inculcate social values is not entirely true. In reality, the degree of social consciousness varied from one congregation to another. Armando Villanueva del Campo, a founder of the Aprista political party, remembers the Christian social orientation he received at San Luis of the Marists in Barranco (Lima).[50] In general, all Catholic schools in the thirties promoted Catholic Action that was inspired by the papal social encyclicals. But Pablo Macera, a leading historian, displayed little affection for Colegio La Salle in that same period. According to Macera, under the direction of the Spanish brothers he and other students were obliged to sing "Cara al Sol," the hymn of the Spanish Falangists.[51] There were in reality a great variety of experiences. At La Inmaculada one could find a very Spanish atmosphere well into the late twentieth century. At La Recoleta the atmosphere was very French. At La Salle and the Marists'

The Teaching Orders and Congregations   169

schools the atmosphere was that of lower class and even rural Spain. The same observation could be made of the girls' schools: the language that predominated at Belén was French; at Villa María, English, and at Santa Ursula, German.

The success of these schools did not depend, however, on the nationality of the teachers, but rather on the fact that they were all religious. They were professional educators with a long institutional experience who gave themselves over to their work with zeal and dedication. As a result of their special dedication, they forged deep affectionate ties with their students. In all of these schools there were always religious who were considered living embodiments of the institution, such as Brother Santos García at La Inmaculada, Father Plácido Ayala at La Recoleta, and Sister Loyola at Santa Ursula.

But the heart of the question is whether these schools fulfilled the mission for which they were created. The ideal proposed by the schools themselves was in general to form Christian men and women who would in some way influence society, socially and politically. The formula used to express this ideal varied from school to school and from period to period. Before the decade of the thirties, when the social teaching of the church was only beginning to be felt in the Catholic world, the personal and academic formation of the students was emphasized over instilling in them a social consciousness. According to the thinking of those times, for a young person to influence society it was merely necessary that he or she receive a solid academic and religious education. By "religious formation" was meant religion classes, attendance at Mass, or participation in pious associations such as the Marian sodalities of the Jesuits. In the decade of the twenties La Inmaculada proposed as its ideal: "To educate young men in a Christian way and to prepare them by means of an adequate instruction to follow a professional career that will help them face the struggle for existence."[52] La Recoleta in the same period was more explicitly social: "To provide students with a profound Christian education that will make them men of knowledge with a well-formed conscience who will be useful to their country."[53] The schools for women expressed their ideals in the same terms, though with less emphasis on professional training. The school of the Sacred Heart (León Andrade) proposed: "To inspire them (the girls) to respect and love Religion, to form their hearts in virtue, to incline them to a simplicity in customs, to enrich their intelligence with useful and agreeable studies, to direct their education to the fulfillment of the needs of the family and society."[54]

The difficulty in answering the question raised is that virtually nowhere in the entire Catholic world have satisfactory criteria been found to judge the influence that Catholic education has had on its students. Certainly, the Catholic schools in Peru gave a strong impetus to the creation of a better-formed laity. The names of graduates from La Recoleta who became leaders of Catholic Action stand out: Ismael Bielich, Javier Correa Elías, Jorge Velaochaga, and Ernesto Alayza Grundy; and from La Inmaculada, Carlos Elías, Carlos Arenas y Loayza, and others. But there were also leaders who did not go to Catholic schools, except for brief moments in their youth; José Dammert Bellido and Gerardo Alarco studied at the German school. Héctor Cornejo Chávez, a founder of the Christian Democratic Party, went to both state and religious schools in Arequipa. But more important than the names of these exceptional leaders are the lives of thousands of more "ordinary" men and women who graduated from these religious schools. The difficulty is that in many cases one does not discover any notable difference in their political or social orientation from that of other persons who went to private but nonconfessional schools or state schools.

Two key elements that most educators would agree on today are the role of the family and the atmosphere within the school. If the formation and the atmosphere in the school reinforce the social and moral values the student learns in his or her own family, then the school will probably have a great influence on the student. But if the social or religious message of the school jars with the values learned in the family, the school will have far less influence. If these observations can be reasonably accepted as valid, then it would also seem to demand too much of the schools to effect a radical change in their students if the schools run counter to a whole structure of values and attitudes deeply ingrained in society or in the families. Furthermore, at times the "atmosphere" within the school, to distinguish it from the strictly academic formation, contradicted the social or religious message that the school taught. Even in schools that taught the social doctrine of the church before Vatican II, middle- and upper-class students had little real contact with the poverty of the vast majority of the rest of the country.

These last considerations entered into the consciousness of many religious only in the decade of the sixties of this century. Before Vatican II it was presumed that the religious formation imparted in Catholic schools would automatically influence the students, and through them, all of society. For most religious who

The Teaching Orders and Congregations   171

taught in the schools, this thought was enough to justify their years of hard work in the classroom. In this sense, the schools played an ambiguous role in the history of the foreign teaching congregations. On the one hand, teaching represented the most direct and concrete way to make themselves a part of society and to be useful to that society. On the other hand, as a consequence of their nearly total absorption in their schools, the congregations found that they had become "ghettos," foreign cultural islands closed in on themselves with little vital contact with the living culture around them, especially the world of the popular classes or that of middle-class groups who were ideologically opposed to the church.

It is, of course, important to repeat that this criticism of the ties between the teaching congregations and their upper-class schools came only with Vatican II. Before then, the great majority of religious educators could not conceive of a better way to serve church and society than by using their educational talents to the fullest extent, some in schools for the middle and upper classes, and others in schools for the poorer classes.

6
The Rural and Andean Church

All through the nineteenth century and to the middle of the twentieth, the church maintained a highly visible presence among the popular classes, especially among the peasants and rural workers. Until the advent of the anarchists, Apristas, and Communists after the First World War, there were no other forces that offered any real competition to the church's influence, especially among the coastal working class. This period also coincides with the vocation crisis and the abandonment of many rural parishes. Until the Second World War the church had no significant rivals in the country or in the Andes mountains. We will treat this theme in three parts: first, the church in general in the rural setting; second, the mentality and pastoral action of the rural and Andean church; and third, peasant religiosity and popular organizations.

The Rural and Andean World: A Panoramic View

For most of its history Peru has been fundamentally an agrarian country. The 1940 census classified two-thirds of the population as "rural."[1] But the words "rural," "Andean," or "agrarian" do not adequately describe the complex social reality of Peru, which includes coastal workers of a mestizo background, Quechua speakers in the valleys of the central Andean mountains, and Quechua and Aymara speakers who coinhabit the great plateau of the southern Andes. There are enormous geographical, ethnic, cultural, and linguistic differences that separate each of these groups. According to the same census, 62 percent of Peru's population lived in the central mountain region, also known as the "Quechua zone;" 25 percent lived on the coast, and 13 percent in the Amazon jungle.[2] With the massive migrations from the mountains to the coast following World War II, the rural population dropped and the urban population picked up. In 1980 nearly 35.87 percent of the population was classified as "rural," and in 1985, 32.9 percent.[3] The census defined an urban area as a "populated center that has a minimum of one hundred houses grouped together contiguously or that is a district capital."[4] It should be obvious from this definition that although thousands of towns in Peru are officially considered urban areas, in reality they belong culturally and psychologically to the world of the rural or Andean peasantry. But at the same time it is also evident that the countryside has gone through a gradual urbanization process throughout Peru's republican history.

Three different periods can be distinguished more or less clearly in this process of transformation. The first period runs from independence to the guano boom (1821–40). During this period the economy in general was in a state of recession and stagnation, even though Peru's mines still continued to be the principle source of wealth. But agricultural production was way down principally because there was little internal or external demand. Furthermore, the great colonial estate, which was virtually a closed feudal-like system, did not have the capacity to produce on a large scale. It continued to depend on black slavery and forced Indian labor. During this period there was little social change and scant social mobility in the cities and even less so in the country. The special Indian poll tax called the "Indian contribution" and black slavery were both abolished in 1854, but other forms of colonial abuses, such as forced Indian labor and debt peonage, continued to exist until the beginning of the twentieth century.

The second period (1840–79) corresponds to the guano and nitrate booms that helped give rise to a coastal, capitalist middle class. The coastal sugar estates also expanded and began to seek out contract laborers from Asia. Between 1849 and 1872 nearly one hundred thousand Chinese arrived in Peru to work on the sugar haciendas, especially along the northern coast, or to shovel guano or lay train tracks. The Indian population, however, remained relatively stable during this period.

The war with Chile (1879–84) interrupted this process rather violently and marked the beginning of the third period, the age of the great coastal oligarchy. A few speculators and adventurers took advantage of the ruin of hundreds of property owners following the war and forged great sugar haciendas. Some of them were Peruvians: the Aspíllagas and the Pardos, for example. Others were foreigners: the Gildemeisters, the Grace and the Larco families. Two radically different types of landholdings emerged:

the coastal estates, which were really modern capitalist complexes based on intensive monoproduction (sugar, and in the twentieth century, cotton) and oriented toward exportation; and the great haciendas of the mountains and the highlands, which were also very large territorially, but much less productive and oriented toward local markets. An exception to this rule were haciendas in the south that exported wool to commerical houses in Arequipa.

These two different systems also had a quite different impact on the peasantry. In the Andes and the southern highlands the haciendas, remote from the modernizing trends on the coast, intensified their feudal grip over the land and society. The abuses committed by the landowners, who worked hand in glove with the local political authorities, provoked frequent Indian uprisings, such as one in Huancané in 1866 and a series of uprisings in Puno between 1895 and 1900. But these uprisings were sporadic and passing explosions that interrupted the normal and monotonous rhythm of life in the Andes. Furthermore, these uprisings never turned into permanent movements with an ideological orientation. Nor did they have much impact on the different governments in Lima that practically ignored the rural and Andean peasantry. Lack of social mobility and economic scarcity were the general characteristics of life in the Peruvian Andes throughout the nineteenth century and the first decades of the twentieth.

The Indian who lived in the Andes, however, enjoyed certain advantages over the hacienda worker on the coast. The latter was absorbed into a system that left no space for small landowners, nor even for the peasant community. But the huge latifundium in the Andes did not need permanent workers during the entire year. As a consequence, the Indian community survived alongside the hacienda as a refuge to which the Indians could retreat and maintain their culture. The peasants in the Andes usually worked part time on the hacienda and the rest of the time on their own communal lands. For this same reason, Andean popular religiosity also remained relatively intact after colonial times until the latter part of the twentieth century.

On the coast, by way of contrast, the sugar and cotton haciendas accelerated the occidentalization process. First they absorbed the black slaves, then the Chinese, and finally the Indians, giving rise to a multiracial proletarian society. The former slaves, emancipated by Ramón Castilla in 1854, generally remained on the same haciendas where they had been slaves and became salaried peons or small sharecroppers. The black population became concentrated around the towns of Cañete and Chincha to the south of Lima and in certain neighborhoods in the capital. The Chinese came to Peru fundamentally in response to the demand for workers on the sugar haciendas in the north. When Great Britain abolished the trafficking in coolies in 1872, the northern hacienda owners had recourse to the Indians in the Andes. Their method was to attract the Indians with money and gifts, but once the Indians began working on the haciendas, they were soon bound to the land by debts. Finally, toward the end of the century, the Japanese came over. Between 1898 and 1923 some seventeen thousand came, almost all to work on coastal haciendas.

The coast became a melting pot of races and cultures during the heyday of the oligarchy. At times the mixture was explosive, producing bitter racial conflicts such as a riot that broke out in the Cañete valley in 1881 during which blacks massacred one thousand Chinese. On other occasions the exploited groups revolted against the system itself. Between 1880 and 1881 the Chinese workers left the haciendas en masse and followed the victorious Chilean armies as they headed toward Lima. At the beginning of the century the hacienda workers began organizing unions and strikes. In the Chicama valley in 1908 and again in 1921 the workers planned and organized strikes that lasted for months. On both occasions they were also severely repressed by government troops. By the twenties and thirties the oligarchy found itself seriously threatened by rising and highly politicized peasant movements.

The Rural Church: A Framework for Understanding

In the middle of this complex cultural and ethnic diversity that characterized rural and Andean Peru, the church continued to be what it had always been during colonial times, the main point of historical and cultural reference. The church served as a bridge with the past, giving cultural stability to the peasants in the face of western and capitalist expansion. The church also served as a bridge between the dominant white culture and the peasant culture. The church fulfilled several roles at the same time.

According to the liberals, the priest in the Andes was a rapacious bird ready to exploit the Indians at the drop of a hat with exorbitant stipends for Masses and sacraments. Furthermore, the priest himself was frequently a landowner who rented out his land to the Indians, thus strengthening the feudal bonds that characterized Andean society. According to the image painted by the liberal, the priest was usually a crude man, with little culture and even less human compassion. He lived at the expense of the peasant's superstitions. He also drank much and usually lived in concubinage. His "nephews" were in reality his own children whom he would never recognize as such. This rather pejorative image of the rural priest was not entirely false. But it also revealed the lack of a critical sense in the liberal himself. Usually it was the priest who lived among the peasants, and not the desk-bound city liberal, who really understood the Indian situation in Peru.

The church was, of course, more traditional and conservative in its thinking than the more progressive-minded liberal. But the church also accommodated itself more readily to the reality of the rural setting, which was characterized by social rigidity and resistance to change. A better question would be whether the church, even if it wished to, could have radically changed the deeply ingrained customs of the rural and Andean inhabitants. On the contrary, the church was widely accepted in that world precisely because it adjusted itself to the style of life there. Gramsci highlighted the contrast between the "progressive" church of the theologians and city intellectuals, on the one hand, and the tradition-laden and less "orthodox" church in the countryside of Italy on the other. The church, Gramsci observed, is strong because it insists on maintaining unity between those two worlds, that of the elite and that of the popular classes. For this reason, the Italian socialist concluded, the church does not impose by force (although it did attempt to do so on a number of occasions in history) a "progressive" church on the peasantry in order not to drive it out of the church.[5] Historically, one discovers in Catholicism a firmness with regard to dogma and doctrine, but at the same time an elastic flexibility when it comes to pastoral practice. Medieval Catholicism entertained the intellectual worldview of Thomas Aquinas alongside the religiosity of the popular classes, the very popular religiosity that would help prepare the way for Luther's reform. It was with a certain irony that González Prada exclaimed, "It is the paganism that you bear within yourself that makes you survive, O Christianity!"[6]

A glance at the social reality of the Latin American rural setting reveals the existence of a rigid social structure coupled with an all-pervasive fatalism toward life. The liberal usually blamed this fatalism on the church, which presumably fostered an "alienating" form of religiosity. However, the religiosity that the people practiced was the one that most fit their circumstances. The anthropologist George Foster wrote a well-known article on the

"Image of the Limited Good." According to Foster, Latin American peasants see the world as a place where there are very limited resources and goods to go around. From their viewpoint, not only are there few goods to go around, but there never will be an abundance of goods, and therefore one should not try too hard to produce more goods.[7] This fatalism is not really the "cause" but rather the "effect" of backwardness. Given this interpretation, the church fit harmoniously in the world of the peasants because it did not run counter to their folk wisdom. To cite a concrete example, although the priests criticized the drinking that went on during the village feast days, they did not demand too much (such as excommunicating the people for drinking) as a condition for having the feast.

The liberals also accused the church of fostering a magical-ritualistic mentality among the peasants. Mariátegui restated this theme in *Seven Interpretive Essays on the Peruvian Reality:* "The missionaries did not instill a faith; they instilled a system of worship and a liturgy, wisely adapting them to Indian customs."[8] Nevertheless, it can also be asked whether the magical and ritualistic worldview of the peasants was the result of the pastoral action of the church or the spontaneous creation of an agrarian and presecularized people. The truth probably lies in the middle. In a presecular rural and illiterate peasant society, the sacred and the temporal blend together and ritualized behavior is perceived as the proper way to control nature. In this setting the intellectual content of a sermon has far less meaning than rituals and symbols. It was principally by means of music, dances, images, and the liturgy that the church communicated the mysteries of Christianity. This was the basic thesis that Víctor Andrés Belaunde presented to refute Mariágetui's claim that the Indians were never really evangelized.[9] In this sense popular religiosity is both a creation of the church and of the people: of the church because it has a rich deposit of rituals and symbols, and of the people because they are used to expressing their deepest feelings in art, music, and ritual. Of course, the lack of intellectual formation also opens the door to the distortions, exaggerations, and deficiencies that characterize many expressions of popular religiosity in the Andes.

Furthermore, the celebration of the feast days of the patron saint, Christmas, Holy Week, All Saints' Day, and many others fulfills an all-important religious and social function. The feasts are rites of collective renovation by which the peasants celebrate important moments in the year and strengthen their community ties. The feasts also represent ties with the past that help the peasants maintain their sense of identity. With the passage of time, however, and as a consequence of the priest shortage and the very limited intellectual formation that the peasants normally receive, these feast-day celebrations have in many cases degenerated into superficial civic and cultural rites. In these cases the church has also ceased to be a dynamic part of the life of the peasants, becoming instead an institution that produces rituals with little theological or ecclesial meaning for the people.

Nevertheless, the pace of secularization is much slower in the country than in the city. Claudio Véliz underlined this fact when he observed that during the entire nineteenth century it was the conservative church, not progressive liberalism, that most influenced the lives of Latin American peasants.[10] The secularizing and rationalistic mentality was typical only of the urban world that received the brunt of the advance of capitalism, the industrial revolution, and modern science. Indeed, popular religiosity even represented a sort of resistance to the values of the progressive elites, in part because they were the very groups that exploited the peasants. However, this tenacious retention of traditional religious practices did not necessarily translate into militant support of the church. The real weakness of the rural church was precisely the absence of an ecclesial life. The peasants and villagers went to church, not because they viewed themselves as living and necessary members of the church, but because they needed the rituals the church provided for the well-being of the community. In the popular mentality, the church was a "patron" who gave out favors to its "clients." And the local priest was generally perceived as a member of the cultural elite and therefore on a social rung above the ordinary people.

Finally, the topic of peasant religion, as well as the transformations that it has undergone since independence, lies outside the scope of this study, which aims rather to analyze the institutional church and its relationship with the people. There are several studies, such as those of Marzal for the sixteenth century in general and for Urcos and Piura in the twentieth century, and that of Garr for Ayaviri, which analyze popular religious beliefs among Indians and peasants in much more depth. These and other studies have helped to clarify our view of that world. A student of Andean peasant religiosity today will not fall prey to certain simplistic generalizations that the pro-Indian writers of the twenties made about the existence of a pre-Columbian religion "hidden" beneath Catholic forms. The widespread popularity of Catholic

The Rural and Andean Church

symbols and ritual everywhere in the Andes and the southern highlands, even with the absence of priests, attests to the fact that Catholicism did make a deep impact on the people. But neither is there much uniformity: the degree of the purity of Christianity or of syncretism varies considerably from period to period and from region to region. Wherever the institutional church has been absent for a long time, because of the priest shortage, for example, one can observe a greater distortion in peasant Christianity. Our object now is to understand the general context in which the church functioned.

The Rural-Andean Church: Basic Realities

The Doctrine

The fundamental structure by which the church related to rural and Andean dwellers was the doctrine, just as it had all through the colonial period. The doctrine was the name given to a rural parish because its principal function from the sixteenth century on was to "indoctrinate" the Indians into the Catholic faith. The Indians gathered every Sunday and on certain other days in the church patio after Mass to learn Christian doctrine and to commit to memory the Our Father, the Hail Mary, the Apostles' Creed, the Ten Commandments, and the precepts of the church. The word "doctrine" was still used in the decade of the forties of this century for rural parishes.

The doctrine parish generally included a main town and two or three satellite villages. Normally there was one priest for each doctrine, an optimal situation that was maintained until the last decades of the nineteenth century. An example of the social control that the church exercised in the country was the census it took with certain regularity. A census was taken, among other reasons, to determine who should pay tithes. The lists used for the census classified the parishioners, who represented the entire population within the doctrine, according to sex, civil status, and age. Furthermore, until the abolition of slavery the lists still classified people according to race and caste, "Spaniards," "Indians," "blacks," and "slaves." The fact that the church did not bother to change this obviously colonial nomenclature until twenty years or more after independence suggests that many of the basic realities also had not changed. The exactitude of a parish census indicates furthermore that the church was better organized than the state bureaucracy, at least for the first decades after independence.

Until the second half of the nineteenth century there were no vacant curates or doctrines in rural Peru. In 1850 Archbishop Luna Pizarro enjoyed the luxury of removing for lack of aptitude seventeen rural pastors (out of 159 parishes in the archdiocese) and naming their assistants pastors in their place.[11] But toward the end of the century as seen in chapter 2, there were reports of abandoned parishes everywhere. According to a "priest from Cuzco," who wrote in 1904, the church in the country was in a sorry state: "churches in disrepair, parish houses in ruins..., parishes left unattended for months and even years...."[12] According to statistics from 1940, of the 673 parishes in all of Peru, 222 were vacant; the majority of those were in the Andes.[13] Increasingly, an abandoned church without Mass or any other activity for months or even years became a normal scene in the Peruvian Andes. This "deinstitutionalization" of the rural church was an additional reason why the peasants emphasized the sacramentals, processions, Holy Week plays, and other activities that they could do themselves without a priest.

The Church's Wealth

A basic consideration for determining the size of a parish was its capability of supporting a priest. The doctrine of Huarochirí reported in 1848 that it did "not need more than one priest because the parishioners do not have the means to support a pastor and an assistant."[14] Since the sixteenth century the minimum income necessary for supporting a priest was called the *congrua*. This basic income came from the tithes, which in the country frequently were in the form of animals and produce. As a supplement to this basic income, pastors also collected stipends for Masses and sacraments. But there were many other sources of income, including rent from properties, the salary that came with a chaplaincy, and especially in the southern Andes, money gained from commerce. Although this last means of income was prohibited by canon law, it did not prevent many rural priests from buying and selling goods well into the twentieth century.[15] Sometimes the rural priest rented animals and collected interest for their "use."

Tithes (frequently called "firstfruits" in the country) constituted the basic source of income throughout colonial times. In 1846 congress abolished all laws that obliged Peruvians to pay tithes or to offer the firstfruits of their harvest. But the government restrained from applying the abolition until such time as the priests could find another means of support. In 1856 congress

The Rural and Andean Church   181

formally abolished the tithes, although it allowed the practice of offering the firstfruits to continue in the countryside. The reason for the exception was the recognition on the part of the state that without that offering the rural church could not exist. But the state understood at the same time that all of these colonial forms of payment should cease to exist. The church defended its right to collect tithes and firstfruits as an ancient Christian practice.[16] It is not clear exactly when the practice of firstfruits disappeared. In a pastoral letter of 1905 the bishops complained that people were losing the custom of offering firstfruits.[17] In his pastoral visit of 1916 Bishop García Irigoyen of Trujillo exhorted the hacienda owners to continue practicing the custom.[18] But in 1941, in the same diocese, Bishop Guevara observed that the custom of firstfruits had disappeared.[19] The reasons for its disappearance were many and obvious: widespread poverty in the country, the absence of any legal obligation, the abandonment of many parishes, and the migrations from the country to the cities.

A second source of income, approved by the church and not affected by the laws of 1856 and 1859, was the stipend established for Masses, sacraments, and paraliturgical acts. These stipends did not depend on the will of the pastor but on a fixed policy laid down by the bishops to curb clerical abuses. To that effect a list of stipends was published in all parishes so that the faithful could have a clear idea of what they should pay. In the first decades of the nineteenth century the scale of stipends depended on such variables as the social and racial condition of the faithful. In a list published in 1837, which in reality was simply a reprint of a colonial list, a "Spaniard" (that is, a white person) had to pay sixteen pesos for a funeral; a nontaxpaying Indian, six pesos; a taxpaying Indian, four *reales*. However, the paying of stipends was much more complicated than what this list suggests. If a churchgoer wished special additions (such as someone to sing the epistle or the gospel, the use of a special stole, bells to be rung, or incense to be used), then it was necessary to pay more.[20] Quite literally, requesting a funeral, a marriage, or any rite of the church turned into a veritable commercial transaction, even to the extent of bargaining with the priest for discounts or paying more for "overtime."

Much more important as a source of income than Sunday Mass or the sacraments were the feast-day Masses in honor of the patron saint of a village. For these occasions a special community collection was taken up to cover the expenses of the feast and the stipend to be offered the priest. Furthermore, the visiting priest made use of the occasion of the feast to baptize, perform marriages, bless houses and harvests, and recite prayers for the dead. Notwithstanding all the admonitions of the episcopal assemblies, the country priests abused the people's dependence on them to exact stipends far in excess of what was due. There are abundant reports that attest to this. In 1884, for example, the neighbors in the village of Sitacocha, near Trujillo, sent a message of protest to the bishop in which they accused the visiting priest who came for the feast of the Immaculate Conception, not only of collecting for baptisms and marriages that he performed during the feast, but also of trying to collect for all the burials that had been done in his absence![21]

Economic scarcity in the country as well as the abusive demands of many priests deeply influenced relations between the church and rural dwellers. There most of all the priest was perceived as a patron or distributor of goods, either temporal or spiritual. This relationship also directly affected the pastoral practice of the church. One reaction toward exorbitant demands on the part of the priest was the widespread practice of clandestine burials in order to avoid paying the priest for a funeral rite.[22] Another consequence, widespread even today in the Andes, is the practice of living together and postponing the marriage ceremony until the couple is able to afford the cost of a suitable marriage feast. This is the background to explain a government measure in 1868 that aimed to reduce by half the church's "rights." As the proposed law stated, ". . . It is a well-known fact that many citizens, especially artisans and Indians, put off marrying in order to avoid paying the corresponding parish rights."[23]

In colonial times there was another sure means of income, the interest that came from land or from the endowment set aside for chaplaincies. According to colonial custom, a family would set up an endowment and stipulate that the interest from that sum should go to a chaplain chosen by the family on the condition that he celebrate a certain number of Masses for the deceased of the family. Very often the priest himself was a member of the family. For this reason, chaplaincies sometimes ceased to exist with the death of a priest or the dispersal of the family. In 1852 congress abolished these endowments. Furthermore, as society modernized, the custom of having a particular priest for a family or for a special group such as a guild gradually faded away. The chaplaincies survived in the rural areas in the form of special spiritual attention given to the hacienda chapels.

The other most important source of income, along with the

The Rural and Andean Church

stipends for sacraments and the feast-day Mass, was rent earned from property. There is still no comprehensive study of the church's landholdings in Peru. Thomas Ford (1955) calculated that the Peruvian church owned 5 to 10 percent of the cultivated land around most cities and towns.[24] This estimate included lands owned by monasteries and convents in the cities. To some, this may seem to be a very low estimate, but it is well to remember that with the expulsion of the Jesuits, the wars of independence, the suppression of many convents and monasteries in 1826, and a law in 1911 that consolidated church mortgages, the church had lost a considerable amount of property since colonial times.

The topic of church properties is somewhat complicated. On the one hand, confraternities and other pious associations were among the principal rural property owners. The typical confraternity rented its properties to help defray the cost of maintaining the devotion to its patron saint. Yet it is open to debate whether the lands owned by the confraternity belonged to the "church" or to the local community, because the members of the confraternities were all laymen. Furthermore, rural priests frequently held property titles in the name of their family, but that property did not belong to the parish.

A glance at the descriptions of their properties made by parish priests reveals two basic facts: their holdings were very small and very scattered. Parish priests in rural Peru never came close to being real hacienda owners. In fact, since their land was usually scattered over a wide area, most priests simply rented their properties out. This system had the advantage of freeing the priests from the need to administer their own holdings. But neither did they become rich. The renters were usually poor peasants who frequently failed to pay their rent, a fact that gave rise to many legal battles between them and the priests. Eyewitness accounts certainly do not give the impression of a prosperous church. A typical example is this report written in 1855 by the pastor of three churches near Cuzco, located in the towns of Faray, Pisac, and San Salvador. In his report the priest observed that the church in Faray had three *topos* for raising corn, and each *topo* brought in six pesos a year. According to the pastor, this was not enough to light the gas lamp or to pay for the candles or the wine for Mass. The church at Pisac had five *topos* for raising corn and the church at San Salvador had twelve *topos*. The pastor concluded, "These are the only properties that belong to the churches under my care. Their produce is not sufficient for paying the costs of the liturgy and maintaining the Blessed Sacrament and his Holy Mother in a decent state...."[25]

Finally, from colonial times on many priests, especially in the southern Andes, engaged in commercial activities such as buying goods to resell to the peasants. Records of this particular abuse are rather scarce, principally because it was expressly forbidden by the church and the priests naturally did not refer to it in their reports. There are, however, other testimonies indicating that the practice was widespread. In a pastoral letter sent to his diocese in 1866, Bishop Ambrosio Huerta wrote, "We must confess with sorrow that one can find many priests who are willing to trade their title of pastor for that of merchant and even that of rapacious wolf."[26]

It would be a bit tedious to make a detailed description of the economic situation of each diocese. One striking impression stands out in the midst of the many reports made by bishops during their visits to their dioceses, or the letters of priests to their bishops: the church had increasingly come upon hard times and sought to maintain itself by practically whatever means possible, legitimate or not. Especially after the elimination of the tithes, priests in rural areas had recourse to every means they could find: stipends, feasts, rent on property, and commerce. In 1901 Bishop Puirredón of Trujillo announced that it was necessary to annex a doctrine to the parish of Chocope. The reason given was that "it doesn't produce enough to support a pastor."[27] There is a letter from the parish priest of Paruro that same year to the bishop of Cuzco in which he requested to be transferred to another parish: "The returns from this doctrine are extremely small. They are not enough to pay even the bishop's ecclesiastical tax or to attend to my personal needs in a provincial capital such as this."[28]

The venal priest of the Andes who demanded exorbitant stipends for the sacraments or the village feast-day Mass and who hounded the peasants to pay up their rent is a stereotype based partially on fact. The background for the stereotype was the bitter poverty that characterized Peru's rural and Andean areas since independence. The church was affected by that poverty, too. But the stereotype does not do justice to the many good priests who suffered poverty in order to carry out their mission. Finally, it also does not take into account the peasant mentality that thrives on haggling and driving a bargain. From colonial times on, most Latin Americans learned not to support the church spontaneously, even though they received benefits from it. This attitude was a direct consequence of the church's dependence on the state for its support. As a result, most Latin Americans, especially the impoverished rural dwellers, did not develop a deeply ingrained habit of supporting the church.

The Rural Clergy

Given Peru's sharp geographical contrasts as well as the long period of time we are covering, one should avoid making quick generalizations about the rural clergy. Still, a few generalizations seem safe to make. Between the end of the colonial period and the middle of the nineteenth century one could find a certain uniformity among the rural clergy. In general, they came from the small white middle class of the towns in the mountains or the coastal cities. They were relatively well educated. But with the passage of time, and especially as a consequence of the crisis of the shortage of priests, the quality of the clergy in rural areas also deteriorated. Toward the middle of the century a doctrine priest looked upon his rural parish merely as a first step up the ladder toward arriving at an urban parish. There existed a certain "social control" over the quality of the clergy. But toward the end of the century, given the priest shortage, it was increasingly difficult to find priests to send to the rural areas. The tendency was to consolidate two or three parishes into one in order to support the priest. The church did not escape another consequence of the priest shortage: increasingly, the rural priest was a man lacking in human qualities and with scant intellectual formation. At the same time, Spanish missionaries began to arrive to fill the vacancies left by the Peruvian clergy.

One very important factor was geography: the vast difference between the mountains and the coast. In general, it was much easier to provide priests for rural parishes on the coast than for parishes in the Andes or the southern highlands. The reasons were evident: since most candidates for coastal parishes came from the middle classes, there was a greater possibility of selecting good candidates. Furthermore, with the greater poverty in the mountains and the southern highlands, parishes on the coast were much more attractive.

In spite of these differences, certain generalizations can be made about the rural clergy from the middle of the nineteenth century until the decade of the forties. First, complaints made about the clergy in rural areas were almost always the same. Also, reports from the pastoral visits of the bishops or their delegates help provide a good idea of what conditions were like in the rural parishes. The visitors were usually critical observers who described with scrupulous care the social and ecclesiastical reality of the parishes they visited. One of the motives for writing reports was precisely to reform the clergy. It is sufficient to cite three of these reports that are especially valuable because of their detailed descriptions: Huaylas, 1848; Puno, 1912; and Trujillo, 1926.

The Episcopal Visits

In 1848 the auxiliary bishop of Lima, José Manuel Pasquel, conducted a visit to the Callejón de Huaylas, in the heart of the northern Andes, the first such visit since that of Archbishop de la Reguera in 1783. According to Pasquel's report, there were approximately one to two thousand parishioners for every priest in that mountainous region. The doctrine of Yuncay had two pastors and seven assistant priests. The town of Huari, with a population of six thousand, had one pastor and one assistant pastor. During his visit the bishop examined all the priests in order to renew their licenses to practice their ministry. Of the eighteen examined, sixteen were approved. In the case of the two who were not, Pasquel suspended their licenses because of "their incorrigibility in the vice of drinking." The bishop also exhorted the tithe collectors not to mistreat the parishioners. Unlike in colonial times, however, when public sins could be punished by the church, the bishop limited himself to recommending that offenders be taken before the justice of the peace.[29]

In the years 1910, 1911, and 1912, Bishop Valentín Ampuero of Puno made pastoral visits throughout his entire diocese, which was practically the same size as the department of Puno. Ampuero observed that in general the clergy was not "up to the standards of their mission," whether for lack of adequate formation or on account of the social milieu in which they lived. Poverty had driven many priests to support themselves by means forbidden by the church. The bishop, however, also noted that many accusations against the clergy were not accompanied by proof. He added that the church's work was made especially difficult by the local political authorities either because they were liberals or because they were simply incompetent.[30]

Of exceptional value is the report made by the two friars, Deogracias de Ondonégui, the visitor, and his assistant, Luis Arroyo, who visited the rural parishes of Trujillo in the years 1924–26. The report, made for Bishop García Irigoyen, describes in great detail the state of seventeen different parishes in the provinces of

Otuzco, Santiago de Chuco, Pataz, and Huamachuco. The report also gives a much more realistic picture of the rural church than that drawn by the anticlerical intellectuals who naturally painted the local priest in the most unfavorable colors. The report, as would be expected, includes bad priests, but it also refers to exceptionally good ones. The majority are in the middle: human beings with virtues and vices, but on the whole much better than the stereotyped "bad" priest of the anticlericals.

Of all the priests in the reports, the parish priests in the towns of Santiago de Chuco and Pataz seemed to be the closest to the stereotype of the "bad" priest. When the visitors reached Santiago de Chuco they noticed that the church building gave the impression of being abandoned and in disrepair. According to the visitors, the pastor did not give a good example of the gospel to his parishioners "because of his irascible temperament" that led him to "treat the faithful with harsh language." When the visitors called this to his attention, the pastor accused the two of taking sides with his enemies. The pastor of the next town, Pataz, did not even bother showing up to receive the bishop's delegates. The visitors noted that he owned several very "comfortable" houses in the town, while his church was nearly in ruins. According to the visitors, he never preached the gospel and rarely celebrated Mass, "except when they paid him to." He also lived in public concubinage. The visitors added, "He even makes a big show of going everywhere with his 'nephews,'" and, finally, "He is ignorant and rude." The two visitors noted in their report that they had little hope for his reform.

In all the towns they visited, the two delegates found a priest who resembled the Curé of Ars: Antonio Rodríguez, the eighty-year-old pastor of Soledad and Parcoy. He always preached the gospel, his moral conduct was beyond reproach, and "he was friendly toward everyone." His parish was poor, among other reasons because the renters who farmed the church's properties rarely paid their rent. The other priests in Ondonégui and Arroyos' report are in the middle of these extremes: they were men who fulfilled their basic duties, but few of them were models of moral rectitude. This description of the priest who cared for the hacienda of Angasmarca in the district of Santiago de Chuco typifies the majority: "The Pastor shows up for Mass fairly regularly on the appointed days; his conduct, though it is not very immoral, is far from exemplary and he drinks too much, a fact that I personally observed...."[31]

The Priest Shortage and Moral Conduct

The shortage of priests considerably weakened ecclesiastical discipline; there are abundant references, especially at the height of the priest-shortage crisis, to moral laxity among rural priests and even outright insubordination to bishops. In a report he made in 1918 to the new bishop of Cuzco, Pedro Farfán, the vicar of the cathedral chapter, wrote that it was necessary to remove five pastors. He gave reasons in four of the five cases: one was removed for "immoral conduct"; another because he never "makes the spiritual exercises"; a third "for secretly selling" a considerable quantity of finely wrought silver that belonged to his own church; and the fourth, "for his immoral living and his unwillingness to fix up his church."[32] The reports frequently refer to eccentric and ill-humored priests who turned their parishes into personal fiefs. These recalcitrant pastors looked upon the bishop as a nuisance who needlessly meddled in their private affairs. Without doubt, José Pedraza, pastor of Huariaca in the department of Huánuco toward the end of the century, was a perfect example of the troublesome priest. For years he carried on a public feud with the ecclesiastical authorities over his properties, the contributions he owed the diocese, and his scandalous way of life in general. The bishop was even forced to publish a public statement to defend himself against charges made by the pastor. In his declaration he offers a description of this insubordinate priest:

> For years Pedraza has been a veritable hacienda owner, and he is the owner of an estate called "Despensa." . . . Pedraza spends his life in the middle of pleasures, surrounded by his numerous family—brothers, sisters, nephews, and nieces. They all live and support themselves by rent from church properties. . . . No one is unaware of the fact that Pedraza is by nature opposed to all church authorities and has been the bane of all the bishops he has had. . . .[33]

It would difficult to say whether the priests of the republican period were more venal or immoral than those of colonial times. There are certainly many testimonies in the colonial period to clerical concubinage and other practices forbidden by the church.[34] What was different, however, was the absence of any kind of "social control" over the clergy. When Luna Pizarro removed several priests in 1850 for their lack of aptitude, there existed a system of advancement according to merits. This system assured, at least for higher posts, a minimum level of quality. But

The Rural and Andean Church 189

with a grave shortage of priests, bishops obviously could not be very selective. In a report made in 1918 by the head of the Cuzco cathedral chapter cited above, the author complained about the fact that there were only four seminarians for the entire diocese and that there were already five parishes without priests. The reason given was that "no priest wants to work in them."[35]

It would also be difficult to say which defect or abuse among the clergy most damaged their image. Although concubinage was a widespread practice up until the middle of the twentieth century, it does not seem to have been a source of great scandal in the Andean regions. The most frequent complaints refer to economic matters: payments for Mass or the sacraments and the endless quarrels between priests and renters over church property. The complaints are abundant and very similar. In 1826 Manuel Atauchi, a tributary Indian in the province of Paucartambo, accused the local priest of stealing twenty-five of his sheep supposedly in revenge for the fact that the accuser's brother had killed two pigs left in his care by the priest.[36] In 1877 Mariano Cuitre, an "Indian who worked on a farm in Ccepa" in the province of Canchi, denounced the local priest because "on the pretext of my not making funeral payments, he appropriated land that was exclusively mine."[37] A lay accountant of a parish in Cuzco in 1910 accused the pastor of investing the interest gained from parish properties in his own private business.[38]

In 1850 the French merchant, Rafael María Taurel, who was also the papal consul in Peru, described with realism and some sympathy the situation of the priest who worked among the Indians in the Peruvian Andes:

> This is what a priest among the Indians is and does the greater part of his time: ... sentenced to live in the midst of an Indian village where practically no one knows Spanish, he must as a consequence spend most of his time studying the language of the people. Beyond that, he attends to his pastoral duties, though many priests also teach classes, too. But most priests end up becoming stultified and forget the better part of their classical education. So much for his intellectual life. As far as customs go, imagine a young priest separated from the affection of his family and legitimate friendship, surrounded by a mass of people who still believe in superstitions tinged with paganism. And one of their beliefs is that close contact with the priest is good for them. From all this you may gather what are the dangers that threaten a Peruvian priest.[39]

Although Taurel wrote in the middle of the nineteenth century, his observations could just as easily apply to a priest in the

Andes in the middle of this century. It is not easy to sum up the general image of the rural clergy. On the one hand, the reports of the bishops clearly reveal that there were problems and deficiencies. On the other hand, one does not find among Andean dwellers anything like a deep resentment toward the priests. With great generosity or perhaps with some naïveté, the mountain dwellers always forgave the bad priests and welcomed new ones.

This last observation leads to certain conclusions, negative and positive. On the negative side, it seems evident that the inhabitants of the rural and Andean world entertained a magical concept of the priest: what mattered was not the person but the office. The priest, whether good or bad, performed rites such as blessing the fields, celebrating Mass, and administering the sacraments, which the Andean worldview deemed necessary for the well-being of the community. But there is a positive conclusion to be drawn, too: the people forgave the bad priests because they really were a minority and because they remembered the good ones, or the relatively good ones. The fact that real anticlericalism is virtually unknown in the Andes may simply mean that the ordinary people have more wisdom and practical experience than the anticlerical intellectuals. In 1870 the Indians in the doctrine of Challabamba in the province of Paucartambo sent a message to the bishop complaining about their priest. The complaints were the same as always: the priest was greedy, he never attended to the doctrine, and he had all kinds of vices. The message stated, "The poor town of Challabamba does not see in him either a pastor or even a simple priest."[40] With this rather sharp but eloquent indictment, the Indians in the town showed that they did have clear criteria for distinguishing a good from a bad priest.

Priests and Landowners

Throughout the entire republican period there was a close relationship between the church and the principal power-wielder in the country: the hacienda owner or the *gamonal* (a small but tyrannical landowner) in the Andes. Very often the local priest or bishop came from one of the powerful families in the area. That was the case of Pedro Pascual Farfán, the bishop of Cuzco, who experienced a dilemma when he attempted to protect the Indians because many hacienda owners in the region were either related to him or were close acquaintances. Furthermore, the priest or itinerant missionary looked upon the hacienda owner and his family as people of his own white, western culture, quite different from that of the Indians. Nevertheless, it is well not to

The Rural and Andean Church 191

judge the church in its relations with the landowners too precipitously. In the first place, until recent times very few people had a clear concept of the relationship between economic and social structures and social injustice. The past-century liberal and the first pro-Indian writers limited themselves to matters of particular abuses against the Indians, and never questioned the system of landholding itself. González Prada was a solitary figure at the beginning of this century. It was not until the twenties, when anarchists, Apristas, and Marxists denounced Peru's feudal agrarian system, that a new mentality emerged.

Basically, the church judged the large landowners according to traditional religious criteria or according to the way the landowners helped the church fulfill its mission. As a normal practice, most landowners maintained chapels on the hacienda where Sunday Mass would be celebrated. In the case of remote haciendas in the higher Andes, the chapel was used for the priest's annual visit. The hacienda owners were supposed to assume the responsibility of seeing that the peasants and field-workers fulfilled their religious obligations. One of his principal duties in that regard was to offer hospitality to a visiting priest, take care of him during his stay, and help prepare for the great religious feast day. Many documents of the period underline this role of the owner as a "patron" of religious activities on the hacienda. Nicanor Larrea, a hacienda owner in the valley of La Convención near Cuzco writing toward the end of the last century, requested the bishop to recognize him as the religious patron of his hacienda. He justified this request by stating, "I made the decision to build a chapel on my hacienda, which is also the capital of the province."[41] The bishop granted him "the rights of patronage and benefactor."[42] In 1937, Rafael Larco Hoyle, owner of the hacienda "Chiclín," asked the bishop of Trujillo to give his approval for the "Confraternity of the Lord of Sugar Cane."[43] Larco, like many other hacienda owners, had accepted the petition of his workers on his own hacienda to be the patron of the confraternity.

In the report made by the visitor, Friar Deogracias Ondonégui, cited above, one can find a description of a "model" hacienda owner, Señor Enrique Ganoza, owner of the hacienda "Calipuy" in the province of Santiago de Chuco. Ganoza was highly praised by the visitors because he was personally on hand to receive them and offered them the best of hospitality. He summoned all his workers to go to Mass during the visit. According to the visitor's enthusiastic description, the hacienda chapel was "a magnificent gothic church," which was evidently kept in a good state. Ondonégui had only words of praise for his host, "Our applause goes to this Christian gentleman, who also fulfills his duties toward his workers in an exemplary way."[44] By way of contrast, noted the visitor, there are other hacienda owners who fail to keep up their chapels and who do not cooperate so openly with the visitors.

From this description one could conclude that there was a complete and unquestionable harmony between the church and landowners. Yet the historical reality was not so simple. A glance at the other fundamental relationship in the country, that between the church and the peasantry, also reveals that on many occasions priests and bishops condemned the landowners for the harsh treatment they meted out to the workers. In a report sent to the central govenment in 1912, Bishop Valentín Ampuero of Puno showed that the church did have a critical consciousness, albeit incipient, in regard to social injustice. The bishop described the local *gamonal* in these words: "[He is] an octopus whose long or short tentacles grab up, by violent and unjust ways, the properties of the Indians who live near him in order to enlarge his own estate."[45]

In general, however, the church did not question the system of landownership. On the contrary, it openly sought the help of the landowners to help carry out its religious mission. There did exist a minority of priests and bishops, however, who from colonial times on had raised their voice against concrete abuses committed against the Indians or hacienda workers. But they did so without questioning the system itself.

Indian Pastoral Legislation

In the sixteenth and seventeenth centuries the great Lima councils gave high priority to the topic of the Indians in order to evangelize them more efficiently. However, in the republican period, generally only the bishops and priests who worked in the mountains and the southern highlands gave much attention to the Indians. The national episcopal assemblies, which reflected more the official, Lima-centered Peru, gave scant attention to the world of the Indians. A review of the pastoral letters of the bishops in the mountain regions as well as of the synods and church congresses they organized will show that the Andean church did speak out very clearly in defense of the Indians. This was certainly not the image of the church the liberals painted. For them, the church was paternalistic and insensitive toward the plight of

The Rural and Andean Church 193

the Indians. Yet there existed a pro-Indian movement within the church that paralleled the pro-Indian movement of the liberals. In general, the Andean church centered its attention on three topics: the cultural backwardness of the Indians, the abuses committed against them by merchants and *gamonales*, and the abuses committed by priests.

One of the liberals' favorite caricatures was that of the priest as a narrow-minded (i.e., antiliberal) reactionary who held the Indian villages in a state of backwardness. The truth was, however, that it was the priests themselves who most complained about the low educational level of the peasants and the village dwellers. In 1848 the doctrine-priest of Cabana in the department of Junín described the cultural level of his doctrine:

> The ignorance of Cabana progresses in direct proportion to its principal defects, its immorality, its stinginess, and its customs in general. The word "custom" has a peculiar force here: it is considered more sacred than any other principle. The women are in general less lazy than the men, and they are also more contentious. The men never govern the women by the force of reason, but rather by the force of blows.[46]

In a circular letter sent to the provinces announcing vacancies for pastors, Archbishop Luna Pizarro referred to the "deep ignorance, the blatant vices of so many unhappy Indians."[47] The archbishop made this comment in the context of exhorting the rural priests to learn Quechua in order to have more influence over the Indians. But these two generalizations made by the priest in Cabana and the archbishop also reveal their own cultural and psychological distance from the Indians. A third testimony is that of Bishop Ampuero of Puno in 1912 who complained about the ignorance and superstitious practices of the Indians: "The ignorance of the Indians is woeful. Their religious beliefs are minimal. Their religion is an adulterated Christianity. It consists in having a Mass said or praying before the image of a saint when someone is sick or dying or when a llama has gotten lost or a *misti* (a white man) tries to steal some land or commit some other abuse."[48]

This rather acid commentary sums up the church's view of the Indians and their beliefs and religious practices. Far from favoring such practices, the rural priests were perpetually perplexed about how to deal with a religious worldview that was foreign to their way of thinking.

Other points of interest for the church were the abuses committed against the Indians either by laymen or by churchmen. The constitutions of the diocesan synod of Puno of 1868, presided over by Bishop Ambrosio Huerta, offer a good sample of church legislation with respect to the Indians. The synod condemned the merchants who extorted the Indians: "The merchants who deal in wool, gold, dyes, and herds have no right to force the Indians to sell their wares. . . . A merchant who does so commits a grave sin that shall be reserved to the bishop to forgive."[49]

The synod also denounced merchants who provoked drunkenness among the Indians in order to increase the demand for alcohol. It also singled out for special criticism the *tinterillo* (so-called because he wrote documents with *tinta*, "ink"), the barely literate mestizo who served as an accomplice of the whites in their exploitation of the Indians. The synod's documents condemned the superstitions practiced by the Indians as well as drunkenness during feast days. Finally, Huerta and the synod delegates censured "any priest who drinks regularly or who lives in concubinage" or "who traffics in prayers, Masses, etc."[50]

The church was especially concerned over the many abuses committed during the community feasts, such as heavy drinking and exorbitant spending. The liberal press accused the church itself of fostering these feasts precisely to earn more money. But the church's legislation in the Andean region clearly condemned those practices. The synod under Huerta also criticized the custom of commissioning a member of the community, called in some localities the *alférez* ("lieutenant"), with organizing the feast. The reason was that the person was expected to spend all his earnings to make the feast a success. The synod, of course, forbade the priests from accepting anything but a reasonable and modest sum for their services during the feast.[51]

The Congress of Social Action, 1921

Undoubtedly the best example of the pastoral concern the church had for the Indians during this period was the Congress of Social Action held in May of 1921 in Cuzco. The dioceses that participated made up the southern Andean region: Cuzco, Puno, Arequipa, and Ayacucho. The main organizers were Bishop Pedro Pascual Farfán of Cuzco and the diocesan clergy of Cuzco, especially the canon Isaías Vargas, and the priest Hernando Vega Centeno. The nearly sixty delegates who attended included priests, religious, and laypersons. The congress was motivated in large part by *Rerum Novarum* (1891) as well the spread of socialist ideas, the new worker's movement, and most of all the frequent Indian uprisings in the south.

The southern Andean region was the nerve center of the Indian problem in Peru, where both exploitation and violence were the greatest. Between 1895 and 1900 a series of Indian rebellions broke out in the region around Lake Titicaca, and in 1915 a mestizo sergeant who assumed the name of "Rumi Maqui" ("Hand of Rock") led a major rebellion in the area. The presence of Albert Giesecke at the inauguration of the congress had important symbolic significance. Giesecke was both the mayor of the city and rector of San Antonio Abad University. An American by birth, he strenuously promoted Indian studies at the university. A year earlier, Haya de la Torre had chosen Cuzco as the site of the first student congress in Peru, which gave birth to the popular universities.

The purpose of the congress was to propose ways and means of bettering the moral condition of Indians, workers, and women.[52] The congress proposed the creation of school-workshops for educating the Indians and the publication of catechisms in Quechua and Aymara. It also called for the founding of Catholic Circles, libraries, and self-help societies for the workers. It recommended that anti-alcohol leagues be founded for Indians and workers. Furthermore, it exhorted Catholics to support the new Catholic University, founded in Lima in 1917. Although most of the reform proposals pertained to educational and humanitarian programs, the congress also addressed the subject of social justice. Concretely, it called upon textile factory owners to lower their prices to lighten the burden for sheep-raisers and peasants in general.

This reformism was tempered by warnings against solutions or movements that the congress considered too radical, including socialism (referred to as "bolshevism"), "revolutionary feminism," and, naturally, Protestantism.[53] One single speaker, Isaías Vargas, stood out for the strong criticism he made of the system of exploitation. The young cathedral canon asked the congress to study "the Indians' right to property" because, he pointed out, the Indian rebellions were provoked by *gamonales* who usurped their lands.[54] Vargas called for the founding of "Indians' unions" to defend their rights, although he also said that these unions should be under government "protection."[55]

Farfán and the Indians

The bishop, Pedro Pascual Farfán, considered himself a defender of the Indians. Born in Cuzco in 1870, his family went back to Lorenzo Farfán de los Godos, a creole who organized a subversive movement in the same year as the uprising of Tupac Amaru. Farfán entered the seminary in 1886 and was ordained in 1894. After serving as rector of the seminary, in 1907 he was appointed bishop of Huaraz, in the north central Andes. Already at that early date he began taking up the cause of the Indians. In 1913 he convoked the first synod of that diocese. The synod called for the creation of a society or "league" of male Indians in each parish in order to raise their cultural and intellectual level.[56] In 1918 he returned as bishop to his native city and from the beginning established the advancement of the Indians as his principal policy. In August of that year he wrote a pastoral letter in Spanish and in Quechua addressed to the Indians. In April 1920 he wrote another to the hacienda landowners, "A Pastoral Exhortation on the Protection of the Indians."[57]

Two years after the Congress of Social Action, Farfán summoned the fourth diocesan synod, which ratified the pro-Indian resolutions of 1921. The synod went on to propose the founding of parochial schools to educate the Indians and a special section in the seminary for Indians.[58]

Farfán played an especially important role as president of the departmental *Junta* of Indian Patronage. In 1922 President Leguía had created the "Patronage of the Indian Race," to be presided over by distinguished citizens, intellectuals, and churchmen, in order to hear the complaints of the Indians and investigate their causes. The official pro-Indian stance of Leguía, however, called for hearing complaints but not for changing reality. Farfán devoted himself zealously to his new task. He received letters and delegations of peasants who presented their complaints about the local *gamonales*. The first few lines of this letter sent by the Indians of Langui-Layo in August 1921 capture the general tenor of the complaints: "We, the undersigned, your sons, parishioners of the parish of Langui-Layo, place ourselves humbly before you and make it known that not only have the *gamonales* taken away our lands but they have also taken away the lands of the church. . . ."[59]

Although the members of the Indian Patronage were well-intentioned, they were completely subordinate to the interests of President Leguía. They never had the power to effect real change. Farfán himself was not very enthusiastic about sending out messages of protest to the great landowners around Cuzco because he knew them all personally.[60] The patronage, as well as the congresses, synods, and pastoral letters of the church, revealed the limits of the church's reformism. Without doubt the church was genuinely concerned about the Indians' plight. But it had no power to change the fundamental structures of the agrarian world. Furthermore, although its pastoral legislation reflected the positive tone of *Rerum Novarum* in favor of the workers, it spoke at times in such paternalistic terms that it weakened the force of its call for reform. The synod of 1923, for example, proposed marriages between Indians and whites as a way to avoid racial tensions![61] The church also called upon the large landowners to practice social justice voluntarily by paying a more just salary to their Indian laborers and by reducing their work load for the good of their health. The synod invited the hacienda owners and the Indians to live in peace, but it made no proposal for a fundamental change in their relations: "The synod calls for reconciliation. It casts a loving eye on whites, Indians, hacienda owners, field and factory workers. It calls upon them not to forget that, no matter what one's station in life, all are brothers and sisters under God, and therefore everyone owes each other mutual respect and love."[62]

The church's reformism was basically educational and humanitarian in scope, as opposed to the more revolutionary orientation of the other pro-Indian intellectuals. The church's reservations about radical solutions were based in part on *Rerum Novarum*, which rejected both communism and violence. But the priests of that period also lacked any training in the social sciences, which, besides being new, were still heavily charged with antireligious bias. Furthermore, most of the priests came from middle-class families and were reluctant to sympathize with radical change. More concretely, many of them depended on the rent they earned from church properties. Finally, religion had been the legitimizing force of order for so long that it was difficult to distinguish between order and religion.

But there was another limitation to all the pro-Indian movements of that period: the nonparticipation of the Indians themselves. In a pastoral letter of April 1920, Farfán wrote with some realism, "Our Indians do not even know that their bishop is concerned about them, nor will they even know about this pastoral letter."[63] Nevertheless, within a few years the peasants did come to know the bishop, judging by the great number of protest letters he received from the Indian communities as head of the Indian Patronage. There were other indications that both he and the canon, Isaías Vargas, maintained a close relation with the peasants. In May 1928 the first eucharistic congress in Peruvian church history was held in the old Inca capital. At a Mass Farfán celebrated at Sacsahuamán, the great Inca fortress outside of Cuzco, more than a thousand Indians attended and received Communion. It was through the liturgy and other rituals, feasts days, and daily parish life that Andean dwellers established vital contact with the church.

Pastoral Action and Politics

The pastoral relationship between the church and the Indians was always complex and ambiguous, and it became more so in republican times. During the colonial period the church, with its preaching and presence, tended to legitimize the established order. Even priests who defended the Indians against abuses or criticized the king's officials did so without questioning the political and social system itself.

With the coming of liberalism, the church grew increasingly hostile toward the various liberal governments, especially when they tried to touch the church's privileges and properties. However, this antigovernment posture was not the same as questioning the social order. Throughout the entire nineteenth century the church continued to fulfill its role of protecting the Indians against specific abuses. There were bishops and priests who courageously took a stand in defense of the Indians against the army or the *gamonales*. But these clergymen, with few exceptions, were also political conservatives who opposed liberalism.

The various Indian uprisings in the last century and at the beginning of the present century help bring to light the complex relationship between the church and the Indians.[64] The church fulfilled three basic roles during those uprisings: that of defender of the Indians against the government and the landowners; that of arbiter between the political authorities and the Indians; and that of spokesperson for the government itself to the Indians. These three roles sum up the relationship of the church to the peasantry: on some occasions, a defender; on others, a moderating force; and on still others, a legitimator of the status quo.

The Church as Defender

A man notably consistent in practice with his pastoral statements was Juan Ambrosio Huerta, the first bishop of the diocese of Puno, established in 1861. The constitutions of the first diocesan synod referred to above condemned certain abuses explicitly, especially the practice of forcing Indians to buy or sell goods. The section entitled "Sins Reserved to the Bishop" specifically singled out the "dealer in wool, gold, coca, or livestock who forces the Indians to sell to him."[65]

This condemnation was no doubt inspired by a personal experience Huerta had when he intervened as a mediator in an uprising in 1866 caused in large part by that particular abuse. In November of that year several thousand Indians from the entire region around Lake Titicaca rose in rebellion and took over the small town of Huancané. Huerta managed to save the lives of the government officials there, but he was soon called upon to defend the Indians. When the army that had been sent to "pacify" the Indians arrived, Huerta went out to meet it, hoping to prevent a bloodbath. The commanding officer paid no attention to him and marched on the town, killing many Indians and their animals.

Years later, when he was bishop of Arequipa, Huerta referred to this incident in a pastoral letter. He blamed the exploiters and the army for the uprising, and he also expressed sympathy for the Indians: "When I made my first pastoral visit, it caused me great sorrow to see the tyrannical and inhuman way the traffickers in wool and gold and the local political authorities treated the Indians. These and many other abuses we could mention provoked the Indians to explode in a violent uprising."[66]

The year after the uprising another one broke out in the same region under the leadership of Colonel Juan Bustamante, a known defender of the Indians and a friend of Huerta. In 1868 Bustamante was defeated and killed by another army commander. On the occasion of these two uprisings, the directors of *El Comercio* in Lima founded the first defense group for the Indians in republican times, the Society of Friends of the Indians. The society proclaimed Bartholomew de las Casas as its patron and among its first activities published a circular letter that criticized the church for being an accomplice in the exploitation of the Indians. What was most interesting, however, was the fact that there were several priests who belonged to the society. Little is known about them. The Catholic press praised them for their "good will" but also warned them against the liberal tendencies of the society's founders.[67]

It is clear that there were churchmen in the last century, like Huerta and the priests in the Society of the Friends of the Indians, who actively took the part of the Indians. Although they never proposed any fundamental structural reform, their mentality did anticipate the more radical stance of a later time.

The Church as Mediator

On other occasions, the church played the role of reconciler between the government and the Indians without necessarily favoring one against the other. In March 1885 the Indians around Huaraz rose up in rebellion under the Indian mayor Pedro Pablo Atusparia and for two months controlled the Callejón de Huaylas. The main causes of the rebellion were the general poverty of the country after the war with Chile, the reimposition of the head tax for Indians, and the violent methods used by the prefect to collect the taxes.

The principal mediator between the Indians and the white population was a young priest named Fidel Olivas Escudero. Throughout the entire uprising, Olivas Escudero acted as an exemplary mediator, representing both sides at the same time. Atusparia respected the young priest and listened to his petitions to preserve the white population. Atusparia was a practicing Christian and he, too, desired peace. When the army defeated the Indian leader, Olivas Escudero interceded for him and the other Indians and managed to save many lives.

Less conciliating in his attitudes, however, was "Uchcu" Pedro, the number two leader of the rebellion. "Uchcu" (which means "mine tunnel") Pedro, a miner from Carhuaz, represented the more radical faction of the Indians. But he, too, accepted the mediatorship of Olivas Escudero on at least two occasions. On the first occasion he sent the young priest as his emissary to demand the surrender of Yungay in April of that year. When the townsfolk refused to do so, "Uchcu" Pedro marched on the town and killed many of the white inhabitants. On the second occasion, when Atusparia had been defeated outside of Huaraz in the first days of May, "Uchcu" Pedro fled toward the Cordillera Negra (the Black Range) between the Callejón de Huaylas and the coast. This time the government sent Olivas Escudero as their delegate to demand the surrender of "Uchcu" Pedro. The Indian leader refused and continued to resist until September, when he was captured and shot.

Two conclusions can be drawn from Olivas Escudero's role in this Indian uprising. In the first place, the priest certainly displayed considerable courage and moral rectitude, qualities that undoubtedly made him a good mediator. But, unlike Huerta in the southern Andean region, Olivas Escudero did not sympathize with the rebellion. In the funeral sermon he delivered for those killed during the uprising, he referred to "our unfortunate helots, who on account of their ignorance and uncontrollable passions were incited to rebel by blind and at times malicious leaders...."[68] Olivas Escudero, a man of peace, did not sympathize with anyone who disrupted the peace that he esteemed so highly. He believed his mission in life was to maintain order as a precondition for peace.

The Church as Legitimizer of the Status Quo

The role the church assumed with greatest frequency was that of collaborator with the government in maintaining order. Examples of that role can be found in letters and reports of the government itself. In 1896 an Indian rebellion broke out in Huanta, in the central Andes. The immediate cause of the rebellion was the government's abusive monopoly on the selling of salt. But in this case there were also two rival hacienda owners who instigated the Indians against one another. The central government sent an expedition under Colonel Domingo Parra to "pacify" the area. Parra reached Huanta in November and by the middle of December had the situation under control. Parra himself expressed his satisfaction over the fact that force was not necessary to take control of one of the towns. The local priest, wrote Parra, "helped very much in pacifying his community and the surrounding areas...."[69]

In another instance, toward the end of the century a series of uprisings broke out in the entire region around Lake Titicaca. Although the fundamental reason for these uprisings was the system of exploitation, the reports of government officials also point to the church as partially responsible. In a report from Puno in 1895 the official in charge of putting down an uprising in Chucuito stated: "It seems rather obvious to me that the frequent uprisings of the Indians are caused not so much by the abject state and apathy of the Indians but by the arrogance and harshness with which the political, judicial, and church authorities treat them...."[70]

In all of these situations the church also participated in the "pacification" process. The subprefect in charge of restoring order in the town of Ilave, where a major rebellion had broken out in 1897, mentioned in his report that he brought an Aymara-speaking priest, Fermín Manrique, along with him "so he can use his religious influence to dissuade the Indians from rebelling."[71] The governor of the same area noted that as a remedy against future uprisings he had brought in a special mission of Franciscans to keep the peace among the Indians.[72] These and other testimonies underline the church's role as legitimizer of the established order.

Popular Religious Organizations

Within the world of Peruvian popular religiosity there is a great variety of devotions, processions, and customs that differ from region to region. These processions and practices are almost always linked to certain organizations with deep historical roots, the confraternities and the brotherhoods. In the sixteenth century the Spanish founded and spread these religious associations, which were copies of similar ones in Spain, as key instruments for evangelizing. The confraternities and brotherhoods were the basic ways by which people belonged to the church. The laity who belonged to them learned the truths of Christianity, received the sacraments, and practiced certain devotions within the context of these popular organizations. Whereas the parish represented the basic juridical reality in the church, the confraternity and similar associations were the basic ecclesial structures within which people lived out their Christianity. In colonial Lima there were only five parishes. But within each one there were a great number of associations, confraternities, and brotherhoods that gathered the faithful together according to their race, sex, profession, and favorite devotion.

These lay organizations shared certain common characteristics. With the church's approval and under the protection of the Virgin Mary, the members committed themselves to fulfill certain religious obligations, such as celebrating the feast of their patron saint. The statutes of these associations usually included the obligation to help one another in moments of need or to perform some work of mercy.[73] Frequently, they had their own chapel or private altar within the parish church, and they had their own chaplain. Although in many cases no real difference existed, a brotherhood was a purely religious association that chose Mary or another saint as its principal object of devotion. The confraternity, in contrast, more noticeably emphasized membership by race, profession, or social status.[74] There were confraternities for Spaniards and others for mestizos, Indians, and blacks. Furthermore, the confraternities possessed goods and properties to defray the costs of the devotion and to carry out their charitable works. In this sense, the confraternities were a mirror of society itself, with its racial and corporative categories.

In the country the confraternities complemented the doctrine.

Whereas the doctrine represented the formal ecclesiastical jurisdiction, the confraternity and other pious associations directly represented the people themselves. They became in time the most popular and deeply rooted organizations anywhere in Latin America. Some authors even believe that the confraternity was a sort of substitution or continuation of the *ayllu*, the basic earth cell of pre-Inca times.[75] Very often in rural areas there was no "confraternity" in the same sense as in the city. Rather, the entire community adopted a single special devotion to the patron saint of the town. In this case the devotion "belonged" to the town, and the townsfolk collectively committed themselves to practice that devotion.[76] A town member participated in the annual procession in honor of the town's patron as a right and as an obligation.

The community's devotion did not always correspond to the territorial limits of the doctrine. The doctrine usually consisted of two or three towns and many smaller clusters of homes close to haciendas. But the basic loyalty of the people was not to the doctrine but to the patron saint of the community. The anthropologist, Richard Adams, studied the case of a conflict between two communities in the department of Junín, near Jauja: Muquiyauyo and Huaripampa. The two communities belonged to a single parish since colonial times, but the parish church was located in Huaripampa. The townsfolk in Muquiyauyo resented the fact they they had to contribute to the support of a priest and religious activities in another town.[77] Such conflicts have always occurred everywhere in the Andes, especially in situations in which the juridical limits do not correspond to social realities. The people in the typical Andean community are so deeply attached to their patron saint that they cannot imagine "sharing" it with another community. On the other hand, there are certain regional devotions that do not fall under this rule. The most notable in Peru are the devotions to the Virgin of Alta Gracia in Ayaviri, the Virgin of Chapi in Arequipa, Qollur Rit'i near Cuzco, and the Lord of the Ascension in Cachuy.[78]

The bond between the community and its devotion was an organic unity that touched all spheres of life, including the economic. From colonial times on, the members of the community cultivated lands set aside for the support of the devotion and the community feast day. Just as the feast was considered a community act, so too the lands "of all the saints" were considered as belonging to the entire community.[79] Originally, these lands were conceded by the church to the communities. But it was never clearly defined whether they belonged to the community or to the church. This ambiguity gave rise to many legal battles between the church and the communities in the twentieth century, especially whenever the church attempted to sell them. The confraternities and the feast days also fulfilled and still fulfill functions that were not strictly religious. The religious feasts, for example, obviously serve as occasions for celebrating, but they also serve as "safety valves" to let off social tensions. In many Andean communities the celebration of a feast or Holy Week is the occasion for competition between two rival bands or confraternities to see which one can put on a better show or organize a better sporting event. The excessive spending during the feasts also serves a social and economic function: to level off wealth and spread it among the entire community. The confraternities also function as social clubs that allow community members to acquire status within the community. To be named the *mayordomo* or the *alférez* (steward) of the feast is considered a mark of esteem. Finally, at least until the advent of the liberals, the confraternities also functioned as credit cooperatives.

These religious organizations suffered the fate of many traditions that have been swept aside by the advance of modernization. They began to decline in the second part of the nineteenth century, which coincides with the crisis of the priest shortage. The liberals greatly restricted their economic activities, and the migrations from country to town and from town to the coast also weakened them. Finally, the advent of Protestantism in many towns hastened their decline.

Bolivar and most successive liberal governments refused to recognize the Indian communities, leaving them without any legal protection from the landowners. In the decade of the fifties of the last century, the liberals intensified their campaign against the church and sought to bring the confraternities under control. In 1855 a junta was created to inspect the confraternities in order to make an inventory of their capital and properties. In 1865 control over their own money was transferred to the benevolent societies. As a result, an open battle broke out between the confraternities and the local benevolent societies.

In fact, the confraternities resisted the laws that ordered them to turn over their wealth. They frequently resorted to legal subterfuges. Celestino and Meyers cite the case of a confraternity in Jauja in the thirties that sold its own goods to different organizations that, it turned out, all belonged to the confraternity.[80] The church, assuming a right it did not really have, attempted to sell the lands owned by the confraternities to forestall their being confiscated by the benevolent societies. In the case of the community of Muquiyauyo, which Adams studied, the bishop of Huánuco tried to sell the confraternities' lands in 1931, but the townsfolk opposed the bishop and finally bought the lands themselves in 1938. Naturally, they were somewhat resentful because they believed that those lands belonged to the "town" in the first place.[81]

The benevolent societies finally won the battle. As the confraternities lost their lands and wealth, they also lost some of their religious and social prestige. They could no longer organize sumptuous feasts, at least on the same scale as before. An interesting example of the relationship between economy and feasts was discovered by the researchers of the Cornell-Vicos project. They observed that a noticeable consequence of the new prosperity in Vicos that resulted from the injection of new changes in the community was that the feasts also grew in number and pomp.[82]

But another important consequence of the liberals' attack on the church was the latter's loss of social control over the peasant communities. With the elimination of the tithes and the growing shortage of priests in rural areas, the church could no longer oblige the communities to pay their dues to the church or go to Mass on Sundays or other days of obligation. In his study of Muquiyauyo, Adams traced the decline of many customs and religious feasts. In 1887, for example, the mayor of the town still fulfilled his ancient obligation of warning the community members to go to Sunday Mass, and even of forcing them if necessary. But the crisis of control had already begun, because that year there were no *mayordomos* for the celebration of some of the big feasts, and in 1891 the governor of the district complained that many people no longer went to the Sunday doctrine classes.[83] Adams concluded that an important factor explaining this change was the relationship between the Indians and the mestizos. With diminished church influence, the Indians who lived in the outlying fields preferred not to go to town except when necessary. The town, as Uriel García stressed in *El Nuevo indio*, was the habitat mainly of mestizos.[84]

Finally, some other social factors accelerated the process of transformation or disintegration of the confraternities. In the latter part of the nineteenth century and all through the twentieth, Andean mountain dwellers migrated to the coast or mining centers looking for work. These migratory waves had their impact on the church. In 1916 Bishop Irigoyen of Trujillo noted that many inhabitants in the town of Olmos had begun to migrate on account of the "poor harvests." The bishop was forced to unite the parish in Olmos with the parish in the neighboring town of Motupe.[85] In the decade of the twenties, President Leguía accelerated the process of migrations with legislation favoring road projects connecting the mountains with the coast. After the Second World War Peru underwent a population explosion. But in the mountains the population increase augmented the poverty, thereby pressuring even more people to leave.[86] As a result, many confraternities and feast-day celebrations disappeared in the Andes. New religious associations have taken their place. They are usually run by the emerging mestizo class.

As the church's social control diminished in the rural areas, many customs and feasts increasingly lost their original religious meaning. The anthropologist Efraín Morote observed that in many of the most outlying towns there are confraternities that are not approved by the church. In these cases, a religious feast is generally a pretext for a celebration. These "spontaneous" confraternities use the feast as the occasion for an all-out splurge, in which eating, drinking, and having a bullfight far outweigh the celebration of Mass, if there is one.[87] Nevertheless, the positive influence of the confraternities and other popular organizations should be stressed, too. Largely because of these organizations the towns throughout the Andes have maintained their cultural identity, especially in the face of the prolonged absence of the institutional church. In view of the accusation of pro-Indian liberals who claimed that Andean dwellers practiced a superficial Catholicism, one is surprised rather by the widespread tenacity of many Catholic traditions and customs in the most remote settlements in the Andes.

Each year twelve "holy men," dressed in white togas, prepare the celebration of Holy Week with great care, while other townsfolk organize the traditional processions in which the risen Christ "encounters" the Virgin Mary. On the feast of All Saints community dwellers go in procession annually to visit the tombs of their ancestors. All these activities are done without the presence of priests. The survival of these and other traditions is due to the popular rural religious organizations. In the post-Vatican II years, priests and pastoral agents have discovered that their task in these priestless areas of Peru is not so much to "evangelize" as to "reevangelize," that is, to build upon a sixteenth century Catholicism that is still deeply rooted everywhere in rural Peru and especially in the Andes.

7
The Militant Laity, 1930-1955

The overthrow of Augusto B. Leguía on August 22, 1930, signaled the end of the peaceful but precarious order that sustained the rule of the oligarchy. During the 1931 presidential elections, the popular classes on the coast emerged as decisive political actors, some favoring Haya de la Torre and others, Sánchez Cerro. Although the latter won, the populist radicalism of the Aprista Party continued to be a permanent force in Peruvian politics. In the face of this politicization of the popular classes, the oligarchy had recourse to the army to restore order. For approximately the next twenty-five years Peruvian society became sharply polarized between two antagonistic forces: on the one hand, the Aprista party (also referred to as APRA), made up of large sectors of the popular classes and some groups from the middle classes, and on the other, the oligarchy, the army, and middle-class groups. The peasantry remained on the margin of this initial politicization process. This state of tension, which broke out into a near civil war in 1932, remained unchanged until the fifties, when new parties and personalities emerged to offer new alternatives.

This turbulent and agitated period also marked a change of direction for the church. Because of his close ties to Leguía's regime, Archbishop Lissón was forced to leave the country and resign. His successors, Mariano Holguín, who acted as apostolic administrator between 1931 and 1933, and Pedro Pascual Farfán, who was named the new archbishop (1933–45), assumed the difficult task of recovering some of the church's lost prestige and of guiding the church in the middle of hostile forces that sharply questioned its role in society. Liberal anticlericalism, already very strong in the national universities and in intellectual circles, became even more recalcitrant. In the constitutional congress of 1931–33 (so called because it wrote a new constitution and legislated at the same time), followers of Sánchez Cerro, Apristas, socialists, and others, irrespective of the differences among themselves, all united in their opposition to the church. But it was APRA that posed the greatest threat. In the 1931 campaign the more radical Apristas called for the separation of church and state, universal lay education, the expulsion of foreign clergy, and the nationalization of church property. After the elections, the persecuted Aprista party turned into a quasi-messianic crusade, with the charismatic Haya de la Torre as its leader. APRA, somewhat like the fascist movements in Europe, functioned as a closed society and demanded absolute loyalty of its members. But anticlericalism had also become fashionable in conservative circles. Increasingly, the church became a fortress in a state of permanent siege.

In order to face this crisis the bishops gave the highest priority to the creation of a well-formed laity. The old Catholic Union of Gentlemen was by then moribund. At the same time a whole new generation, educated in religious schools or formed in certain select groups, displayed a militant enthusiasm comparable to that of the Apristas. This was the generation that gave rise to Catholic Action, founded in 1935. The new laity also characterized itself by its greater independence from the hierarchy and by its greater awareness of the church's social teachings. The Catholics in the congress of 1896 had also expressed their social concern for Indians and workers, but they never realized the ideological implications of *Rerum Novarum*. The militants of the thirties studied the writings of Jacques Maritain and listened attentively to lectures by Víctor Andrés Belaunde on the church's social doctrine. In the fifties and sixties they were also influenced by the French Dominican, Louis-Joseph Lebret. These were the years that gave birth to "social Christianity," a movement inspired by the papal social encyclicals that proposed to create a new social order, neither capitalist nor Marxist.

Social Christianity also represented the first substantial advance in Catholic thought since the conservative positions of Bartolomé Herrera. But the new thought currents also gave rise to differences among Catholics. In the thirties Catholicism in Peru encompassed a wide spectrum of tendencies, ranging from the democratic views of Víctor Andrés Belaunde to the authoritarian concepts of José de la Riva-Agüero. But these differences were not very noticeable at the time because Catholics were drawn together in a common cause against outside enemies. The laity of this period also displayed an intellectual creativity that had been missing before in the church. The laity were often better formed than the clergy. With the exception of some priests, the clergy lacked the necessary education to serve as guides or moderators to the new lay groups.

The thirties and forties were years of formation and preparation. Under Presidents Bustamante (1945–48) and Odría (1948–56) many leaders of Catholic Action went into politics, giving rise to the Christian Democratic Party. Others became priests, thereby interjecting a new social consciousness into the ranks of the clergy. This was a period of transition from a relatively monolithic and closed church to one that would become more pluralistic and open. But not all within the church experienced this change of mentality, and not all changed at the same rate. The more progressive groups were really small enclaves within a still generally conservative church. In fact, the majority of priests and religious women changed very little during those years. The rural and Andean church continued to be a bulwark of tradition. The arrival of the priests of Maryknoll in 1943 rather abruptly introduced a modernizing influence into the southern Andean region. Small though they were, these progressive groups paved the way for the changes that typified the period of Vatican II.

Early Groups

From the end of the last century on, the church had promoted the concept of "Catholic Action." But the pope who really gave meaning to the phrase was Pius XI (1922–39). Similarly, the bishops in Peru referred to "Catholic Action" long before it really existed. Catholic Action emerged as the spontaneous creation of many smaller groups created at different times and by different people. When Catholic Action was formally founded during the eucharistic congress of 1935, it was really constructed on other groups that had existed for many years.

In their collective pastoral letter of 1905 the bishops emphasized the importance of "Catholic Action." Under that term they included the Catholic Union, the Catholic Youth, and the Catholic Worker's Circles.[1] In 1912, in another collective message, the bishops added a nuance when they spoke of "Catholic Social Action."[2] By "social action," however, they principally meant defending the church. Again in 1923 the episcopal assembly called for the creation of "Catholic Social Action" throughout the entire country.[3]

One of the most important promoters of Catholic Action was Pedro Pablo Drinot y Piérola. Born in Callao, he studied at Santo

Toribio seminary and later entered the congregation of the Sacred Hearts. He continued his studies in Chile where he encountered some Catholic Action groups. In 1904 he was named bishop of Huánuco. In his pastoral letters he displayed deep concern for the Indians and associated the concept of Catholic action with defense of the Indians: "With the Indians and for them we should organize a modern, strong, and loving Catholic Action."[4] In 1920 he resigned his post for health reasons and was then named national moderator of the Catholic Union of Women, based in Lima. He also set about promoting the idea of a national Catholic Action movement. In 1928 he personally distributed Pius XI's letter on "Principles and General Bases of Catholic Action," and in 1929 he organized and presided over the first general meeting of all the different groups of Catholic youth in Lima.[5]

The Center for Catholic Youth

In 1895 the Jesuit Manuel Fernández de Córdoba founded one of the earliest groups, known as the "Center for Catholic Youth," in Colegio La Inmaculada. Most of the members of the center, which was based on the model of the Marian sodalities of the Society of Jesus, were students or former students of the Jesuits. The principal moderators in those years were Manuel Abreu and Juan Albacete, both Jesuits. In 1931 the steering committee was made up by Cargín Allison, Manuel Vélez, Jorge Arce, Henry Loveday, and David Vega Christie, all to be founders of the national Catholic Action movement.[6] The center celebrated its fortieth anniversary in 1935 with three hundred former students on hand, including Víctor Andrés Belaunde (a graduate of the Jesuit school in Arequipa) and Carlos Arenas y Loayza, a former president of the Catholic Union and at that time prime minister of the country.[7]

The Center of Catholic Extension

In 1915 Father Jorge Dintilhac of the Sacred Hearts founded a group called "Catholic Youth Action." Most of the members were students at Colegio La Recoleta. Among the principal founders were Ismael Biélich, a future minister under President Bustamante y Rivero, and Javier Correa y Elías. In 1930 Father Dintilhac changed the name to the Center of Catholic Extension. It was open to all university students, most of whom came from the Catholic University. Some of the leading lights of the center were César Arróspide de la Flor, Gerardo Alarco, Ernesto Alayza

Grundy, José Pareja Paz Soldán, David Vega Christie, and Alberto Wagner de Reyna. The moderator for years was Father Plácido Ayala of the Sacred Hearts Fathers.[8]

There were other groups on the university level, but of short duration. In 1924 José León Bueno founded the literary club "Novecientos" (The Nineties) at San Marcos University to discuss the ideas of novelists and well-known Catholic thinkers in Europe such as Paul Claudel, Jacques Maritain, and Gilbert Keith Chesterton. The group lasted a year.[9]

Youth Social Action

In 1926 César Arróspide founded one of the more important movements, Youth Social Action. Arróspide, destined to be the key figure in Peruvian Catholic Action, graduated from La Recoleta and studied law at San Marcos University. His movement was modeled on the YMCA, precisely because the "Y" was believed to be the avant-garde of Protestant proselytism. Youth Social Action attracted several hundred youths who engaged in sports and religious and other cultural activities. Although Arróspide and his aides maintained cordial relations with the hierarchy, and a Jesuit priest, Vicente Sánchez, acted as their adviser, they intentionally played down their clerical ties in order to emphasize the lay character of their movement.

In spite of their initial success, by 1928 Arróspide had doubts over his own foundation. In a letter he sent that year to Bishop Farfán in Cuzco he revealed what the problem was: "The association grew rapidly, bringing together a multitude of young men, perhaps seven hundred altogether; but, to be truthful, only a handful were really practicing Catholics. . . ."[10]

Quite obviously, the youths had more interest in sports than in religion.

Fides Center

This lesson led Arróspide, Gerardo Alarco, Roberto Pérez del Pozo, Ernesto Alayza Grundy, and others to found a new and more select organization, Fides Center. Founded on August 22, 1930, Fides represented many of the best and committed lay youth of Lima, drawn mainly from university and professional circles. Fides functioned as a forum for ventilating the major intellectual and social topics of the day. Among the more frequent speakers were Víctor Andrés Belaunde, José de la Riva-Agüero, and Raúl Porras Barrenechea. In 1933 Fides combined forces with another group, Center of Catholic Students, but as a consequence it lost its original character. In 1940 it appeared once again as an independent group but ceased to function in the years 1944–47. In 1949 it was reborn again with a new generation formed in Catholic Action and UNEC (the student wing of Catholic Action). Frequent speakers in this second period of its existence were Luis Bedoya Reyes, Fernando Belaúnde Terry (the future president), Ernesto Alayza Grundy, Edgardo Seoane, Fernando Stiglich, and the priests Eduardo Picher and Angel de la Puerta. It also had its own publication, *Fides*, directed at various periods by Antonio Espinosa Laña, Alfonso Baella, and Antonio Lulli. Although Fides Center was not directly founded by Catholic Action, it nevertheless served the same purpose for young professionals. It also followed the same path as Catholic Action and by the middle of the fifties had ceased to exist.[11]

The Catholic Center of Miraflores

In 1929 Amelio Placencia, a Vincentian priest, founded the Catholic Center of Miraflores (Lima). Placencia, who had lived in Mexico for eighteen years as head of the seminary in Oaxaca, was deeply influenced by the Mexican revolution. He believed it urgent to teach Latin American Catholics the church's social message. In weekly meetings with the youth at his parish, he devoted himself to doing just that. The youths he directed also taught night classes to workers at a center he had founded in Surquillo, a lower middle-class district of Lima. A direct fruit of this experience was the creation of a Center for Catholic Working Youth in 1936. Placencia was also the moderator for the Catholic Center of Barranco, and in 1943 he was named national moderator of UNEC.[12] Among the best-known youth leaders of the Miraflores center were Ernesto Alayza Grundy and Germán Stiglich. Alayza, a student at La Recoleta, was a cofounder of the Christian Democratic Party and later on of the Popular Christian Party.

Other Centers in Lima and in the Provinces

In 1931 Eduardo Suárez Jimena cofounded the Catholic Center of Chorrillos (Lima).[13] Raúl Rebagliati was another of the founders, and he served as president of the Catholic Center of Barranco. Gerardo Alarco was the president and moderator of Labor Center in Callao.

Similar groups sprang up in the provinces. In Arequipa in 1925 Father Juan Guevara, later on to be Cardinal Guevara, founded the first Catholic Action group in that city. Among its members were certain very well known names: Rafael Belaunde,

Guillermo Marcó del Pont, Manuel E. de Piérola, and the brothers Alberto, Roberto, and Alfredo López de Romaña.[14] In the diocese of Trujillo from 1912 on there were several small parish groups with the name of "Catholic Action," especially in Simbal and Ascope.[15] The most important promoter was the bishop, Carlos García Irigoyen (1910–36). In 1920 he created the Diocesan Council of Catholic Action, principally as an arm to fight against legislation in favor of civil marriage and divorce.[16] In 1926 another group appeared, the "League of Catholic Action for Gentlemen," with the Claretian priest Conrado Oquillas as moderator.[17] But progress was not uniform; the diocese of Cuzco reported in 1929 that as yet no Catholic Action groups existed there.[18]

Women's Catholic Action

Many of the earlier groups that flourished were women's groups. In 1931 the Sisters of the Sacred Heart began promoting Catholic Action groups in their schools. Some of the names that appear on the list of members of the Central Council of Women's Catholic Action in 1934 are Rosina Dugenne de Cebrián (the president), María Alvarez Calderón de Mujica (vice-president), Virginia Candamo de Puente (secretary), Carolina Elmore de Cobián, and Rebeca Bellido de Dammert.[19] In 1935 the moderator, Father Benito Jaro, S.J., proposed changing the name to "Catholic Action of Peruvian Women." According to Jaro, "Eventually all social classes will participate in the movement."[20] In Arequipa Father Francisco Cabré founded the group "Women's Social Action" in 1931. The majority of members were former students of the Sacred Hearts school.[21]

The 1931 Elections and the Popular Union

After a period of relative tranquillity, new tensions arose between church and state under the Sánchez Cerro regime. Among the first decrees of the "Hero of Arequipa" were obligatory civil marriage for everyone and the right to divorce (both in October 1930). In October 1931, after the presidential elections, the bishops published a collective pastoral letter condemning both these measures and several other proposals that had threatened to become laws, such as the separation of church and state, the expulsion of foreign clergy, and the imposition of lay education.[22] In spite of this protest congress ratified Sánchez Cerro's decrees and they became part of Peru's civil legislation. Most of the anticlerical measures were proposed by the Apristas. In the face of the upsurge of anticlericalism, many Catholics decided to organize themselves politically. The most important action was to create the Popular Union Party under Carlos Arenas y Loayza, a lawyer and president of the Catholic Union and for many years vice-rector of the Catholic University.

Toward the end of 1930 Arenas y Loayza called together a group of people connected with Catholic organizations with the aim of founding a political party. Among the cofounders were Gerardo Alarco and César Arróspide of Fides Center; Cargín Allison, president of the (Jesuit) Center for Catholic Youth and director of *Verdades*, a polemical Catholic newspaper founded in 1930; and Gonzalo Herrera, founder of another newspaper, *Patria*, that became an organ of expression of Popular Union.

On December 28 these Catholic lay leaders met with representatives of fifty-three Catholic institutions and associations, principally confraternities, such as the Workers of the Heart of Jesus of Santo Domingo, the Lord of Miracles, the Catholic Crusade, the Confraternity of the Rosary, and others. The Workers of the Heart of Jesus acted as host at the meeting, which was held in the monastery of Santo Domingo. These groups represented about four thousand Catholics. At this first meeting an agreement was made to found a party based on Christian social democratic principles.[23] At a second meeting in January 1931, the party was formally founded and Carlos Arenas y Loayza was elected president. At a third meeting on January 18, at the monastery of the Discalced in Rímac, a declaration of party principles was read in public. The main orator was Cargín Allison, who spoke on the concept of a "Christian democracy." Finally, when the nearly three hundred delegates were awaiting their turn to sign the declaration, the new party received an unexpected baptism of fire. The police, believing that the meeting represented a communist conspiracy, rushed in and marched the entire assembly off to jail! The following day *El Comercio* summed up the tragicomic incident with this headline: "214 Catholics and 13 friars arrested for conspiracy."[24]

The exact number of members of the Popular Union Party is difficult to determine. The foundation declaration had 235 signatures. In July of that year, when the presidential campaign was getting under way, *El Deber* (Arequipa) claimed that in Lima alone there were seven thousand affiliated to the party.[25] In reality the Popular Union (UP) was but one of twenty-seven parties that entered the presidential contest. And in the final stretch it

The Militant Laity, 1930–1955

entered into an alliance with other parties to stop the advance of the two big blocs, APRA and Sánchez Cerro. The leaders of the UP were mainly middle-class professionals and university professors, whereas the rank-and-file supporters came from the lower middle class. In general, they were the members of the confraternities of the more popular devotions. According to one witness, the party consisted of "distinguished elements of our social and professional world, and outstanding artisans and workers..., that is to say, people of every social class."[26]

The declaration of the party was inspired by the social teachings of the church (principally *Rerum Novarum; Quadragesimo Anno* was just published in May of that year). It called for the creation of a social democracy governed by a corporative state based on geographical and functional representation. The senate would be based on economic groups: farmers, merchants, employees, workers, and professors, while the house of deputies would be based on territorial divisions.[27] Many of these corporative elements were similar to those proposed by Víctor Andrés Belaunde.

The declaration recognized two kinds of property: private and social. The state would have the right to expropriate nonproductive private property, but only after indemnization. The state would also have the right to nationalize key natural resources, so that Peru would no longer have to "pay tribute for the wealth of other nations." Finally, the party program also called for a policy of protectionism in order to secure this "economic independence."

The program covered a wide range of social reforms. It called for the state to guarantee a "just salary" (a concept out of the papal encyclicals) that would insure a decent living for workers and their families. It called for social insurance against industrial accidents, sickness, problems related to maternity, and involuntary unemployment. The program recognized the right of workers to form unions and defend their rights by having recourse to strikes, but without violence. It favored the partial or joint ownership of companies by workers and employees. In other points, the program called for greater protection for women and children against work exploitation. Finally, it favored promoting the Indian communities, giving them back land that had been usurped, and providing them with more educational opportunities.

The UP and APRA

What is most striking about the UP's program is its rather advanced position on social reforms. The apologists of the new party held that Catholics could no longer belong to the "extreme right" nor be characterized by a "narrow conservativism." Indeed, they enjoyed pointing out that their party put Sánchez Cerro "very much to our right."[28] Even more surprising, however, was the resemblance of the UP's program to that of APRA. During the campaign, spokesmen for the UP, aware of the similarities, were at pains to stress the differences.

In a series of articles in *Verdades* the editors compared the two programs. Both favored protectionism for industry, a more just and efficient tax-collecting system, the recognition of women's rights, and more protection for the Indian communities; and both called for the creation of a corporative state (what the Apristas termed the "economic congress" of Haya de la Torre). *Verdades* even praised the Aprista program and in that context cited a reference to socialists made by Pius XI in *Quadragesimo Anno:* ". . . They undoubtedly come close to certain truths that the Christian tradition has always taught, and it cannot be denied that their demands come close to what Christians want for society."[29]

But the editorialists of the Catholic newspaper also rejected the laicist tendencies in APRA as well as their advocacy for a strong state, which was little different from a totalitarian corporativism. The UP also spoke of creating a corporative state but quickly denied any relation between that and fascism. In a talk he gave in June 1931, Arenas y Loayza praised the concept of "Christian democracy" as a solution for caudillism and statism. Although he expressed admiration for Mussolini (a common attitude at that time in the western world), he also condemned fascism's aggressive campaign against Catholic education and Catholic Action in Italy.[30] It is quite clear that the UP considered APRA to be the greatest threat to Peru because of its anticlericalism and totalitarian tendencies. *El Deber* in Arequipa was even led to affirm that only two parties had spoken frankly on the religious issue: the UP and APRA. The first clearly defended religion and the second clearly opposed it.[31]

The Provinces: Regionalism and Catholicism

Barely a month or two before the elections, the UP began establishing party committees outside of Lima. In September the party set up a base of operations in Callao. The main nuclei of the party in the port city, as in Lima, were the confraternities and brotherhoods, such as the Society of Gentlemen of the Sacred Heart, the Lord of the Sea, the Catholic Center of Callao, and the Society for the Bearers of Our Lady of Carmen de la Legua.[32] In the

The Militant Laity, 1930–1955 217

same month the party established bases in Ayacucho and Puno. In Cuzco and Arequipa the party's history was more complicated because it was founded as an alliance of other early movements.

In September 1930, Catholic Action of Cuzco, under the leadership of Teófilo Marmanillo, created the "Popular Committee of Cuzco" to propose candidates for the constitutional assembly. In the beginning this committee had no ties with the Popular Union in Lima. The committee, under the presidency of Moisés Corvacho and with Emilio Vega Centeno acting as secretary, drew up a list of acceptable candidates for the "Catholic cause," although the people selected had not been previously consulted. The list was based on the corporative scheme; the candidates were selected largely on the basis of their occupation. The list included David Samanez Ocampo to represent "politicians"; Félix Cosío to represent "lawyers"; José Ferro, "dairy farmers"; Luis E. Valcárcel, "teachers and intellectuals"; Juan M. Jara Vidalón, "workers"; etc.[33] When Samanez Ocampo was named provisional president of the country to succeed Sánchez Cerro in March 1931, this was perceived as a victory for the southern Andean region and for Catholicism. In reality, regionalism and religion converged to become one single force.

The bishop of Cuzco, Pedro Pascual Farfán, openly supported this political activity on the part of Catholics. In January 1931 he sent an "instruction" to all the pastors in his diocese on the coming elections. He urged them to support candidates who would offer the "best guarantees for Catholic interests."[34] When the UP was finally founded in Cuzco in September, the groundwork had already been laid.

In Arequipa the UP played an even more important role. There especially regionalism and Catholicism converged to form a most harmonious symbiosis. Leguía's fall had the effect of providing an opportunity for different regional forces to challenge Lima's dominant economic and political role. In January 1931, the Decentralist party was founded. It included merchants, farmers, and middle-class professionals. In February a civilian-military movement spread throughout the south that ended up forcing Sánchez Cerro to step down in March and to hand power over to the provisional government of Samanez Ocampo (Sánchez Cerro returned as a civilian candidate for the elections in October). The Decentralists supported Samanez, an old pro-Piérola veteran, because they believed that he best symbolized southern sentiments. In July the League for Autonomy, an association of farmers, merchants, and professionals, was founded to foster development projects. Many members of the decentralists were also in the league. All these organizations symbolized a resurgence of southern regionalism.[35] In Cuzco this regionalism often took the form of a radical pro-Indian sentiment. But in Arequipa regionalism was expressed in its Catholicism.

In viceregal times Catholicism symbolized authority and centralism. But after independence it acquired a new meaning: defense of tradition and local self-determination. Lima increasingly became the center for advanced ideas, especially liberalism and positivism, whereas the provinces, in order to withstand Lima's centralism, emphasized their own local, and usually more conservative, values. In the provinces Catholicism became a banner of defense against "foreign" ideas. This was the stance of Arequipa's upper classes. For them Catholicism acquired the ideological connotation of defending local economic and political control. But for the middle classes Catholicism meant also advocating a just social order as outlined in the papal encyclicals.

The man who most represented the latter tendency was Víctor Andrés Belaunde. In January 1931 Belaunde returned to his native city after a lengthy exile (1921–30) and delivered a lecture on decentralism and democratic corporativism.[36] Yet, curiously enough, Belaunde never sought to associate himself with the Popular Union Party. He personally knew Carlos Arenas y Loayza; the two were among the leading figures at the Catholic University. Furthermore, Belaunde explicitly acknowledged the fact that it was the "Catholic Party" of Arequipa that sent him to the constitutional assembly of 1931.[37] The real explanation for Belaunde's independent course of action was his rejection of the idea of a "Catholic" party. For him Catholicism was such a deeply rooted reality in Peru that it should not be reduced to a mere political cause.[38] Along with his brother Rafael, he devoted his efforts to seeking a centrist solution or candidate as an alternative for APRA or Sánchez Cerro. He evidently did not see in the UP the viable solution for which he was searching.

In the absence of Bishop Holguín, who had been called to Lima to act as apostolic administrator of the archdiocese, the clergyman who lent most support to the Catholic cause was Juan Gualberto Guevara, the founder of Catholic Action in the "White City" and editor of *El Deber*. He kept his readers informed of the progress of the UP in Lima. Finally, in August 1931 the UP was founded in Arequipa, too. The president of the organizing committee was José María A. Corso. The organizers described the UP as "a party of all social classes, but especially of the most qualified persons."[39] This populist declaration notwithstanding, the regional party committee was made up of some of the most powerful men in the department:

President	Alfredo López de Romaña
Vice-President	Pedro José de Noriega
Secretaries	Roberto Chocano
	Carlos A. Benavides
Treasurer	Carlos L. Bouroncle
Subdirectors	Gustavo A. Llosa
	Guillermo J. de Belaunde
	Adolfo Wagner
	Alberto López de Romaña
	Rafael Bustamante de la Fuente, etc.

This list not only looks like the social register of Arequipa, but it is also striking for its similarity to another list. In July of that year the League of Hacienda Owners published the names of their executive committee:[40]

President	Pedro José Noriega
Vice-President	Alfredo López de Romaña
Secretary	Arturo López de Romaña
Treasurer	Carlos L. Borouncle
Subdirectors	Alberto Rey de Castro
	Adrián Arnillas
	Carlos Cánepa, etc.

Comparing the two lists, it is difficult not to arrive at the conclusion that the UP was virtually the party of the hacienda owners. Three of the executive members of the League of Hacienda Owners (Noriega, Alfredo López de Romaña, and Bouroncle) were also founders and directors of the UP. Pedro Noriega and Corzo also appear on the list of leaders of the League for Autonomy.[41] But these revelations pose a problem. What possible ideological relation could there be between the UP in Lima, made up of the middle and lower-middle classes and with a very progressive social program, and the UP of Arequipa, which was dominated by great landowners?

In reality, the party in Lima did not share the same ideological perspective as the same party in Arequipa. The UP in Lima did, however, have far more similarity to the ideas of Víctor Andrés

Belaunde, but Belaunde, in spite of his pride in being from Arequipa, did not represent the economically powerful of that region. He did share with them his Catholicism, but for him and the Lima group that meant the social teachings of the church.

A month before the elections, the centrist parties, resigned to the fact that the lower classes favored either Sánchez Cerro or Haya de la Torre, decided to form an alliance and present a single candidate. On September 7, the leaders of the Popular Union and of the Democratic, Liberal, and Progressive parties met and founded the "National Alliance."[42] Shortly afterwards the alliance chose José María de la Jara as its candidate.

In Arequipa the UP published a list of candidates acceptable to Catholics, though they were not necessarily affiliated to the party. The list included the names of Augusto Pérez Aranibar, José Luis Bustamante y Rivero, Víctor Andrés Belaunde, Manuel J. Bustamante de la Fuente, Alberto Rey de Castro, Carlos Gibson, and Adolfo Wagner.[43] In mid-September, acknowledging the fact that in reality there were no real differences between them, the UP and the Decentralist party joined forces to present a single list. But given the fact that the UP had already incorporated members of the other party into its own list (such as Manuel Bustamante de la Fuente, who was the president of the Decentralists), the final list was not very different from the UP's list.[44] With that, Catholicism and decentralism in Arequipa made their final step toward unification.

The Elections and Their Aftermath

Toward the end of September a conflict that arose within the ranks of the UP motivated Carlos Arenas y Loayza to resign as head of the party. In his letter of resignation Arenas accused the party's directing committee of making decisions in his absence.[45] The remaining party leaders, Gerardo Alarco, Cargín Allison, César Arróspide, José Bonilla, and Gonzalo Herrera, decided to rotate the direction of the party among themselves.

The centrist candidates received relatively few votes (de la Jara: 21,291; Arturo Osores: 19,654) compared to Sánchez Cerro (152,062) and Haya de la Torre (106,007).[46] Clearly, the big winners were the strong and charismatic leaders, not the "principled" and moderate ones. For the constitutional congress Sánchez Cerro's Revolutionary Union party won eighty-three seats; APRA, twenty-nine; the Decentralists and independents, thirty-three. The UP's candidates were included in the latter group.

The Militant Laity, 1930–1955   221

Of Arequipa's twelve seats, Sánchez Cerro won eight; then in the order of votes won came Víctor Andrés Belaunde, Manuel J. Bustamante de la Fuente, Colonel González Honderman, and Guillermo Lira. Rafael Belaunde was also a candidate but failed to win the minimum number of votes. The winners in the south were, first, the Sanchezcerristas, and second, the Decentralists and Catholics.

After the elections the UP ceased to exist. In a letter he wrote to Bishop Farfán in November 1931, Arenas y Loayza confided that both Belaunde and Riva-Agüero had committed themselves to supporting the UP after the party reorganized itself.[47] But that reorganization never occurred. As a result, the Catholic cause no longer had a party and therefore had to express its will through individuals, such as Belaunde in congress, or through the lay organizations of the church, such as Catholic Action. Carlos Arenas y Loayza continued working at the Catholic University as a professor and a university administrator. In 1935 President Benavides named him president of the council of ministers and minister of justice, cult, and public welfare. One of his most important acts was to make religion an obligatory course in all state schools.[48] Years later he became Peru's ambassador to Colombia and then director of the Central Bank. He died in 1955.

In spite of the meager results obtained in the 1932 elections, the idea of a Catholic party continued to persist. In 1932 Sánchez Cerro created the "Junta of Social Defense" to combat what he termed the "Apro-Communist sects" in the country. He asked Bishop Farfán of Cuzco to lend his support to the junta. Farfán not only offered his support, but he even wrote with enthusiasm of the need to regroup all "forces on the right" into a single "conservative party."[49] But the most vigorous defender of that idea was José de la Riva-Agüero. Riva-Agüero had supported Sánchez Cerro in 1931 as the only realistic alternative to APRA. In the beginning of 1935 he gathered former members of the Civilist party, Sanchezcerristas (Sánchez Cerro was assassinated in 1933), and personal friends and founded the Patriotic Action party. He also sought the support of the bishops. He wrote to Bishop Holguín in 1936 and emphasized the importance of Arequipa for his plans: ". . . Arequipa is the indispensable base for a right-wing campaign."[50]

In 1936 he entered into an alliance with other groups on the right. They agreed to support Manuel Vicente Villarán for the elections that year. When the elections were called off, Riva-Agüero declared his party to be in recess.[51] It is not clear whether that party merited belonging to the category of "Catholic" parties. His right-wing corporatist tendencies were quite distant from the social teachings of the church. Since Leo XIII's time the church spoke in favor of the concept of a "Christian democracy." The aggressiveness of fascism also served to discredit corporative inclinations in the church.

With the disappearance of the UP, Catholics with a social conscience no longer had a party that responded to their desires. APRA was still tainted by a belligerent anticlericalism. Riva-Agüero and the newspaper *El Comercio* represented upper-class interests, with little social consciousness. It was not until Bustamante y Rivero's time that Catholics attempted to regroup and to lay the basis for the Christian Democratic party. In the meantime, bishops, priests, and laypeople concentrated their efforts on the task of strengthening lay movements within the church. The 1931 election showed what little influence the bishops had on the conscience of thousands of Peurvians of the middle and popular classes. This fact, of course, reinforced their conviction that the church needed a better-formed laity.

The Intellectual Revitalization of Catholicism

In the midst of the political and social agitation of the thirties, and after a long period of stagnation, the church began to experience an intellectual rebirth. The principal center of the movement was the Catholic University, founded in 1917. Its two stars were Víctor Andrés Belaunde and José de la Riva-Agüero. These two contributed to the formation of an entire generation of young professors and professionals who helped turn the university into an institution of national prestige. Also intimately associated with the university was the Jesuit historian Rubén Vargas Ugarte, who assumed the task of writing the first complete history of the church in Peru.

The thirties were characterized by an aggressive sectarian spirit: the military and the oligarchy opposed the Apristas, and the Apristas opposed them and the communists. The church denounced Marxism and did not hide its antagonism toward Aprismo. Both Riva-Agüero (in spite of his more conservative concepts) and Belaunde gave an example of the compatibility between faith and reason and between faith and the world. They were also men of strong personalities. Belaunde was noted more for his joviality while Riva-Agüero seemed more aloof and grave.

But both of them were also characterized by certain personal qualities that made them similar in some respects to, ironically, González Prada, especially their Hispanic elitism that tended to create a barrier between them and the popular classes. Although they both addressed their message to the ordinary person, neither came close to establishing the same charismatic rapport with the popular classes that Haya de la Torre or José Carlos Mariátegui were able to do. Nor were they practical organization men; they did not participate actively in Catholic Action, for example, a movement directly inspired by their own ideas.

Víctor Andrés Belaunde (1883–1966)

Throughout his life Víctor Andrés Belaunde always pointed to the two primary influences in his own formation: Arequipa, his native city, and his Catholic faith. For him, Arequipa represented the perfect synthesis of what Peru should be, a spiritual and psychological fusion of Peru's Spanish and Indian cultures. He also extolled the virtues of the city's leading families—small property owners with a long colonial history—because they had given rise to a middle class with a social consciousness. And he himself came from that class. For that reason Belaunde felt no affinity with the great sugar oligarchy on the northern coast. The small property owners in Arequipa were much closer to the Indians and mestizos who worked on their lands. They were bound together in a relationship that at times was paternalistic but rarely characterized by arrogance or racism. In his opinion the great sugar-estate owners in the north did not really constitute an "aristocracy" but rather a "plutocracy," an ambitious get-rich-quick class with no social values.

The other important factor in his life was his Catholicism. His father, Mariano Andrés de Belaunde, founded the Catholic Union of Arequipa and the newspaper *El Deber*, with its explicit Catholic orientation. Along with his younger brother Rafael, he studied in the school founded by Father Hipólito Duhamel, a French Vincentian who had a great influence on the religious life of the city, and also for a brief period in the Jesuit school of San José. His brother Rafael went on to become prime minister of Peru in the years 1945–48. His nephew, Rafael's son, is Fernando Belaúnde Terry, twice elected president of the country (1963–68; 1980–85).

Not only his family but the city itself was steeped in Catholic traditions. The clergy always played a prominent role in the city's social and political life: Luna Pizarro, Gualberto Valdivia, and Mariano Arce were all precursors of the independence movement. Although he was not a native of the city, Bartolomé Herrera ended his days as bishop of the "White City." Ambrosio Huerta, who also became bishop, was one of the best orators of the last century. One of Belaunde's classmates was Juan Gualberto Guevara, later to be archbishop of Lima and Peru's first cardinal. In other parts of Peru the clergy's image had become tarnished, but not in Arequipa.

In 1901 Belaunde began studying at San Marcos University in Lima. He soon fell sway to positivism, which led him to drift away from the religion of his youth. He struck up friendships with many of the professors, and with author and fellow student José de la Riva-Agüero. In 1908 he led the Peruvian delegation to the first all-Latin American Student Congress held in Montevideo. Upon returning he founded a University Center that aimed to offer courses to workers. Earlier, in 1903, he had begun working in the Archive of National Frontiers. From then on his two principal professions were teaching and diplomacy.

Belaunde developed his basic ideas in a series of public lectures in the university and in various political circles. In 1914, as a new professor at San Marcos, he gave the inaugural talk on the "Present Crisis." He asserted that the Peruvian middle class was destined to regenerate the nation after the long period of disorientation and moral disorder following the war with Chile. But that class needed first to break its dependency on foreign capital. In 1915 he presented himself as a candidate in Arequipa for the National Democratic party founded by Riva-Agüero. Though he lost the election he impressed many with the clarity of his thinking, especially in a talk he gave on "The Social Question in Arequipa," in which he decried the exploitation of Indians and called for state institutions to protect them. In 1917 he addressed the newly founded Federation of Peruvian Students and touched on the theme of the lack of vital contact between the university and the social reality of the country.

This rapid and brilliant career was cut short abruptly by Leguía. In March 1921, Belaunde delivered a speech at San Marcos protesting the suppression of civil liberties under the latter. The police interrupted the speech and sent Belaunde into exile. He spent his nine years of exile principally in the United States and France. In the United States he taught in various universities that had Latin American studies programs. His exile also marked his rediscovery of Catholicism. He returned to Peru in 1930, after Leguía's fall, a more mature man intellectually and spiritually.

But his return was also full of disappointments. The country had changed radically since his exile. After a brief moment of freedom, it was once again under a dictator, Sánchez Cerro. Furthermore, a messianic fervor was sweeping through the lower classes, who opted either for APRA or Sánchez Cerro, the candidate supported by the army and the oligarchy. The era of goodwilled dialogue had passed; demagoguery and sectarian passions filled the vacuum.

The Catholics of Arequipa voted Belaunde into the constitutional congress, where he took up the "Catholic cause." He defended his ideas on a corporative Christian state and sustained heated debates with the Apristas and others on the questions of lay education and the right of women to vote. The opposition to the latter measure came from the anticlericals, who feared that the clergy would manipulate the women. In February 1932, Sánchez Cerro expelled the Apristas from congress. As a gesture of protest Belaunde resigned, too, and left congress. He went back to the United States to teach, but the church asked him to return and to continue to be its unofficial representative in congress.

Belaunde's greatest disappointment, however, came when he failed to be elected rector of San Marcos University. He returned to his university in the hopes of defending basic liberties as he had done before. But he discovered instead a hostile atmosphere created in large part by the Apristas who objected to his Catholicism. Given that sectarian milieu, he left San Marcos and in 1932 joined the faculty of the Catholic University at the invitation of Father Jorge Dintilhac. The Catholic University offered him the necessary breathing space in which to develop his ideas further and to influence others. In reality, he had already taken up the thread of his pre-exile years when he wrote *La Realidad nacional* (The National Reality) in 1930, a reply to Mariátegui's *Seven Interpretive Essays on the Peruvian Reality*. His book, along with Mariátegui's, soon became a political classic and a mandatory work for all students of contemporary Peru.

La Realidad Nacional (1930)

Belaunde conceived *La Realidad nacional* as a Christian response to Mariátegui's Marxist interpretation of Peruvian history. Nevertheless, he did not intend simply to dismiss Mariátegui's ideas, but rather to enter into dialogue with him. He was in the middle of his own work when he learned of Mariátegui's death. He thereupon dedicated his work to the memory of Peru's first socialist intellectual. Belaunde paid tribute to Mariátegui's nobility of spirit and praised his capacity for synthesis and powers of criticism. Most of all, he shared with Mariátegui the latter's keen sense of justice. He expressed his complete agreement that the northern oligarchy and the dominant role of Lima had both had a pernicious influence on Peru's development.

But Belaunde also criticized Mariátegui's tendency to polarize the country's Spanish and Indian heritages so radically and the way he confused the colonial period with feudalism and race with class. In opposition to Mariátegui's pro-Indian socialism, Belaunde noted that there existed a mestizo Peru that was built upon the best of the Indian and Spanish past. In a later book, *Peruanidad* (1943), he described Peru as a "living synthesis" in which two races had fused together to form a new psychological and spiritual unity. Belaunde accused Mariátegui of not appreciating how deeply Spain had influenced the Peruvian psyche, or how deeply the Indian had influenced the Spaniards in Peru. The great exception to this racial interaction was Lima, where the Spanish culture predominated.

For this very reason Belaunde did not agree with Mariátegui's thesis that the Indian problem came down essentially to the land question. Belaunde pointed out that the Indian is not just a peasant but also a member of a particular race and culture. Nationalization or "collectivization" of the land (which Mariátegui proposed) would not resolve the "Indian problem." Belaunde called rather for the Indian communities to be protected. Better education should be provided for adults. Cooperatives should be created. Belaunde noted that the Indians themselves had always had different types of property: private and communal. But he agreed with Mariátegui that nonproductive haciendas in the Andes should be expropriated.

Belaunde approved of Mariátegui's call for decentralizing the country, thereby freeing it from the northern oligarchy and Lima's excessive control. But socialism was not the answer to these latter realities. Belaunde called for decentralizing the country by taking into account the acute regional differences. The great sugar barons of the north should not be confused with the small property owners of the south, who displayed greater social sensitivity. Peru's problems, asserted Belaunde, were not just class, but also race and cultural divisions. The basic problem was how to foster a true civic and social consciousness.

In the second part of his work, Belaunde presented a few of his own solutions. Basically he called for the creation of a "social democracy" as opposed to Soviet collectivism or oligarchic capitalism. Peru should retain and strengthen the best elements of modern western culture, such as political freedom and human rights, but it should also recover, and reconstruct in modern form, some of the best features of Catholic medieval Europe, such as the guilds and other functional associations. The state would have the usual separation of three powers, the executive, the legislative, and the judicial. But Belaunde also called for a corporative legislature. The lower house would be based on population and the senate on regional and functional concepts. The idea was to have representatives from the workers, the employers, the universities, the businesspeople, and from the different economic units according to the varying regions of the country.

Both Mariátegui and Belaunde agreed that religion was a fundamental aspect in the life of the country. But Belaunde disagreed with Mariátegui's thesis, common among pro-Indian advocates, that the Indians had been evangelized only superficially while continuing to practice pagan ways under Catholic forms. Through the liturgy and devotion in honor of the Virgin Mary, contended Belaunde, the church had touched the soul of the Indian very deeply. Furthermore, Belaunde thought that Mariátegui failed to appreciate sufficiently the role that the church had played in history. It was the church most of all, claimed Belaunde, that had forged the Peruvian nation. The church evangelized the Indians and brought them into western culture; but it also "Christianized" the Spanish and forced them to acquire a social consciousness with respect to the Indians. This was the living spiritual and cultural synthesis that became the basis of the Peruvian nation.

In the midst of his duties as a member of congress, Belaunde was sent by the government in 1932 to carry out special diplomatic missions in Europe and the United States. In 1942 he was named vice-rector of the Catholic University, and when Father Dintilhac died, he became provisional rector (1946–47). In 1943 he published *Peruanidad*. In 1945 he was named head of the Peruvian delegation to the United Nations, and from 1949 on he practically remained in that post until his death in New York in 1966. He interrupted that mission once, in 1958, when he was named minister of foreign relations.

Belaunde was a true forerunner of contemporary social thought in Peru. Bartolomé Herrera had proposed the idea of a corporative state, but within a clerical and conservative mold. But Belaunde's corporativism was social and democratic. The Apristas also had their own corporative scheme under the label of the

"Economic Congress." But for Belaunde, economic justice was not sufficient in itself to forge a nation, much less a community. He believed that it was also necessary to build the nation on spiritual and moral values. In his view service to the common good was the ideal for all citizens. For this reason he criticized Apristas and Marxists alike for their obsession with state control of everything. Yet Belaunde also believed that there was a basis for dialogue with Marxism. He announced in his writings that the day would come when the only option would be to chose between Marxist collectivism and social Christianity. For him a Catholic "right" no longer had any meaning, especially after the papal social encyclicals.

In spite of his friendship with Riva-Agüero, therefore, he did not share the latter's authoritarian and elitist mentality. But in the context of a highly polarized Peru of the thirties he found himself a rather solitary figure. Keenly aware of the fact that he stood outside the political mainstream, he wrote, "My Catholic and corporative reformism in regard to fundamental liberties and progressive social change had no listeners at the time."[52]

But there was no room for permanent disillusionments in his life. In 1959 he reached the height of his career when he was elected president of the General Assembly of the United Nations, an enviable distinction for any diplomat but especially for one from a poor third world nation.

José de la Riva-Agüero y Osma (1885–1944)

The most articulate voice of the Catholic right in the thirties bore the same name as his great-grandfather who was the first president of Peru. He was somewhat similar to Bartolomé Herrera in that his right-wing politics did not necessarily signify an identification with the great oligarchy or with capitalism. Rather, Riva-Agüero proposed the creation of a new national elite that would distinguish itself for its superior moral and intellectual capacity. He had a dim view of the colonial aristocracy and the republican oligarchy for their incapacity to assume responsibility and forge a real nation. He has frequently been labled a "Hispanist." More accurately, Riva-Agüero was a nationalist who, though he praised the values that Spain had left Peru, also greatly admired the Inca empire, not so much for its presumed socialism but for its sense of order and historical mission. He also admired Mussolini and proposed the creation of a corporative state.

As a youth he had studied at La Recoleta, run by the Sacred Hearts Fathers. At San Marcos University he stood out for his intellectual capacity. He wrote two doctoral theses, each of which became a classic in intellectual history: *Carácter de la literatura del Perú independiente* (1905) and *La Historia en el Perú* (1910). In 1912 he visited the southern Andean region and other parts of the Andes. Impressed by what he saw, he wrote another work, *Paisajes peruanos*.

Like Belaunde he too fell away from his faith, but the positivism he professed was more pronounced than in Belaunde's case, and he eventually declared himself an agnostic. In 1911 he had his first political skirmish with Augusto Leguía. In 1915 he founded his own party, the National Democratic party, which represented the progressive wing of the Civilist party. In 1921 he left Peru in protest over Leguía's dictatorship and did not return until 1930.

When he returned he was named mayor of Lima by David Samanez Ocampo, then the provisional president, and in 1933 President Benavides named him president of the council of ministers. He also occupied the post of minister of justice, instruction, cult, and welfare. In 1934, however, when congress approved the decrees promulgated by Sánchez Cerro on civil marriages and divorce, he resigned for reasons of conscience. In 1931, like Belaunde, he too joined the faculty of the Catholic University. In the years 1935–37 he served as dean of the College of Lawyers in Lima. In 1936 he founded another party, Patriotic Action, which represented his rightist positions. The party lasted for a brief time. He took a trip around the world in 1938 and returned in 1940.

The political ideas of Riva-Agüero would not have had much impact on Catholics if it were not for the singular fact that in 1932 he publicly retracted his agnosticism and returned to the Catholic faith. Unlike Belaunde, who returned to his faith in a more discreet way, Riva-Agüero turned his conversion into something resembling a campaign. In an address to his former classmates at La Recoleta he blamed his loss of faith on imprudent readings and a bad assimilation of certain philosophical currents. But, "between sorrows and wounds," he announced that like the prodigal son he had finally returned.[53] For then on he identified himself with the Catholic cause in politics and in the university. In Riva-Agüero most of all one can find a fusion of four elements: Hispanism, nationalism, Catholicism, and corporativism.

When he died in 1944 he donated his house and other properties to the Catholic University. In honor of his memory Belaunde founded the Riva-Agüero Institute in 1947. For years the institute was a prestigious academic center devoted to advancing studies based on Riva-Agüero's ideas.

The Catholic University

The principal center of the Catholic intellectual renovation in Peru was the Catholic University, founded in 1917 by Father Jorge Dintilhac. Luis Eugenio Dintilhac (his real name) was born near Paris in 1872, and in 1895 he entered the congregation of the Sacred Hearts. After completing studies at Valparaíso, Chile, he arrived in Lima in 1902, and that very year he was ordained a priest by Archbishop Tovar. As a young teacher at La Recoleta colegio he became familiar with the intellectual and religious world of Lima. Out of this knowledge grew a desire to found a Catholic university: "Around 1916 it seemed that the Catholic faith was on the point of disappearing among the upper social and intellectual levels in Lima and Peru. The religious schools that existed then seemed to bear very little fruit because the majority of their students left and then declared themselves atheists or at least became indifferent toward religion."[54]

He set about promoting the idea of a Catholic university among some prominent families in Lima and was soon aided by a benefactor, Josefina Araraz, who donated her entire fortune to his project. La Recoleta colegio offered him the use of some its classrooms. But he had barely petitioned the government to found a new university when voices of opposition were raised, especially at San Marcos University. The opposition came from anticlericals and San Marcos professors who feared that another university in Lima would compete with them. Finally, on March 24, 1917, ignoring the protests, President José Pardo signed the decree permitting the university to exist. It opened its doors in April of that year to a total of seven students.[55]

The first crisis had just subsided when Archbishop Lisson created another one. When he became archbishop in 1918 he came up with his own plans for a university, to be named in honor of Bartolomé Herrera. He failed, however, to find the necessary support for his project.[56] Lisson thereupon decided, along with the other bishops, to lend his full support to Father Dintilhac's university.

The new university led a very precarious existence for its first twenty years. In fact, it was hardly more than an extension of Colegio La Recoleta in the Plaza Francia in the center of Lima. Then the turbulent politics of the thirties gave the university an unexpected boost. In March 1932 Sánchez Cerro closed down San Marcos, and many of the students there transferred to the Catholic University. At the same time well-known intellectuals such as Riva-Agüero and Belaunde also abandoned San Marcos and joined the Catholic University. As a consequence, the new university experienced a sudden increase in enrollment and in quality. In 1931 the Higher Institute of Science was founded, and in 1932 the Institute of Advanced Studies for Women. In 1933 the Faculty of Engineering was created, and that same year the Normal Teachers School for Men, under the direction of the Brothers of La Salle, was also founded. In 1936 a teachers school for women was founded in the university and placed under the direction of the Canonesses of the Cross. In 1934 the university had 1,167 students and by 1942 it had grown to 2,320. That year, while celebrating its silver anniversary, it was raised to the dignity of a "pontifical" university.

The university soon became an important center of the new Catholic lay movement. Besides Belaunde and Riva-Agüero there were many other professors who took an active role in promoting the movement: Jorge Velaochaga, Carlos Arenas y Loayza, Pedro Benvenutto, Javier Pulgar, José Pareja Paz-Soldán, Ernesto Alayza, Raúl Ferrero Rebagliati, and Beatriz Cisneros. Among priests, Ruben Vargas Ugarte and Luis Lituma stand out, and after the Second World War Gerardo Alarco and José Dammert Bellido also played important roles. Father Dintilhac, known affectionately by all as "Father Jorge," with the exception of two trips he made in 1919 and 1940, was the rector of the university all through those years until his death in 1947.

Although it was relatively small in the beginning, the university soon won a name for itself as a serious center of studies. Given its small size there was a family spirit among its faculty and students. Nor was it as elitist as its critics claimed. In fact, the great majority of the professors were from the middle class and 80 percent of the student body came from the provinces.[57] In 1944, with the donation made by Riva-Agüero, its economic future became far less uncertain.

But at the same time the university, like most Catholic universities in that period, was characterized by a certain provincialism with respect to the modern world. It was also closely associated with the political right. Many professors gave a Hispanist orientation to their teaching, ignoring the cultural reality of Peru's popular classes. It would not be until the sixties, under the rectorship of Father Felipe MacGregor, that the university would go through a radical transformation and become a really modern academic institution.

The International Catholic Student Movement

In 1933 the first congress of the Ibero-American Confederation of Catholic Students was held in Rome. Peru was represented by César Arróspide, Gerardo Alarco, Ernesto Alayza, David Vega Christie, Raúl Ferrero, and others. Present also were Eduardo Frei and Rafael Caldera.[58] In 1939 the second congress of the organization was held in Lima. The most prominent spokesmen among Peruvian Catholics attended: Víctor Andrés Belaunde, José Jiménez Borja, Rubén Vargas Ugarte, Luis Lituma, Mario Alzamora Valdez, César Arróspide de la Flor, Jorge del Busto, Ernesto Alayza, Félix Denegri Luna, Alberto Wagner de Reyna, and many others. The identification of Catholicism with *Hispanismo* reached its culminating moment. Many of the delegates did not hide their admiration for Franco, who had recently achieved victory in Spain. The congress condemned all "dechristianizing influences in Hispanic America," including Protestantism, liberalism, Marxist socialism, materialism, and racist *indigenismo* (pro-Indianism). The delegates also warned against the materialist and secularizing influence of the United States. But some of the Peruvians present, such as Mario Alzamora Valdez, resented this imposition of *Hispanismo*. Alzamora borrowed Belaunde's concept of *Peruanidad* (Peruvianity) to oppose "Hispanism": "*Peruanidad* is not a synonym for 'Hispanism' because it takes into account the contribution of the Indian culture to Peru's identity. *Peruanidad* is a new term: it symbolizes the new path toward that universal and unique ideal of culture, which is Christianity.[59]

Already at this early date the social Christians were distinguishing between themselves and the "Hispanists" who defended Spain's culture heritage as the only one worth considering. But that latter current began losing force during the Second World War. In 1944 Peru did not send a delegation to the congress of the organization held in Bogotá. On the positive side, however, these congresses provided Peruvians with a more sophisticated view of the international scene and an opportunity to come into contact with other Catholic leaders from the rest of Latin America, such as Eduardo Frei and Rafael Caldera. Long before the hierarchy, it was the laity that began to acquire a vision of a Latin American church.

The Revitalization of the Church

Farfán and Holguín

Emilio Lissón symbolized the church of the twenties. In the thirties the two most prominent representatives of the official church were Mariano Holguín and Pedro Pascual Farfán. In many ways they were alike. Both had a somewhat austere countenance and were not nearly as eloquent as many lay speakers. But both displayed notable leadership qualities in steering the church with firmness and discretion through troubled times. Both were closely identified with the regionalist sentiment, one in Arequipa and the other in Cuzco. Furthermore, within a conservative framework, both demonstrated an openness toward the social question. And both gave a strong impetus to the nationwide lay movement.

Born in Arequipa, Holguín joined the Franciscans of La Recoleta and was named bishop of Huaraz in 1904. From 1906 until his death in 1945 he was bishop of Arequipa. Only Goyeneche, who presided over the diocese for forty-two years in the last century, lasted longer than Holguín. Between 1931 and 1933 Holguín was also the apostolic administrator of the archdiocese of Lima following Lissón's resignation. He enjoyed the somewhat dubious honor of being the president of the nation for a few hours when Sánchez Cerro resigned in March 1931. The two principal candidates to be archbishop of Lima were Holguín himself and Farfán of Cuzco. In spite of the best efforts of Belaunde, a native of Arequipa like him, Holguín did not win the necessary votes in congress. But, Arequipa still continued to play a leadership role in the Peruvian Catholic church. In 1896 Holguín had founded the Catholic Worker's Circles and in 1925 he encouraged the creation of Catholic Action in his diocese.

Pedro Pascual Farfán succeeded Holguín as bishop of Huaraz, where he resided from 1906 until 1918. Then he was named bishop of Cuzco, his native city. As archbishop in Lima Farfán was faced with enormous problems. *Aprismo*, socialism, and positivism had taken nearly total possession of San Marcos and other intellectual circles. Yet Farfán was not closed to the social question. In a pastoral letter he wrote on the occasion of the feast of St. Rose of Lima (August 1937) he certainly sounded like a conservative. He stated that poverty is "the best road to eternal happiness."[60] Yet in the same letter Farfán also pointed out that earthly wealth was "empty of spiritual contact." A better idea of his social thinking can be gathered by reviewing all of his pastoral messages from Huaraz to Cuzco to Lima. An interview in *El Amigo del Clero* in June 1936 reveals his thought more clearly. In it he declared that social justice had the highest priority: "Of course, everything cannot be solved by charity. It must be preceded by justice, as the Roman Pontiffs have insisted so many times; . . . There is no greater sin than to rob a worker of his salary."[61]

Even more striking was the following statement, made in the same interview: "There are good Christians in all the parties, on the right and on the left."[62] Such a statement, unthinkable for a last-century bishop, was quite in harmony with Farfán's pastoral actions. In general, Farfán attempted to reconcile Catholics on the right with Catholics in the Aprista party. In one dramatic incident a priest by the name of Ambrosio Ruiz was killed during an Aprista uprising in Huancavelica in November 1934. The perpetrator of the crime was a certain Cirilo Cornejo, who was not an Aprista but rather a member of an allied group. In Lima the enemies of APRA planned to turn the priest's funeral into an anti-Aprista mass meeting. After listening to the opinion of political independents who were close to APRA, Farfán ordered the coffin to be taken directly to the cemetery in order to avoid the protest meeting.[63] And unlike other clerics, such as Rubén Vargas Ugarte, the Jesuit historian who wrote a polemical tract denouncing the Aprista Party, Farfán never explicitly condemned that party as such, only some of its laicist tendencies.

The National Eucharistic Congress, 1935

Toward the end of 1934 Farfán set into motion plans for the first national eucharistic congress in Peru. The first eucharistic congress had been held in France in 1882 as part of the reaction of the church to laicism and anticlericalism. The eucharistic congress paralleled the devotion to the Sacred Heart; both entailed large public manifestations in which the faithful made reparation for attacks against the faith. These great public assemblies also served to strengthen the faithful in their convictions and to demonstrate the strength of Catholicism. In this sense the congress of 1935 was the culmination of the period of the militant church that had arisen in the last century.

In preparation for the congress, "eucharistic weeks" were held in parishes all during the year. The congress was held between October 23 and 27. According to all criteria it was a great success. It was calculated, and photographs confirm this, that about one hundred thousand men and the same number of women attended.[64] Thousands of children received Communion. Many different groups and associations marched in the processions: the old Catholic Union of Gentlemen, the Catholic Union for Women, students of the Catholic University, youth of the Diocesan Federation of Catholic Youth, and the faithful from the parishes. President Benavides and his entire cabinet attended. The principal speakers were Víctor Andrés Belaunde and José de la Riva-Agüero. All the bishops of Peru were present, as well as many prelates especially invited from neighboring countries.

Farfán achieved his goal. The congress was a demonstration of Catholic strength that impressed everyone present but especially Catholics who had become lax or indifferent. Many Catholics now displayed a militancy that had previously characterized only small groups. In 1940 in Arequipa a second national congress was held under the direction of Bishop Holguín. A third was held in Trujillo in 1943, a fourth in Cuzco in 1949, and a fifth in Lima in 1954. All were characterized by their solemnity and pageantry. Furthermore, the individual dioceses also held smaller regional eucharistic congresses, such as the one Farfán had organized in Cuzco in 1928.

But the real intention of Farfán and the other bishops was not so much to impress Catholics with external signs, as to give a more permanent structure to the Catholic cause. With the birth of Catholic Action during the congress, this objective was also fulfilled.

Catholic Action

Beginning in 1929 the various parishes in Lima organized youth groups, and in 1931 all of these were fused into the "Diocesan Federation of Catholic Youth." The Marian sodality of the Jesuits joined the new organization. The moderator was Father Juan Albacete, S.J., and the principal lay leaders were César Arróspide, Gerardo Alarco, and Ernesto Alayza Grundy. When Catholic Action was founded in 1935, it absorbed the federation, which thereupon ceased to exist.

During the eucharistic congress Holguín pointed to the need to give new impetus to Catholic Action: "The bishops of Peru, realizing how important the mission of the laity is, especially in this country with such a shortage of priests, conceived the idea of founding Catholic Action from the year 1921. . . ."[65]

In the "Resolutions of the Congress" the bishops stipulate what the activities of Catholic Action should be: "To maintain organs of expression; to hold study circles; to teach religion and catechism in schools and outside the classrooms; to carry out crusades against indecent spectacles, especially in the movies; to defend our holy religion against Protestant propaganda by employing the press, setting up free schools, and offering medical aid in areas where these services are not provided for the sick."[66]

But the bishops also declared that "Peruvian Catholic Action is not to be confused with any political party or action," although its members were called upon to defend "the legitimate and unalienable rights of religion."[67]

Peruvian Catholic Action followed the model created in Italy. It had a national committee and four branches for men, women, young men, and young women. Later on, specialized branches were founded, such as the UNEC (National Union of Catholic Students), professional associations for educators, engineers, pharmacists and lawyers, the Agrarian Catholic Action, the Christian Family Movement, and the Young Christian Workers. With the passage of time, only the specialized associations continued to function. The first president of the national committee was César Arróspide. His successors were Cristóbal de Losada y Puga and Ismael Biélich, whom he followed for another term. The ecclesiastical moderator was Father Amelio Placencia.

First Period: Organization (1935–49)

For its first few years Catholic Action led a very dynamic existence with a high degree of responsibility on the part of the members, though some sections were more active than others. Numerically, of course, these groups represented a very small percentage of practicing Catholics in general. Nevertheless, Catholic Action was far more vigorous than the old Catholic Union. The records of Young Catholic Women for 1936 show that that branch had 918 members in the entire country.[68] Some two hundred men and women delegates attended the first archdiocesan congress of Catholic Action, held in Lima in 1937.[69] For the first national congress of Catholic Action, held in Lima in 1955, there were 130 lay men and women and thirty-three ecclesiastical moderators on hand.[70] Finally, in a report written by Jorge Alayza Grundy in 1959, when Catholic Action had begun to decline, the author stated that there were nearly five hundred men and 1,623 women who were active members of Catholic Action in the entire country. That year UNEC had 115 members and the Young Catholic Workers had 190 members of both sexes.[71]

The Militant Laity, 1930–1955 237

In general, though some of the leaders came from prominent upper-class families, the great majority of the members came from the urban middle classes. In this sense, Catholic Action was much less elitist than the Catholic Union. A glance at some of the reports of Catholic Action will confirm this observation. Of the thirty-two members of Young Women's Catholic Action in Cuzco in the year 1949, nine were secretaries, four were students, nine were school teachers, and ten were "housewives."[72] In the case of the specialized groups such as the Young Catholic Workers or the Association of Educators, the social background of the members is clear. In Trujillo, to cite one example out of many, there was a "Center for Secretaries of Young Women's Catholic Action."[73]

During the first stage the leaders of Catholic Action were the same ones who had directed the earlier organizations: César Arróspide, Ernesto Alayza Grundy, Cristóbal de Losada y Puga, and Ismael Biélich. Other important leaders were Javier Correa Elías, Enrique Cipriani, Germán Stiglich, David Vega Christie, and Gerardo Alarco. In the forties and fifties a second generation appeared: Ernesto Alayza, Roberto Pérez del Pozo, Jorge Alayza, and Enrique Echegaray. Through all these periods César Arróspide in particular came to symbolize the model layman: a cultured and well-bred man, receptive to the social message of the church, respectful of the hierarchy while retaining his own critical spirit. In the seventies and eighties, when Catholic Action had virtually disappeared, Arróspide was one of the few veterans of the lay movement of the thirties who made the transition to the new church of Medellín and Puebla. Along with José Dammert Bellido he had a major influence on the generation that forged liberation theology.

Some of the militants began as laymen and ended as clerical moderators for the same movement. Two men especially stand out in this respect: José Dammert Bellido and Luis Vallejos Santoni. Dammert was influenced by his own mother, Rebeca Bellido de Dammert, who was a leader of Women's Catholic Action in the thirties. Dammert pursued graduate studies in Italy, where he joined the Italian Catholic Action. When he became a professor of the Catholic University in Lima he worked as a lay adviser to Catholic youth groups. He entered Santo Toribio Seminary and was ordained a priest in 1947. Shortly afterwards he was named adviser to the National Committee of Catholic Youth. In 1958 he was named auxiliary bishop of Lima and in 1962 he was designated bishop of Cajamarca. He was without doubt the most important pioneer in the hierarchy of the socially progressive church of Medellín and Puebla.

Luis Vallejos Santoni, a pharmacist by profession, was also a lay militant of Catholic Action. He came to hold two different posts: president of the Archdiocesan Council of Catholic Action in Lima (1945) and president of the National Council of Young Catholic Men (1948). He was a "late" vocation, entering the seminary in Lima at the age of thirty. He was ordained a priest in 1957 and in 1971 was named the second bishop of Callao, his birthplace. In 1975 he was appointed archbishop of Cuzco and in that post became one of the architects of the progressive southern Andean church. He died in an automobile accident in 1982.

Among other priest-advisers who began as lay militants in Catholic Action were Gerardo Alarco, Eduardo Picher, and Gustavo Gutiérrez. Alarco, a civil engineer by profession, was the cofounder of Fides Center and the Popular Union Party, and for a while director of the newspaper *Verdades*. After studying for the priesthood in Europe he returned to Peru in 1945 and became national adviser to UNEC and later on national adviser to Catholic Action. Finally, Gustavo Gutiérrez, while studying medicine at San Marcos, served as president of the Catholic Center of Barranco. When he returned in 1960 from his studies in Europe he became archdiocesan adviser to UNEC and later on the national adviser.

In the provinces some other leaders of Catholic Action stood out. In Arequipa the main ones were Jorge Cornejo Polar and Jorge Bolaños; in Cuzco, Máximo Vega Centeno; in Chiclayo, Edgardo Seoane. In general, the women's branches showed more dynamism and had more members. Among the more prominent women leaders were Rebeca Bellido de Dammert, Virginia Candamo de Puente, María Alvarez Calderón, Rosina Dugenne de Cebrián, and María Rosario Araoz. María Rosario Araoz was also a cofounder of ONDEC (National Office of Catholic Education).

Second Period: Self-Criticism (1949–53)

During the Fourth National Eucharistic Congress, held in Cuzco in 1949, the leaders of Catholic Action critically examined the first fifteen years of the organization's existence. They came to the conclusion that Catholic Action had not fulfilled many of the objectives for which it was created. They decided that it had been an error to take the European church as their model. In Europe, for example, the parish was the basic nucleus of Catholic Action. But in Peru the parish was very often not the center of the religious life of Catholics. Their principal criticisms, however, were the lack of a clear definition of what they proposed to achieve, and excessive clerical interference. Some bishops and priests had conceived of Catholic Action as a sort of lay arm of the priests. The leaders requested the bishops to reexamine their expectations so that Catholic Action could really be a lay organization and act with some autonomy with respect to the bishops. The request was not received with enthusiasm by the hierarchy.[74]

Third Period: The Social Question and Decline (1953)

Increasingly the "social question" became the central issue in the existence of Catholic Action, not only in Peru but in the rest of Latin America as well. In 1945 César Arróspide, along with the president of Catholic Action in Bolivia, Armando Gutiérrez Granier, and Fernán Luis Concha, president of Catholic Action in Chile, organized the first inter-American week of Catholic Action in Santiago, Chile. A second week was held in Havana in 1949. The Peruvians and other delegates who attended were dissatisfied with the formality characteristic of those meetings and the consequent lack of real dialogue. They were especially resentful of the fact that the meetings were dominated by groups that did not want to address social issues. Accordingly, in 1953, with the support of Bishop Manuel Larraín of Talca, Chile, the adviser to the inter-American secretariat of Catholic Action, the Peruvians themselves organized the third week in the small fishing city of Chimbote along the northern coast of Peru. They achieved a double objective: in the simpler surroundings of Chimbote the dialogue was much more fluid and natural and, in the face of the poverty of the fishermen and their families, the social question received more serious attention.

The meeting at Chimbote also marked a new phase in Peruvian Catholic Action; from that point on, the social question became the dominant theme at all other meetings. Ironically, it also signaled the beginning of the end. In the decade of the fifties many leaders of Catholic Action came to the conclusion that their mission in life was to change all of society through direct political action. Among them were many of the founders of the Christian Democratic Party. Also UNEC, which had absorbed the majority of militant Catholic university youth, began following a more independent course. Finally, when the official church itself in the sixties made the social question a concern of the entire church, Catholic Action ceased to be the specialized, exclusive forum where social issues would be aired among Catholics. After Vatican II Catholic Action began to decline. The specialized branches for professionals and students, however, continued to function.

The National Union of Catholic Students

In 1941, Fernando Stiglich Gazzini, a Catholic Action militant, founded the organization "Catholic Youth Students" (JEC), with affiliated groups in Lima, Arequipa and Cuzco. In 1943 these groups coalesced to become the National Union of Catholic Students. The UNEC was one of the more dynamic branches of Catholic Action. With eight hundred members in the beginning, it represented about 10 percent of all university students. One of its important activities was the annual Easter Communion. At the first Easter Communion in 1943 nearly 1,300 students attended.[75] UNEC joined Pax Romana, an international association of Catholic university students. The Peruvians sent delegations to meetings of Pax Romana in New York and Washington in 1939 and to Santiago, Chile, in 1944. They also hosted the first inter-American assembly of Catholic Universities in Lima in 1946. A key figure in these interchanges was Rudy Salat, a German Catholic leader who was forced to remain in Peru during the war years. In 1946 UNEC sent a delegation to congresses of Pax Romana in Salamanca and Freiburg. Juan Landázuri Ricketts, the future cardinal, accompanied the delegation as moderator. In the fifties Father Gerardo Alarco served as national adviser to UNEC, and in the sixties Gustavo Gutiérrez assumed that responsibility.

UNEC went through many changes that reflected the different stages in the church's evolution. It was born in a period when anticlericalism reigned at the national universities. For this reason the annual Easter Communion symbolized the militant church: to receive the sacraments in public required courage because it set one off from the majority of students, who were either indifferent or hostile toward religion. In the fifties and in the beginning of the sixties, two phenomena especially affected UNEC: the increase of the student population and the appearance of an aggressive Marxism stimulated by the success of socialism in China and the Cuban revolution. That same Marxism also declared open war on *Aprismo*, which until then had dominated student life. In the face of the sectarian dogmatism of both Apristas and Marxists, UNEC, highly influenced by Christian Democracy, took up the banner of social Christianity. In the sixties, however, UNEC began to radicalize its positions; it went beyond social Christianity, giving rise to a Catholic left. But the other problem,

The Militant Laity, 1930–1955

the population explosion, could not be met by changing one's ideological postures. By the late sixties the "Unecistas" constituted only very small groups within an ever-growing student population, especially at the national universities.

The Workers Movement

Catholic Action also organized a branch for workers, but with less success than among professionals and students. In Arequipa and Cuzco the Catholic Workers Circles continued to function, but these associations were really made up of artisans, chauffeurs, and employees, not factory workers. In Lima in the twenties and thirties confraternities and mutual aid societies for workers were founded. In 1931, for example, the Dominicans founded the Society of Workers of the Sacred Heart, which had nearly five hundred members.[76] In 1932 the Federation of Societies of Catholic Workers was founded to coordinate the activities of all existing groups in the country.[77]

These associations were not "unions" but rather mutual aid societies. Morever, they were usually of a politically conservative nature and had nothing to do with the national union movement, dominated by anarchists and Apristas. In 1931 the Catholic Workers Circle of Arequipa even lent support to the creation of a "Steering Committee of Workers Unions on the Right."[78] During the eucharistic congress held in Arequipa in 1940 the workers who participated called for forming a "United Front of Workers on the Right."[79]

There were also several attempts to found JOC (Young Christian Workers) in Peru. JOC was first founded in Belgium by Father Joseph Cardijn and it came to have considerable influence among workers in Europe. In the thirties Amelio Placencia organized the first groups of JOC in Surquillo and Santa Beatriz (Lima). The Catholic Center of Barranco founded a branch of JOC in 1939.[80] In 1948 the first national convention of JOC in Peru was organized and Mariano Noriega, a Jesuit, was named as national adviser to the movement. He was succeeded in 1951 by Father Augusto Camacho. JOC managed to establish affiliated branches in Arequipa, Mollendo, Toquepala, Huancayo, Paramonga, Casa Grande, La Oroya, and Chiclayo. But it was never large numerically. According to the report of Catholic Action in 1959 cited above, the total number of men and women "militants" and "sympathizers" in JOC in the entire country was 373.[81] One reason the report gave for such a low number was the lack of moderators to form new groups.

The Catholic Press

The new militant spirit of the thirties gave new life to Catholic journalism. Two of the most important new newspapers were *Verdades* and *Patria*. *Patria* was founded and directed by Gonzalo Herrera as the organ of the Popular Union party. It came out daily in 1931 and 1932. *Verdades*, a weekly, was founded in 1930 by the Diocesan Federation of Catholic Youth, under the direction of Cargín Allison and Gerardo Alarco, partly to respond to *La Libertad*, an anticlerical newspaper that favored the Apristas.[82] *Verdades* consisted of six pages full of news of the Catholic world in general. It continued until the sixties. Between 1921 and 1976 *Acción Católica Peruana* was published as the official voice of Catholic Action. In 1949 Fides Center published the newspaper *Fides* under the direction of Alfonso Baella and Antonio Lulli. It lasted only a few years. In Lima the other Catholic publications of importance were *La Rosa del Perú* and *El Amigo del Clero*.

The principal newspapers in the provinces were *El Deber* and *La Colmena* in Arequipa, *El Diario* in Cuzco, *El Estandarte Católico* in Ayacucho, and *El Heraldo* in Puno.

Progress and Decline

Catholic Action represented the culmination of the militant church. On the positive side, it fulfilled its two principal objectives: it inculcated in hundreds of middle-class Catholics a deeper sense of belonging to the church and it infused in them a zeal for social change. The Catholic militant of the thirties and forties felt himself or herself to be a soldier at the service of a great and noble cause that demanded a total commitment in the battle against the enemies of the church. A special "mystique," not unlike that found in messianic political movements, pervaded Catholic Action groups. Participating in the eucharistic congresses or even in the ordinary weekly meetings made the Catholic Action militant feel a member of the church. Although Pius XI was esteemed as the founder of Catholic Action, members identified more readily with Pius XII because he symbolized even better the militant church at war with the forces of disorder: liberal Protestantism, fascism, and atheistic communism.

Of course, Catholic Action also had its limitations, some of which were imposed by the ecclesial reality of that moment and others by the social reality of Peru. Like a soldier, the Catholic Action militant's participation in congresses or the liturgy was also somewhat passive. The militants of that period did not have

The Militant Laity, 1930–1955 243

a theological and biblical formation that would have imparted greater understanding to that participation. Nor did they know about modern techniques of group dynamics that would have helped them communicate on a deeper, more personal level. César Arróspide, who followed Catholic Action throughout its entire history, made this criticism of the great congresses and other meetings: "They were very external and formal events, full of oratory, but it was difficult to perceive in them a deeper Gospel resonance."[83]

But the greatest limitation was in the social order. Catholic Action was a middle-class urban movement and did not reach the immense majority of the rest of the country that lived in the rural and Andean areas. Nor did it have much impact on the workers. On the occasion of its twenty-fifth anniversary, Arróspide underlined this limitation: "The Indian problem, which constitutes one of the more serious obstacles in the path of national unity, was simply left untouched by Catholic Action, which was a middle-class, urban movement, quite distant from the world of the peasants."[84]

Nevertheless, one of the principal contributions of Catholic Action was precisely that it did create greater sensitivity to poverty in Peru and to the need to close the enormous gap between social classes. It was in Catholic Action that many professionals, university professors, and school teachers learned the basic elements of the church's social message. For the first time hundreds of Catholics in Peru began to identify social justice with their own Christian faith. At times the militants of that period looked upon the social message not as a guide to change society but as an arm with which to refute the arguments of their enemies. In fact, Catholic Action harbored many different tendencies. The social Christianity of the thirties gave rise to the Christian Democratic party in 1956, but that party splintered into two factions in 1966: one under the leadership of Héctor Cornejo Chávez, of a more leftist tendency, and the other under Luis Bedoya Reyes, who was considerably more to the right. But these differences were not evident during periods dominated by dictators who cut off all democratic dialogue. The militant laity arose first under Leguía, organized itself more solidly under Benavides, and turned into a political party under Odría.

But Catholic Action's historical role was not limited to its contribution to Peru's political life. Undoubtedly, its most important contribution was the change it brought about in the church itself. A high point of Catholic Action was the First Social Week held in

1959. The week was convoked by the hierarchy to bring the church up to date with the larger social questions of the day. Many of the organizers of the week and principal speakers were veterans of Catholic Action, César Arróspide, José Dammert Bellido (a bishop by then), and Ernesto Alayza Grundy. Of the 348 delegates present, two hundred were active members of Catholic Action. The week was practically a congress of Catholic Action.

Ironically, the First Social Week coincided with the beginning of the end of the movement that made it possible. In the meantime, new social and church phenomena of the postwar period were substantially changing the milieu that had given rise to Catholic Action. In the more pluralistic and democratic era of the western world, the church of Pius XII gave way to that of John XXIII. The militant church was transformed into the "modern" church.

8

The Challenge of Modernization and the Social Question

The period between 1955 and 1975 constitutes the most decisive moment in modern Peruvian church history. During this brief space of time a conservative and relatively closed church became transformed into a modern, open church that was also decidedly committed to the cause of social justice for the poor and the oppressed. This period can be subdivided into two phases: the "modern church," 1955–68, and the "social-political church," 1968–75. The modern church, influenced by the developmentalist doctrines in vogue after President John Kennedy's election as well as the "revolution of rising expectations" that swept across all of Latin America, was characterized by its enthusiasm for external changes (new churches, seminaries, and schools) and for development projects (credit cooperatives). "Modernity" manifested itself in other external signs such as the use of clerical suits instead of cassocks. But there were internal changes, too, such as the adoption of a "modern" mentality that esteemed efficiency and rational planning.

Modernization corresponds especially to the transition in the church from Cardinal Guevara (1945–55) to Juan Landázuri Ricketts, his successor. Under Landázuri (named a cardinal in 1962) the ecclesiastical bureaucracy was reorganized to be more in tune with changing national realities. In 1954, for example, the National Office of Catholic Education (ONEC) was created. At the same time new offices and departments were created both in Peru and in the rest of Latin America to coordinate the church's activities more efficiently. In 1955 CELAM (Permanent Council of the Latin American Bishops) and in 1956 the Conference of Religious of Peru were founded. In 1963 a conference for religious women was also established. Although the Latin American church still had far to go in emulating the church in the United States, the model par excellence of efficiency, nevertheless it too began to acquire some of the traits of a modern well-managed enterprise: long-range planning, the rational use of personnel and capital, and efficient coordination of different departments. The national bishops conference, with its commissions and subcommissions, seemed more and more like the board of directors of a large company with multiple interests at many different levels.

In the middle of the modernization process the social question loomed increasingly larger. In the space of a few years, under the impact of Vatican II and the march of events in Latin America in the sixties, the church went from a passive spectator of those events to a direct participant in shaping them, especially during the military regime of Juan Velasco Alvarado. In those years the church was propelled into the unusual role of legitimizing radical change.

What were the factors that combined to produce this dramatic transformation in the church? It would be difficult to single out any one factor. The intellectual sources of inspiration came from within the church and from "without," or better, from the church in dialogue with the world. Long before Vatican II many people in the church had been in quest of this dialogue with the secular world. The highly politicized atmosphere of the thirties had radicalized many Peruvians, who opted either for Marxism or for *Aprismo*. But the Catholics who gave rise to social Christianity were not immune to that atmosphere. They were forced to examine their own Christianity more deeply and to take the social message of the church more seriously. It is no surprise, therefore, to find among the pioneers of the socially progressive church of the sixties and seventies veterans of Catholic Action such as José Dammert, Luis Vallejos, Gustavo Gutiérrez, César Arróspide, and Héctor Cornejo Chávez.

At the same time, the postwar church, though it still maintained a closed attitude toward communism, began to open itself up more positively to the values most esteemed by the western world: pluralism, dialogue, respectful intellectual criticism, and psychological maturity. Although the high point of the new openness occurred during the pontificate of John XXIII, these values were already in full circulation among progressive Latin American Catholics some time before. Some of the promoters of the new church, such as Gustavo Gutiérrez, the Alvarez Calderón brothers, Ricardo Antoncich, and Romeo Luna Victoria, studied at the more advanced Catholic academic centers in Europe in the fifties and sixties. Others, such as Felipe MacGregor and Ricardo Morales Basadre, pursued further studies in the United States.

Of great importance for understanding the changes was the presence of numerous foreign missionaries who went to work among the popular classes in the cities and in the rural areas. Many of them came from parts of Europe that traditionally sent missionaries to the New World: Spain, Italy, and France. But others came from new areas of Europe and the New World: the United States, Canada, Ireland, and England. Many of the new missionaries were more democratic and open in their thinking than older generations of missionaries. In many areas they became the principal catalysts of the new church among the popular classes.

But more important than this confluence of ideas was a new "mystique" that pervaded the Catholic world, and especially Latin America, in the wake of Vatican II. The Christians of the sixties went through their own "revolution of rising expectations," especially when faced with the exciting challenge of being witnesses to and participants in two great "crusades": the radical transformation of the Catholic church after Vatican II and the reshaping of Latin American society, either by revolution or by peaceful means, into a more just and democratic society. The newly arrived missionaries and the Peruvian Catholics who had already set the changes into motion felt themselves called upon to perform a task even more ambitious than that assumed by the militants of Catholic Action days. The lay militant of the thirties sought to defend the church and Christianity against its enemies. But the Christian of the sixties and seventies was called upon to change all of society.

The velocity with which these changes occurred can only be understood by taking into account the impact of political and social changes on the church. Once open-minded priests, religious, and laypersons set to work to change the world in which they lived, they were caught up in a process that radicalized them even more. Foreign missionaries, for example, who found themselves working with the marginalized popular classes soon acquired a greater social sensitivity and political awareness than they had before going to Latin America.

There were, of course, some people who played key roles in promoting change within the church: Landázuri and Dammert in the hierarchy, Felipe MacGregor in the Catholic University, Romeo Luna Victoria among teachers, and Gustavo Gutiérrez in university circles and in the new popular church. Toward the end of the sixties and throughout the seventies, Bishops Luis Bambarén and Germán Schmitz set the example of the new pastoral style in the "young towns" where they worked.

Not all church groups accepted the changes. Some bishops directly opposed them. Others resigned themselves to the changes as necessary evils. In spite of this lack of uniformity, however, there is no doubt that the church as a whole experienced a decisive transformation in its mentality in the fifties and beyond. Some people and events merit special attention for their contribution to the changes: the foundation of the Christian Democratic party; Cardinal Landázuri; the initiatives taken to face the crisis of social marginalization; the Vatican Council, and finally, the foreign missionaries.

The Christian Democratic Party, 1955–1956

Social Christianity, a fruit of the thirties, underwent several trials before emerging formally as a political party in Peru. It was founded about the same time as other Christian Democratic (CD) parties in the rest of Latin America, though much later than the most famous ones, the CDP in Chile, founded by Eduardo Frei in 1937, and the COPEI of Venezuela, founded by Rafael Caldera in 1945.[1] These two "stars" among the Christian Democrats both came to power and exercised a decisive influence over the course of events in Chile and Venezuela. But the CDP of Peru became a victim of adverse circumstances and internal quarrels, provoked by both ideological and personality clashes. It never became an electoral force. It did, however, come to exercise an important intellectual influence far beyond its small membership in university and political circles.[2]

Peruvian CD leaders had become acquainted with other leading Latin American CD personalities, such as Frei and Caldera, in different encounters since the thirties. In 1949, for example, Luis Bedoya Reyes, David Vega Christie, and Carlos Gandolfo made up the Peruvian delegation to the second meeting of the Latin American CD parties, held at Montevideo.[3] Along with Christian thinkers and humanists such as Jacques Maritain, Emmanuel Mounier, and Nikolai Berdyaev, the French Dominican Louis-Joseph Lebret played an especially important role in their development. In 1941 Lebret founded a center called "Human Economy" in Marseilles to study social problems and their impact on human beings. After the war he directed his attention to the problem of worldwide underdevelopment. It was precisely in centers like that run by Lebret that the concepts of "first" and "third" worlds and "development" and "underdevelopment" were fashioned. Lebret was soon sought out by different "third-world" governments to carry out research in their countries in order to find solutions to their problems.[4] In 1958 the Peruvian senate gave its approval to the "Lebret Mission," which was comissioned by the government to study the *barriadas* (marginal urban settlements) of Peru.[5] Lebret and other thinkers, with their sociological and economic training, helped Latin American Christian Democrats translate the papal social encyclicals into concrete concepts applied to the reality of Latin America.

The first steps toward the creation of a Peruvian CDP were taken under José Luis Bustamante y Rivero. The president from Arequipa was a perfect example of a Catholic gentleman; he was modest, austere, but very conscious of his duties to the poor. And he practiced his religion. The pioneer group of the Peruvian CDP arose around him. In 1947 Fernando Stiglich Gazzini, Héctor Cornejo Chávez, and Luis Bedoya Reyes, all of whom were presidential advisers, formed the "Christian Democratic Association" to channel political support for Bustamante. Other members of the association were Javier Correa Elías, Carlos Gandolfo Corbacho, Jorge del Busto Vargas, and César Arróspide.[6] In 1948 Stiglich organized a "Popular Democratic Movement," which pulled together several hundred young people, most of whom were university students or professionals.[7] These efforts to support Bustamante, however, were doomed to failure. First, the promoters had little political experience. Second, they were unable to galvanize real popular support. And third, Bustamante himself did not support them publicly because he did not want to give the impression of using his high office to create a political party.

Bustamante finally fell, a victim of the instability inherent in being a political independent, without a party or organized groups to support him. He found himself caught between two extremes: on the one hand, the Aprista party, which had become increasingly belligerent in congress, and on the other, the oligarchy and its conservative representatives. He tried to save the situation by governing through the military, but to no avail. In October 1948, General Manuel Odría overthrew his government.

Odria's coup d'etat radicalized the social Christians, who now joined the forces of resistance to the dictatorship. In Arequipa, Javier Belaunde led an antigovernment movement in the elections of 1950 (in which Odría allowed no other candidates but himself). The Arequipa movement drew together men who were to play prominent political roles later on: Enrique Chirinos Soto, Jorge Bolaños, Roger Cáceres, and Héctor Cornejo Chávez. Finally, after several meetings, in September 1955 a group of professionals, the director of *El Pueblo*, a major daily, university professors and students, and a few workers founded the "Christian Democratic Movement." The key founders were Mario Polar Ugarteche, Javier Belaunde, Cornejo Chávez, Roberto Ramírez Villar, and Jaime Rey de Castro.[8] In October of that year another group was formed in Lima under the leadership of Luis Bedoya Reyes. In January 1956 the two groups coalesced and formed a single national party.

The militants of the Peruvian CDP represented a new type of Christian in Peru: they were modernminded middle-class professionals with a keen sense of social awareness. They were not hesitant to enter politics, which earlier generations of Catholics had looked upon as sordid and unseemly. Although they were respectful of the hierarchy, they had a clear sense of their own identity as laypersons. Many of them knew the social message of the church better than most priests and bishops, and in general they possessed a broader and more sophisticated view of the world than the local clergy. In many ways the man who came to be the most visible representative of the Christian Democrats, Héctor Cornejo Chávez, incarnated these qualities. He had studied in both national and religious schools in Arequipa and graduated as a lawyer at San Agustín University. He was one of the founders of JEC (Young Christian Students), and in 1943 he presided over the Archdiocesan Commission of Young Men's Catholic Action. Catholic Action for him and other CD leaders was a school of preparation for political involvement. In 1948 he served as a secretary to President Bustamante y Rivero. He participated in many of the protest marches in Arequipa during the Odría years. In 1956 he was elected to the house of deputies, and in 1962 the party nominated him as its candidate for the presidency. In 1963 he was elected to the Peruvian senate. He was also twice elected president of the party, in 1961–62 and 1966–68. He served as an adviser in the Velasco military government and was appointed director of *El Comercio* when the military expropriated the press in 1974.[9] He was elected to the constitutional assembly of 1978–79. Then, quite abruptly, he withdrew from politics altogether. One reason he gave for that decision was his belief that he was personally in part responsible for the divisions in his own party. Partisan politics notwithstanding, he continued to maintain close ties with the church. As a lawyer he specialized in legislation affecting the family and served on numerous occasions as an adviser to the church, especially in such sensitive areas as divorce, birth control, and children's rights.

Yet in spite of these obvious close ties, Christian Democracy was never a party "of the church." Party leaders were careful to stress their independence from the official church. Furthermore, Catholic Action militants who joined the party had to resign from leadership posts in the former as a condition for participating in politics. In spite of this formal independence from the church, the Peruvian CDP did contribute to the maturing process in the church. It represented the first attempt to spread social Christianity outside strictly church circles. In time social Christianity went beyond the confines of a particular political party. In the sixties many military personnel were influenced by Christian Democratic doctrines, and the Velasco government openly courted CD leaders such as Cornejo Chávez. By then a Catholic left had arisen, which for a time found its principal expression in the Revolutionary Socialist party founded in 1976. Earlier, in 1966, Luis Bedoya Reyes had broken off from the CDP and taken with him other important original founders of the party: Ernesto Alayza Grundy, Mario Polar, Roberto Ramírez del Villar, Jaime Rey de Castro, and others. Bedoya's Popular Christian party constituted a sort of rightist "social Christianity." Naturally, the CDP of Cornejo Chávez dismissed Bedoya's group as a deviation from the ideal.

CD leaders were frequently invited to address church groups, in parishes or schools, as guest speakers. In the First Social Week (1959) many of the speakers and commission heads were CD militants. Progressive clergymen looked upon Christian Democracy as a concrete expression of their own message. Yet the CDP's influence on the church was not uniform. The progressive wing of the church was much smaller and less influential than the corresponding wing of the Chilean church. In Peru many priests and bishops sympathized, not with the CDP, but with Fernando Belaúnde's Popular Action Party or some of the more conservative parties. The Peruvian CDP represented a moment of transition for the church from the period of the militant laity that functioned mainly within closed church circles to a new period in which the militants joined the general political fray. In so doing, they also challenged the church to leave its siege mentality behind and come to terms with the modern world.

MOSICP

The creation of the Christian Democratic party also led to the founding of the Christian Union Movement (Movimiento Sindical Cristiano) in 1955. MOSICP was the international worker's branch of the Christian Democratic parties. In Peru it absorbed many members of the JOC. Ideologically, it rejected both Marxism and *Aprismo*, the first because of its emphasis on class struggle and its hostility toward religion, the second because of its fascist tendencies. It called for solidarity between exploited classes, though in the sixties it radicalized its positions and condemned North American economic imperialism in Latin America. It received financial and technical support from the European CD parties, especially those of Belgium and West Germany. Like the Peruvian CDP, however, it never became a mass movement. According to one specialist, it had between twenty and thirty-thousand members in 1968.[10]

Landázuri and the Peruvian Church

Juan Landázuri Ricketts is certainly one of the key figures in modern Peruvian church history. Between 1955 when he was named archbishop of Lima after the death of Cardinal Guevara and until he formally ceased to be archbishop in January 1990, he was a witness to all the important changes that contributed to the radical transformation of the church. In fact, he was one of the principal architects of many of those changes. Born in Arequipa in 1913 and baptized Eduardo, he belonged to one of the most prominent families of the "White City." His maternal grandfather was William Ricketts, the founder of a commercial house that eventually became known as Gibs Ricketts and Company. After two years at San Agustín University he entered the Franciscans of the Missionary Province of San Francisco Solano. He did most of his ecclesiastical studies at the great monastery of Santa Rosa de Ocopa (near Huancayo) and was ordained a priest in 1939. His rise within the church was very rapid. He taught for a while at Ocopa and then in 1946 was named moderator of the delegation of Peruvian students who went to the congresses of Pax Romana in Salamanca and Freiburg. After studying for three years in Rome he received a doctorate in canon law. He returned to Peru in 1950 and took up teaching at Ocopa once again. In 1951 he was named superior of the missionary Franciscans in all of Latin America. In 1952 he was named coadjutor archbishop of Lima.[11]

From the moment he was named archbishop he was recognized by the other bishops as virtual "head" of the Peruvian church. Although the archbishop of Lima is de facto primate of the Peruvian church, in principle any bishop (among the thirty-six there were in 1960 and the fifty-four in 1985) can be elected president of the bishops conference. But largely in recognition of his leadership qualities, the other bishops elected Landázuri president of the conference for almost the whole period that he served as archbishop. During that long period he personally consecrated nearly half of Peru's bishops. He became, in short, sort of a patriarch of the Peruvian church. Furthermore, he was always the most visible representative of the Peruvian church at all major international church meetings.

Given his social background, as well as his good-natured and nonaggressive personality, he seemed called upon to play the role of a nonassertive conservative. Nevertheless, after thirty-five years as archbishop, this initial assessment clearly proved to be inaccurate. Landáruzi's style of governing was to use the art of persuasion and the "soft" approach. He avoided authoritarian gestures, preferring dialogue instead. He encouraged people to take the initiative and took the role of conciliator between parties in conflict. It was largely due to Landázuri's gift of diplomacy that the Peruvian church went through the period of the Council, Medellín, and Puebla without any major internal crisis, at least compared with other parts of Latin America.

In the style of a conciliar bishop, Landázuri emphasized dialogue with other bishops and with his own clergy. This also explains to a large extent why there was relatively little resentment on the part of either conservative or progressive groups. Furthermore, as Lima grew the church became notably more pluralistic, but without losing its common identity, once again a fruit of the cardinal's pastoral tact.

CELAM, 1955

In July and August of 1955 the first General Conference of the Latin American Episcopate was held in Rio de Janeiro. The principal fruit of that conference was the creation of CELAM, the permanent Council of Latin American Bishops, an organization designed to coordinate the pastoral work of the church throughout all of Latin America. Later on CELAM established its headquarters in Bogotá. Among the founders of CELAM, and who also became its president and vice-president, were Manuel Larraín of Talca, Chile, and Dom Helder Câmara of Recife. Other key figures in the history of CELAM, before and after Medellín, were Marcos McGrath of Panama, Eduardo Pironio of Argentina, and Aloisio Lorscheider of Brazil. Landázuri was elected co-president of the Second General Conference of CELAM at Medellín and served as vice-president of CELAM in the period just before the third conference at Puebla in 1979. Other Peruvian prelates who also served in key CELAM posts were Luciano Metzinger as head of the department of social communication, Luis Bambarén as head of the department of social action, and José Dammert in the department of the laity.

CELAM played an all-important role in helping the Latin American church to mature. First, it broke down the barriers that isolated the different churches from one another. Until the creation of CELAM only the militants of Catholic Action and a handful of bishops and priests had any vital contact with other parts of Latin America. Through CELAM the bishops began to acquire a real sense of identity as part of a single Latin American church. CELAM also served as a channel of expression for the social concerns of the various national churches. And CELAM itself became a vital instrument for conscienticizing the local churches as well. Finally, CELAM organized the major bishops conferences at Medellín and Puebla.

The Mission of Lima, 1957

The most urgent problem that the new head of the archdiocese of Lima had to face was the population explosion. Lima climbed from a population of 645,172 inhabitants in 1940 to 1,652,000 in 1961. But by 1985 the population had jumped to six million.[12] With this enormous growth rate, Landázuri set into motion an ambitious building plan. In 1955 there were fifty-one parishes in the archdiocese. But by 1985 that number had risen to 136, without counting the many small satellite chapels belonging to parishes.

But change was not just quantitative. The church also adopted a "missionary" mentality to face the challenge of the fast-growing new settlements (then called *barriadas*) that ringed the city. The demographic explosion also forced many in the church to realize that there was an entire structural problem in Peruvian society that was primarily responsible for the growth. The church built new parishes and also adopted new pastoral strategies to face the crisis. For example, the church frequently collaborated in development projects or humanitarian relief programs. The new parishes in the *barriadas* had a strong social orientation from the very beginning.

At a press conference held in May 1957, Archbishop Landázuri announced the creation of the "Mission of Lima," which was to be the first part of his pastoral plan for the *barriadas*, which then had about 120,000 inhabitants.[13] In fact, since 1955 small groups of priests and lay volunteers had been visiting the *barriadas* regularly, usually on weekends. In October 1957, the first house of the mission was founded in Villa María (a barriada).[14] The house had a chapel, a medical post, a meeting room for members of the credit cooperative, and a center for mothers. In 1958 the mission consisted of fifteen priests and 124 lay volunteers. The principal source of financial aid for the mission as well as for many other projects of the church in the *barriadas* was Cáritas, an international Catholic relief agency, which established a branch in Peru in 1954. Cáritas channeled the contributions of other agencies, such as the Catholic Relief Service of the United States, into the church's centers in these settlements. A key organizer of the Mission of Lima was María Rosario Araoz.

The mission projected a somewhat paternalistic image in the beginning. Nevertheless, the full pastoral plan called for creating a stable and independent church some day in the *barriadas*. In fact, as time went on the new parishes began absorbing many of the original tasks assigned to the mission, which finally ceased to have a reason for existence. It continued to function, under the direction of Rafael Hooij, a Redemptorist priest, for twenty years after its foundation.[15]

Abbé Pierre, Daniel McClellan, and Father Iluminato

Abbé "Pierre," a former soldier who became a symbol of social consciousness in the postwar years for his work among the destitute of Paris, also had an influence on Peru. In 1958 Bishop Dammert quoted Abbé Pierre in defense of the right of settlers in the *barriadas* to live in "unoccupied houses."[16] And in 1959 Abbé Pierre himself went to Peru to visit the *barriadas*. He attended the First Social Week and spoke of his experiences.[17] One direct fruit of his visit was the foundation of a movement to help the poor called the "The Ragpickers of Emmaus."[18]

In the same period Daniel McClellan of the Maryknoll Fathers won praise for his enterprising spirit. In 1955 he founded the Savings and Credit Cooperative of San Juan in Puno. A year later the cooperative had eight hundred members.[19] Soon an entire chain of similar cooperatives sprang up throughout the southern highlands. Also in 1955 Father Iluminato de la Riva Liguri, an Italian Capuchin, founded the "Children's City," an orphanage for abandoned children. The three together, Abbé Pierre, McClellan, and Iluminato gave moving examples of the church's social sensitivity and creativity in the face of new social realities.

SENATI, 1961

SENATI (National Service for Industrial Job Training) was founded in 1961 as an ambitious program to offer both technical education and humanistic formation to young workers. Although it was not directly a work of the church, it was conceived by a group of educators and businessmen linked to UNDEC (National Union of Catholic Employers), which in turn was founded as a fruit of the national eucharistic congress of 1954. The moderator of this new branch of Catholic Action was Father Felipe MacGregor, S.J. The founders of SENATI aimed to train young workers and arm them with a humanistic background so that they in turn could create their own centers of work. In 1957 Alejandro Tabini, a civil engineer, proposed the idea to the National Society of Industry, which not only approved the idea but even assumed responsibility for getting the project started.[20] By 1966, after only a few years of existence, SENATI, besides its big complex in Lima, had branches in Chiclayo and Arequipa, and during that time had provided free education for some 12,903 workers. The same group of businessmen were also responsible for creating the University of El Pacífico.

A New Social and Political Mentality

The Pastoral Letter of 1958

The church's new mentality is reflected most of all in a pastoral letter the bishops wrote in 1958 on the social question. It was the first real social message of the Peruvian episcopate. In the thirties and forties the bishops had spoken of creating a just social order, but they limited themselves to criticizing concrete examples of injustice and did not question the very social structures that had produced those abuses.

Further, the earlier messages gave more emphasis to the evils that accompanied certain ideologies than to the positive need for change. By way of contrast, the 1958 letter called upon Christians positively to change society. The bishops even pointed to the "accumulation of wealth in the hands of a few" as one of the causes of the current social crisis.[21]

The bishops repeated many key themes of the church's social

doctrine from Leo XIII on, but the thinking of Pius XII is especially evident. They denounced the evils produced by materialistic technical society, especially dehumanizing and depersonalizing relations. The bishops stressed the obligation to pay a just salary and pointed to the workers' rights to participate in the ownership of companies. They singled out for praise the parish cooperatives in Puno and Lima as models of free associations that fostered community development. Finally, they exhorted government authorities to find a solution to the problem of the *barriadas*. The letter ended by convoking the First Social Week.

The First Social Week, 1959

The First Social Week in Peru, held between the first and the ninth of August 1959, took as its model similar weeks that had been held in other parts of the Catholic world: in France since 1903, in Italy since 1907, and in Latin America at different times in Argentina, Brazil, Colombia, Mexico, and Uruguay. The principal organizer was José Dammert Bellido, auxiliary bishop of Lima since 1958. The president of the preparatory committee was Rómulo Ferrero, who was also the president of the National Union of Catholic Employers. The vice-president was Jorge Alayza Grundy, president of the National Committee of Catholic Action. Two priests, Augusto Camacho, moderator of the JOC, and Felipe MacGregor, adviser to the Union of Catholic Employers, also belonged to the committee. Representatives of fifteen dioceses and 106 various Catholic groups, making up a total of 348 delegates, which did not include the organizers and speakers, attended the week.[22]

The Social Week generated great expectations in part because it was a novelty. It represented the first time in contemporary history that the Peruvian church had organized a meeting of clergy, religious, and laity to discuss the major social problems of the country openly. José Luis Bustamante y Rivero, the former president, delivered a talk on "The Social Classes in Peru." Felipe MacGregor, S.J., spoke on "Notions of Community and the Common Good," and César Arróspide addressed the theme of "Promoting Culture." In his talk Bishop Dammert stressed the urgency of making the church's social message known among teachers and university students. Abbé Pierre inspired the delegates by his very presence. The final result was an increase of social consciousness in the church. In that sense, the week was the culmination of the work of Catholic Action, and indeed the majority of delegates were veterans of that movement. The week was also characterized by the absence of a polemical tone typical of earlier meetings of Catholics.

In August 1961, the Second Social Week was held in Arequipa. The main organizer was Father Santiago Delgado Butrón, moderator of the UNEC. He in turn was aided by the Catholic Action groups of the "White City." The second week took a stronger social stance than the first week because it openly criticized the system of land tenure in Peru.[23]

Jurgens and the Agrarian Reform in Cuzco, 1963

Following recommendations made in the various social weeks, the church began to examine its own properties. But only a few dioceses came up with concrete proposals. In Cajamarca, José Dammert, recently named bishop there, not only carried out a reform of church properties, but also gave impetus to many development projects to benefit the peasants. Another striking example was the ecclesiastical agrarian reform carried out by Archbishop Carlos María Jurgens in Cuzco. Since 1956 he had begun a process of selling church lands to land-hungry peasants, and in April 1963 he formally initiated a major church land reform. But Jurgens's initiative provoked criticism from among the peasants themselves who claimed that the church was selling the lands of "all the saints," which really belonged to the communities. Many observers believed that Jurgens was acting under pressure to avoid having those properties expropriated by an imminent national land reform. In fact, very little land was actually sold or distributed; between 1963 and 1972 the church gave over some 1,136 acres to the peasants.[24]

The Elections of 1962 and 1963

In two different collective pastoral letters, "Catholics and Politics" (October 1961) and "On Social and Political Action at This Moment" (May 1963), the episcopate touched upon the theme of politics more directly. The background of the letters was the presidential elections of 1962 and 1963. In 1962 Haya de la Torre, Fernando Belaúnde, and Manuel Odría competed for power, but in the midst of accusations of electoral fraud and fear of an Aprista victory, the military called off the elections and took over the government. A military junta under General Ricardo Pérez Godoy ruled the country for a year and convoked new elections in 1963. The same three candidates ran again, but this time the winner was Fernando Belaúnde Terry, supported by his own Popular Action party, the Christian Democrats, and sectors of the left. The left was represented by the National Liberation Front, with former General César Pando Egúsquiza as its candidate. A curiosity that caused many eyebrows to be raised was the presence of a priest, Salomón Hidalgo Bolo, who was the Front's candidate for the vice-presidency. Although he was suspended from his priestly functions, "Cura Bolo," as he was popularly called, appeared at assemblies of the Front in his cassock and invoked the names of Marx and Christ.[25]

In both letters the bishops pointed out the finality of politics: service to the common good. At the same time they warned against totalitarian and laicist tendencies, which were obvious references to the Aprista party. But the most important aspect of the letters was the exhortation to Catholics to acquire a new "social mentality" and the call to carry out major social reforms. The bishops condemned the concentration of economic power in the hands of a few and explicitly supported the idea of an agrarian reform.[26]

Vatican II and New Pastoral Orientations

Nearly six hundred Latin American bishops attended the Second Vatican Council, held between 1962 and 1965. Cardinal Landázuri himself was a member of the Conciliar Commission for Religious, and after the council Paul VI named him vice-president of the commission. The ecumenical council convoked by John XXIII was without doubt one of the most dramatic moments in the history of Catholicism. But the council did not have nearly the same impact in Latin America as it did in Europe and the United States. To a large extent the council was dominated by European bishops and theologians who addressed themselves to first-world realities. Nevertheless, it was important for the Latin American church because, among other reasons, it strengthened the growing sense of unity and common identity among the bishops, who came to know one another better during the sessions. In this sense the council helped solidify the work of CELAM and paved the way for the episcopal assembly at Medellín in 1968.

One of the key documents of Vatican II was the constitution on the church, *Gaudium et Spes*. The document used biblical metaphors to describe the church as the "people of God" at the service of a humanity in search of its destiny. Church history was conceived of as an open and dynamic process in which new experiences are welcome and healthy for growth. This new way of looking at the church motivated many bishops to encourage experiments and to try out new pastoral methods in their respective dioceses.

The Conciliar Mission of Lima, 1967

In February 1962 the First Pastoral Week was organized in Lima. Over one hundred priests attended. The principal promoters of the week were Bishop Dammert, Father Jorge Alvarez Calderón, and the canon Fernando Boulard, who was also a sociologist. The following year a second week was held with two hundred priests from twenty different dioceses in attendance.[27] The central themes of these weeks were in general the same as those at the Vatican Council. In the third week, held in 1964, the principal theme was the liturgical reform. In 1965 the Latin American Pastoral Institute of CELAM organized a series of pastoral "encounters" for priests and religious women in Arequipa and Cajamarca. By means of these weeks and encounters the central ideas of the Vatican Council began to reach the basic levels of the Peruvian church.

The high point of this campaign to make the council known was the Conciliar Mission of Lima in 1967. Under the direction of Vicente Guerrero, a Dominican, an ambitious project to reach all Catholics in Lima was set into motion. Between June and October of that year a major sociological study was conducted in the archdiocese to determine the religious practices of most Catholics. The study showed that only slightly more than 25 percent of Catholics who were obliged to do so went to Sunday Mass on a regular basis.[28] But the study also served as a pretext for establishing contact with thousands of people in the 117 parishes of the archdiocese who had ceased to practice their Catholicism. To carry out the project 119 Spanish priests volunteered to go to Peru especially for the occasion, and they were joined by another 250 priests working in Peru.[29] In addition, four hundred religious women left their schools and convents to visit houses in the *barriadas* and to give talks on the meaning of the council.[30] The conciliar mission of 1967 reinforced the Mission of Lima of 1957 that had already established a bridge between the church and the *barriadas*. But the conciliar mission also suffered from a few defects. The home visits were carried out like popular missions in the Andes—quick visits but no follow up. Furthermore, the foreign missionaries who went for the project were not acquainted with local customs.

Dammert in Cajamarca

Although the application of the conciliar reforms received more attention in Lima, the best all-round example of putting the council into effect was in the diocese of Cajamarca. José Dammert Bellido, born into an upper-class family in Lima, was a veteran of Catholic Action and a former professor at the Catholic University. He did not seem the best candidate for bishop of a diocese in the middle of the northern Andes, far removed from the cultural and intellectual life of the national elites. However, after a brief period as auxiliary bishop of Lima, he accepted the challenge and within a few years managed to transform a sleepy mountain diocese into a model of the progressive, conciliar church. He put into operation a comprehensive pastoral plan that aimed to reorient the priests, religious women, and laity of the diocese. Most of all, he stressed the formation of rural catechists who virtually became lay "deacons"; they were trained to prepare paraliturgies, administer the sacrament of baptism, and in general assume responsibility for the religious formation of their local communities.

In addition, he fostered many development projects: credit cooperatives, home building, and the establishment of medical posts. In 1964 the Institute of Rural Education, which had other centers in the country, was invited to Cajamarca. The institute, which functioned within the diocesan seminary, offered courses for training peasants. After Medellín it stressed even more the formation of rural leaders with a community consciousness.[31]

At the same time the diocese critically reexamined many traditional practices, such as the exploitation and drinking associated with religious feasts. The reforms that were put into effect to eliminate these practices provoked the hostility of different groups, especially the landowners and churchmen who were opposed to giving church lands to the peasants; and in the decade of the seventies, SINAMOS (the military government's bureaucracy in charge of popular level projects) blamed the church for the coldness with which their agents were received. But the diocese had already helped the peasants to organize themselves, and the peasants looked upon the government agency as an intruder. Toward the end of the sixties other dioceses, especially those in the southern highlands, also put into effect other kinds of renovations. But Cajamarca had already led the way.

The Christian Family Movement and the Cursillos de Cristiandad

These two movements really belong chronologically to the pre-Vatican II period, but they had their greatest impact in the sixties and in many ways represented concrete ways of implementing the council's call for greater lay participation. The Christian Family Movement had its origins in France and the United States in the forties and was founded in Peru in 1953 as a direct outgrowth of the meeting of Catholic Action in Chimbote. It soon spread to other cities: to Arequipa in 1959 and Puno and Cuzco in 1960. In the sixties in Lima alone there were four hundred families making up sixty teams to direct other families that belonged to the CFM.[32] The CFM sought to strengthen marital ties and foster greater dialogue within families, naturally within a Christian context. The movement had its biggest impact on middle-class families and was largely responsible for the return of many couples to the practice of Catholicism.

The *cursillos de Cristiandad* (literally, short courses in Christianity), by way of contrast, were oriented more specifically toward men. Founded in Majorca in 1949, the cursillos consist of intensive weekend retreats that aim to help Catholics reexperience their Christianity in a more vital and deeper way. The movement relies heavily on the modern techniques of group dynamics. The cursillo movement arrived in Peru in 1958 and its first center of diffusion was Arequipa, but like the CFM it soon spread to other parts of the country. In 1964 the First National Assembly of the Cursillos was held in Trujillo. Some five hundred *cursillistas* attended.[33] In the early years the cursillos were criticized by some because they employed psychological techniques designed to have the maximum emotional impact, but which did not necessarily lead to a deeper faith commitment. Nevertheless, for hundreds of men they signified a second beginning as Catholics and even had political consequences: some of the military who took power in 1968 were *cursillistas*.

Both the CFM and the cursillo movement were oriented primarily toward the urban middle classes. In this sense they did not go beyond the class barriers that had been one of the limitations of Catholic Action. But they did represent an advance over Catholic Action by going beyond a purely formalistic and intellectual presentation of Christianity. Both stressed the affective component essential in family relationships and in the Christian commitment in general.

The Foreign Missionaries

The Peruvian church would not have been able to put into effect many of the changes called for by Vatican II, nor maintain a significant presence among the popular classes especially in the midst of the population explosion that began in the forties, without the collaboration of hundreds of men and women missionaries who came from Europe, North America, and other parts of the world in the postwar years. The majority of religious personnel in the jungle, in many rural areas especially in the southern highlands, and in the popular settlements that ring the cities are missionaries who belong to this new wave. Mainly through their efforts the reforms of Vatican II and the new mentality of Medellín reached the basic Christian groups in the popular classes.

This missionary wave also signified a notable increase in the number of clergy and religious women. Among men's religious orders and missionary associations a total of forty-two new groups came to Peru after 1940, and of these twenty-five arrived after 1960.[34] This phenomenon was due to a combination of several factors. First, the churches of the United States, Canada, and Ireland had come to maturity and enjoyed an abundance of vocations. Second, China and other parts of the Orient had closed their doors to the missionaries as a consequence of the Second World War and the coming to power of the communists. And third, the two popes, Pius XII and John XXIII, made repeated calls to the established churches of the first world to send personnel to Latin America to help face the grave priest shortage.

Pius XII first, and John XXIII with even greater insistence, called upon Catholics in Europe and North America (Canada and the United States) to assume greater responsibility for Latin America. These papal exhortations corresponded chronologically to a period of great prosperity in the United States and to a moment when Europe's economic recovery was well under way. On both sides of the Atlantic the papal summons was received as a call to a new "crusade."

The belief that they were participating in a great "crusade" was especially characteristic of the North American missionaries. In 1961 Monsignor Agostino Casaroli, later named secretary of state of the Vatican, spoke in the name of Pope John at the University of Notre Dame when he called upon American Catholics to face the great crisis that affected the Latin American church. He suggested that each religious community send 10 percent of their personnel to Latin America.[35] Cardinal Richard Cushing of

Boston became an enthusiastic promoter of this call, and he chose Peru as a special object of his missionary efforts. In Washington Father John Considine of the Maryknoll Fathers, who was director of the Latin American bureau of the United States bishops conference, turned the papal call into a publicity campaign among American orders and congregations. The papal nuncio in Peru, Rómulo Carboni, also took up the cause and visited religious communities in the United States urging them to send personnel to Peru. As a result of the combined efforts of Cushing and Carboni, and with the full support of Rome and the Peruvian church, Peru received an especially high percentage of the American priests, sisters, and brothers who went to Latin America. In the sixties, when the influx of Americans to Latin America reached its apex, nearly 68 percent of all American diocesan priests in Latin America were in Peru.[36]

Three common traits characterized the majority of the new missionaries who came to Peru. First, almost all belonged to religious orders or congregations. Some belonged to associations of diocesan priests sent by particular bishops; in this case they were not strictly speaking "religious." But they shared with the religious many of the external signs of the religious way of life, especially the call to be missionaries, which gave them special bonds of unity. Second, although the largest group of missionaries to Latin America still came from Spain (of the 982 religious priests in Peru in 1984, 451 were Spaniards), the increase of missionaries from English-speaking countries, Irish, Canadians, and Americans, was nevertheless striking. After the Spanish the largest group of foreign missionaries in Peru (including associations of secular clergy such as the Society of Maryknoll and the St. James Society) are Americans, followed by Italians, Irish, Canadians, French, and Germans. After these large blocks, there follow many smaller groups of other nationalities that have between two and fifteen missionaries: Mexicans, Maltese, English, Polish, Swiss, Yugoslavs, Australians, Dutch, and Belgians.[37]

Third, the great majority of these new missionaries came with a social mentality that they identified closely with their missionary vocation. They left the United States, Canada, or Western Europe with the understanding that one of their tasks was to contribute to the economic and social development of Latin America. Many of them conceived their mission as part of a great battle against communism. But after the sixties most missionaries left behind some of their more simplistic views of Latin America and came to understand the need for fundamental structural change in all of Latin American society.

In general, in recognition of the fact that Latin America had already been evangelized in the sixteenth century, the new religious personnel avoided the rather paternalistic word "missionary" and labeled themselves simply as "helpers" or "volunteers." The Peruvian church sent most of them to the areas where they were most urgently needed: the *barriadas*, the Andes, and the jungle. In some cases the new personnel belonged to an order or congregation already working in Peru, such as the Jesuits or the Franciscans. The four largest groups of new missionaries that came to Peru in this period were the Comboni Fathers, the Society of Maryknoll, the Columbans, and the St. James Society. These four groups in different ways all serve as examples of the new missionary groups in general.

The Comboni Fathers, 1938

Founded in 1867 by Daniel Comboni in Verona, Italy, for work in central Africa, the Comboni (or "Verona") Fathers split into Italians and Germans in 1923 as a consequence of the First World War. The first Comboni Fathers who arrived in Peru in 1938 were Germans; the Italians came in 1966. In 1979 the two groups reunited on a worldwide basis. The first three Comboni Fathers in Peru were invited by Bishop Berroa of Huánuco to work in Pozuzo.[38] After the war, the Comboni Fathers took charge of the seminary in Huánuco. In 1958, in recognition of their notable pastoral activity in parishes throughout the central Andean region, the city of Tarma was made a prelature and placed under the responsibility of the Comboni Fathers. The first bishop was Antonio Kühner. Another bishop of the Comboni Fathers was Lorenzo Unfried, who arrived in Peru in 1951. He served for a number of years as auxiliary bishop of Arequipa and was then named bishop of Tarma in 1980. Kühner was reassigned to be bishop of Huánuco.

In 1954 the Comboni Fathers founded the parish of San Pío X in Mirones, Lima, and in 1970 they founded the parish of Los Doce Apóstoles in Chorrillos. The Italian Comboni Fathers, who arrived in 1966, established themselves in Yanahuanca and Cerro de Pasco, cities of very high altitude in the central Andes. In 1979 the newly reunited congregation began publishing the missionary magazine *Esquila misional*, which changed its name in 1983 to *Misión sin fronteras* (Mission without Frontiers). By 1985 there were forty-five Comboni priests and two bishops in Peru. That same year they had thirty students in the congregation, all Peruvians. Their congregation is strictly missionary; they only accept candidates who intend to work in another country.

Maryknoll, 1943

Two basic factors explain Maryknoll's coming to Peru: the pressing priest shortage in the southern highlands and the closing of their missions in China. In 1943 the diocese of Puno had fifty-five parishes, but only twenty-eight of them had priests. The superior general of Maryknoll visited Peru in 1942, and the bishop of Puno, Salvador Herrera, invited the Society of Maryknoll to his diocese. In 1943 the first five priests of Maryknoll arrived in Puno.[39] Founded in 1911 as the Catholic Foreign Mission Society of America, the priests and brothers of the society are better known by the name of their mother house in New York State: "Maryknoll." Their first objective was to send missionaries to Asia, especially China. This explains why the first Maryknoll priests in Lima worked initially with the Chinese colony.

In Puno the Maryknoll missionaries took charge of several parishes and in 1944 took over the direction of the seminary of San Ambrosio. The first rector of the seminary was Edward Fedders, who was later named superior general of Maryknoll in Peru. In 1957 he was named prelate of the *prelatura nullius* of Chucuito and Huancané and in 1963 was consecrated bishop of the area, with residence in Juli. He died in 1973.[40]

In 1945 Maryknoll established a permanent house in Lima and another one in Arequipa as rest stations for their personnel working in the highlands. Encouraged by María Rosario Araoz of Catholic Action they founded the parish of Santa Rosa in the district of Lince in Lima, and in 1952 they also founded a parish school that was placed under the direction of the sisters of Maryknoll. The pastor of the parish, John Lawler, became a popular symbol of Maryknoll's presence in Lima. He turned the parish into a model of "modernity," fostering a strong sense of unity between priests, religious women, and the laity.

In the southern highlands the Maryknoll missionaries distinguished themselves for their American "know-how" and the application of new pastoral methods. Father Daniel McClellan with his credit cooperatives and Robert Kearns, founder of the radio schools "Onda Azul," were prime example of these qualities. After his first experimental cooperative in Puno in 1955, McClellan set up a central consulting office in Lima to help found other cooperatives in the rest of the country. In 1961 Father Kearns founded the first radio school in Puno, and in time he created a chain of these schools throughout the highlands. The more than twenty thousand peasants who attended these schools could listen to programs in either Quechua or Aymara.[41] In 1969 Kearns was named director of the National Council of Mass Means of Communications recently created by the bishops. In 1970 he was officially acclaimed by the Peruvian government for his work in restoring communications during the disasterous earthquake that year in the Callejón de Huaylas.

Members of Maryknoll in Lima also demonstrated their impressive organizational capacities. Between 1962 and 1974 Father William McCarthy, one of the original Maryknoll priests in Peru, served as director of Cáritas, a job that made him the key liaison in coordinating the church's social works in the *barriadas* (later named *pueblos jóvenes*). In 1962 Father Joseph Michenfelder, trained in journalism, founded the Catholic Information Center and in 1964 began directing *Latin American Press*, a weekly news summary of the Latin American church. In 1956 Maryknoll founded another parish in Lima, Nuestra Señora de Guadalupe, in La Victoria. In 1975 they turned that parish over to the diocesan clergy. They also founded a parish, El Niño Jesús, in San Juan de Dios, one of the newer *barriadas* of Lima. After years as pastor of the parish of Nuestra Señora de Guadalupe, Father Thomas Garrity founded in 1978 the Peruvian Association of Missionaries, a lay organization for volunteers who wished to spend a few years working in projects of the Maryknoll Fathers or Sisters.

The priests, brothers, and sisters of Maryknoll, with their successes and setbacks, typify more than any other group the American presence in Peru. During their first years they displayed a vital creative energy that drew the admiration of friends in Peru and abroad. The parishes they founded, complete with cooperatives, medical posts, and schools, were models of efficiency. Their schools reproduced the best of American education. When other American missionaries arrived in the sixties the Maryknoll priests, brothers, and sisters were already well known in Peru. But they did not escape the effects of the two crises that affected all foreign missionaries in Latin America in those years, the crisis generated by the Second Vatican Council, and the crisis produced by a rising frustration over the absence of visible signs of progress. The best example of the latter crisis was the case of the minor seminary in Puno. During the twenty-five years that the Maryknoll Fathers ran the seminary, some eight hundred young men studied there. Of that total only twelve reached the priesthood. And half of those twelve left the priesthood later on. Disillusioned by those meager results, they decided to close the seminary in 1969.[42]

This failure as well as other problems led the members of Maryknoll to question their presence in Peru seriously. They came to the conclusion that they had based much of their pastoral planning on faulty, preconceived notions of the reality of Latin America. In their enthusiasm they had applied the North American model of church to Peruvian situations. In the midst of this crisis, the changes ushered in by Vatican II led many priests and religious men and women to question their own vocation. In the middle of the sixties there were nearly seventy priests and brothers of Maryknoll in Peru. But between 1965 and 1976, thirty-five of their members left the priesthood, among them Daniel McClellan.[43] Once these crises were faced and overcome, Maryknoll continued to maintain its works with a reduced personnel (in 1985 there were thirty-six members), but at the same time with a more mature vision of its mission in Peru.

The Columbans, 1952

The Missionary Society of Saint Columban was founded in 1918 in Ireland to send missionaries to the Orient, especially China. Like the priests of Maryknoll, the Columbans are an association of secular priests. Although their principal base is in Ireland, many of their members came from other parts of the English-speaking world, including Australia, New Zealand, and the United States. Their decision to come to Latin America was motivated in part by the closing of their missions in China. In 1951 Cardinal Guevara invited them to take charge of a large semiurbanized area that included the districts of San Martín de Porras, Independencia, and Naranjal in Lima. In 1952 the first three Columbans arrived, and by 1956 there were six, all Irish.[44]

The Columbans witnessed practically all the major social changes in the marginal areas under their care. By 1982 they had founded fourteen parishes, three complete primary and secondary schools, and fifty-two primary schools. The Columbans also felt the impact of Vatican II. In the sixties there were fifty Columbans and associated priests in Peru. In 1982, however, there were only thirty-two. Like the Maryknoll Fathers and Sisters they too made readjustments. Before Medellín the typical newly ordained Columban would go directly to the missions after having gone through a traditional pre-Vatican II seminary. After Medellín, however, new reforms were put into effect, such as the requirement to spend two years in the missions during formation. Furthermore, almost all who are assigned to Peru spend six months at the Maryknoll Language Institute in Cochabamba, Bolivia.

Like the Maryknoll priests and brothers, the Columbans do not accept native vocations for themselves. Their policy is to orient youthful candidates toward the diocesan clergy in order to strengthen the local church. Financially, they receive the greater part of their support from mission collections in Ireland and other dioceses throughout the English-speaking world, especially Sydney, Australia. However, some of the first parishes they founded are now virtually self-sufficient. The principal self-criticism the Columbans make is their overconcentration in Lima. As a result of that concentration in the capital, many of the newly arrived missionaries lack a more ample vision of Peru. On the other hand, their pastoral work has been a model of coordination and efficient planning.

The St. James Society, 1958

Like the members of Maryknoll and the Columbans, the priests of the St. James Society are secular priests. Unlike the former, however, their society was founded by an archbishop, Cardinal Cushing of Boston, for priests of his own archdiocese. Richard Cushing personified the generosity and perhaps also the impetuosity of the American church. He was a living incarnation of the immigrant church that became transformed into an established and economically and politically powerful church. Born in a poor neighborhood of Boston, he became a friend of and pastoral counselor to the Kennedys. The archdiocese of Boston that he governed had 2,623 priests and 5,370 religious women—more priests and sisters than in all of Peru! When Pope John XXIII urged the North American church to send personnel to Latin America, Cushing made himself a spokeman for the cause, not just in Boston but in the entire United States and elsewhere. The idea of founding a mission society of diocesan priests was first conceived by Frank Kennard, a priest from the diocese of Portland, Oregon, who had worked for some time in the mountain diocese of Abancay.[45] In 1958 Cushing formally founded the St. James Society, and the first group of missionaries arrived in Peru in 1959.

The first centers of work were Apurímac, Abancay, and Andahuaylas in the southern central Andes. The society also founded a parish in Lima, San Ricardo in La Victoria. The pastor, Joe Martin, a dynamic innovator, became a popular figure in the neighborhood. One of the society's most important works was the language school at Barranco. The first volunteers of the society went to the Maryknoll Language Institute in Cochabamba, but in 1962 the society founded its own school. The school functioned first in Cieneguilla and then in 1967, under the direction of Father Jerry Pashby, it moved to Barranco (Lima). Until it closed in 1977 as a result of diminishing numbers in the society, hundreds of incoming missionaries of different groups studied there.[46]

After several years of experience in Peru the founders of the St. James Society in Peru decided to separate themselves from the archdiocese of Boston and constitute themselves an autonomous group. One of their motives was to free themselves from the obligation to return to the archdiocese after five years of work in Latin America, a standard rule for diocesan missionaries.[47] Nevertheless, the society continues to maintain close bonds with the archdiocese of Boston, although a large percentage of the thirty-six priests (1982) who work in Peru come from many other dioceses, especially in England, Australia and New Zealand. The society administers twelve parishes in Peru, in Apurímac, Chimbote, and Lima. A consequence of the separation from Boston is that the priests of the society are now directly under the local Peruvian bishops.

Concentration by Regions

Besides these larger groups there are smaller groups that stand out because they are the principal ones in charge of a particular area or region. Following a practice already established long before in the Amazon jungle region, the church sought to face the priest shortage by assigning certain areas to specific groups. Many of the *prelaturae nullius* (areas set aside to be dioceses some day but that lack sufficient population or do not fulfill certain other conditions) began as territories entrusted to certain congregations or orders. The head of a *prelatura* is known as an "apostolic administrator" or at times a "vicar apostolic." Although he is not a bishop, he does have the powers of a bishop while he remains in charge of that jurisdiction. An example of this relationship of a special group with a mission territory are the American Carmelites who came to Peru in 1949. The archdiocese of Lima entrusted them with the parish of San Antonio in Miraflores. In 1959 they were also asked to administer the *prelatura nullius* of Sicuani, which had been separated from the archdiocese of Cuzco. The first two prelates of Sicuani were both Carmelites, and both happened to have been pastors of the parish in Lima, Nevin Hayes (1959–70) and Albano Quinn, a Canadian by birth (1971–).[48] Another example is the Italian Oblates of St. Joseph. They came to Peru in 1952 and took charge of several parishes in Lima and Chimbote. In 1958 one of their members was named prelate of the *prelatura nullius* of Huari, high in the north central Andes. His successor in 1966 was Dante Frasnelli of the same congregation. In both Sicuani and Huari, the Carmelites and the Oblates maintain an institutional commitment to their respective prelatures.

In the fifties two new Spanish groups came to Peru: Opus Dei and OCSHA. In 1957 Ignacio María de Orbegoso was named prelate of the *prelatura nullius* of Yauyos, which was broken off from the archdiocese of Lima. The Society of the Holy Cross and Opus Dei, founded in Spain in 1928, had six priests in Peru in 1959: four Peruvians and two Spaniards. In 1968 two other members of Opus Dei were named bishops: Luis Sánchez Moreno, of Yauyos, and Enrique Pelach, of Abancay. Orbegoso was transferred to the diocese of Chiclayo. OCSHA (Work of Hispanic Priestly Cooperation) was founded in 1958 by the Spanish bishops to coordinate the task of sending diocesan priests to Latin America. The "cooperators" of OCSHA in Peru were sent to work in Cajamarca, Lurín, Trujillo, and Chimbote. Since they were diocesan priests, they were placed directly under the bishops of each place. For that reason they have not maintained the same tight organizational ties characteristic of members of a religious order. After the first few years many returned to Spain.

Some foreign groups "adopted" a special territory. In 1961 the Canadian Oblates of Immaculate Mary, who came to Peru in 1957, founded the Centro Jesús Obrero in Comas, one of the major *barriadas* of Lima. The center was a forerunner of many similar programs of technical training for workers. In 1958 the Canadian bishops founded the Society for the Foreign Missions to coordinate Canada's missionary activity in Latin America. The society has concentrated most of its personnel in Peru in Pucallpa, in the central Amazon region.

Another example is the Irish Priests of Santo Toribio, an association of priests of the diocese of Cork founded in 1965 specifically for work in Peru. They founded many parishes in the "young towns" (the new name for *barriadas*) in Trujillo. A group of Dominicans from New York established themselves in Chimbote when one of their members, James Burke, was named prelate of Chimbote in 1967. Also in the sixties the Benedictines of

St. Meinrad in Indiana founded a monastery in "Los Pinos" in Huaraz. In 1964 American Augustinians took charge of the prelature of Chulucanas in northern Peru. John McNabb, of the same order and nationality, was named the first prelate and also the first bishop when Chulucanas was made a diocese in 1967. In 1962 the diocese of Jefferson City, Missouri, assumed responsibility for several parishes in Ica, south of Lima, and in the mining town of Marcona.[49] These are only a few of the many foreign groups and the territories assigned to them.

Finally, there were also many different groups of lay volunteers. The best-known in this period was PAVLA (Papal Volunteers for Latin America). Frequently described as a sort of Catholic "Peace Corps," PAVLA was founded in 1960 by the Pontifical Commission for Latin America. In the sixties it sent nearly one thousand young men and women from the United States to Latin America to work in parishes, schools, and medical posts. PAVLA had an annual average of twenty to thirty personnel in Peru until it was dissolved in 1971, a casualty of the criticisms of the period of the massive and undiscerning sending of foreign missionaries to Latin America.

Critical Assessment

Between the Second World War and the beginning of the seventies several hundred foreign priests and religious women and men joined the Peruvian church. The great majority of them came during the sixties in response to the papal calls to aid the Latin American church. The fundamental instinct that motivated these men and women, most of whom came from the middle classes and many of whom had university degrees, was a missionary idealism, not very different from the drive that sent thousands of missionaries to Latin American in the sixteenth century. But there were certain political and social realities peculiar to this period that formed the background of this new missionary wave. For example, most of the missionaries were products of the cold-war period, which reached a dramatic climax in the confrontation between Kennedy and Khrushchev in Cuba in 1962. In this context Pope John XXIII's summons to work in Latin America acquired the connotation of an anticommunist crusade. Many priests and religious women came to Latin America with the intention of preaching the Gospel and combating communism. Also, conscious of the material wealth and technical superiority of their home countries, the missionaries came, not unlike the sixteenth-century ones, with a triumphalistic spirit that expressed itself in the form of paternalistic attitudes toward the receiving church. Many missionaries limited their preparation to the task of studying Spanish and did not bother to study the culture or the history of the land where they were to work.

At the same time, the sending of so many missionaries was not adequately evaluated from the perspective of the receiving church. On the contrary, the policy of many bishops, and especially the papal nuncio, Rómulo Carboni, consisted in inviting all groups whatsoever in the hope of solving the priest shortage as quickly as possible. Very often the decisive criterion was economic; the foreign missionaries, with more economic backing, could support themselves in the "young towns" and in the poorest parts of the mountains or jungle, while the national clergy could not. In most dioceses in Peru the majority of foreigners were assigned to work with the poor, while the Peruvians continued to work in middle- and upper-class parishes. In general, there was no overall pastoral planning for receiving and distributing the new personnel. The foreigners often formed national "ghettos" with little contact with the local church.

The new missionary wave reached its peak in the sixties; thereafter it declined notably. One reason for the decline was the vocation crisis that the Second Vatican Council produced throughout the entire Catholic world. The fall in the number of vocations was so great that some orders, congregations, and missionary societies drastically reduced the number of personnel sent overseas and in some cases even called their people back. One striking example is the archdiocese of Boston. In the sixties the ordination class at the seminary averaged forty-five to fifty men each year. By the eighties, however, the average ordination class in Boston consisted of twelve to fifteen.

In addition to this generalized crisis, many volunteers who came to Latin America discovered that they did not really have a "missionary" vocation. At the same time, many missionary groups submitted their presence in Latin America to a critical evaluation in the light of Medellín. One of the more celebrated criticisms of the new missionary wave was the article published in 1967 by Ivan Illich in *America*, "The Seamy Side of Charity." In it Illich warned against the indiscriminate sending of hundreds of foreign personnel to Latin America. Prescinding from individual generosity, the new wave constituted a sort of cultural invasion in which the newcomers simply transplanted their own model of church to Latin America without ever really understanding the historical factors that had led to a crisis in the church there in the first place. Instead of solving problems, the newcomers created a new form of dependency.[50]

Between 1968 and 1972 the Maryknoll Fathers and Brothers held a series of meetings to reexamine their own presence in Peru. In an atmosphere of great intellectual honesty, they recognized that they lacked a deeper knowledge of the Peruvian culture and religious traditions.[51] They questioned some of their original triumphalistic attitudes and stressed the need to work more closely with the local bishops to help give rise to an authentically Peruvian church.[52] This kind of self-examination also led some missionary groups to be more selective in accepting volunteers. Not all groups, however, have followed the example of Maryknoll. There are still congregations and missionary associations that transplant foreign church models and maintain a paternalistic relationship vis-à-vis the local church.

The years right after the Council constituted a springtime of new expectations in the entire church. At the same time a new generation of young priests appeared on the scene who promised to be the standard bearers of the changes: Harold Griffith Escardó, Gustavo Gutiérrez Merino, Jorge and Carlos Alvarez Calderón, Romeo Luna Victoria, Ricardo Antoncich, Alejandro Cussiánovich, and others. Besides these Peruvians there were many foreign-born priests who contributed to the process of change, such as the Jesuit theologian José Luis Idígoras, professor at the seminary in Cuzco, and the North American Dominican Enrique Camacho, a chaplain to the fishermen in Chimbote. All of these men represented the new conciliar mentality, especially in their openness to dialogue with the modern world. There existed among them a consensus on the need for the church to update itself intellectually and socially. Gustavo Gutiérrez in his theology classes at the Catholic University and Harold Griffith in his column in *Oiga* spoke with enthusiasm of the new awakening in the church.[53]

But this uniformity among "modern" priests, the fruit of the euphoria following Vatican II, soon dissipated under the pressure of the political and social events that ushered in a new wave of militarism and placed severe strains on democracy everywhere in Latin America in the sixties and seventies. Especially after the episcopal conference of Medellín in 1968 the social question turned into a double-edged sword, dividing Catholics into opposing factions. Within a few brief years, some of the priests who were considered "progressives" in the sixties were labeled "conservatives" in the seventies and eighties, while others were termed "radicals." In Peru this polarization became most acute during the military regime of Juan Velasco Alvarado.

9
The Church and the Military, 1968-1975

> *Although the Peruvian church had been conscious of the problems of social injustice in Peru for quite some time, it was especially in the years between 1968 and 1970 that it acquired a really critical awareness of that reality and assumed an institutional commitment to the poor who suffered the consequences of that injustice*[1]
>
> BISHOP LUIS BAMBARÉN, 1972

Under the reformist military regime of General Juan Velasco Alvarado, known as the "First Phase" (1968–75), the Peruvian church became a model for the church in the rest of Latin America. Also during this period numerous groups of avantgarde laity and priests sprouted up everywhere in Latin America. This progressive movement was inspired by the Council and the social encyclicals of popes John XXIII and Paul VI. It was also encouraged by the revolution of rising expectations that affected Latin Americans everywhere. Finally, the foreign missionaries who went to Latin America in those years strongly supported these progressive tendencies. In Peru, the phenomenon of the *pueblos jóvenes* (young towns), an intensification of the level of peasant political activity in the Andes, especially in the southern highlands, and the reformist military regime itself, all exercised pressure on the church to change its mentality.

The demographic explosion and mass migrations to the cities on the coast literally turned the *barriadas*, which some authors termed "squatter settlements," into new, albeit satellite "cities." In these new urban areas the church assumed an active role in helping the inhabitants organize themselves socially and even politically. In the Andes and in the southern highlands the church also took an active role in supporting the peasants' demands for land. The military regime that took power in 1968 reinforced these progressive tendencies in the church. Never before had the church been faced with the challenge of giving its opinion on structural social and economic change affecting the entire country. During the Velasco regime, the church became directly involved both on the level of the government and on the popular level during the reform process. As a consequence, it acquired a more panoramic and sophisticated vision of the relation between politics and society. These were also the years when liberation theology was born. That thought current in particular served as an intellectual instrument for many Christians who were trying to understand the changes from the perspective of their religious faith. These few short years constituted the period of the "social-political church." During the period of modernization the key concepts that prevailed were "dialogue," "development," and "openness." Now the dominant concepts became "conscientization," "liberation," and the "popular struggle."

From the Council to Medellín

The two conciliar popes, John XXIII and Paul VI, decisively changed the course of the entire church. Although the council did not have the same immediate impact in the third world as it did in the first, the social messages of these two pontiffs were particularly encouraging for Latin American Christians. For them the most urgent issues were social injustice, human rights, and economic dependency. In *Mater et Magistra* (1961) and *Pacem in Terris* (1963) Pope John considerably amplified the social teaching of the church, which up until then was largely concerned with European questions. The new encyclicals touched directly on the theme of the fundamental division in the world between the northern and the southern hemispheres. In *Populorum Progressio* (1967) Paul VI highlighted the themes of worldwide hunger, poverty, and economic dependency. This encyclical in particular seemed to be addressed especially to the third world. Earlier, in 1966, on the occasion of an extraordinary meeting of CELAM in Mar del Plata, Pope Paul sent a message to the Latin American bishops in which he exhorted them to take seriously the need to carry out thoroughgoing social reforms in Latin America.[2]

Medellín: A Decisive Watershed

In 1965 Bishop Manuel Larraín of Talca, Chile, then the president of CELAM, formally proposed that the Latin American bishops use the occasion of a eucharistic congress scheduled for 1968 in Bogotá to hold a meeting of the bishops also. Paul VI approved the proposal and decided to confer on the eucharistic congress and the bishops meeting a special solemnity by being present to inaugurate both events, the first papal visit to Latin America. In multiple preparatory meetings the bishops, aided by theologians and specialists, worked out the basic documents to be discussed at the general assembly. Finally, between August 20 and September 6 in Medellín, Colombia, some 130 bishops, representing all the episcopal conferences of Latin America, debated and approved the final documents. The Peruvian delegation was made up of Cardinal Landázuri, Archbishop Ricardo Durand, and bishops Luciano Metzinger, José Dammert, Fidel Tubino, and Eduardo Picher. They were accompanied by two priests, one of whom was Gustavo Gutiérrez, and two laypersons. Landázuri served as one of the two vice-presidents of the assembly. He also gave the inaugural and closing speeches.

The more socially progressive bishops set the tone for the Medellín meeting. Among the seven principal presentations were those of Eduardo Pironio, the secretary general of CELAM; Samuel Ruiz, the bishop of Chiapas; Leonidas Proaño, of Riobamba, Ecuador; and Marcos McGrath of Panama. The most important of the documents are those that refer to peace and justice. Bishop Helder Câmara and Fathers Joseph Gremillion and Gustavo Gutiérrez were among the principal authors of these documents. In the document on peace the authors underline the themes of dependency, the progressive indebtedness of the third world countries, world monopolies, the arms race, and violence. The document drew attention for its affirmation that peace is the fruit of justice.[3]

The Medellín conference stirred up much interest throughout Latin America and the entire Catholic world. Never before had the church spoken so clearly and energetically on social, economic, and political themes. Medellín signified most of all the birth of the Latin America church with a sense of its own identity as well as a sense of mission to secular society. It was an "ecumenical" council because it spoke in the name of Christians from Mexico to Chile. Given its solemnity and impact, it was comparable to the great councils held in Mexico and Lima in the sixteenth century, but with one all-important difference: unlike those earlier councils, in which the church represented the dominant power, the church at Medellín severely questioned the ruling elites. Indeed, in the years after Medellín the church would be called upon to take a prophetic role in denouncing political repression and violations of human rights.

It has frequently been observed that the Medellín conference was really the work of progressive "elites" within the church, not the expression of the entire church.[4] To a large extent this was true. The more socially advanced groups among bishops and their advisers certainly took the lead at the meeting. Several of the founders of liberation theology left their imprint on the documents. The progressive groups themselves looked upon Medellín as a beginning, not a final step. By way of contrast, the Third Episcopal Conference of CELAM, held at Puebla in 1979, did represent more authentically a grass-roots movement. But that movement itself was inspired to a large extent by Medellín.

The Progressive Elites

ONIS

In March 1968 a group of sixty priests and twenty laypersons held a meeting at Cieneguilla, on the outskirts of Lima, to discuss the socio-economic situation of Peru. One of the principal promoters of the meeting was the Jesuit Romeo Luna Victoria. The group decided to convert itself into a permanent body and adopted the name ONIS (National Office of Social Information). At the end of the first meeting the group published a document in which they denounced, in the light of the Gospel and the church's social teachings, the general state of social injustice in Peru. Shortly afterwards another twenty-eight priests signed the document. Among the signers were Gustavo Gutiérrez, Alfredo Pastor, Jorge Alvarez Calderón, Harold Griffiths, Luis Fernando Crespo, Gastón Garatea, Luis Velaochaga, and Germán Schmitz.[5] In successive meetings the more radical members in the group took over the leadership, and some of the original founders, including Luna Victoria, abandoned ONIS.[6]

In time ONIS created its own organizational structure and defined its positions more sharply. Soon ONIS divided itself into regions: ONIS-Lima, ONIS-North (Chimbote-Trujillo-Piura), ONIS-Arequipa, etc. In September 1968, under the direction of Jorge Alvarez Calderón who acted as secretary general, ONIS published a second document on national affairs. In a meeting held at Santa Anita, outside of Lima, in September and October of 1969 the 120 participants present discussed the Medellín documents. Besides Gustavo Gutiérrez and Jorge Alvarez Calderón, one of the principal authors of the ONIS documents was Alejandro Cussiánovich, a Salesian priest. The basic orientation that guided ONIS's discussion was liberation theology.[7]

Throughout the military regime ONIS took a very active role. It published numerous statements on the critical issues of the moment, such as the agrarian reform, workers' and teachers' strikes, and the political conduct of the military themselves. ONIS's statements were published in newspapers or simply handed out in the form of fliers. Along with "Golconda" in Colombia and "Priests for the Third World" in Argentina, ONIS became one of the best-known progressive priests movements in Latin America. Some Peruvians even identified it as the voice of the progressive church in general.

Nevertheless, even though ONIS did have considerable influence on several episcopal messages, it never represented more than a very small percentage of the clergy. According to most calculations it had about two hundred active members, which represented about 8 percent of the clergy in all of Peru. Also, the majority of the members were foreign-born. Only 38 percent of the members were Peruvians by birth. Of the rest, 23 percent were Americans, 9 percent were Canadians, 8 percent Spanish, and 7 percent Irish.[8] Besides this somewhat "elitist" character, ONIS also manifested traits typical of other avant-garde movements in history that assumed a prophetic role: the adoption of an apocalyptic perspective that tends to see everything in terms of extremes; the pretense of understanding major social and political problems better than the experts; and the claim to be the true interpreters of the sentiments of the popular classes. ONIS also adopted a critical stance vis-à-vis church authorities. However, unlike other similiar groups, ONIS generally avoided direct clashes with the bishops.

These limitations notwithstanding, ONIS contributed positively to the new image of a church committed to the poor and oppressed. Ironically, ONIS's major contribution may have been the service it performed for the more moderate sectors in the church. Compared to the somewhat aggressive and hyperbolic rhetoric of ONIS, the proposals of the moderates seemed most reasonable and therefore acceptable for the majority.

The Laity

A new generation of lay men and women began to fill the vacuum left by Catholic Action. The new lay groups were advised by priests with the new conciliar or Medellín mentality. In Ñaña, outside of Lima, in June 1968 a group of laypersons representing many different movements—the Legion of Mary, the *cursillos de Cristiandad*, JOC, UNEC, etc.—wrote a document that stressed the importance of the laity in the new postconciliar church.[9] The students of UNEC (National Catholic University Students) took more radical positions in a meeting they held in July and August of that year. In different camp meetings and workshops held throughout the sixties, the *unecistas*, influenced by their adviser, Gustavo Gutiérrez, and others, had assimilated the basic tenets of liberation theology. In a seminar held in Chosica the thirty-five participants of UNEC published a strongly worded document that supported the changes in the church but also severely censured the upper-class church schools for their "antitestimony." Among the signers were some veterans of Catholic Action, such as César Arróspide and Carlos Gandolfo, as well as representatives of the new generation, such as Carlos Amat y León, Enrique Bernales, Miguel de Althaus, and Rolando Ames.[10]

In May 1971 some of the these same lay leaders met with the idea of resuscitating the social weeks. The meeting was organized largely by Ricardo Antoncich, a Peruvian Jesuit who acted as secretary to the Bishops' Commission on Social Action. The principal fruit of the meeting was the foundation of Faith and Solidary Action, which constituted a lay parallel to ONIS. The new group also published its own communiqués and statements on strikes and other public issues.

The Peruvian Church Assimilates Medellín

In January 1969 the bishops held the thirty-sixth National Bishops' Conference of the Peruvian church. The principal topic on the agenda was the Medellín assembly, held only a few months earlier. Several lay and priest advisers were especially invited, a novelty for the bishop's meeting. The bishops not only discussed Medellín, but they also analyzed, for the first time, the significance of the new military government that had taken over barely two months before. The assembly naturally reaffirmed Medellín and, in unusual language for bishops, denounced the "colonial feudalism" that still existed in some regions of the country. It also accused the national oligarchy of being an accomplice to "international money imperialism" and of being one of the principal causes of the poverty in Peru.[11] This rather strong language clearly reveals the influence of Medellín and liberation theology. And following the example set by Pope John and the Vatican Council, the assembly also submitted the church itself to a critical examination. The assembly called for an evaluation of the church's properties in the light of the Gospel.

The Episcopal Commission of Social Action

The Episcopal Commission of Social Action, created in 1965, was now suddenly thrust into the limelight, especially after the thirty-sixth General Episcopal Assembly. Shortly after Medellín the recently named auxiliary bishop of Lima, Luis Bambarén, was elected head of the commission. His executive secretary was another Jesuit, Ricardo Antoncich, who was one of the principal authors of many of the episcopal documents relating to social themes. The 1969 bishops' assembly charged the commission (known by its initials in Spanish, CEAS) with the tasks of advising the hierarchy on social issues and of helping in the social formation of priests, women religious, and laity. Many laypersons, notably César Delgado, Oscar Espinosa, Helan Jaworski, Rolando Ames, and Marcial Rubio, offered their professional advice to the commission on numerous occasions. Father Antoncich was succeeded by Ernesto Alayza, a layman, as executive secretary of the commission. Soon CEAS became the principal channel by which the bishops were informed of the problems that affected especially the popular classes. When the military government took a repressive turn in 1974, CEAS became one of the principal forums in the country in which human rights violations could be ventilated. After being reorganized in 1977, CEAS subdivided its work into five departments: human rights, peasants, jails, the Amazon, and labor issues.[12] Under Bishop Bambarén's energetic leadership, CEAS came to exercise a decisive influence on all episcopal assemblies during the military period.

The Church and the Military's Reforms

It is not a coincidence that the church's thinking, today in total harmony with the original Gospel message, should manifest itself in Medellín the very year of the Peruvian revolution.[13]

GENERAL JORGE FERNÁNDEZ MALDONADO, 1973

A Catholic Corporativism?

The reformist military government that seized power in October 1968 soon gave an unexpected impulse to the changes within the church. Especially during the first years of the Velasco regime the military's reforms created a climate that favored the acceptance of Medellín. Unlike the tense situations in Brazil or Chile where the church had to face repressive, rightest military regimes, the church in Peru enjoyed a special relationship with the reformist military. One important reason was that the Peruvian military had virtually appropriated the social doctrines of the church to justify their reforms ideologically. This fact also tended to strengthen the progressive sectors in the church that were frequently selected to serve as mediators between church and state.[14]

In reality, there were many remote and proximate antecedents for this special relationship. In the sixties and seventies the Jesuit Romeo Luna Victoria gave lectures on several occasions at CAEM (Center for Higher Military Studies) on the social doctrines of the church. And during the Velasco regime the Jesuit from Trujillo continued to influence key military personnel.[15] Furthermore, some of the military had made the *cursillos de Cristiandad*, an experience that served to stimulate their social consciousness. Between 1973 and 1974 nine of the eleven ministers who belonged to Velasco's cabinet, known as COAP (Committee for Advising the President) were *cursillistas*.[16] The military leader who most explicitly described or justified the Peruvian "revolution" in Christian terms was General Jorge Fernández Maldonado, the minister of mines and energy and for a while prime minister. Others among the military reformists were graduates of religious schools, such as Francisco Morales Bermúdez, who studied with the Jesuits, and General Edgardo Mercado Jarrín, a graduate of the Marist Brothers. Some had family links with the church, such as General Ernesto Montagne, the brother-in-law of Cardinal Landázuri, and General Pedro Richter Prada, brother of the auxiliary bishop of Piura and later archbishop of Ayacucho.

Although there were civilian advisers to the military of many different ideological tendencies, ex-Apristas, leftists, and Christian Democrats, the military did not identify itself explicitly with any one tendency. In frequent public addresses General Velasco spoke of the "humanist, libertarian, socialist, and Christian" values that inspired the revolution. However, upon closer examination of the documents and statements produced by the military, as well as a glance at the reforms themselves, it becomes evident that the principal concepts of the military were borrowed from the Christian Democrats. Although some of the reforms had long ago been proposed by the Apristas, and the military encouraged the left to support them, they still did not feel comfortable with either APRA, whom they had persecuted for over thirty years, or the Marxist left. By way of contrast, however, the "third way" of the Christian Democrats, enunciated in the formula, "neither capitalism nor communism," was particularly attractive to these middle-of-the-road military reformers. The key ideological slogan of the military, "a social democracy of full participation," reflected many basic tenets of Christian Democracy, such as its concept of "communitarian participation," social property, cooperativism, and joint capital-worker ownership of enterprises.

Besides these ties, there was a certain affinity between the military and the church that had deeper historical roots. Some authors saw in the corporativist tendencies of the Velasco regime a reincarnation of the Catholic corporative state, which was the basic political model in the Hispanic world since the Hapsburgs. The church, which was and is a perfect model of a corporatist society, lived quite in harmony with such a state. Indeed, the concept of the Christian corporative state appears in different ways in the writings of Thomas Aquinas, Thomas More, Francisco Suárez, and Pope Leo XIII. For these thinkers the state should not limit its functions to maintaining order. Rather, it should actively seek to serve the common good. To that end it should help organize the different parts within society so that they all contribute to the common good to the fullest of their capacities. When Leo XIII rejected liberal capitalism and communism in *Rerum Novarum*, he did so because he believed that neither system really looks out for the common good or the good of the individual: the former because it places the economic interests of a few before the common good, and the latter because it destroys individual liberties in the name of an abstract justice. Given this perspective, the Velasco regime was a new version of this older tradition. Velasco's government sought to regulate the activities of private enterprise, unions, and other institutions, not to suppress them, but to insure that they fulfill a social function for the benefit of all of society.[17]

Nevertheless, the concept of the corporative state, supported and legitimized by a corporative church, though it is based on certain historical examples, had been losing credibility in the church since the very beginning of the twentieth century. Both Leo XIII and his successor, Pius X, strongly favored the concept of a "Christian democracy" and both defended political and religious liberty as basic human rights.[18] During the period of fascism the concept of a Catholic corporative state reappeared, but it took hold only in nations on the periphery of fascist states: Austria under Dollfuss, Portugal under Salazar, and to some extent, Spain under Franco. In Germany and Italy the state and church did approach each other in the beginning for reasons of mutual convenience. But in both of those cases the church ended up being persecuted and silenced.

Therefore the church had already abandoned theories of a privileged church in a Catholic state long before Vatican II. And the council categorically declared that political and religious liberty are fundamental human rights. For this reason the church from the beginning adopted a posture of critical reservation toward the military regime, and that was probably the attitude of the majority of Peruvians as well. The church did approve of the reforms of the military as long as those reforms offered the possibility of guaranteeing a more stable democracy in the future. But the church also condemned the violations of human rights that resulted from certain heavy-handed measures of the military.

In this sense the church did not "legitimize" the military government; it limited its approval to the reforms the military carried out. This distinction can be observed in the reactions of Cardinal Landázuri and the other bishops toward the military. Shortly after the October coup Cardinal Landázuri published a message in which he supported the expropriation of Standard Oil (which occurred a week after the takeover), but in the same message he called for elections and a return to normal democracy.[19] But when the military began to put into effect a whole series of major reforms, the cardinal and the other bishops no longer spoke of immediate elections. Rather, they sought dialogue with the military to influence the course of the reforms. But after a few years the Velasco regime began to show signs that the reformist thrust was over. At the same time it also began to have recourse to overt repression in order to maintain itself in power.

In that situation the church took a more critical stance and began questioning the reason for the existence of the military government.

Another distinction is worth making. Not all groups within the church supported the "Peruvian revolution" (as the military termed it) with the same degree of enthusiasm. One very visible sign of the church's support was the presence in the government of two Jesuits, Ricardo Morales Basadre and Romeo Luna Victoria, who worked in the ministry of education as advisers. Luna Victoria especially became well-known as a sort of public relations apologist of the educational reform. Neither of them, however, were acting on their own; both were designated by the bishops to serve as mediators between state and church. Father Morales was chosen by General Velasco after consulting with church authorities. But there were other priests and religious, especially members of ONIS and sympathizers with liberation theology, who took a more critical stance toward the military and their reforms. They chose to support the reforms "from below," but not to be involved in the government.

The military approached the church for another, more pragmatic motive: they perceived the need to gather all the support they could especially since they had no party of their own. Given the widespread acceptance of Catholic symbols in Peru, they saw the wisdom of using terms like "Christian" and entering into dialogue with the church as ways of winning popular legitimacy.

The Social Reforms

In other historical contexts the church is normally the first to issue a protest in defense of private property. But in Peru the church fully supported the military reforms affecting property. The key decree-laws in this area were the agrarian reform of 1969, the Industrial Community Law of 1970, and the Social Property Enterprise Law of 1974. A month after the proclamation of the agrarian reform, the bishops published a statement approving the measure.[20]

On the occasion of the social property law, CEAS published a short pamphlet in which it justified the law in terms of the social doctrine of the church.[21] These statements and documents show that the church not only followed the reforms but actively contributed to the process by helping ordinary Peruvians to understand why the reforms were necessary. Even before the hierarchy had spoken, a group of 136 American priests in Peru sent a letter to the American ambassador defending the expropriation of

The Church and the Military, 1968–1975

Standard Oil. In their letter the priests urged the American government not to apply the Hickenlooper amendment, which called for the suspension of aid to any country that expropriates American interests without indemnification.[22]

The Educational Reform

Another area of potential conflict was education. Nevertheless, the Educational Reform Law, promulgated in March, 1972, was a fruit in part of a dialogue between church and state. When the military took power in 1968, the church was already in the process of expanding its educational presence among the popular sectors. Many in the church questioned the church's upper-class schools. In fact, it was due largely to a decree-law of the military junta of 1962–63 that the church was able to staff its schools among the poor (see chapter 10). In 1971, of the 1,051 primary and secondary educational centers run by the church, 342 were completely free and 626 were semifree.[23] After Medellín many religious congregations looked for ways to free themselves from their upper-class schools and dedicate more of their efforts to the poor. In short, there were many groups within the church who were favorably disposed toward the military's educational reforms. The hierachy, too, lent its support, but on one condition: that the state not manipulate the law in order to expand its control to the detriment of freedom of thought.

From the beginning, however, the government consulted the church before making any important move. In September 1970, the government published the general outline of the educational reform. The philosophy behind the proposed law reflected the humanistic and Christian tendencies of the civilian advisers, especially those of Augusto Salazar Bondy, who had recourse to the ideas of Paulo Freire on education as an instrument of "concientization" and "liberation," and to a lesser extent, the ideas of Ivan Illich on deinstitutionalized education.[24] In October of that year, in the middle of the Second National Congress of Catholic Educators, the bishops gave their response to the government's plan. In their message they offered to "collaborate actively" with the reform.[25] At that moment, however, there was no official church representative on the commission in charge of writing the reform law. The bishops therefore decided to assign Father Ricardo Morales, S.J., to the commission. In 1971 Father Morales was named to fill the post of vice-president of the superior council on education, which was a sort of civilian cabinet under the general in charge of the ministry of education. When Salazar Bondy, who served as president of the council, died, Morales Basadre was named by the government to succeed him. Morales acted as president of that body between 1974 and 1976. When the educational reform law was promulgated in March 1972, therefore, it had already been studied at length and approved by the church.

But the educational reform law was also the occasion for protest on the part of many private and religious schools of the middle and upper classes. In May 1973 the Consortium of Catholic Educational Centers published a caustic criticism of the reform in the pages of *El Comercio*.[26] Under pressure from these groups the state and the church agreed to appoint a "mixed (state and church) commission" to resolve their differences. Archbishop Durand presided over the commission, while Romeo Luna Victoria, S.J., acted as the government's representative. The campaign organized by the consortium signaled the beginning of a Catholic "right" in the Peruvian church, a theme to be developed in chapter 10. In general, however, the majority of religious congregations and parishes that administered schools among the popular classes looked upon the educational reform as a ratification of their own work.

Population Planning

In another sensitive area, population planning, the military government was careful to listen to the church's views. In reality, the two institutions were in substantial agreement on this topic. This harmony was achieved in large part because two Jesuits, Enrique Bartra and Juan Julio Wicht, collaborated closely with the government in preparing the official state document. In 1974 the bishops published a pastoral letter entitled *Familia y Población* (Family and Population) in which they set forth the church's vision of the Christian family as well as its norms for "responsible parenthood." The bishops singled out the "breakdown of family life" as one of the fundamental evils in Peru. They also criticized birth control campaigns that purported to check population growth but that actually undermined family values. In 1976 the National Institute of Planning, a state agency, published its own document, *Lineamientos de política de población en el Perú* (Policy Orientations on Population Growth in Peru), which virtually restated many of the church's positions. The government document, for example, blamed the population explosion on poverty and underdevelopment. It also rejected government-enforced family control programs as both inefficient and immoral. Both documents agreed that the population problem can be met realistically only by fostering more development and assuring better health care and education for everyone.

"Justice in the World," 1971

Progressive groups within the church had their maximum influence on the hierarchy under the reformist military. There were two episcopal documents that especially revealed this progressive influence: *Justicia en el mundo* (Justice in the World, 1971) and *Evangelización* (Evangelization, 1973). The two documents also commented on the military and their reforms. The first document, "Justice in the World," was written in August during the fortieth General Assembly of the Peruvian Episcopal Conference in preparation for the bishops' synod in Rome in December of that year. The assembly and the document it produced represented the "Medellín" of the Peruvian church. The Episcopal Commission of Social Action played a significant role in preparing for the assembly and in writing the document.

In the document the bishops praise the efforts of the military government to effect a profound social transformation of the country and they cite specific reforms: the recovery of national resources (the case of Standard Oil), the agrarian reform, and the laws favoring the creation of industrial communities. They also censure the different international interests that block the efforts of a third-world nation like Peru to lift itself out of underdevelopment. Even more specifically, the bishops criticize for their lack of social consciousness and concern for their nation the owners of modern means of communication who manipulate the press and the media in order to advance selfish economic interests.[27] This was the very justification the military government used when it expropriated the press in 1974. The bishops' document also condemns political repression and warns against regimes that suppress basic human liberties in the name of Christianity.[28] This last warning was the basis for growing tension between church and state.

The key unifying theme of "Justice in the World" is liberation: liberation from dependency, political and economic oppression, and from "all that prevents men and women from fulfilling themselves as human beings and as members of a community . . . ."[29] The most original proposal in the document was the call for the church to support governments that seek to construct "socialist societies based on Christian and humanistic values."[30] This was the first time in a document of the Peruvian church that socialism was explicitly mentioned as a valid option for a Christian. In an explanatory note the authors add this nuance: ". . . the Christian community and its pastors do not aim to support any kind of socialism whatsoever, nor do they wish to suggest that socialism in itself can resolve social problems."[31] Finally, the authors remind readers that the church's mission is not to propose concrete technical solutions or specific political models to follow, but rather to set down the theological and moral norms to orient the politicians and ordinary Christians in making decisions.

"Evangelization" (1973)

While "Justice in the World," like the Medellín document, exhorted Christians to become more involved politically and socially, "Evangelization" was directed more to the church itself. There was another important difference between the two documents. The first document was the work of a relatively small group, while the second was the fruit of a wide consultation throughout the entire country. Anticipating the method that would be used to prepare for the bishops' conference at Puebla, the episcopal assembly of 1972 divided the church into regions, each of which in turn invited interested parties to analyze and criticize the ways in which the church transmits its own message. The conclusions of all these regional assemblies were then presented at the national bishops' assembly of 1973. The objective of this new procedure was to help foster a stronger sense of pastoral teamwork throughout the country.

The 1973 document also reveals a subtle change in church-state relations. The bishops repeat their praise of the reforms, but they also insist on the distinction between human reforms and the Christian faith commitment. The latter is not reducible to the former. Finally, the bishops make a not-too-veiled criticism of the military: "Every liberating effort carries within itself the danger of turning into a force for repression."[32] The 1973 document is more restrained and less euphoric than the 1971 one, a fact that reflected the growing number of incidents of human rights violations committed by the military.

But the central thrust of "Evangelization" was to criticize not the government but the church itself. In the document the bishops recognize the existence in Peru of a superficial religiosity that lives on "external practices and sentimental devotions that at times represent economic interests."[33] The document further warns of a crisis of faith the young undergo when they discover the "apparent lack of connection between religion and the great problems of life and society."³⁴ Reference is also made to deficient religious programs in the schools, usually due to the lack of qualified teachers who fail to communicate the Gospel message in a creative and attractive way. Finally, the bishops propose to renovate religion programs and to stimulate the use of creative teaching methods.

Internal Tensions

Although the Second General Conference of the Latin American Episcopate, held in Medellín in 1968, generated much enthusiasm, it also marked the beginning of a period of tensions within the church itself. These tensions had in fact been building up for some time, and Medellín served as a safety valve. But when various church groups perceived that many bishops did not intend to make significant changes after Medellín, they became increasingly vocal in their criticisms. The appearance of groups such as ONIS signaled the end of the age of intellectual uniformity and passive resignation in the Latin American church. Unlike other critical moments in the history of the church, however, the nonconformist clergy in this case based their arguments on official church documents. Their banners of protest were Vatican II and Medellín. The real battlelines were not drawn, however, between bishops and priests, but between progressive bishops and priests on the one hand, and certain minority groups of other bishops and priests of a more conservative mentality on the other. In Peru, given the fact that the progressive bishops more or less set the pace, confrontations between priests and bishops over Medellín were relatively rare and scattered.

The Letter to the Thirty-sixth Episcopal Assembly

On the eve of the thirty-sixth Episcopal Assembly, held in 1969, which dealt with the themes of Medellín, 330 priests from all the dioceses of Peru sent a collective letter to the bishops with a series of proposals to be treated during the assembly. Some of the proposals clearly represented a criticism of the church itself. The very concept of the clergy sending a letter recommending agenda for the bishops to discuss would have been unheard of before the sixties. Although they did not go to the extreme of outright disobedience or lack of respect, much less of forming an autonomous "sect," the priests of ONIS and others who signed the letter did constitute a sort of "parallel church," which had its own conclaves, deliberations, and public declarations. Some of the proposals had already been scheduled for discussion, including greater poverty in the church, greater participation on the part of the religious in the decision-making of the bishops, and greater lay participation and more attention to the economic plight of priests living in rural areas. But the letter also contained more radical proposals, such as reducing the sphere of influence of the papal nuncio, the separation of church and state, discussing whether the church should continue to run upper-class schools, and more rational planning for the use of foreign clergy. The authors ended by exhorting the bishops to denounce abuses of power and concrete cases of exploitation.[35]

ONIS-Trujillo, 1969

The first dramatic case in Peru of a clash between priests and bishops occurred in Trujillo shortly after the bishops' assembly of 1969. The priests of ONIS-Trujillo lent their public support to a strike of the workers in the city's major steel factory who claimed that the company (Triumph) did not recognize their union rights. In February the workers occupied the cathedral as a sign of protest. The priests also organized a march to protest the inauguration of a new Country Club (that was literally its name) because it symbolized luxury in the midst of poverty. These protest gestures soon led to an internal crisis in the church itself. Archbishop Jurgens announced his decision to dismiss several priests who taught at the seminary because they had participated in the protest activities of ONIS and because they inculcated their ideas in the students. On March 24 the seminarians took over the seminary in protest of Jurgens's decision and demanded the return of the priests. The affair was smoothed over after a dialogue between the archbishop and the priests in question.[36]

But in the middle of that crisis another more scandalous one loomed. Luis Baldo Riva, an Italian-born Redemptorist, was named auxiliary bishop of Trujillo and presumably would be in line to succeed Jurgens. The progressive clergy considered Baldo too conservative. They organized protests and on the very day of his consecration as bishop they distributed fliers in which they denounced the ceremony as "antievangelical and contrary to the new orientations of the church laid down in Medellín and in Lima."[37] Although Jurgens managed to calm tensions once again, ONIS continued to exercise considerable influence in the city, especially in the the "young towns."

The Carboni Affair

In their letter to the bishops' assembly, the priests requested that the role of the papal nuncio be submitted to a critical evaluation. The immediate background of that request was the increasingly larger role the papal nuncio, Rómulo Carboni, had assumed in the Peruvian church. Many priests and laypersons believed that Carboni had gone beyond the limits of discreet diplomatic collaboration with the church and directly interfered on a regular basis in internal Peruvian church matters. Carboni, who had been named nuncio in 1960, took upon himself the mission of contributing to the development of the church. He invited priests and religious women to Peru and appealed for economic assistance to the church. These positive actions, however, were offset by the nuncio's volatile personality and tendency to react to criticism with a heavy hand.

When Bishop Carboni learned of the protest against the naming of Luis Baldo as auxiliary bishop of Trujillo, he sent out a circular letter in April 1969 criticizing not only the priests of ONIS-Trujillo, but all priests whom he considered radical, with specific reference to Gustavo Gutiérrez, Jorge and Carlos Alvarez Calderón, and Alejandro Cussiánovich. But the real indiscretion of the nuncio consisted in the fact that he sent the letter not only to the cardinal and other bishops, but even to the minister of the interior, which ministry in Peru is the police![38] The minister at that time was General Armando Artola. The nuncio's letter provoked anger among many church groups. In the beginning of May some 155 priests sent their own letter to the cardinal to protest the nuncio's meddling in affairs they believed did not lie within his sphere of competence.[39] At the end of the month Carboni left for a new assignment and another nuncio was named to Peru. Although no official explanation for the sudden change was given, it was presumed that the Peruvian church had asked him to leave.

Other Crises

There were other crises in this period that do not fall under the heading of conflicts with authority but that were accelerated in one way or other by Vatican II. In 1969 the young auxiliary bishop of Lima, Mario Cornejo, left the priesthood and married. That year also Daniel McClellan, the founder of the savings cooperatives in Puno, left the priesthood and married.[40] In March

1972 the bishop of Puno, Julio González, was suspended from the government of his diocese.[41] Although his admirers claimed that his removal was the work of conservatives, the real cause seemed to have been manifestations of an unbalanced personality. Throughout the entire church the decade of the seventies signaled the climax of the crisis of the abandonment of the priesthood and the religious life.

Church-State Tensions

The new awakening of the church at Medellín also led to tensions between the church and the military. Although the church initially favored the reforms of the military, it did not approve of its authoritarian style. Some sectors of the clergy, such as ONIS, were openly critical of the military from the beginning. But in the years 1973 and 1974 the moderates also became more vocal in denouncing violations of human rights as well as the government's incapacity to bring about the "participatory democracy" that it preached. The first church-state conflicts were isolated incidents. In general, the military prudently backed down so as to avoid further tension. In June 1969, for example, the police pushed their way into the central administration building of the Catholic University in the center of Lima in reaction to student protests over a new university law.[42] When Cardinal Landázuri censured this action, the government immediately sent a note of apology.

The Bambarén-Artola Affair

The most celebrated church-state clash was the confrontation between Bishop Luis Bambarén and the minister of the interior, General Armando Artola. In the first months of the military regime, both were designated as the liaisons between their respective institutions and the "young towns." Although the ministry he headed had little to do with the designation, Artola had been chosen as a sort of informal public-relations man to deal with the new urban settlements. And Bambarén, as the new auxiliary bishop of Lima, had been chosen to coordinate the church's pastoral efforts in the young towns. Bambarén had also participated in discussions held by a government agency in charge of the young towns.[43]

On various occasions in 1969 the bishop and the general exchanged criticisms over the correct way to resolve the problems of the young towns. Artola made several attention-drawing visits in which he gave out clothes and *panetones* (large sweet bread loaves). Bambarén termed those gestures "paternalistic" and declared that the poor needed changes much more substantial to better their lives. The sensationalist press dramatized the "rivalry" between the two. The final act of the verbal duel between the bishop and the minister occurred in May of 1971 when a group of so-called "invaders" squatted on private property near the Jesuit *colegio* in a neighborhood called "Pamplona." The police attempted to dislodge the invaders, and this resulted in the death of one of them.

On Sunday morning, May 9, Bambarén and the other auxiliary bishop, Germán Schmitz, accompanied by five priests, celebrated a Mass in the midst of the invaders. Bishop Bambarén's intention was to express solidarity with the new dwellers, whom he called "living Christs," but without condoning their action of seizing private property. The following day Artola had him detained presumably for inciting the invaders. That same night, however, President Velasco ordered the bishop to be freed. A few days later Velasco and Cardinal Landázuri discussed the matter and both declared in public that the incident of Pamplona, far from constituting a church-state clash, was really the result of a "misunderstanding." Shortly afterwards Artola resigned as minister, and the government mobilized its resources to move the invaders to a new site, known thereafter as "Villa El Salvador."[44]

In one very strict sense the Pamplona incident did not constitute a church-state confrontation. In fact, one of the positive results of the incident was the decision of both Velasco and the church to give high priority to building the new young town. Velasco personally took Villa El Salvador under his wing with the aim of turning it into a model project of his government. Bambarén's prestige grew after the confrontation and he virtually became the principal spokesman for the young towns. The collaboration between the "bishop of the young towns" and the government was so harmonious that years later the political right would single out Bambarén in particular as a symbol of the Velasco regime.

From another point of view, however, the Pamplona incident revealed the existence of a latent tension between the church and the military. The church itself had its own dilemma: to what extent should it collaborate with an authoritarian government, reformist though it may be, if that collaboration also caused it to lose credibility among the popular classes? Bambarén himself had participated in talks in a government agency in charge of helping the young towns. But when the poor (and some unscrupulous developers who urged them on) seized property in order to build their homes, Bambarén decided that his pastoral duty was to express solidarity with the people even at the risk of being accused of being an "agitator" by the government.

The Tensions Grow, 1971–74

There were many other incidents that highlighted the ambiguous relationship between the church and the military of the "First Phase." When the government censured the press, the church increasingly became the only institution that could criticize the military with relative impunity. In February 1971, two months after the Pamplona affair, Bambarén published a statement of CEAS that denounced the police for shooting at some peasants in Carhuaz. In this particular case the peasants had attempted to seize a hacienda. CEAS's message censured the police and bureaucrats in the government for lacking "an authentic revolutionary zeal." [45] In August of that year the bishops in the Amazon copublished with CEAS a document in which they denounced the many abuses government authorities and the police had committed against the natives.[46] A year later, Bishop Dammert of Cajamarca, on the occasion of the installation of an electric generator, criticized the government for not carrying out some of its promised reforms. The minister of mines and energy, General Jorge Fernández Maldonado, who was also present, listened to the bishop but made no objections.[47]

For the more radicalized clergy there was no need to adopt such an ambiguous posture of cautious collaboration with the government and solidarity with the people at the same time. Beginning in 1971 ONIS opted for supporting the "popular movement," even if it meant clashing with the military. This was of course the position of the political left. This decision led to even more incidents and tensions within the church. In February 1972 two priests, a Frenchman and a Spanish Jesuit, were detained and deported. Both had publicly supported a strike organized by a newly founded teachers union, SUTEP, that the governnment refused to recognize.[48] In reality, the government had a longer deportation list, but after pressure from the church, only two were finally expelled from the country. The two in question apparently did not enjoy the confidence of their respective bishops.

There was also an increase in frequency of a new protest tactic, the seizure of churches. Between 1969 and 1973 at least twenty churches were taken over by strikers or peasants.[49] Frequently the priests of ONIS expressed their solidarity with the strikers, and at times a priest turned his own church over to the strikers!

The Expropriation of the Press, 1974

For the first few years the Velasco regime allowed a relative freedom of the press. *El Comercio, La Prensa,* and other major dailies that opposed the government were allowed to criticize the government as long as they did it within certain limits. But the military were very arbitrary in their application of that norm and on several occasions expelled journalists for crossing the boundary. In 1970 the government expropriated *Expreso,* a Lima daily, and turned it into an official government organ. Finally, on July 27, 1974, the government nationalized all the other principal newspapers in the country. The military claimed that the newspapers represented only the voice of the oligarchy and narrow economic interests that used the press to undermine the reforms. The military announced that the newspapers, after a year under state-named directors, were to be converted into the organs of expression of the principal groups in the country according to profession and occupation: peasants, industrial workers, professionals, and teachers.

The church's initial reaction was cautious. The episcopal conference exhorted the government to fulfill its stated intention of turning the press over to the different organized sectors of society.[50] ONIS, on the other hand, was openly enthusiastic about the move. It expressed the hope that the modern means of communication would now become the authentic voice of the people. During the year of "transition," Héctor Cornejo Chávez, who was named director of *El Comercio,* practically turned the editorial page of that major daily into a platform for social Christianity. Romeo Luna Victoria, S.J., contributed to it numerous articles on the education reform. But after a year, when it became evident that the military were not about to turn the press over to others, both the hierarchy and ONIS adopted a more critical line toward the nationalized press. In December 1975 CEAS published a document with the title *Participación popular* (Popular Participation) in which it warned against the dangers of manipulating public opinion, especially if that heralded the imposition of a totalitarian state in Peru.[51] This was the harshest criticism to date the church had made of the military government. The document clearly signaled the end of the conditional support which it had lent the military since 1968.

On August 29, 1975, General Velasco was removed from power by fellow officers of his own government. His fall from power put an end to the "First Phase" and ushered in the "Second Phase" of the military regime. During the Velasco years many rapid changes occurred. One of the most important was the emergence of the marginal popular classes as political actors. The reforms and the revolutionary rhetoric of the government had engendered enthusiastic expectations of the arrival of a new and just social order in Peru. This atmosphere of rising expectations affected the church, too, which in addition had only recently committed itself in Medellín to doing many of the things that the military put into effect. At times some of the more radicalized groups turned their enthusiasm into a dogmatic and naive messianism. But most church groups responded with cautious optimism. Bishops, priests, religious women, and pastoral agents all looked for ways to contribute positively to what promised to be a major transformation of Peruvian society.

The church underwent a major transformation of its own during those years. Although it is not always possible to measure attitude changes with much precision, it is interesting to cite some of the conclusions of a survey conducted in 1974 by Thomas Maloney, an American Jesuit. Maloney surveyed the opinions of a cross section of the clergy in Lima regarding the military government and its reforms. Of those surveyed, 42.5 percent stated that they favored a "capitalist model" of development. But 43.8 percent said that they favored the model proposed by the Peruvian military, that is, a nationalistic model of development that emphasizes social property, but without excluding capitalism, as long as it is kept under certain control. Finally, 13.7 percent said that they preferred a socialist model.[52] From this survey it can be deduced that the clergy in general were rather centrist and moderate in their political and economic preferences. In this sense they were not very far from the opinions of the majority of Peruvians.

The clergy in general and some sectors of men and women religious displayed a far greater openness to social change and interest in politics than the clergy and religious thirty years before. The militants of Catholic Action absorbed certain ideas of the social encyclicals in order to point out the errors of communism or other ideologies. But the committed Christians of the sixties and seventies went far beyond this apologetic mentality; they saw in the social message of the church a challenge and a call to work for real change. They studied ways to translate that

The Church and the Military, 1968–1975

message into concrete economic and political policies. At times the public differences among them scandalized other Catholics. But the new pluralism also reflected a new maturity among Catholics that was not typical of pre-Vatican II days.

The end of the "First Phase" of the military government also put an end to the hopes of many who believed that Peru was about to undergo a thoroughgoing social transformation. Nevertheless, all was not in vain. It was precisely during those few short years that the foundations of the newly renovated church of Vatican II and Medellín were laid. After Velasco the church, without losing sight of its social goals, intensified its efforts to renew its pastoral action in the light of those two great church events. In the years shortly before and after the Third General Conference of the Latin American Bishops' Conference at Puebla (1979) the "social-politcal" church gave way to the "social-pastoral" church.

10

The Social-Pastoral Church, 1975–

During the "Second Phase" (1975–80) of the military regime, relations between church and state were even more ambiguous than they were during the "First Phase." In general, they were characterized by a superficial cordiality that barely hid the real tensions that existed underneath. In the beginning, Velasco's successor, General Francisco Morales Bermúdez, limited himself to consolidating a few of his predecessor's reforms, but after a year in power he put an end to the entire reformist movement. Given this abrupt change in direction, the government did not look favorably upon the work of priests, religious, or pastoral agents who continued to raise the consciousness of the popular classes politically and socially. The church, too, began to distance itself from the government and on several occasions it criticized the government for violations of human rights.[1] However, in light of the fact that Morales Bermúdez had formally committed his government to return to constitutional democracy, the church chose not to adopt an aggressive antigovernment stance, at least publicly. For this reason church-state relations in Peru never reached the extremes of antagonism that were produced in Chile or Brazil in the same period.

Toward a Pastoral Church

It was especially during the "Second Phase" that the "social-pastoral" church grew to maturity. This period corresponds to the years previous to the Third Episcopal Conference of the Latin American bishops at Puebla in 1979. Concern for social change continued to occupy the highest priority in the church's agenda. But once the euphoria of Medellín had passed, and in Peru especially after the reformist stage of the military had

The Social-Pastoral Church, 1975–   301

ended, a subtle change affected ecclesial circles in all of Latin America. In preparing for the Puebla conference emphasis was given to the pastoral mission of the church, and this became the key concept in the final document approved by the bishops. Some clarification is needed here, however, as the church has always been "pastoral." Obviously, the meaning of "pastoral" had been updated and nuanced. Part of the problem consisted in the fact that many Christians had practically identified pastoral action with political action or consciousness-raising. In Peru in particular, the failure of the "First Phase" led the bishops and many Christians to lose confidence in the efficacy of political slogans or ideologies for transforming society.

Second, it became evident to some in the church that the overemphasis on political action in many cases also represented a certain spiritual immaturity and a failure to integrate other values that both Vatican II and Medellín had stressed. The dominant note in the church before and after Puebla therefore became a quest for a new integration of the various dimensions that in theory should form part of the life of a contemporary Christian, the spiritual and affective dimension as well as the political and the social. In this sense, the word "pastoral" referred to the call to harmonize these distinct dimensions in the development of each Christian without diminishing or eliminating any one of them.

This change in orientation could be perceived, not only in the declarations of the official church, but also on a more grass-roots level. Concretely, in the sixties and seventies many new movements sprang up that incarnated or emphasized one or another of these dimensions in Christian life. Liberation theology was without doubt the ecclesial movement that most stressed the call to political and social change. But there were movements at the other extreme of the spectrum, such as marriage encounter or charismatic renewal, that highlighted the affective development of Christians. It would be difficult to say which of these movements had a greater impact on the life of the Peruvian church in general, those that stressed political commitment or those that emphasized affective growth. Furthermore, in the beginning these movements looked askance at each other. The "liberationists" accused the charismatics and others of being "alienated" and of relying on imported American techniques. But after a number of years, each of these movements went through a period of maturation and purification; liberation theology began emphasizing much more the spiritual and contemplative dimension and marriage encounter and the charismatics began speaking openly of the political commitment incumbent upon each Christian.

Dialogue and Unity

Another salient note of the post-Puebla church is the search for a new basis of unity within the church as well as a newer and deeper dialogue. Vatican II itself questioned the existence of a vertical authoritarian structure within the church, a reality reinforced by the Council of Trent and Vatican I, while at the same time it called for the laity to participate much more in the life of the church. In Latin America, Medellín called upon Christians to express solidarity with the victims of injustice. This call had the effect of uniting priests, religious women, and laity together in a common cause that broke down barriers between them. But the new freedom within the church also gave rise to some confusion about the limits of responsible dialogue (which included constructive criticism) and irresponsible dissent. Confrontations between bishops and priests broke out generally because one or other of the two sides did not accept the new pluralism approved by the church or because they did not understand the difficult art of dialogue. In general, the greatest tensions in the post-Medellín years occurred between "conservatives" and "liberals," usually in reference to political issues. But in the post-Puebla years many bishops and priests made their peace in an effort to arrive at a new intrachurch harmony. On the ecclesiastical map, for example, one can find groups of "liberals" in the diocese of a conservative bishop, or conservative groups in the diocese of a liberal bishop. Although a perfect harmony has not been achieved, in general wherever a basic mutual respect exists, there is dialogue between both sides. The confrontations in the period of the "social-pastoral" church have occurred, not so much between those who are politically more conservative or liberal, but rather between "pluralists" and "sectarians," that is, between those who are capable of real dialogue and those who are not.

The Church Leader as Companion and Guide

One of the important notes of the "social-pastoral" church is the emergence of a new role for priests, religious, and pastoral agents, that of "companion" or guide for the people. Although Vatican II called upon the laity to assume leadership roles in the church, the steps taken for implementing this call were very slow in practice. In the young towns or new urban settlements where new parishes were literally being founded every month, priests and religious women assumed practically all leadership functions in the beginning. Yet it was precisely in these new parishes that lay leaders were most encouraged to display their talents, with the help of short courses and Bible-study groups. Within a short space of time the old-fashioned authoritarian model of the priest or sister as leader gave way to a new role, that of a "companion" or a "guide" who offers support to the laity. In some middle-class parishes a real spirit of teamwork has been achieved between priest, religious, and laity. The *cursillos de Cristiandad* and, even more so, marriage encounter have contributed much to this new sense of team spirit because they use group-dynamic techniques that break down the formalistic barriers that once separated the priests from the laity. In the social-pastoral church priests and religious have taken on the role of advisers and spiritual guides, thereby leaving open the possibility for the laity to assume leadership roles.

Liberation Theology

The intellectual current that created the greatest interest in the Latin American church since Medellín has been liberation theology. This new theological current marks the beginning of a new stage in the history of the Latin American church because it symbolizes more than any other movement the emergence of a socially committed church in the southern hemisphere. It represents the coming of age of the Latin American church because theologians, once so highly dependent upon European authors, broke that dependency and charted their own original course, which in turn influenced universal Christian thought. Since its beginnings in the decade of the sixties, liberation theology has given rise to a sort of "school" that includes many well-known intellectuals, each with his own particular perspective: in the southern cone the Jesuits Juan Luis Segundo and Juan Carlos Scannone and the Chilean diocesan priest Segundo Galilea; in Brazil, Hugo Assmann and Leonardo Boff, a Franciscan; and in El Salvador, Jon Sobrino. Among Latin American Protestants, Rubem Alves, a Brazilian, and José Miguez Bonino, an Argentinian, stand out. The Belgian priest José Comblim is considered one of the initiators of the new current. The Argentinian historian Enrique Dussel has also made significant contributions to the field. In this constellations of stars, however, there is none who is more identified with the very concept of "liberation theology" than the Peruvian priest Gustavo Gutiérrez Merino.

Gustavo Gutiérrez

Gustavo Gutiérrez is the only liberation theologian of international fame in Peru. For this reason he has become a symbol of an entire ecclesial movement that finds its inspiration in his ideas. Since the publication of his work, *Liberation Theology* (1971), he has become one of the best-known persons in the entire Catholic world in the twentieth century. In spite of this international fame, however, he is known in Peruvian and Latin American church circles simply as "Father Gustavo." His simple life-style as well as his direct and affectionate approach to people are qualities that have endeared him to the popular classes. He is a priest of the secular clergy and his immediate superior is the archbishop of Lima.

His personal history is a guide for tracing the development of liberation theology. He was born on June 8, 1928, in the center of Lima, and he spent his youth in lower middle class enviroments. He studied at the Marist Brothers' school in Barranco, a suburb to the south of Lima. He was forced to suspend studies, however, as a result of a bone disease (osteomyelitis). He went to San Marcos National University in 1947 to study medicine. He also participated in Catholic Action and in 1950 held the post of president of the Catholic Center of Barranco. He became a friend of the leaders of Catholic Action, such as César Arróspide, Eduardo Picher, José Dammert, and Gerardo Alarco. While he studied at San Marcos he took courses in philosophy at the Catholic University. He was especially impressed by the course in moral theology taught by Father Felipe MacGregor.[2]

In 1950 he entered the seminary in Santiago, Chile, where he studied for a semester. With the help of a scholarship he went to Europe in 1951 to study philosophy and psychology at the University of Louvain. One of his fellow students there was Camilo Torres, the Colombian priest who died in 1966 while fighting for a guerrilla movement. He wrote his licentiate thesis in 1955, entitled "Psychic Conflicts in Freud." Between 1955 and 1959 he studied theology at Lyons, France. He was influenced especially by Gustave Thils, the christologist Christian Duquoc and Gustave Martelet, S.J. He was tutored privately by Henri de Lubac, S.J., one of several prestigious intellectuals in the church at that time who were forbidden to teach publicly on account of their advanced ideas. Through this contact with Jesuits he also developed an interest in Ignatian spirituality. In 1958 he made the thirty-day Ignatian spiritual exercises. Other progressive thinkers who influenced him in those years were Ives Congar, Edward Schillebeeckx, and Karl Rahner, all key voices at the Second Vatican Council. He was familiar, as were most progressive Catholics in that period, with the works of Pierre Teilhard de Chardin. He was ordained a priest in Lima in 1959 by Archbishop Landázuri. Between 1959 and 1960 he complemented his studies with a semester at the Gregorian University in Rome. In 1960 he returned to Lima and was incorporated into the teaching faculty at the Catholic University. He also assumed the role as national moderator of UNEC (National Union of Catholic Students).

It was in these university surroundings, especially in workshops and meetings of UNEC, that the basic elements of liberation theology were forged. In 1964 Father Gutiérrez attended a meeting at Petrópolis, Brazil, organized by Ivan Illich. The paper he presented there was later amplified and delivered to student leaders at the Catholic University of Montevideo in 1967 under the title, *La Pastoral de la Iglesia en America Latina* (The Church's Pastoral Action in Latin America). In July of 1968 in Chimbote he delivered a talk to priests belonging to ONIS entitled, "Toward a Theology of Liberation." From that moment on, the man and the concept became closely identified. That same year he attended the bishops' conference at Medellín as an advisor. Liberation theology was incorporated into the final documents as one of the key themes. In Switzerland in 1969 he gave another talk nuancing some of his ideas and in Lima in 1971 he published his celebrated work.[3] Since that time the book has been translated into many languages and is considered one of the basic texts in both Catholic and Protestant seminaries throughout the world for studying liberation theology.

In the Process of Being Created

In general lines liberation theology conceives the efforts of the third world to leave behind its dependency on the first world and to overcome its underdevelopment as a creative process of self-liberation. In religious terms this quest for freedom can be compared to the flight of the children of Israel from slavery in Egypt. Father Gutiérrez relies considerably on the most important theological currents of postwar Europe and the United States, the social sciences, and especially dependency theory, in order to arrive at a new synthesis between history and theology, with particular reference to Latin America. His work awoke the admiration of many and at the same time provoked an impassioned controversy, typical reactions toward a new concept. In general, the criticisms of his work come down to two: on the one hand, in spite of his announced intention of forging an authentically new Latin American theology, liberation theology, at least in the initial stages, relied heavily on European authors; and, on the other hand, it absorbed dependency theory and certain Marxist categories a bit too simplistically.[4]

In later works Father Gutiérrez nuanced and expanded on his original message. In *The Power of the Poor in History* (1979), for example, there is a noticeably greater emphasis on the reality of Latin America. In other articles and essays the Latin American roots of liberation theology are stressed, especially in the ideas of Bartolomé de las Casas or in the thought of the contemporary Peruvian novelist, José María Arguedas. In other works, notably, *We Drink From Our Own Wells: The Spiritual Journey of a People* (1983) and *On Job: God-Talk and the Suffering of the Innocent* (1986), one can perceive the effort to underline the spiritual dimension of liberation. Liberation theology is not a finished product, but rather a thought still being fashioned. In spite of its rather brief history, however, it has already had considerable influence on church, academic, and political circles throughout all of Latin America.[5]

Collaborators and Sympathizers

In Peru there are certain persons and groups closely associated with the liberation theology movement and Father Gutiérrez. First, several professors of theology at the Catholic University, especially the diocesan priests Luis Fernando Crespo and Felipe Zegarra, are close collaborators. Until his death in 1979 so was Hugo Echegaray, a young and very popular priest, and author of *La Práctica de Jesús* (The Practice of Jesus, 1980). In 1974 Father Gutiérrez founded Bartolomé de las Casas Center in Rímac (Lima) in order to continue research. The team of laypersons at the center carry out research projects and organize short courses and workshops for Christian leaders, especially from the popular classes. The center also provides a documentation and news service on the progressive church in the rest of Latin America. Closely tied to the center is the editorial house, Centro de Estudios y Publicaciones, which publishes the magazine *Páginas* and distributes books that reflect the thought currents within the progressive sectors of the Latin American church.

Furthermore, there are certain lay groups that draw their basic inspiration from liberation theology: UNEC (National Union of Catholic Students), the national moderator of which is Gustavo

The Social-Pastoral Church, 1975–   307

Gutiérrez; JOC (Young Catholic Workers); and MTC (the Movement of Christian Workers). The moderator of the last two groups is Father Jorge Alvarez Calderón, one of the most visible spokesman for the progressive church in Peru. The priests' movement, ONIS, which began to decline after Puebla, was a direct offshoot of liberation theology. In Lima, a majority of the teachers and students at the Institute of Higher Theological Studies (ISET) for religious are sympathetic toward the general lines of liberation theology. Finally, some Jesuits, especially Ricardo Antoncich and Manuel Díaz Mateos, have sought to discover the links between liberation theology and Ignatian spirituality.

An Ecclesial Movement: The Summer Course

Liberation theology cannot be understood merely as an intellectual current. Nor is it really a school of thought in the traditional sense. Rather, it is a sort of banner for an entire ecclesial movement that includes all kinds of people of different tendencies and outlooks. For many Christians who work in parishes and projects among the popular classes, liberation theology represents a message of hope that they associate with the post-Medellín church. The best example of liberation theology as a "movement" is the summer course organized each year by the theology department of the Catholic University. The first course, officially termed a "Workshop in Theological Reflection," was offered in 1971. Since that year the course has become a special event in the life of the progressive church in Peru. It also reflects the growth of that sector. In 1974, for example, there were 464 participants. But by 1983 that number had risen to 1,500.[6]

The organizers and speakers are usually theology professors from the Catholic University. The key drawing speaker, however, is Father Gutiérrez. Although it is not presented as a course in liberation theology as such, that is the general perspective that pervades most of the talks and discussions. The course, which lasts about two weeks, is truly an ecclesial event because it draws together church people from all walks of life and all parts of Peru. Although there are many priests and religious women present, lay men and women are far more numerous. In 1978, for example, of the 1,126 participants that year, there were 405 priests and religious women; the remaining 721 were laypersons.[7] Further, although all social classes are represented, the great majority come from the popular classes, either from the "young towns" or from the rural Andes. The course is also a big attraction for people in the provinces. Many students of UNEC and workers belonging to the JOC and the MTC attend regularly. Finally, groups of Christians from the rest of Latin America, especially Ecuador, Chile, Bolivia, and Brazil participate, as well as theological students from the United States, Canada, and Europe.

The basic motivation of the majority of participants is a desire to deepen their own faith. Most of the laity who attend the course have had very little formal education. Among them one can find workers, peasants, secretaries, and domestic workers. Almost all are involved actively in their local parishes or in a church movement. Almost all, especially those from the young towns, have gone through a process of politicization since the decade of the sixties. For them the course represents a way to harmonize their new political awareness with their religious faith. The course attempts to do just that, to relate the great biblical themes to the major themes of the twentieth century. Of course, opening up one's intellectual horizons is not the only reason for attending the course. The two weeks of sharing ideas with hundreds of other Christians from the rest of Peru and from other parts of Latin America is also an experience of church. This experience strengthens the sense of belonging to a common movement. The atmosphere of friendship and fraternity heightens this sense of belonging. The course begins and ends with a liturgy, usually presided over by one or two bishops.

The Popular Church and Politics

In different messages the bishops of Latin America have expressed their concern over a possible Marxist "infiltration" in the church as well as the creation of a "popular church" that is parallel to and even in opposition to the official church. These fears notwithstanding, with a few exceptions neither of these two phenomena have occurred in Peru. Within the liberation theology movement there are a great number of interpretations and ways of understanding the relationship between faith and politics. Liberation theology in Peru does not represent a closed movement, least of all a "sect." In spite of allusions to Marxism in Father Gutiérrez' works, there are no real Marxists among the Christians who identify themselves with liberation theology or who work among the popular classes. There are some professors at the Catholic University who belong to leftist parties and who are practicing Catholics. But both the professors and the parties to which they belong claim explicitly to be "non-Marxist." Among the thousands of ordinary Christians who live in parishes in popular neighborhoods or in the country there is far less intellectual rigor than in the academic world about the correct way to apply the social teachings of the church to concrete political realities. The political and religious worldview of many grass-roots Christians oscillates between traditional popular religiosity, which contains some conservative elements, and liberation theology. Being "left" for many of these Christians consists in supporting one or other leftist candidate, not because he or she is a Marxist, but because the candidate promises social reform. The vast majority of practicing Christians, especially those from the popular classes, instinctively reject Marxism as a philosophy and as a political system.

Nor has a "rebel" or parallel church arisen among the popular sectors in Peru. This is due to a great extent to the efforts of the spokespersons and leaders of the "popular" church, especially those identified with the liberation theology movement, to strengthen unity with the bishops. Father Gutiérrez maintained a close relationship with Cardinal Landázuri, so much so that many considered the cardinal a sort of protector of liberation theology. In reality, Landázuri followed the same policy with respect to liberation theology that he applied to all church groups, including certain very conservative ones: pluralism and dialogue within the basic context of obedience and respect for authority. Although it is premature to measure the full impact of liberation theology on the Peruvian church, it has been considerable. The summer course alone has been responsible for helping thousands of Christians relate their faith to current social and political realities, and for many it has meant practically a second evangelization.

The Conservative Groups

The use of the word "conservative" as well as the word "progressive" is arbitrary; its meaning depends much on the historical context in which it is used. In Latin America in general there is a key criterion to distinguish a "conservative" from a "progressive" Catholic: his or her degree of acceptance of Vatican II and the bishops' conference of Medellín (which was reaffirmed in Puebla). One is a conservative if one does not practice the letter or live the spirit of the council. The council exhorted Catholics to broaden their horizons and to enter into dialogue with the modern world. This exhortation cannot be reduced to certain fixed formulas because it refers most of all to a mental and psychological attitude. One can make a further distinction between "traditionalists" and "conservatives." More often than not, these are two sides of the same coin. There are Catholics who long for certain traditions of the church (the Mass in Latin, the use of more explicit religious symbols), but they are not necessarily closed to the fundamental values that the council stressed: tolerance of new ideas, openness to other cultures and religions, and a spirit of adaptation to new pastoral needs.

The conservatives in contrast usually insist on retaining not only pre-Vatican II forms but attitudes as well. Or they accept a change in the forms but not of the underlying dispositions that give meaning to the change. The conservative groups are usually characterized by a closed outlook toward others, a rigidity in personal relations that manifests itself in the liturgy, and emphasis on certain devotions that reinforce a pietistic and individualistic religiosity. Most of all, they stand out for their sectarian approach in regard to others in the same church. In the context of Latin America there is another note of special importance: a group's fundamental attitude toward social change. The episcopal conference of Medellín called upon Catholics to incorporate into their lives a commitment to promote social justice for the poor. Latin America's Catholic conservatives do not appear to have heard this call of the church. Many of them are directly connected with the political right and display a near obsession with the "Marxist infiltration" in the church. But for them, "Marxism" seems to refer to practically any serious reform project. The conservative groups usually classify Marxists, leftists, and progressive Christians indiscriminately under the same heading.

In Peru there are several bishops, many small groups of laypersons, some religious orders and associations, and certain factions and individuals within otherwise mainstream religious orders that incarnate these qualities. Two groups especially stand out, Opus Dei and Sodalitium. Opus Dei was founded in Spain in 1928 by Josemaría Escrivá de Balaguer (1902–75), a diocesan priest. It is an association of both laypersons and priests. It had close ties to Franco's regime in Spain, although now it has grown into a worldwide association. It first established itself in Peru in the prelatures of Cañete and Yauyos and currently there are five Opus Dei bishops: Ignacio María de Orbegozo in Chiclayo, Luis Sánchez Moreno in Cañete, Enrique Pelach in Abancay, and the two auxiliary bishops, Juan Antonio Ugarte in Cuzco and Juan Luis Cipriani in Ayacucho. Furthermore, Opus Dei runs the University of Piura, founded in 1968. Opus Dei administers several houses in Lima for the formation of students and others.

The Social-Pastoral Church, 1975–

Sodalitium Christianae Vitae, on the other hand, is strictly Peruvian in origin. It was founded in 1971 by Luis Fernando Figari, a layman who studied at the Catholic University and the Theology Faculty of Lima. He cofounded his group with a Marianist priest, Gerald Haby. Sodalitium is a pious association of laypersons and priests modeled on the Marian Sodality and inspired in part by the counsels of the founder of the Marianists, Guillaume Joseph Chaminade. Nevertheless, the propensity of the founder toward certain pre-Vatican models of the church as well as a tendency to condemn Catholics on the left also form part of the outlook of the members. Many of the first members came from Santa María Colegio, run by the Marianists, where Figari taught for some time. There is a women's branch called the "Association of Mary Immaculate." Sodalitium is present in the Faculty of Theology, where some of its members study for the priesthood, and at the Catholic University. In general, its members come from the middle and upper classes. There are some bishops, especially Archbishop Fernando Vargas of Arequipa, who lend support to the movement.[8]

Puebla

The Conservative Reaction

The Third Episcopal Conference of the Latin American church, held in Puebla de los Angeles, Mexico, between January 27 and February 13, 1979, laid down the basic lines of the "social-pastoral" church and gave rise to a new consensus in the church. Most of all, it reaffirmed Medellín. However, its origins were very different from those of Medellín. The general atmosphere at the 1968 bishops' conference was one of relaxed cordiality and openness. Although the final document of Medellín clearly represented the mind of the progressive groups, there was no attempt to stifle dialogue or to close the meeting to outside influences. By way of contrast, the Puebla conference was carefully planned by conservative groups that sought a way to impose their mentality on the meeting, especially by excluding the progressives. In 1972 the coadjutor archbishop of Medellín, Alfonso López Trujillo, was elected secretary general of CELAM. From that post he became the principal spokesman for conservative groups in all of Latin America. With the Belgian Jesuit Roger Vekemans as an intellectual adviser and with the support of Cardinal Baggio, the president of the Pontifical Commission for Latin America in

Rome, López Trujillo set about preparing the way for the conference.[9]

In December 1977 the organizers of Puebla distributed a preliminary document (called the *Documento de consulta*) that laid down certain basic lines of orientation for the coming meeting. It virtually constituted a rejection of the Medellín conference. Although it rendered tribute to Medellín, the preliminary document declared that Medellín, which aimed to apply Vatican II to Latin America, "did not explicitly place itself in continuity with the episcopal history" of that region.[10] López Trujillo's document stressed "secularism" as the basic problem of Latin America, thus placing a basically European theme at the core of the discussion. By way of contrast, such key Latin American themes as massive exploitation or the dehumanization that results from social and political oppression were given a low priority.

The preliminary document had an unforeseen and, in the long run, positive effect: it stimulated thousands of Christians throughout Latin America, alarmed over the obvious attempt to annul Medellín, to rethink their original position in order to defend it better. In the years between Medellín and Puebla the fundamental ideas of Medellín had spread from the elites to the masses. As a result, the *Documento de consulta* was discussed and debated everywhere, in parishes and ecclesial base communities. During the process, grass-roots Christians became even more conscienticized theologically. The original document met with massive resistance throughout Latin America. In September 1978 Cardinal Aloisio Lorscheider, at that time president of CELAM and principal voice of the progressive church in that organism, published a second document known simply as "The Working Document" (*Documento de Trabajo*) as an alternative basis for discussion. As a result of these initial skirmishes, battlelines were drawn up several months before the meeting at Puebla, each side armed with its own document.

Medellín Reaffirmed

The Puebla conference, held three months after the original date set in order to welcome Pope John Paul II, who had recently been elected, began in the midst of great expectations and tensions. One major source of tension was the attempt on the part of the organizers to exclude from the conference the liberation theologians, who also were the most prominent theologians in the Latin American church. Given that impasse, many bishops invited their own theologians to become counterweights to the officially designated ones. As a result, leaders and thinkers of the progressive church were also present at Puebla. The more conservative theologians gave their advice inside the conference and the progressives from outside. Gustavo Gutiérrez himself was invited to be an adviser by eight different bishops, among them Dom Helder Câmara from Brazil and Leonidas Proaño of Ecuador.[11] In spite of the efforts of López Trujillo, therefore, a confrontation of two distinct theological visions did occur. Finally, the presence of John Paul II influenced the movement of the conference considerably. Many conservatives hoped that the pontiff would condemn liberation theology, given his militant anticommunist background. But the enormously charismatic pope surprised everyone, including the progressives, by his strong condemnation of social injustice in Latin America. Furthermore, the fact that liberation theology was not censured encouraged bishops and theologians to take that as a positive sign in its favor.

For two intense weeks the participants huddled in committees and debated Cardinal Lorscheider's working document. A criticism frequently made of the final Puebla document is that it seems to be the work of a commission, that is, it lacks synthesis and organic unity. Nevertheless, the positive far outweighs the negative. The Puebla document is more theological and in some ways more profound than the Medellín document. For the progressives, Puebla clearly signified a victory because the basic lines of Medellín were reaffirmed. Not only did it underline the preferential option for the poor, but it also affirmed in no uncertain terms the validity of the concept of liberation in Christ. But the document also added that Christian liberation can never be confused with mere political liberation, and certainly not with the Marxist concept of freedom.[12] Finally, Puebla marked the beginning of a new era of consensus between the progressive sectors and the conservatives. Even though each side had a different interpretation of the same document, at least they shared a common basis for working together.

The Peruvians at Puebla

As in the rest of Latin America, the preliminary document for Puebla provoked much heated discussion in Peru. In March 1978 Gustavo Gutiérrez delivered a talk at the Andean Pastoral Institute (Cuzco) criticizing the main lines of the document.[13] In different regional assemblies throughout the country, criticisms and suggestions were proposed to be placed on the agenda at Puebla.

In May 1978 the Peruvian episcopal conference published its own document based on the proposals made in the regional assemblies. The episcopal document clearly stressed its differences with the preliminary document. Under the title "General Observations," the bishops stated their opinion that Puebla should seek its "inspiration in the spirit of Medellín and express itself in the same clear and simple language of that historical conference." Furthermore, the Peruvian document rejected the attempt to impose a document on the rest of the church and called for a wider consultation that would "take into account the testimonies of bishops, priests, religious, and laypersons...."[14] The bishops went on to analyze the structural causes of poverty in Latin America and called for fundamental structural change as the only real remedy to that problem. The document also denounced armament and the doctrine of national security that served as a justification for many military regimes in Latin America.[15] The Peruvian bishops' document clearly did not limit itself to making suggestions for Puebla; it also used the opportunity to level criticisms at the military government of the "Second Phase."

The Peruvian bishops went to Puebla, therefore, with an agenda that represented the feelings of a wide spectrum of Christians throughout the entire country. More so than in any previous assembly the bishops could claim that they spoke in the name of the entire church. Cardinal Landázuri, who was both the president of the Peruvian episcopal conference and the first vice-president of CELAM, led the delegation of twelve bishops. The other bishops were Luis Bambarén (Chimbote), Manuel Prado (Trujillo), Lorenzo León Alvarado (Huacho), Ricardo Durand (Callao), Germán Schmitz (auxiliary bishop of Lima), Luciano Metzinger (secretary to the bishop's conference), Javier Ariz (Puerto Maldonado), Fernando Vargas (Piura), Ignacio Orbegozo (Chiclayo), and Eduardo Picher (Huancayo). Besides the eleven who were elected, Bishop Alcides Mendoza, the chaplain of the armed forces, was designated by the Holy See. The official theologian who accompanied the bishops was Enrique Bartra, S.J. Father Hugo Garaycoa Hawkins, later to be named a bishop, was sent as a representative of pastoral action for the youth. Sister Esther Capestany was sent as the representative of the Conference for Religious. The Peruvian delegation also included a layman, a married deacon, and a representative of the native cultures of the Amazon jungle. There was a total of 188 bishops at the Puebla conference, including both elected and appointed participants.

Further, as indicated above, several Peruvians were present by

The Social-Pastoral Church, 1975–

way of invitations from different bishops. Father Gustavo Gutiérrez was present as well as Father Ricardo Antoncich, who was invited as an adviser to the Latin American Conference of Religious (CLAR). The official theologian, Enrique Bartra, S.J., played an important role in the commission on "Preferential Option for the Poor" by insisting on not watering down that key issue of Medellín. The Peruvian delegation in particular helped to make the "preferential option for the poor" a key point at Puebla as well.

Post-Puebla: The Limits of Tolerance

In the years shortly before and after Puebla, some incidents occurred that were out of harmony with the spirit of consensus. Sensationalist newspapers somewhat inaccurately described the incidents as conflicts between "rightists" and "leftists" in the church. It would have been more precise to speak of "sectarians" versus "pluralists." The groups who provoked the tensions were generally characterized by their incapacity to dialogue and a lack of real desire to work in harmony with the rest of the church. They exhibited many of the traits of a "sect" within the church, whether they were sympathetic to the political right or the left. Two examples that attracted attention were the priest-workers called EMO in Callao and the IEME priests in Chimbote. Among groups on the right, the unrelenting campaign to condemn liberation theology carried out by certain lay groups represented the same sectarian mentality.

EMO-Callao

Between 1974 and 1978 a group of priest-workers, a number of whom were Dutch, established themselves in the port city of Callao. They called themselves EMO: (Equipo de Misión Obrera—Team for the Mission among Workers). The group had been founded among workers and university students in Chile in 1971 and was also known as Calama, a reference to the mining city of that name. Calama had ties with the movement Christians for Socialism that was led by some very intellectually capable priests such as Juan Caminada and Theo Hansen. Hansen, who was the subdirector of the Faculty of Theology at the Catholic University of Santiago, had become so radicalized that he became virtually a Marxist. After Pinochet's takeover in 1973, Calama was forced to flee the country. Some of the members went back to Europe, but EMO decided to make another try in Latin America and chose Peru as a new base for its work. Once in Callao, other priests and some married couples joined them.[16]

In one sense, EMO seemed like the famous priest-worker movement of France in the forties and fifties. But there was one important difference: the goal of the priests in Callao was not so much to Christianize the workers as to conscienticize them politically and to inculcate in them a greater sense of class solidarity. The priests of EMO believed that these actions responded to the biblical call to prepare for the coming of the kingdom of God in the most efficacious way possible. But given their overt political mission, the priests of EMO usually concealed the fact that they were priests. Furthermore, the EMO team led a type of community life that demanded total commitment to their ideals. Among other activities, for example, they held lengthy sessions in which they used the techniques of group dynamics to fortify a sense of solidarity within the group. On the other hand, EMO had little interest in the overall pastoral planning of the diocese. When the bishop, Ricardo Durand, realized what EMO was about, virtually a political cell dedicated to Marxist proselytizing, he refused to renew their contract. The group left Peru in March 1978.

Chimbote

The incident in Callao seemed to be a typical confrontation between progressives and conservatives because Bishop Durand was popularly labeled a "conservative." In Chimbote a similar incident occurred, but this time the bishop in question was Luis Bambarén, a symbol of the progressive church in all of Latin America. In both cases the real difficulty was not so much the ideological orientation of the actors as their aggressive sectarianism. In May 1981 Bishop Bambarén announced his decision not to renew the contract with six Spanish priests who belonged to IEME: Instituto Español de Misiones Extranjeras (The Spanish Institute for the Foreign Missions).[17] All were diocesan priests in charge of different parishes in Chimbote and nearby towns. In public the bishop played down the existence of underlying tensions. Nevertheless, his disapproval of the pastoral methods of the group was well known. For years the IEME priests had practically reduced their pastoral work to supporting various strikes and political causes. Furthermore, in the face of repeated warnings from the bishop, the priests turned their parishes into centers of protest against the bishop himself. In the two cases, Callao and Chimbote, attempts were very clearly made to create a parallel church.

The Campaign against Liberation Theology

Although the episcopal conference at Puebla affirmed the validity of the concept of liberation as a Christian theme, liberation theology became the center of controversy once again in the period preceding and following the first papal visit to Peru in 1985. Liberation theology had already been amply discussed in academic journals long before Puebla. Indeed, for many Christians in academic circles, it was a topic that had already ceased to be a fad. Nevertheless, when liberation theology turned into a popular grass-roots movement, the official church grew increasingly concerned about its possible impact on ordinary Christians. What began as a more academic movement in the early seventies became the center of a theological storm by the end of the decade.

What the general public did not always perceive, however, was the existence of two different levels: one level was that of the examination conducted by the official church, carried out for pastoral motives; but a second level consisted of a sensationalist campaign carried out by journalists, politicians, and some persons from within the official church. In the latter case, the aim was to discredit liberation theology in order to have it condemned. Unlike the official church examination, however, the campaign was characterized by a vehemence that did not stop at calumny, personal insult, and outright distortions. In many aspects it was similar to the crusade carried out by Senator Joseph McCarthy in the fifties. For this reason the campaign to discredit liberation theology was an example of sectarianism on the right. The principal promoter of the campaign was Archbishop López Trujillo, the man who had been in charge of organizing the Puebla conference. After Puebla, López Trujillo was elected president of CELAM. He used that highly visible post to attack liberation theology, but by so doing he also turned CELAM into an instrument of the conservative groups in the Latin American church.

The official examination of the church grew out of the concern of many bishops and other pastoral leaders that liberation theology had become a source of confusion for many ordinary churchgoers. The aim of the examination was not to condemn a theological current that had already been approved at Puebla, but rather to clarify certain points, especially in regard to the juxtaposition of Marxist concepts with biblical concepts. The bishops were also reacting to complaints that in some cases priests and other pastoral agents had introduced partisan political themes into the liturgy.

In Peru the examination process began when Cardinal Joseph Ratzinger, the prefect of the Sacred Congregation for the Doctrine of the Faith, requested the bishops to render an opinion on the works of Father Gutiérrez. Given the level of authority from which the request emanated, the topic of liberation theology was moved to the top of the agenda at the annual sessions of the bishops' assemblies in 1983 and 1984.[18] In September 1984 Ratzinger himself issued a document, *Instruction on Certain Aspects of Liberation Theology*. Although the document was intended for the entire church, it had special relevance for the Peruvian bishops who were in the process of discussing that subject. Finally, in October of that year the episcopal conference issued its own document.

The essential message of the two documents is the same: liberation theology is an authentically Christian perspective as long as it is not based on a worldview born outside of Christianity. However, the tone and style of the two documents is different. Ratzinger's document is more severe and less positive than the bishops' document. In fact, in the period between the two documents a third influence was felt, that of the pope himself. In June and in October of 1984 the pope addressed two different groups of Peruvian bishops in Rome. With an eye to his coming visit to Peru, the pope touched upon certain themes that he would later repeat during the visit. He called the attention of the bishops to points in the *Instruction*, especially the presence of "ideologies foreign to the faith" that had surfaced in some Christian circles. However, what most impressed the bishops was the strong and positive tone adopted by the pope when he exhorted them to take a stand for social justice and to defend the poor. On the other hand, the pope rather conspicuously abstained from mentioning any particular theological line of thought.[19] This emphasis on the positive mission of the church was the decisive factor that influenced the final draft of the Peruvian bishops' document. Finally, in March 1986 the Congregation for the Doctrine of the Faith issued a new document, *Christian Freedom and Liberation*. This second Vatican document highlights the history of political, economic, and social freedom in the West as in large part a fruit of Christianity itself. The document further declares that the social doctrine of the church contains the necessary elements for a "Christian praxis of liberation." Very clearly, liberation theology was once again validated as a legitimate option for Catholics.

The entire examination process was carried out in an atmosphere of intellectual seriousness and sincere dialogue between bishops and theologians. Father Gutiérrez offered much to the dialogue by way of written answers and conversations with the bishops. The document of the bishops was a model of clarity and dialogue in the spirit of Vatican II. On a totally different level, however, was the campaign to condemn liberation theology. In Peru, some right-wing journalists, with the moral support of a few bishops and priests and especially Sodalitium Christianae Vitae, not only did not help to clarify issues, but usually created more confusion than before. On several occasions the press turned the criticism of liberation theology into a personal attack on Father Gutiérrez. In September 1984 the secretariat of the bishops' conference publicly disapproved of the use of the word "Catholic" in a "Catholic Press Service" run by Sodalitium. The service had published a story to the effect that Father Gutiérrez would be a candidate for the vice-presidency of the United Left in the presidential elections of 1985.[20]

Along with this kind of journalism, sectarian groups on the right also engaged in activities of a similar nature. The most notorious example occurred during the papal visit in February 1985 when two former seminarians, with the approval of one of the organizers, changed the official text of the message that the youth were to read to the pope. The changed text turned out to be a diatribe against all the tendencies in the progressive church.[21] These kinds of actions, done either by the "right" or the "left," clearly represented the limits of tolerance.

Special Pastoral Areas

In the Peruvian church there are areas or regions that stand out because they share certain common characteristics and because they have put into practice exceptionally dynamic pastoral programs. The "young towns," especially those on the coast, are an obvious example. But two other regions also fall into this category, the southern Andean plateau and the Peruvian Amazon River basin.

The Young Towns

The "Young Towns"—a euphemism inherited from the military government of the "First Phase"—are a distinct sociological reality within the urban context of Peru. They are urbanizations in the process of development and they share common problems. They are not all the same, however, given the different degrees of development that some have attained. Some settlers could really be classified as "lower middle class." But the most recent arrivals live in conditions of abject poverty, frequently without water, electric light, and paved roads. According to one study, in 1984 approximately 37 percent of Lima's six million inhabitants lived in "young towns," another 23 percent lived in "popular urbanizations" (a step up from a young town), and another 20 percent lived in "slums, alleys, and backyards."[22]

The church was present from the beginning of the creation of these communities. The Mission of Lima of 1957 was the first important step toward establishing the church among the outlying poor, and the Conciliar Mission of 1967 reinforced that presence. The confrontation in 1971 between Bishop Bambarén and the minister of the interior, General Artola, highlighted the active role the church was taking in organizing the young towns. Of a total of 136 parishes in the archdiocese of Lima in 1984, approximately twenty-two are found in the young towns. Another nineteen are located in the popular neighborhoods. From the beginning the church recognized these settlements as a special pastoral area. In 1968 Luis Bambarén, the newly consecrated auxiliary bishop of Lima, was named the principal representative of the archbishop to the young towns. Even though the young towns of Lima were officially under the archbishop, they enjoyed a considerable amount of autonomy for the first years of their existence. The church in these areas is characterized by features that sharply distinguish it from the church in well-off neighborhoods.

One noticeable characteristic is that the majority of religious personnel, priests and religious women, are foreign-born. In this and in other aspects the church in the young towns is highly "missionary" in character. In general, the works of the church in these areas are financed with the help of Catholic organizations and dioceses in Europe and North America (the United States and Canada). In districts such as San Martín de Porras in northern Lima one single group is in charge, the Irish-based Columban Fathers. In Trujillo on the northern coast priests from the diocese of Cork, as well as the St. James Fathers, are especially evident. In Lima, many religious groups took on parishes in response to the call of Medellín. The Maryknoll Fathers took charge of a parish in Ciudad de Dios, the Jesuits took over another one in El Agustino, and the English Benedictines did the same in Las Flores.

A parish in a young town is a many-faceted center that offers a number of services to the community. Besides the main church there are generally many smaller satellite chapels scattered

The Social-Pastoral Church, 1975–

throughout the parish. Almost all young-town parishes have a medical post that offers free services, a popular soup kitchen, and a vocational training school. Within the typical parish there will be many different clubs for mothers and for the youth. During school vacation the parish will offer a multitude of courses for children and adults. In the church of the young towns people experience a high degee of identification with the parish, which in turn is the fruit of systematic pastoral planning from the early sixties. During the sixties and seventies the parish became the natural focal point of unity in the community. This fact led to tension with the military government because the parish hall was frequently selected as a public forum to discuss community planning. And community planning often involved criticizing the government for not helping the community.

But the parish is not the only church presence. One of the principal goals of many migrants from the Andes is to educate their children. So the church's educational centers also became an important part of its pastoral planning. The most notable example are the Fe y Alegría (Faith and Joy) schools run by the Jesuits. In Lima alone there were eighteen of these schools in 1987. Frequently, the school and the parish work together. The women religious who run the schools also take charge of the pastoral planning for their own area.

In 1978 Bishop Bambarén was tranferred to the prelature of Chimbote. On the occasion of this change, the church reorganized itself in the young towns. Given the enormous population growth, especially in the young towns, it was decided to break them up and reapportion them among several auxiliary bishops. With this reorganization the young towns lost some of their original pastoral unity. Nevertheless, three of the six vicariates (the basic division of the archdiocese above the parish level) retain their "popular" character: the first vicariate, under Bishop Alfredo Noriega, covers the "northern cone"; the second vicariate, under Bishop Augusto Beuzeville, covers el Agustino, San Juan de Lurigancho, and Caja de Agua; and the third vicariate, under Bishop Germán Schmitz (until his death in 1990), corresponds to the "southern cone" of Lima.

In general there are strong ties among the pastoral teams that work in the young towns. But not all church groups adhere to the same mentality. In Arequipa two different pastoral plans function in competition: on the one hand, the parishes, and on the other, the schools run by CIRCA, the "Catholic Circles" founded in 1958 by the Jesuit Carlos Pozzo. CIRCA is an impressively well-knit organization of schools and social projects throughout the young towns of Arequipa. In 1982 CIRCA operated twenty-three centers for mothers, twenty primary schools, three complete primary and high schools, many medical posts, and several vocational training schools.[23] It is a model of efficiency and organization, but it is also criticized by the pastoral agents who work in the parishes in the young towns for being "paternalistic" and out of step with Medellín.

The most characteristic note of the church in the young towns is its orientation toward the future, a fact reinforced by the great number of youth who participate in parish activities or who attend schools. Although the settlers easily identify with causes and movements in favor of social justice, they are not prone to dogmatism or sectarianism. The general rule is tolerance, hospitality, and pluralism, a rule imposed by the fact that almost all of them come from different parts of the Andes. For most of them the parish is a source of stability that helps them to retain their cultural identity. Belonging to the parish also represents a way of becoming integrated into the community. The young-town parish is a melting pot in which traditional popular Catholicism fuses with the new liberation theology mentality, thus giving the settlers a new common identity.

The Southern Andean Church

During the military regime the church in the southern Andean plateau was considered the most progressive region in the Peruvian church. Bound together by common geographical and cultural characteristics, the bishops and apostolic vicars of the region displayed an uncommon moral leadership that not only inspired their own people but the rest of the country as well. Furthermore, by means of the Andean Pastoral Institute and other regional centers, the church also became one of the principal promoters for studying the indigenous cultures in the area. The area's pastoral planning also became a model for forming the laity. The key prelates who helped create the southern Andean church were Luis Vallejos, archbishop of Cuzco (1975–82), Luis Dalle, vicar apostolic of Ayaviri (1971–82), Albano Quinn, vicar apostolic of Sicuani (1971–), Jesús Calderón, bishop of Puno (1972–), Albert Köenigsknecht, vicar apostolic of Juli (1973–86), and Lorenzo Miccheli, vicar apostolic of Chuquibambilla (1968–86).

The southern Andean church began to take shape in the fifties and sixties with the creation of the *prelaturae nullius*. Some of these new jurisdictions were given over to missionary groups with a modern mentality, such as Juli to the Maryknoll priests and brothers, Ayaviri to the Sacred Hearts missionaries, and Sicuani to the American Carmelites. The forerunners of this regional effort were the first prelates of the new jurisdictions: Edward Fedders in Juli, Luciano Metzinger in Ayaviri, and Nevin Hayes in Sicuani. Ricardo Durand, the archbishop of Cuzco (1966–75) was one of the driving forces behind the creation of the Andean Pastoral Institute in 1968. The institute soon became the principal nexus for interregional activities. Its main function was to help priests, religious women, and laity in general to become better pastoral workers. It emphasizes especially courses in the Quechua and Aymara languages and culture. The first director of the institute, Luis Dalle, of the Sacred Hearts missionaries, also founded a magazine, *Allpanchis Phuturinga*, which specializes in anthropological and regional cultural topics. It soon became the principal organ for a revival of interest in the local native cultures.[24] In 1974 the institute began to publish another magazine, *Revista de Pastoral Andina* (Andean Pastoral Review), of a less academic and more pastoral nature.

This effort was complemented by the foundation of two other centers, the Bartolomé de las Casas Center for Rural Andean Studies in Cuzco and the Institute for Aymara Studies run by the Maryknoll Fathers in Chucuito. The Las Casas center, run by French and Belgian Dominicans, notably Juan Hugues and Guido Delrán, carries out research on the social and religious situation of the region and publishes studies along those lines. Father Juan Baptista Lassegue, of the same order, reorganized the church archives of Cuzco.[25]

The southern Andean church distinguished itself for the quality of its intellectual production and for its social concern. In various pastoral messages the bishops of the region denounced injustices and violations of human rights. The most famous pastoral letter, published in September 1978, bore the title "Accompanying our People."[26] Their explicit identification with the peasants who were the principal victims of exploitation in the region provoked much criticism from the political authorities and the local *gamonales* (landowners).[27]

Another criterion to judge the vitality of the church is its capacity to foster lay participation and to form leaders. During the decade of the seventies the dioceses of the southern Andean church with the help of IPA trained hundreds of highly motivated committed catechists and "animators." As late as the sixties the concept of the "sacristy-catechist" still prevailed in most parts of the

Latin American church, that is, the catechist who was a pious person, but who was never more than a lackey of the priest. But after Medellín the new tendency was to foster lay leadership from among natural community leaders, men and women who in fact were role models in their respective communities. In IPA, for example, the catechists of this new generation participated along with priests and religious women in short theology courses. In October 1984 the first convention of "Peasant Animators" of the diocese of Puno was held. Some 550 animators (the words "animator" or "pastoral agent" are frequently used instead of "catechist," given the pejorative image that many have of the traditional catechist), men and women, all with a keen social sensitivity and a simple but solid biblical formation, attended.[28] Given this phenomenon of numerous committed laypersons, who are highly motivated to take the initiative to organize church activities in their local communities, the shortage of priests and nuns is not as urgently felt as it was in the early sixties.

On the other hand, the church in the southern Andean region does have problems, most of which are the result of the type of pastoral action that existed before Medellín. To begin with, the great majority of the progressive clergy are foreigners, while the majority of the members of the native clergy belong to the more traditional and conservative groups. In many cases, the priests born in the area come from very poor peasant families for whom being a priest meant ascending the social scale. This native clergy does not look at all favorably on the progressive clergy, who are perceived as a threat to them and their "control" over the church. This division within the clergy is most noticeable in Cuzco. The majority of the parishes are in the hands of priests born in the Cuzco area itself. They have shown few signs of updating their parishes along the lines of Vatican II. Although some of these priests know the Quechua language very well, they shun contact with the very progressive groups that foster courses in inculturation. They are conservatives both ecclesiastically and politically. The exceptions to the rule, such as the Aymara priest Domingo Llangue in the prelature of Juli who has done advanced studies in the United States, stand out. In this sense both IPA and the Las Casas Center seem like enclaves of foreigners in the middle of an otherwise conservative church. Nevertheless, the progressive groups in that region have set the pace as far the church's pastoral planning goes, a fact largely due to the support they receive from the bishops. With the death of three of the founding bishops of the region, Luis Vallejos and Luis Dalle in 1982 and Albert Köenigsknecht in 1986, all in highway accidents, the church of the southern Andean plateau suffered a major setback.[29]

The Peruvian Jungle

Given its distance from the centers of power and influence the church in the eastern Peruvian jungle has not attracted as much attention as other parts of the church, but its pastoral planning has been just as creative and forward-looking as in the southern Andean region. The church in the Amazon jungle has managed to carve out a common identity in an immense territory that is the equivalent of two-thirds of Peru and that includes some four hundred different human groups. The modern history of the church in the Amazon basin began in 1894 with the exhortation of Leo XIII to send missionaries to the area (see chapter 4). Three apostolic prefectures were founded, that of the Augustinians, the Franciscans, and the Dominicans. In a sense a sort of common identity existed from the very beginning. Nevertheless, given the great distances and the difficulties of moving from one place to another, the missionaries in the jungle maintained very little contact among themselves before the decade of the sixties.

During the first decades of the twentieth century new groups went to the jungle to work. As a consequence, new subdivisons were made to facilitate the church's pastoral action. The original prefecture of the Augustinians was subdivided into three new jurisdictions: the vicariate of Iquitos, still under the Augustinians of the Province of the Most Holy Name of Jesus of the Philippines (based in Spain); the vicariate of Yurimaguas, given over to the Passionists in 1921; and the vicariate of San José de Amazonas (the Peruvian political province of Indiana) entrusted to French Canadian Franciscans in 1945. The Passionists were also entrusted with the apostolic prefecture of Moyobamba (1948), which was made up of territory separated from the diocese of Chachapoyas. In 1945 the Jesuits took charge of the apostolic prefecture of San Francisco Javier by the Ecuadorean frontier. In the central Amazon region the apostolic prefecture of Ucayali was subdivided in 1956 into three vicariates: San Ramón, Requena, and Pucallpa. The first two are under the care of the missionary province of the Franciscans and the last is administered by the Canadian Society for the Foreign Missions. Finally, the apostolic prefecture of the Dominicans of Urubamba changed its name and its status; in 1949 it became the apostolic vicariate of Puerto Maldonado.[30]

With these territorial divisions the church in the Peruvian jungle began to acquire its definitive features. Currently, there are eight vicariates and one apostolic prefecture (Moyobamba) under the responsibility of seven different religious groups. In five of these groups, the Augustinians, the Franciscans of San Ramón and Requena, the Passionists, the Dominicans, and the Jesuits, Spanish missionaries predominate. In Pucallpa and San José de Amazonas, missionaries of French Canada make up the majority of church personnel. Nevertheless, within each of these jurisdictions there is a growing number of native vocations to the priesthood and the religious life. There are also many lay volunteers, mostly from Europe, and a great variety of congregations of religious women.

The growth of the church in the jungle can be judged from statistics taken from the mid-seventies. At that time there were 204 priests, twenty-seven religious brothers, 394 religious women, and one hundred lay missionaries. Furthermore, there were some seventy thousand students studying in 1,250 schools of different levels, ten normal schools for teachers with 1,060 students, fifty-five medical posts, twenty-three cooperatives, eighty-five centers for adult literacy, thirty-one technical schools, and five educational radio transmitters.[31] These works include the Colony of San Pablo for persons with Hansen's disease run by the Franciscans in Indiana, and a medical river boat run by the Passionists in Yurimaguas.

It was this growth, as well as increasing contacts between the bishops of the region, that helped give a common identity to the church in the Peruvian jungle. In 1971 the first Pastoral Encounter of the Missions of the Upper Amazon was held. Present for the meeting were bishops, anthropologists, sociologists, and medical doctors. It was especially at this encounter that the church in that region carved out a common pastoral identity. Under the leadership of the Augustinian priest Joaquín García, the Center for Theological Studies of the Amazon (CETA) was founded in 1972. The center trains catechists for the entire Peruvian jungle. In 1974 the bishops of the area created the Amazonic Center of Applied Pastoral Anthropology (CAAAP) to foster research on the social and religious situation of the Peruvian Amazon region. CAAAP also aims to facilitate the evangelization of the native cultures and to foster development projects. In 1976 it began publishing the academic journal *Amazonía peruana*, which has distinguished itself for the quality of its articles. It also publishes *Shupihui*, a more pastoral magazine. CAAAP has centers in Lima, Iquitos, and several other places scattered throughout the jungle.

The first three directors have all been Jesuits trained in the social sciences.

The church in the jungle has emphasized pastoral studies and action adaptable to the region. Most of all, it has taken a strong stand in defense of the local native cultures. In the Peruvian jungle there are approximately one thousand native communities that represent about fifty-three distinct ethnic and linguistic groups.[32] From the sixteenth century on, the inhabitants of the jungle have been victims of exploitation from coastal white explorers and adventurers. But in the nineteenth and twentieth centuries what was a trickle before turned into a flood of invaders: merchants, rubber extractors, soldiers, white settlers, road constructors, and oil drillers. The outsiders have threatened the ecological stability of the jungle and have also placed the lives and cultural identity of the jungle folk in jeopardy. In a collective pastoral letter in 1971, *Justicia, un clamor de la Selva* (Justice: a Cry from the Jungle), the bishops denounced the twin evils that imperiled the native communities, genocide and cultural destruction. The letter cited abundant concrete cases of abuses and crimes that had been committed against the natives. CAAAP, CETA, and the various bilingual educational centers run by the church have established strong links of friendship with the native communities. In this sense the church has contributed very positively to the efforts of the natives to forge a common Amazonic identity among themselves in order to defend their way of life better against the onrush of occidental society.

Although there exists a common pastoral plan, actual pastoral practice varies from place to place. In general, the Franciscans, Dominicans, and Passionists are more traditional in their methods than the Jesuits and the Canadian missionaries. Gustavo Prevost of Pucallpa is the most progressive of the bishops in the region. Joaquín García, the Augustinian priest in Iquitos, has stood out as one of the most dynamic leaders in organizing this far-flung church territory. As a group the Jesuits have stood out the most for their studies on the jungle. José María Guallart, Manuel Rendueles, and James Regan, all Jesuits, have written much on the popular religiosity of the jungle.[33] The Augustinian Jesús San Román wrote one of the first histories of the Peruvian jungle, *Perfiles históricos de la Amazonía peruana* (1975). Other missionaries have stood out for their creative experiments in inculturation. Carlos Diharce, a Jesuit, created a movement among the Aguaruna Indians called the "Big Family." Gastón Villanueva in Pucallpa is a known defender of the Shipibos and Cunibos, and the

Dominican Ricardo Alvarez, a cofounder of CAAAP, is well-known for his work among the Piros Indians.

The church in the Amazon River basin faces problems similar to those in other areas, but there are certain problems peculiar to the jungle. More than in other areas, the missionaries in the jungle live in what appear to be foreign enclaves. To a large extent, the isolation imposed by living in the jungle is responsible for this phenomenon. But another factor also enters the picture, the enormous cultural difference that separates white middle-class European or Canadian missionaries from the local native cultures. It was only after decades of effort that the first native vocations to the priesthood began to come forth. With the foundation of the Summer Language Institute at Yarinacocha, near Pucallpa, in 1945, another challenge was posed, that of evangelical proselytism. Officially, the institute was founded to facilitate communication between the jungle tribes and western culture by teaching the natives to read the Bible in their own languages. But in reality the institute, which is financed by fundamentalist groups in the United States, refuses all contact with the Catholic church and creates small evangelical enclaves with anti-Catholic bias throughout the Amazon region. As a consequence, these groups also place obstacles in the path of integration among the tribes.[34] Finally, working in the Amazon region presents special risks and dangers. A number of missionaries have lost their lives in boat accidents on the fast-moving tributaries of the Amazon River. Others have contracted intestinal diseases that can be cured only after years of treatment. In spite of these and many other obstacles, the men and women who work in the church in eastern Peru, like frontier pioneers, are characterized by a certain inner "toughness" as well as an expansive optimism.

The Lay Movements

The clearest sign that the Peruvian church has revitalized itself after Vatican II is the presence of a great variety of very active lay movements. Indeed, giving a new status to the laity in the church was one of the aims of the council. Some of the groups, such as UNEC or JOC, in fact existed before the council. Others, such as the Christian Life Communities, represent new expressions of older groups, in this case the Marian congregation of the Jesuits. On the other hand, Marriage Encounter and Choice are completely new, though they were somewhat modeled on older movements such as the Christian Life Movement or the *Cursillos de Cristiandad.* Some movements, especially charismatic renovation and the restored catechumenate, arose out of the liturgical reform fostered by the council. The permanent diaconate, although inspired by the model of the primitive church, was in reality a creation of Vatican II.

Although each of these movements has its own specific purpose, all of them share certain common traits and values that were stressed at the council. The model of the layperson proposed by the modern church is that of a creative agent who is both critical and open to change. Most of all, the model layperson is one who not only thinks and acts ecclesially, but who feels himself or herself to be a real part of the church. The council broke down barriers that for centuries had separated priests (and religious men and women) from the laity. Instead of the vertical clericalism that existed before, the council called for a more communitarian Catholicism in which priests and laity would form a team or pastoral unity that stresses complementary role-playing. The council also emphasized the need for a new lay spirituality to help the laity assume their new role in the church. The Spiritual Exercises of the Jesuits, after a period of updating, experienced a new surge of popularity, to a large extent because the Ignatian exercises were originally designed to help the laity live their vocation in the world.

Student and Youth Movements

The principal student movements in Peru are UNEC, the Christian Life Movement, and the university branches of Sodalitium. There are certain other smaller groups, such as Héctor de Cárdenas, Bishop Vallejos, and "Siempre" in Lima, notable for their dynamism and stability. In the youth subculture movements arise and disappear very quickly. Under the influence of Gustavo Gutiérrez, national moderator since 1960, along with local moderators such as Luis Fernando Crespo in Lima and Alfredo Pastor in Arequipa, UNEC (National Union of Catholic Students) radicalized its outlook and absorbed many aspects of liberation theology. UNEC followed the same evolution that the generation of the social Christians of the sixties went through, from Christian Democrats in the sixties to leftists in the seventies. However, UNEC never lost its ecclesial character. Especially after Medellín, it emphasized the spiritual development of its members as well the maintenance of close ties with the hierarchy.

UNEC, like the Jesuit groups "Siempre," Héctor de Cárdenas, and others, is small numerically because it places many demands on its members. The "unecistas" make retreats, hold days of reflection, and study, and carry out some kind of apostolic work. In the decade of the eighties there were approximately 150 members in Lima.[35] Though small in number, UNEC regularly organizes forums for university students that, like the annual Hugo Echegaray University Seminar, draw up to five hundred or more participants.[36]

The Christian Life Community of the Jesuits is very similar to UNEC. In the sixties and seventies Father Pablo Vásquez, S.J., directed a youth movement called the Christian Community of Leaders. When the founder died in 1980 the movement was reorganized and under the direction of other Jesuits, especially Roberto Dolan, the Christian Life Community, a modern day version of the older Marian sodality, was substituted in its place. The CLC is also very demanding and selective. In 1985 there were 150–200 members in Peru.[37] The basic spirituality is of course Ignatian. Another group called "Siempre" in Miraflores, Lima, founded in 1970 by the Jesuit José María Granda and directed for years by Angel Palencia, S.J., is a variant form of CLC. In 1985 it consisted of ninety young professionals and university students.

In 1972 Father Héctor de Cárdenas of the Sacred Hearts Fathers organized a group of young people to help him give retreats in the Marist schools in Lima. In time the group turned into a permanent lay movement that also began to carry out various apostolic activities. When the founder died in 1980 the group took his name and adopted the spirituality of the Sacred Heart congregation. In 1985 it had some seventy members. In 1972 Father Jorge Cuadros, a Dominican, founded a group for students in the University of San Martín de Porres to give them a deeper Christian formation. In 1974 the group constituted itself legally under the name Institute of Christian Studies. The institute organizes short courses and prepares programs for Radio "Santa Rosa" run by the Dominicans. The group's most important moderator for years was Father Juan Leuridan, O.P., aided by Armando Borda, a lay leader. In 1985 Borda founded the Peruvian branch of Communion and Liberation, a movement based in Italy.

In the University of San Marcos, especially in the San Fernando Medical School, a number of Christian groups sprang up spontaneously. Some of the groups are "charismatic" while others are more "liberationist" in tone. All groups come together for the annual Christmas and graduation Masses, both of which have been celebrated since 1981. In the context of San Marcos, with a

The Social-Pastoral Church, 1975–

long anticlerical history, the celebration of these Masses represented a major change in direction.

Besides these strictly university or professional groups there are a multitude of parish groups for youth. The typical parish group helps prepare the Sunday liturgy, teaches catechism, and holds days of reflection and prayer.

Professional Groups and Workers

With the demise of Catholic Action, the professional groups of the thirties and forties ceased to have a noticeable presence in the church. No new nationally based group came to take their place. On the other hand, several new groups were founded for teachers and workers. The Movement for Christian Workers is a branch of the Latin American Workers Movement of Catholic Action. It was founded in Peru in 1971 by Father Jorge Alvarez Calderón, who continues to be the group's moderator. It has about 150 men and women members, most of whom come from lower-class neighborhoods. The Brotherhood of Workers, founded in 1966 in Peru by the Missionaries for Workers, is Spanish in origin. In the first years it had nearly a thousand members, but when the founders left Peru, membership dropped to fifty. The Christian Teaching Community Teams were founded by Father Michel Duclercq in France in the postwar period in order to offer a Christian formation to teachers. Duclercq had contact with Latin American bishops at the Vatican Council, and during visits to Peru in 1965 and 1966 he founded the first groups of his movement. Since 1975 Father Juan Dumont has been the national adviser of the movement that in 1985 had some forty-eight teams and some three hundred members altogether. The teams function especially in state schools and isolated regions. Since 1980 the teaching teams have held an annual pedagogical workshop in Lima for training teachers who work among the popular classes.[38]

These groups of professionals and workers are very small. For most Latin American workers religion is still perceived as an activity restricted to the church or the home. Another factor that enters the picture is that the workers, tired after a heavy working day, look upon belonging to a religious group as an additional weight to bear in life.

Charismatic Renewal and the Restored Catechumenate Movement

These two movements share a common emphasis on intense participation in liturgical acts and community prayer. Further, unlike the professional and student movements, these two have had a much wider impact on the popular classes. The restored catechumenate movement was born in Spain in 1964 as a pastoral experiment to help fallen-away Catholics return to the faith. It took as its model the liturgical and community life of the primitive church. A new member is invited to form part of a small community that then encourages him or her to follow the "way," a step-by-step process toward full participation in the life of the church.[39] The movement was founded in Peru in 1976. The first communities were based at six different parishes in Lima. By 1985 there were some two hundred of these small communities throughout Peru with an average of forty to sixty persons in each community. The movement has a high perseverence rate: nearly eighty percent of those who start finish the process of eight to ten years. It has also been very successful in transforming the lives of persons with family problems or who suffer from alcoholism and drug addiction.[40]

Charismatic renewal began in Peru in 1969 with the visit of a team of Catholic and Protestant charismatics from the United States. The team offered an experimental retreat in Union Church in Miraflores, Lima. Some one hundred persons participated. Soon, two basic groups of charismatics grew up in Lima: one led by the Canadian Oblates in Comas, a young town, and another run by the American Carmelites in San Antonio, Miraflores. The two principal promoters of the movement have been Father Neil Macaulay of the Oblates and Father Michael La Fay of the Carmelites. In 1985 there were some 150 different groups in Lima and a number of other groups in the provinces. The biggest group in Lima, "Alabaré," which meets at the church in San Antonio, Miraflores, normally draws three hundred to four hundred persons.[41]

These two movements, but especially the charismatic renewal, were considered alienating by the more politically oriented church groups because of their emphasis on the emotions and their lack of stress on social commitment. But this criticism, applied to the popular classes, turned out to be a stereotype. In general, the degree of social consciousness of each group depends upon the moderator and his or her capacity to help the group integrate the social message of the church into its piety. There are charismatics of the popular classes who attend the Catholic University's summer course conducted by Gustavo Gutiérrez. Although the charismatics come from all social classes, the majority come from the popular neighborhoods. A special problem in the case of this movement is its similarity to the Protestant Pentecostals. Some Catholic charismatics do not have a clear sense of "church" and go to both Catholic and Protestant meetings.

Marriage Encounter and Choice

Marriage encounter began in Spain in 1964 and was later adapted and perfected in the United States. Marriage encounter is a sort of retreat for married couples who aim to deepen their level of mutual communication and also their commitment to the church. Priests, brothers, and religious women also participate in the marriage encounter weekend. The first encounter was given in Peru in 1976 with the help of Mexican couples and Chicano couples from the United States. By 1986 some 712 marriage encounter weekends had been given in Peru in which 17,075 couples participated.[42] The founders of the movement in Peru were Enrique Camacho, a Dominican, and Luis Martínez, a Jesuit. The couples and priests who make a weekend form the teams that offer new weekends.

Marriage encounter has had a considerable impact on thousands of marriages. In the first years it was strictly a middle-class movement, but in time changes were made to adapt the experience to the popular level. Several spin-off programs have been created, modeled on the original marriage encounter concept. For example, a weekend encounter called "Afternoons for Engaged Couples" has become popular as a preparation for marriage. In 1979 Luis Martínez, the Jesuit, and Ennio Leonardi, a Salesian, visited the United States and made a special adaptation of the marriage encounter principle for youth groups. The result was "Escoje," from the word in English for "choice." "Escoje" has also become very popular in many parishes not only in Peru but throughout Latin America. Like marriage encounter, "Choice" aims to create a deeper communication between youth and their parents. It also helps young people develop a more affective prayer life. It has been notably efficacious: in many parishes it has become the principal instrument for attracting youth to participation in the church. Other variants of the same experience are "Reflection Days for Parents" and "Youth Encounter."

The evident popularity of this type of experience, whether charismatic renewal or marriage encounter, is due largely to the fact that with the aid of modern techniques of group dynamics, these pastoral programs touch people in a direct and very personal way, especially on the level of the sentiments. Furthermore, the techniques used help the participants to have a greater self-knowledge and capacity to communicate with others. Whereas major political and social problems seem so difficult to solve, some pressing personal problems can be solved here and now. Most moderators of these groups, however, look upon solving personal problems not as an end in itself, but as a first step toward orienting the people toward social and political involvement. In spite of their emphasis on intercommunication, all of these pastoral movements have suffered internal divisions, frequently the result of personality conflicts, a phenomenon that affected the first Christian communities as well.

Deacons, Catechists, and Animators

Some contemporary pastoral programs concentrate on forming laypersons so that they can be more effective leaders of their local ecclesial communities. In 1971, at the behest of the cardinal, two Maryknoll priests, Peter Ruggere and Thomas Garrity, founded the Program for Deepening Christian Commitment. The program, which consists of one weekly meeting for a period of three years, aims to impart a more solid theological and liturgical formation to the laity. By 1985 there were four hundred participants in the program in Lima, many of whom were married couples.[43] The majority came from the lower classes. The same program was used in the beginning to train lay deacons, and in 1975 the first married deacons were ordained in Peru. But that same year a special diaconate program was set up to give future deacons a more-than-ordinary formation. According to the church's norms the permanent diaconate is only for married men who have shown themselves to be model laymen and model family men. In 1985 there were forty permanent deacons in Peru, all in Lima. The bishop most responsible for both programs was Germán Schmitz, who also taught in both of them.

In Lima, as well as in all other dioceses, there are catechetical schools that train catechists and religion teachers. The Catechetical School of Lima, founded in 1967 and directed for many years by Father Santiago Izuzquiza, S.J., functions during the year and in the summer months. Each year an average of thirty to forty graduate. The summer program regularly has 600–700 students.[44]

Other Lay Associations

Some pre-Vatican organizations, such as the confraternities and the Legion of Mary, are still fairly active. Few studies have been done on the multitude of confraternities that exist everywhere in Peru. In Lima there is a great variety of these colonial institutions, all founded in honor of a particular saint.[45] Without doubt, the Confraternity of Our Lord of Miracles is the largest (nearly four thousand members) in Peru. But others are of comparable size. The Confraternity of San Martín de Porras and San Juan Macías, founded in the monastery of Santo Domingo in Lima in 1922, has 1,095 members divided into twelve *cuadrillas*, or local branches.[46] The great majority of the members of the confraternities come from the lower middle class. Some confraternities have resisted the changes in the church after Vatican II. Others, with the help of an up-to-date moderator, have managed to incorporate the changes into their pious practices.

Founded in Ireland in 1921, the Legion of Mary was established in Peru in 1952. The Legion is a pious association of men and women whose spirituality and organizational patterns are based very noticeably on the pre-Vatican model of the "militant" church. Nevertheless, the Legion has updated itself in the light of the Council. Its members are subdivided into "Senatus," "Curia," and "Presidia." They help parishes by making home visits, teaching catechism, and preparing youth for the sacraments. In Latin America the great majority of the members are women. The number of "legionnaires" in Lima is estimated to be around ten thousand.

Consecrated Religious and Laywomen

The various groups of religious women and consecrated laywomen, like the men's orders and congregations, experienced many sweeping changes as a result of Vatican II. In many senses the women suffered more crises than the men. Nevertheless, religious life for women came through the crises not only transformed but with a highly positive public image. Women religious, as well as women belonging to secular institutes that were renewed along the lines of Vatican II, are characterized by a far greater degree of liberty and creativity than the religious of pre-Vatican II days. Of course, not all groups have changed, and not all changed at the same pace. As in the world of men's orders and congregations, there are progressives, traditionalists, and conservatives among the women.

Everywhere in Peru, on the coast, in the mountains and in the jungle, women religious and consecrated laywomen form the backbone of the church's pastoral activity. Without them the church's pastoral work would be seriously limited and in some cases it would simply cease to exist. In Peru in 1984 there were some 2,265 priests. That same year there were 4,835 consecrated women, including religious women in the active and contemplative life and women belonging to lay secular institutes.[47] The transformation that occurred in women's religious life was not limited to external changes (the type of habit used) but went straight to the core of the very concept of religious life, and this involved most of all a fundamental change in attitude toward the relationship between religious life and the world.

In the sixties and seventies powerful currents and pressures arising within the Catholic world gave impetus to the move to reform religious life. Some of the new currents stressed the need to deinstitutionalize religious life in order to foster a more personalized experience of community. Other, more spiritual currents emphasized the importance of types of prayer more in harmony with the demands of contemporary existence. Certain modernizing trends called for updating external signs, such as the habit or dress, in order to make the religious vocation more attractive to young people. Most of all, the call of the church to opt preferentially for the poor and the dispossessed of the world constituted, especially in Latin America, the greatest incitement to the religious.

In general, the post-Vatican crises caused greater stress for the women than for the men. The great majority of women religious in preconciliar days worked in institutions with fixed routines, such as hospitals or schools. They lived a convent existence that more or less protected them from the vicissitudes of the daily life of the laity. By way of contrast, most parish priests and even religious men who worked in institutions always had greater contact with the ordinary world of the laity. The first steps toward modernization for women religious involved aspects of their life that for outsiders may have appeared to be of small significance but that in reality constituted critical and even threatening innovations for the religious: the change in religious garb and the change in fixed routines for prayer. For many religious women, altering the religious habit not only seemed to be a step toward "secularization," but even seemed to represent an affront to their identity as religious. The second "reform" refers to the obligation of many congregations, even active ones, to maintain perpetual adoration of the Blessed Sacrament. But this obligation, if adhered to according to rigidly fixed schedules, created a conflict between religious life and service in the world. For many religious women, allowing greater flexibility for fulfilling that obligation represented a real liberation that made it possible to harmonize

The Social-Pastoral Church, 1975–   337

daily prayer with the call to serve in the world. But a minority of religious objected that such changes constituted an assault on the order and stability that are intrinsic to religious life.

Along with these more external changes, religious communities experimented with new life-styles: smaller communities were created to accentuate personal relations, and new works were created among the popular classes to attend to the poor. Although in the long run these changes were perceived as positive, they generated many tensions among the religious. For example, the smaller communities were frequently made up of younger religious; but their leaving to form new communities left the traditional big convents half empty. Older religious felt "abandoned." At the same time, many religious were not prepared for life in small communities; greater flexibility in life-styles also gave rise to the need for greater tolerance toward others. Life in smaller communities demanded greater personal responsibility and a greater spirit of adaptation to new circumstances, and that often meant experiencing real poverty.

Another bone of contention involved formation programs. Many religious superiors pushed changes so rapidly that they provoked resentments among younger religious. For example, part of the updating that came with the Second Vatican Council called for raising the intellectual level of religious women, who generally received far less formal education than the men. But many religious women objected that they did not enter religious life in order to study. Some women simply abandoned religious life as a result. The challenge that Vatican II posed for religious superiors and those in charge of formation programs was how to implement the changes without alienating either of two groups: those who feared the changes and those who complained that the changes were happening too slowly. The greatest challenge was how to avoid the creation of pockets of resentful religious within the communities.

Finally, the changes affected the vocation situation of the congregations of women religious in unexpected ways. In general, the teaching congregations that had schools for the middle and upper classes suffered the most. By way of contrast, the congregations that worked principally among the popular classes continued to attract many vocations. This phenomenon is open to different explanations. In the third world where poverty is much more visible than in the first world, religious life repesented much more of a status symbol for the lower classes. When the religious who worked with the upper classes began orienting their work toward the popular classes, they ceased to be "attractive" for the upper classes. Ironically, the religious who taught in upper-class schools were frequently the most progressive, given their higher level of formation and closer contact with the modern world. But it was precisely their progressive attitudes that often dissuaded their own upper-class students, who entered religious life in pre-Vatican II days for the security and the social status that it offered, from following their way of life.

Of course, these sociological explanations do not do justice to the motivation behind many individuals. Between the two extremes, the congregations that worked principally with the wealthy and those that worked principally with the poor, there were others that never fell into either category. Furthermore, some congregations managed to maintain a greater equilibrium during the post-Vatican II years: they practiced flexibility but not at the cost of losing their identity as religious. In general, these congregations came through the process and project a harmonized image of women who are clearly "religious" and "progressives" at the same time. These latter groups experienced, after a period of decline, a surge of vocations in the late seventies and early eighties.

One of the major consequences of the new orientation is that women religious abandoned many of their traditional apostolates, especially work in institutions. In 1961 in Peru, for example, there were seventy-four different congregations of women religious. Two-thirds of the personnel in those congregations worked in schools. The other third worked in hospitals and clinics or carried out some type of social work.[48] But twenty-five years later only one-fourth of all religious women in Peru taught in schools. The majority of the rest worked in parishes, in medical posts, and retreat houses. The women who still continue to teach or to attend to the sick no longer do so in the traditional way. Many religious teach part time in a school in a young town, while the rest of their time is dedicated to working with mothers' clubs or similar social activities. Religious who worked before in hospitals now spend most of their time in medical posts in the young towns, the mountains, or the jungle. The contemporary religious woman in Peru is typically a combination educator, nurse, social worker, family counselor, spiritual director, coordinator of parish activities, and assistant to prison chaplains. In many towns in the Andes and the jungle she is also the extraordinary minister who baptizes the people and organizes paraliturgies.

Foreign Women Religious

In 1984 in Peru there were 2,053 foreign-born religious women, slightly less than half of all religious women in the country. Although many of them were already in Peru before the Second Vatican Council, a significant portion came in response to the various papal calls made in the sixties for missionaries to help the Latin American church. In this sense it is interesting to note that of the 212 different groups of religious women in Peru in 1984, some 138 arrived since 1960. The new groups are characterized by the influence of the council in their mentality and by their strong sense of social commitment. But even before them there were forerunners that led the way in acculturating themselves to the Peruvian situation. The Little Sisters of Jesus, founded by Charles de Foucauld, stand out in this regard. They established themselves in 1953 in Cerro de San Cosme, a young town built on a hill in Lima. They are motivated by a special vocation to share their daily lives with the poorest of the poor. They also follow a lay spirituality that calls for giving testimony of their solidarity with the poor by working in factories and market places. Some of the new groups represented the women's branch of a men's order or congregation already in Peru. The Sisters of Maryknoll who arrived in 1951 and the Missionary Sisters of Saint Columban who arrived in 1962 both fit this description. Sister Joan Sawyer, whose death in the middle of a gun battle during a prison breakout in Lurigancho Penitentiary in 1983 made a dramatic impression on the entire country, belonged to the Columban sisters.[49]

The new groups also manifest the universal character of Catholicism more than the pre-Vatican II ones. Missionaries continue to come from Europe, especially Spain, France, and Italy, from where they have always come. But two new nationalities are very evident, the English and the Irish. The new missionaries also include North Americans and Canadians. Among Latin Americans the Mexicans and Colombians are the most visible. In the last few years religious women have been coming to Peru in increasing numbers from the Philippines, Thailand, Vietnam, Japan, Australia, and New Zealand. The Sisters of Mercy of Mother Theresa of Calcutta founded two homes for the sick and the dying in "La Parada" in Lima and in Chimbote on the northern coast.

In general, the new groups have sought to offer a service that is more explicitly social and pastoral than traditional work in schools, hospitals, and other institutions. One North American congregation that typifies all these changes is the Sisters of Saint Joseph of Carondolet. This congregation was founded in France in 1650, but by the nineteenth century it had become firmly rooted in North American soil. The sisters of Saint Joseph went to Peru in 1962 following an invitation by the papal nuncio, Rómulo Carboni. Their first work in Peru was predominately institutional in character. Some of the sisters worked as nurses in the Military Hospital in Lima, others in schools in Chimbote and Ica, and others at the Catholic University of Santa María in Arequipa. But by 1975, under the influence of the council and Medellín, the sisters made a critical self-evaluation and decided to abandon almost all of those commitments. Since 1972 they began working as pastoral agents in Moho, in the department of Puno. Furthermore, they expanded from their teaching work in private schools to include teaching in state schools and performing neighborhood pastoral activities in Ica, Arequipa, and Chimbote. In Sicuani (southern Andean church) they collaborate with health programs, and another group of sisters works among peasants in San José de Lourdes in the northern department of Cajamarca. There were fourteen sisters in the original group. By 1985 there were thirty-two sisters in Peru, nine of whom were Peruvian, but this does not include the large number of Peruvian postulants and novices. Two members of the Saint Joseph of Carondolet sisters have been elected to important posts in the Conference of Women Religious, another clear sign of successful inculturation in the Peruvian church.[50]

The Conference of Religious and ISET

In the decade of the fifties the Holy See began pressing the local churches to unify forces and pastoral efforts. In response to that initiative, the Conference of Religious Men of Peru was founded in 1955. The conference consisted of a permanent assembly of major superiors, that is, superiors of the principal religious orders and congregations, in order to coordinate plans and activities and to discuss common problems. In reality, the Consortium of Catholic Schools, which for decades coordinated the activities of religious schools, was a forerunner of the conference. The first president elected to head the conference was Father José Ridruejo, the provincial of the Jesuits. A year later Father Ridruejo served as an adviser for creating the Conference of Women Religious. With twenty-five provincials present at the

The Social-Pastoral Church, 1975–

first meeting, Carmen Cubero of the Sacred Heart Sisters was elected the first president of the women's conference.[51] The two conferences functioned as autonomous organizations until 1969 when they fused into one single conference. The conference has fulfilled an especially important role in renovating religious life in Peru. Of equal importance the conference became an influential source of opinion on the national scene for influencing the public on key issues of justice and morality.

In the decade of the sixties the conference of women pushed for the updating of religious women along conciliar lines. To that end it organized days of reflections and short courses, especially for superiors, on the Bible and theological topics. In 1969 it also founded a common juniorate (the years after novitiate) for all the congregations that wished to participate. In the seventies the conference felt the impact of the divisions between progressives and conservatives. Some of the more conservative groups simply left the conference and never returned. Nevertheless, in the middle of these tensions, the conference strove to maintain a pluralistic character and to make the conference a clearinghouse where real dialogue could be achieved. In this sense it has been highly successful. All of the religious superiors who have served as presidents or secretaries of the conference have distinguished themselves as conciliators and unifiers. Among the most notable of the presidents have been Nicolás Gobert (Dominican), Gastón Garatea (Sacred Hearts Father), Noé Zevallos (Brother of La Salle), Esther Capestany (Ursuline), José Luis Fernández-Castañeda (Jesuit), and Jorge Cuadros (Dominican). The secretaries of the conference, especially Margarita Recavarren (Sacred Heart Sister), Catherine Judge and Theresa Avalos (Saint Joseph of Carondolet), and María Teresa Razquín (Franciscan Missionary of Mary), have also played key roles.

In 1975 several of the major religious superiors, especially Father Nicolás Gobert of the Dominicans who took a leading role, founded the Superior Institute of Theological Studies (ISET), named in honor of Pope John XXIII. Their objective was to have a formation center especially designed for religious. Until that time most religious received their basic humanistic and theological formation in their own communities, outside the country, or in the local Faculty of Theology closely tied to the archdiocesan seminary. Many of the religous were less than satisfied with the formation that was offered in the Faculty of Theology. First, the faculty existed principally to train seminarians destined for the secular clergy. Second, in their opinion the Faculty of Theology had not updated itself sufficiently after Vatican II. Most of all, the courses offered there did not seem to have much application to the Peruvian situation. ISET was founded to fill these lacunae. The new center for religious began to function formally in 1976 with seventy-five students. Under Brother Noé Zevallos, named director in 1979, ISET became a model of interecclesial cooperation. By 1985 it had 340 students. The professors represented some sixty-six different congregations and many different nationalities.[52]

Catholic Education

The Consortium and ONDEC

In no other area were the tensions between conservatives and progressives so visible in the decade of the seventies and eighties than in that of education. The tension between the two groups was so bitter that the Catholic educational system in Peru finally broke down into two different systems: one that represents schools for the rich and the other for middle and lower class schools. Further, the campaign organized by the conservative groups constituted the first step toward the formation of a Catholic right in Peru. With some simplification, the battle between the two forces came down to a battle between the Consortium of Catholic Schools, which represented the older, traditional schools, and ONDEC (National Office of Catholic Education), which represented Catholic schools among the middle and popular classes.

Toward the end of the fifties the older Catholic schools that had been founded by the leading teaching orders and congregations, such as the Jesuits, the Sacred Hearts fathers and sisters, the Immaculate Heart of Mary sisters, the Ursulines, and others, created a central coordinating office of Catholic education in Peru. In fact the church did run many schools for the poor at that time, but their presence was not particularly noticeable in the light of the more famous upper-class church schools. In 1929 these latter schools formed an association among themselves to advance their mutual interests. In 1939 this association was transformed into the Consortium of Catholic Schools. The Consortium, which had 180 member schools at the time, acquired legal status in 1953.[53] The following year the episcopal conference founded the National Office of Catholic Education (ONDEC: Oficina Nacional de Educación Católica) to coordinate more effectively the multiple educational activities of the church. Catholic schools at that time represented about eight and a half percent of the total primary and secondary student body in the country. Private, nonconfessional schools represented another nine and a half percent of the national student body.[54] ONDEC did not limit its activity, however, to the running of Catholic schools. According to Peruvian law, reaffirmed in the constitution of 1979, religion is an obligatory course in all state schools. One of the most important activities of ONDEC, therefore, was to produce textbooks for these courses and to train religion teachers. At the time of ONDEC's creation, there were 9,866 state schools in all of Peru.[55] By 1982 that number had risen to thirty thousand.[56] The consortium, which continued to represent the Catholic schools, was incorporated as a subdepartment of ONDEC. In the first few years the relations between the governing entity, ONDEC, and the subdepartment, the consortium, were quite harmonious, especially since for years the president of the consortium and the director of ONDEC were one and the same person, Father Felipe MacGregor, S.J.

Although the Peruvian government had aided Catholic education, especially in the jungle and other frontier areas, since the last century, that aid did not reach significant proportions until the military government of General Odría (1948–56), especially as a result of the policies adopted by General Juan Mendoza, the minister of education. Under the military junta of 1962–63 that official aid was not only increased but institutionalized in the form of an agreement between church and state. The initiative for the agreement was taken by the junta's minister of education, Admiral Franklin Pease, who promulgated a decree-law in March 1963 that established a new category in the national educational system, "subsidized private education." The purpose of the decree was to utilize all national educational resources, state and private, to extend primary education to areas of the country where practically no schools existed.[57] The government set aside a small percentage of its educational budget to be channeled through ONDEC for Catholic schools that functioned in remote or marginal areas.

This new policy of regular state aid affected the educational presence of the church in Peru radically. Many parishes and teaching congregations, now freed from the need to depend on the upper classes, began to open schools in marginal areas. In the decade of the fifties there were 497 schools run by the church in Peru.[58] But largely due to the influx of state aid, that number jumped to 1,051 schools throughout the country by 1971. Of that total, 342 were completely free and 626 were semifree.[59] As a consequence, even before the eductional reform of 1972 more than two-thirds of all Catholic schools in Peru received some type of state aid. Further, the church's presence was not limited to its own schools. In 1971 some 241 strictly state schools had as their directors members of religious orders.[60] In this case, the schools depended totally and directly on the state, which chose members of religious congregations to direct some of its schools. The military government of the seventies ratified all previous agreements with the church and at the same time stressed the social aim of those agreements. The *Reglamento de Centros Educativos Parroquiales* (Statutes for Parochial Educational Centers), promulgated in 1977, stipulated that church schools aided by the state must "offer educational services to families of low income."[61]

The impact of this change of emphasis in Catholic education was dramatic. In a relatively short period of time, the traditional schools for the rich became a minority within the total Catholic system. Although the consortium continued to be a subdepartment of ONDEC, the tension between the two became increasingly evident; ONDEC had become the official voice of Catholic schools for the middle and lower classes, and the consortium fulfilled that function for upper class Catholic schools. According to one estimate, by 1975 only forty percent of all Catholic schools recognized the corsortium as its official representative.[62]

In the midst of these changes of a more sociological order, the social question increasingly became a bone of contention between the two sides. Both offices reacted quite differently toward the educational reform law of 1972. ONDEC responded very favorably to the law. But the consortium, concerned over the effect the law would have on its schools, chose the occasion to organize a campaign to criticize not only the educational law but the entire social thrust of the military government as well. In 1972 the Christian Family Movement published a series of statements in the newspapers criticizing the reform law, and in 1973 the consortium itself took the lead in the campaign. In May of that year it published a statement in *El Comercio* that constituted virtually a declaration of war on the educational reform. In essence, the statement denounced the reform because it represented a "growing and stifling statism" that threatened to suffocate the private schools.[63] Further, in the beginning of 1975 the corsortium announced its intention to call off matriculation in its schools that year.[64] That defiant gesture was, of course, a tactic to pressure the government not to apply the reform to private schools. In this case the government backed down, among other reasons because the reformist momentum of the "First Phase" had already been spent and the military had no appetite for a major confrontation with religious schools or the church in the middle of an economic and social crisis that was increasingly destroying their base of popularity.

All of these initiatives of the consortium were taken without previous consultation with ONDEC. As early as 1971 the consortium had requested permission from the bishops to become an entity independent from ONDEC. In the midst of this conflict, Bishop Ricardo Durand, president of the Episcopal Commission on Education, sought to establish peace between the two. Finally, in 1975 the bishops gave their permission for the consortium to establish a separate office in another part of Lima, although it continued to be nominally a "department" of ONDEC. In reality, however, the divorce between the two offices was final and complete. In 1976 the consortium changed its name to the Federation of Catholic Educational Centers (but changed it back again to Consortium a few years later). The federation took with it the major portion of schools of the upper class and a certain number of middle-class schools of a more conservative tendency. ONDEC, somewhat unburdened by the removal of a bothersome subordinate, remained as the principal coordinating office for religious and parochial schools among the popular sectors.

The division between the two Catholic educational offices represented, however, but one aspect of a conflict that deepened even more in the last years of Velasco and during the entire "Second Phase." Besides the educational reform, there were two other thorny issues that increased tensions: the religious textbooks published by ONDEC and the different teachers' strikes that occurred during the Morales Bermúdez regime. In 1973 ONDEC began to publish the *Cuadernos de religión,* which were auxiliary textbooks for religion teachers, especially those who taught in state schools. The *Cuadernos,* written and published by Father Eduardo Bastos, S.J., not only reflected the general lines of Medellín but very clearly displayed sympathy toward liberation theology. Furthermore, they were written in a nontraditional style that made them seem very much like newspapers, with humorous caricatures and comic-striplike dialogues on theological and current social themes. They had hardly begun to circulate in the schools when many parents with children in the consortium schools began to organize a campaign to denounce the presence of what they believed to be Marxist elements in the texts. Some bishops and priests lent their support to the campaign. The cardinal himself tried to intervene to calm down passions, but with little success. The majority of corsortium schools rejected the *Cuadernos* as unfit for their classrooms. ONDEC, on the other hand, looked favorably on the texts and distributed them to religion teachers throughout the entire state educational system.

The Teachers' Strikes

Since its foundation in 1972, SUTEP (*Sindicato Unico de Trabajadores en la Educación del Perú*: United Peruvian Teachers Union) constituted a problem not only for the government but for the church as well. The military government attempted to deny the right of the union to exist, especially since the leaders belonged to *Patria Roja* "Red Fatherland", a Maoist-oriented political party. In 1978 and again in 1979 SUTEP organized nationwide strikes that galvanized the majority of the teachers in state schools. But for teachers in private schools, participating in the strikes turned out to be a major dilemma, because the teachers in the ONDEC system received their salaries from the state. Finally, the majority of teachers in religious schools in popular sectors (ONDEC schools) decided to join the strike. The federation (ex-consortium) attempted to stay aloof from the strike. Once again, the two Catholic systems found themselves on opposite ends of the spectrum.

The 1978 strike was relatively peaceful and ended as a victory for SUTEP. The 1979 strike, however, which lasted from June until September, was characterized by violence and ended as a defeat for the union. In the middle of the two strikes the government hardened its position and adopted a policy of no appeasement to the union's demands. For its part, the church was caught in the crossfire. During the 1978 strike, at the request of the union, the church played the role of mediator between SUTEP and the government. But the situation was radically different in 1979. Like the government, the church did not view with favor the decision of the union to paralyze the entire educational system of the country exactly one year after their last strike. This time the Episcopal Commission for Education, then under the direction of Bishop Emilio Vallebuona, accused SUTEP leaders of acting in bad faith.[65] In practice, however, the church adopted a more subtle policy: on the one hand, it condemned the radical Marxist orientation of the union leaders, but at the same time it expressed sympathy for the teachers who were trying to better their standard of living. During the strike ONIS and the bishops of the southern Andean region published statements expressing their solidarity with the teachers. This distinction between support for the teachers but not for the union that represented them did not please the government. In fact, on a number of occasions, priests and religious women who taught in state schools were fired from their teaching posts for participating in the strike.

In August and September of that year the federation and ONDEC held joint assemblies in order to heal the divisions between themselves and to attempt to formulate a united policy with respect to the strike. However, the assemblies turned out to be the occasion for stormy debates that belied the attempt at reconciliation. The federation's policy consisted in supporting neither the teachers on strike nor the union. This hard line produced open conflict in many schools. The most dramatic example occurred in the Salesian school in Ayacucho. In September a group of teachers, some of whom were from the school itself, seized control of the school building to express their disapproval of the passivity of the private schools toward the strike. The teachers were forced out of the building, but in the middle of the scuffle shots were fired and a lay teacher and a religious sister were wounded. When the strike ended, the Salesians refused to take back their own teachers who had gone on strike.[66]

At the end of the decade of the seventies the Catholic educational system, in spite of its own internal divisions, enjoyed the prestige of having a far higher level of education than the state schools, although the degree of social consciousness in the system varied sharply from school to school. Also, in spite of their differences, ONDEC and the federation still maintained contact and were able to cooperate in a number of areas. Furthermore, as a consequence of strong political and church pressures, some middle- and upper-class schools did incorporate many socially oriented activities into their programs. But the most impressive feature of Catholic education in Peru is its capacity to maintain high educational standards in its many schools in the popular sectors. The Fe y Alegría schools and the hundreds of parochial schools that are to be found everywhere in Peru annually educate thousands of children from impoverished backgrounds gratuitously. The moral and educational level in those schools is notably superior to that of the state schools, and it is only the conditions of poverty in which the children live that hold them back from attaining an even higher cultural level.

Higher Education

The classification "higher education" includes a wide range of institutions of different levels that are associated in one way or another with the church: teachers normal schools, seminaries, and universities. In 1984 there were twelve major seminaries officially recognized by the church in Peru. Furthermore, the Faculty of Theology in Lima, frequently confused with the diocesan seminary because they exist side by side, not only offers a theological and university formation for seminarians but also for some two hundred laypersons in attendance.

The number of teachers schools run by the church has varied greatly throughout the twentieth century. In 1960 there were thirteen teachers normal schools run by the church, and these included one administered by the Marist Brothers and another by the Theresians, both at the Catholic University in Lima. In 1974 the number of schools rose to thirty throughout all of Peru. But, as a result of the military government's policy of reducing the number of these schools, by 1984 there were only ten teachers normal schools run by the church, five state schools and five private. Seven of these schools are directed by religious orders. One of the better known of these schools is the Normal School of Champagnat, run by the Marist Brothers in Lima, one of the principal centers in Peru for the training of teachers of religion. The state schools obviously do not "belong" to the church. However, since their directors are members of religious orders, there is a loose, de facto church connection. In all of these church-run schools the atmosphere of order and work is immediately evident. Undoubtedly, the most famous church-run teachers school in Peru is still the National Pedagogical Institute in Lima directed by the religious of the Sacred Heart.

In contrast to the seminaries and teachers schools, which are really more akin to professional schools, the universities associated with the church have a more ambiguous status. The ambiguous situation of these universities with respect to both the church and the state can be better appreciated by referring to the long-standing regalist tradition in Peru by which governments normally intervene in the private sector. An important example of that mentality was the decree-law promulgated in February 1969 by the military government in order to reorganize the universities. The decree obliged private universities to adopt the same system of internal government as that of state universities. According to the law, no higher educational institution could depend on an "external entity," even if that entity happened to the religious order that founded it. The highest authority in the university had to be a university assembly made up of university authorities, professors, and students. The assembly elects the rector (in Latin America presidents of universities are called "rectors") and other university officials. The 1969 law, reaffirmed by the University Law of 1984, therefore created a barrier between the founding entity and the university. The Catholic University in Lima published a letter of protest in which it accused the government of attempting to convert the private universities into "replicas" of the state universities, without regard for their right to have greater freedom in order to be different from the latter.[67]

Until 1961 the Catholic University in Lima was the only church-administered university in the country. Around that time many different private groups, especially businesspeople and religious orders, saw the importance of founding new universities. Their reasons were various: the demographic explosion, which by then had reached the university level; the lack of modern specialties in most Peruvian universities; and the increased politicization in many of the state universities with the resulting disorder that reigned in them. In 1961 Father William Morris, an American Marianist priest, founded the University of Santa María in Arequipa. In 1962 three more universities were founded, all in Lima: the University of El Pacífico, the University of San Martin de Porres and the Women's University of the Sacred Heart. In 1969 Opus Dei founded the University of Piura. That same year the Víctor Andrés Belaunde University of Ayacucho was founded, but it closed down in 1976 for lack of sufficient funds.

Two of these new universities, Santa María in Arequipa and San Martín de Porres in Lima, suffered the impact of the 1969 university law the most, to the extent that currently neither can really be considered "church" universities. In both cases the founding party lost control of the university as a result of the law. The causes for the loss of control were practically the same: an inordinate growth in student population with very loose standards for selection; the emergence of cliques of professors opposed to the aims of the founders; and, for their part, the failure of the founders to assure a sufficient level of quality among the professors. In the case of Santa María in Arequipa the Marianist congregation never attempted to assume full responsibility for the university. In 1973, under pressure from the National Council of Peruvian Universities, Father Morris was forced to cede the virtually absolute personal control he exercised over the university. During the period of reorganization the laymen who were elected began to establish their own policies.[68] In the second case, the Dominicans who founded San Martín de Porres in Lima were very few in number. When one of them, the rector himself, left the order to marry, this caused an internal crisis that favored the move to turn the running of the university over to the lay professors.

The University of El Pacífico and that of Opus Dei are essentially business schools that train businesspeople, economists, and accountants. Both are small and both enjoy a high degree of internal stability. The University of El Pacífico, which was founded by several private businesses, with the Jesuit Fathers acting as advisers, stands out for its research center that draws together economists, who have influenced several governments. It maintains its Christian orientation, based on the intellectual pluralism of the Society of Jesus under Pedro Arrupe. The University of Piura, in contrast, took as its model the Opus Dei University of Navarre and functions in a far less pluralistic atmosphere. The Women's University of the Sacred Heart (UNIFE) is also small. Its program for teachers who work with children with learning disabilities is one of the best in Peru.

The Catholic University

Under Father Rubén Vargas Ugarte, S.J., the rector from 1947 to 1952, and his successor, Father Fidel Tubino (1953–63) the university founded by Father Dintilhac in 1917 came to occupy a special place among the other universities in Peru. But gaining acceptance was not easy. The state universities tended to resent the Catholic University because it was the only private one in the country and because of its somewhat elitist character. At the same time it enjoyed the prestige of being a stable institution with a high standard of education. The state finally recognized its importance in Peruvian national life by conferring upon it the title of "national university" in 1949. From that moment on, it participated in all meetings of the other universities and even began to receive limited government aid. But it not until the advent of Father Felipe MacGregor (1963–77) that it turned into a really large and modern university. "La Católica," as it is commonly known, had 5,093 students in 1962. But by 1985 this number had jumped to 9,129.[69] Further, in contrast to the anarchy that reigned in many of the state universities, this increase in number was accompanied by an increase in quality. Several new faculties,

The Social-Pastoral Church, 1975–

notably the Faculty of Social Sciences (1964), were added during the process.

One factor that favored this transformation was the increased presence of professors and students who left the state universities in discouragement at the disorder that existed there. But without doubt the dynamic leadership of Father MacGregor, who was successful in securing a considerable amount of financial aid from the Dutch and German bishops, was another key factor. Also, under MacGregor's leadership, the university opened itself to the pluralistic winds of the western world. In the Catholic University, professors of the old Catholic Action found themselves teaching side by side with younger professors who belonged to the liberation theology generation. Such pluralistic openness was practically nonexistent until recent times in most state universities in which Marxist ideologues tended to dominate.

In 1985 the university had eight faculties, without counting the two years of general studies that students must attend before entering a faculty. Altogether there were thirty-seven different professional specializations offered. Among the most prestigious faculties are Law, Science and Engineering, Social Sciences, and Humanities. The Faculty of Education with 575 students in 1985 was considered one of the best in the country. Some professors have achieved worldwide fame: Adolf Winternitz, born in Austria, known for his stained-glass windows, and Gustavo Gutiérrez, a founding father of liberation theology. The Center of Television Education (CETUC), established in 1972, is considered one of the most important centers of its kind in Latin America. The summer theology course attracts thousands of persons each year. In 1975 the Pastoral Counseling Center (CAPU) was founded as a symbol of the religious orientation of the university. The founder was Father Alberto Rodríguez, S.J., who was succeeded by Father Luis Martínez, S.J. In the eighties the government began reducing its aid to the university drastically. This change in policy forced the university to face the dilemma of how to remain a pluralistic, middle-class university and not become an upper-class and elitist one.

The ties between the university and the church continue to be cordial. However, they have also become more complex than what they were during the first decades when the bishops themselves made public appeals to support the university. In 1942 "La Católica" was raised to the rank of a "pontifical" university. This meant that the official church began to take a more direct hand in the running of the university, which until that year had been administered exclusively by the congregation of the Sacred Hearts Fathers. Under the new statutes, the archbishop of Lima was named the "Grand Chancellor" with power to name the rector. But the law of 1969 radically changed that situation. Currently, the archbishop limits his function to that of "confirming" a newly elected rector in office. The church does, however, maintain a permanent representative on the University Council that governs the university. Beyond this juridical relationship, there did occur an incident that led the cardinal to distance himself from the university for a number of years. In 1973 the vice-rector in line to be rector left his family to marry his secretary. Although this minor scandal was partially resolved by having the vice-rector resign, Cardinal Landázuri refused to visit the university as a sign of protest because the university official in question continued to function as a professor at the university. Finally, in 1981, the cardinal ended the period of separation by presiding over the Christmas Mass on campus. In 1984 he confirmed Dr. José Tola Pasquel in his second term as rector of the university, and in 1989 he did the same for Tola's successor, Hugo Saravia, from the Faculty of Engineering.

Finally, there is a purely sociological factor responsible for creating some distance between the bishops and the university: the marked contrast between the worlds in which both function. The majority of bishops are far too occupied with daily pastoral problems in their dioceses to be overly concerned about academic affairs. With the exception of the bishops who have been university professors or officials at one time, such as José Dammert Bellido, Guido Breña, Oscar Alzamora, Hugo Garaycoa, and Alfredo Noriega, very few understand the inner dynamics of university life. Although there is mutual influence between one and the other, in practice the university functions with relative autonomy with respect to the hierarchy.

Relations with the State

The constitutional assembly of 1978–79 put an end to the system of state patronage over the church that had existed since colonial times. Unlike the assembly of 1931–33, which was heavily charged with anticlerical feelings, the representatives of the new assembly entered into a dialogue with the church, which was characterized by openness and sincerity on both sides. In fact, the concept of patronage had been questioned within the church for many years, and in practice the state had reduced its right to name bishops to the mere formality of seconding candidates that the church proposed. Finally, the church itself, through its two representatives, Bishops Dammert and Metzinger, took the initiative for putting an end to the patronage system. The formula that the bishops proposed, and that appeared virtually unchanged in the 1979 constitution, states: "Within a framework of independence and autonomy, the state recognizes the Catholic church as an important element in the historical, cultural, and moral formation of Peru. The state offers it its cooperation. The state may also establish different types of cooperation with other confessions." (Article 86)

In the formula the word "separation" is conspicuously absent. The bishops and legislators chose the more positive word "cooperation" in order to avoid giving the impression of a rupture or the type of antagonistic split that characterized the relations between church and state in Europe or other parts of Latin America under liberal governments. Later, in July of 1981 a more concrete agreement between the state and the Holy See was drawn up. Article Seven of the agreement declares that the president of the republic reserves the right to "recognize" (but not to name) a candidate that the church proposes to be a bishop. The other articles reconfirm previous agreements between church and state regarding education and chaplaincies in state institutions.[70]

But the church did not limit its interest to the question of the old state patronage. The bishops also entered into dialogue with other commissions in the constitutional assembly to express their views on such sensitive topics as the teaching of moral values in educational programs and the right to life of the unborn. The church firmly supported full religious freedom for other religions.[71] The atmosphere of goodwill between the church and the assembly clearly reflected the many changes that had occurred since the assembly of 1933. Above all, the church had taken an energetic stand in favor of human rights since Vatican II, and after Medellín it actively participated in popular movements that aimed to promote a more just society. For their part, politicians, especially those in the APRA and the left, had long ago eschewed their laicist prejudices and openly endorsed the call for strengthening moral values in society.[72]

Although the second period of Fernando Belaúnde Terry (1980–85) began in an atmosphere of church-state cordiality, many small incidents soon occurred that revealed an undercurrent of tension. Many leaders of the ruling party, Popular Action, resented the progressive church, and especially the cardinal, for cooperating with the military that overthrew Belaúnde in 1968. During holy week of 1984, Francisco Belaúnde, a deputy in congress and the president's brother, accused the cardinal of being an "accomplice" of the military regime. President Belande's conspicuous absence during the traditonal holy week services that year underlined the government's coldness toward the church.[73] But the tensions had deepened as a result of the church's criticism of the government for its human rights violations and its apparent indifference toward mass poverty and hunger. In July 1981 the Episcopal Commission of Social Action accused the government of torturing a young man held for terrorism. The young man in question, whose innocence was not so clear, also happened to be the nephew of Bishop Augusto Beuzeville.[74]

After that first incident many others followed. In January 1983 the president himself accused various research centers and charitable foundations, especially those run by foreign religious, of giving aid to subversives.[75] No proof was produced to support the accusation. In January 1984 a French woman, who had left her religious congregation but who continued to work as a pastoral agent in the diocese of Cajamarca, was detained by the police and accused of being a "terrorist." Although she was quickly proved to be innocent of the charge, she was held in jail for three months.[76] In October 1984 a Salesian priest in the district of Angaraes near Cuzco was arrested along with several pastoral agents for the same charge. Once again, their innocence was easily established.[77] In these and other incidents it appeared that the government was deliberately goading the church, perhaps as a sort of reprisal for its criticisms of the government. Or perhaps the attacks reflected the frustration the government experienced at not being able to resolve the escalation of terrorist violence in the country. In this case, the church served as a sort of "scapegoat."

Modern Means of Communication

With the exception of *El Deber* in Arequipa, Catholic journalism ceased to be an influential force toward the end of the last century. Since the decade of the fifties new media, such as the radio, began to fill the lacuna. The most notable radio stations of the church have been: in Lima, Radio Luz, Radio Santa Rosa of the Dominicans, and Radio Unión; in the provinces, the radio schools of the Maryknoll Fathers (Onda Azul) in Puno and another school in Cañete. In 1985 there were five radio stations of the church in Peru: Onda Azul in Puno, the "Voice of the Jungle" in Iquitos, Radio Marañón in Jaen, and Radio Santa Rosa and Radio Omega in Lima. There are also several centers for producing radio programs: Cajamarca, Chimbote, Cuzco(IPA), Juli, Pucallpa, and Lima (CETUC at the Catholic University).[78]

There are also several centers that publish books, magazines, and teaching materials. Centro de Estudios y Publicaciones (CEP: Center of Studies and Publications) founded in 1970, and closely associated with the Bartolomé de las Casas Center in Lima, publishes the magazines *Páginas* and *Informativo quincenal*. The Centro de Proyección Cristiana of the Jesuits publishes *Encuentro*, a magazine of selected articles. The International Movement of Catholic Students (MIEC) publishes *ICLA, Informativo Católico Latinoamericano*. The Maryknoll Fathers publish *Noticias Aliadas* (which appears in English under the title *Latin American Press*). The Comboni Fathers publish *Misión sin fronteras* (founded in 1979 under the title *Esquila Misional*). The most prestigious research center associated with the church is DESCO, founded in 1965 with the financial support of European Catholics (CEBEMO, Misereor, etc.). DESCO has fostered the publication of a great number of studies of the popular classes in Peru. The episcopal conference publishes *Iglesia en el Perú* (1973–) and the archdiocese of Lima puts out a small news magazine, *Boletín del Arzobispado de Lima* (1978–). CELADEC, an interdenominational publication center that especially sympathized with liberation theology, closed its Lima offices in 1985. The regional centers, such as IPA in Cuzco and CETA in Iquitos, were treated under the subtitle "Special Pastoral Areas" in this chapter. For many years the bishop who most fostered the use of modern means of communication in the church was Luciano Metzinger, president of the Episcopal Commission on Social Communication.

Protestantism and Other Religions

The 1981 census listed the religions practiced by Peruvians in this order: "Catholics," 89.1 percent; "Non-Catholic Christians," 4.7 percent; "Other Religions," 0.3 percent. According to the 1972 census "non-Catholic Christians" made up 3.2 percent of the population.[79] In all of Latin America the historical Protestant churches (Lutherans, Methodists, Presbyterians, etc.) have grown rather slowly. By way of contrast, the more missionary churches, such as the Adventists, Pentecostals, and Baptists have grown very rapidly. The so-called "sects" (groups that retain Christian elements but do not belong to mainstream Christianity), such as the Mormons and Jehovah's Witnesses, have also grown considerably. During the first half of this century the Adventist church was the largest Protestant group in Peru.[80] But in the last twenty years the fastest-growing group has been the Pentecostals. Pentecostalism began in Peru in 1911 and by 1982 had some 212,822 members.[81]

The Adventists first, and later the Pentecostals, Jehovah's Witnesses, Mormons, and others, found their most fertile field to be the marginated popular classes. The rapid growth of these sects especially among those classes is not difficult to understand because a similar phenomenon occurred in the United States and in other parts of Latin America, especially Brazil and Chile.[82] The sects fill a vacuum in the lives of many poor people who have either lost contact with the Catholic church or do not find an answer to their felt needs in their local Catholic parish. The nearby Pentecostal or Mormon temple, in contrast, offers them a sense of community and security. Further, the new members of the sects participate a lot more than in the traditional Catholic parish, and many are quickly promoted to positions of responsibility, an experience that contributes to their self-esteem. The religious conversion that the new members experience is usually the first such experience in their lives. They feel interiorly motivated to change their conduct: many cease to consume alcoholic beverages and begin to lead more orderly lives. These religious changes, however, frequently produce tensions within families and within the local community. Furthermore, as the Jesuits Manuel Marzal and José Luis Idígoras have noted, the sects exhibit many traits typical of the Old Testament: rigid codes of conduct, the practice of tithing, and messianic expectations. The affinity with the Old Testament may be explained by the fact that the poor in Peru and the rest of Latin American live in social, economic, and psychological conditions that seem like Old Testament times.[83] In this sense, one of the most important "para-Christian" sects that has appeared in Peru is the Israelites of the New World Pact, founded in 1958. This new religion is especially replete with Old Testament practices, including veils for the women, beards for the men, and animal sacrifices.[84]

Another fast-growing group is the Church of the Christian and Missionary Alliance, founded in Peru in 1923 as an interdenominational Protestant enterprise. In 1986 it had 20,425 members in Lima and Callao.[85] Unlike the sects, however, the Church of the

The Social-Pastoral Church, 1975–

Alliance is largely based in the middle class. It has been especially successful in attracting youth in search of more communitarian and dynamic religious services than those found in many Catholic parishes. There are other religions, or pseudoreligions, such as the sects of an oriental inspiration like Hare Krishna or Baha'i, that attract middle-class youth but are small in number.[86]

The ecumenical movement, of great importance for the Catholic church in Europe and North America, has not had the same significance in Latin America. The reason is that the great majority of Protestants in Peru, for example, belong to sects that do not participate in the ecumenical movement, which involves both the mainline Protestants and Catholics. In general, the sects look upon all of Latin America as an open field for proselytizing, and the Catholic church for them is an obstacle in the way. They do not have the same historical ties with the Catholic church as do the older Protestant churches. In contrast, the Lutheran, Methodist, and Anglican churches in Peru have all maintained ecumenical contact with the Catholic church since the sixties. Two examples of ecumenism are CELADEC and the "Faith and Prayer Outings." CELADEC (Latin American Evangelical Commission for Christian Education) was founded in Lima in 1962 as an ecumenical effort, although most of the financing came from the Protestant churches. CELADEC espoused the liberationist line and cooperated with like-minded Catholic groups. The "Faith and Prayer Outings" is a movement that emphasizes shared prayer among Catholics and Protestants. Ministers, pastors, and priests preside at the meetings. During his 1985 visit Pope John Paul II invited representatives from the Protestant and Jewish communities to an ecumenical breakfast.

The rapid spread of the sects could be interpreted as a reflection of the deficiencies of the Catholic church: the lack of creative liturgies, of a more dynamic participation of the laity, or of a greater sense of community in the parish. But these deficiencies exist most of all in the older churches in the city centers or in parishes run by conservative congregations. By way of contrast, the parishes in the young towns and in the special pastoral areas like the jungle or the southern Andean region stand out for their creative liturgies and dynamic participation. The typical Catholic parish in a young town offers all of the "attractions" that the sects offer: a strong sense of community, biblical courses, and group dynamics for the youth. The real nature of the problem is that the church has been overwhelmed by the population explosion. Many young-town inhabitants go to the nearest Pentecostal temple simply because there is no other religious service available. Very often they are invited by their neighbors to accompany them to the temple. In this sense, the Catholic church is not really "losing" practicing Catholics to the sects. The persons who join the sects are usually baptized Catholics who do not have a strong sense of identification with the church. They belong to a religious frontier zone that is claimed by everyone and by no one at the same time. Given this situation, the sects and evangelical Protestantism will surely continue to grow. But the Catholic church will also expand into the same area.

To a large extent, all of the topics treated in this chapter—a committed laity, the renovation of religious life, the inculturation of the church in popular sectors, and the creation of an original theological current—are the fruit of Vatican II and the episcopal conferences of Medellín and Puebla. The "social-pastoral" church represents a stage of growth and maturity. But it is also an unfinished stage. Nevertheless, it seems safe to say that the basic tendencies considered in this chapter—the search for consensus between "conservatives" and "progressives," the effort to form a laity increasingly conscious of its role within the church, the attempt to foster pastoral experiences that lead to a greater integration of the Christian message in the daily life of the faithful, and a search for greater maturity in religious life and in the clergy—will continue for some time to come. But the dominant note, as Medellín and Puebla made clear, will continue to be the effort to make the church pastorally responsive to young people and the popular classes that continue to live in extreme poverty.

Conclusion

Pope John Paul II's visit to Peru in February 1985 seems a convenient moment to conclude this work and make a general assessment of the state of the Peruvian church. During the five days of the pope's visit (February 1–5) Peruvians of all walks of life were caught up in a festive spirit. John Paul's presence came as a great consolation to a country that was in the middle of one of the worst social and economic crises in Peru's modern history. Also, systematic terrorism had taken thousands of lives. A collective pessimism pervaded all conversations in the last year of Fernando Belaúnde's second term as president (1980–85). Like a hardy sixteenth-century missionary, John Paul visited city after city without rest: Lima-Callao, Arequipa, Cuzco, Ayacucho, Trujillo, Piura, and Iquitos. The entire nation was tuned in by television or transistor radio to hear him speak. A foreign missionary who had been in Peru for many years commented, "I haven't seen the Peruvian people so happy for quite a long time." A dramatic event such as a papal visit to a Catholic country (and Peru, as Peruvians like to claim with pride, gave the pope one of the most enthusiastic welcomes in all of Latin America) is also an appropriate occasion to review the church's evolution since that country's independence and to make a few summary observations on what it has accomplished and what it has not.

Since the time of González Prada and the positivists, Peruvian intellectuals have asked whether Peru is really a nation or not. The question refers in part to the great diversity of ethnic groups and cultures that exist side by side in Peru. But the question also refers to a harsher economic reality, the enormous inequality between social classes. Finally, the persistence of certain colonial attitudes and practices, such as public corruption, paternalism that is sometimes a veiled form of racism, lack of civic spirit (few Peruvians pay taxes), elitism, etc., are other motives for doubting whether Peru is a "real" nation or simply a collection of groups in conflict living together. At times, of course, intellectuals, especially those on the left, have exaggerated this criticism and failed to see what Jorge Basadre, Peru's leading historian in the twentieth century, termed the "promise of the Peruvian way of life." The pope's visit brought out the best of Peru and helped people see that promise in a more visible way. At least for five days, there reigned an atmosphere of civic cooperation and spontaneous good will. Most of all, from the Inca fortress of Sacsahuamán (where the pope addressed the peasantry of Cuzco) to Tumbes in the extreme north and to Iquitos on the headwaters of the Amazon river, one could palpably perceive the existence of a common identity. Throughout Peru the display of common religious symbols, including the symbol of the papacy itself, all deeply rooted in the country's collective historical memory, gave witness to a deeper unity that binds the country's twenty-one million inhabitants together. The papal visit brought to light the best of what Peruvians are and what they can be.

To a great extent, the achievement of this common identity was the work of the church. Beginning in the sixteenth century, the church evangelized the people and implanted the first common symbols to be shared by all cultures and social groups in Peru. The pope's visit symbolized four hundred years and more of historical continuity. Besides this fundamental contribution to Peru's sense of national identity, the church also contributed to Peru's development by way of its many educational and humanitarian works. It is important to emphasize these positive points because they far outweigh the church's shortcomings and limitations. But these limitations, too, should be mentioned to help fill in the picture.

In the first chapter we pointed out some of the basic weaknesses of the colonial church in Peru as well as in the rest of Latin America. Although the church influenced everyone at all levels of society, it too was influenced by the society in which it functioned. In this sense church and society have grown together since the sixteenth century and both have at times shared the same defects. If Peru is an "adolescent country," to use the phrase of Luis Alberto Sánchez, then in many ways the church too is "adolescent." Although the church was already nearly three hundred years old at the end of the colonial period, it nevertheless had to start all over again after independence. During the colonial period it led a protected and privileged life. Because of that, it was not prepared to live without state support in the postindependence period. Most of all, it had not inculcated in the vast majority of believers a strong sense of "church," that is, a common identity as Catholics above and beyond the myriad local devotions. The Indians, the half-castes, and the creoles all professed

Conclusion 361

to be Catholics, but they lacked the spirit of militancy that characterized Catholics in post-Reformation Europe. For most Peruvians, to be a Catholic was part of one's natural heritage as a Peruvian, but not necessarily a personally internalized conviction achieved at the cost of great effort. During the first few decades after independence the church did not see the need to make that distinction. But when various hostile forces began to question its role in society, the church reacted to those forces by summoning the faithful to its defense. This struggle to forge a sense of militancy and of belonging to the church is one of the central themes running through all of the church's history from independence to Medellín and Puebla and beyond.

In the period of the "militant church" and that of Catholic Action, the church managed to communicate this sense of belonging to small groups from the middle and upper classes. The inhabitants of the rural areas and the Andes, although profoundly religious, did not participate in this process. Vatican II and much more so the two episcopal conferences of Medellín and Puebla signified a decisive new step forward in the church's maturation; this sense of a deeper identification with the church, including the adoption of a militant spirit, now reached the level of the popular classes. The Council and the episcopal conferences held up as a model the "committed Christian," a Christian who participates actively in the church and who also works to promote social justice and peace in society. This criterion also serves as a measuring stick to determine more or less how much the church has accomplished and how far it still has to go. According to this somewhat demanding norm, only a small percentage of Peruvians could be considered "committed Christians." On a positive note, the number of committed Christians who participate in parish and national lay movements has grown considerably in the years since Medellín. But beyond this core of "militants" there is a multitude of ordinary Peruvians who relate to the church "in some way," such as going to Mass, receiving the sacraments, and participating in one or other procession. The majority of them belong to the world of popular religiosity.

Popular religiosity is, almost by definition, the religion of the majority of Peruvians. On the one hand, it contains many practices, symbols, and artistic expressions that have enriched Peru's culture. But popular religiosity also reveals most of all the weaknesses of the Peruvian and Latin American church. Although the symbols of popular religiosity are taken from Catholicism, the content of its devotions is not based on a theological understanding that leads to a deeper identification with the church itself. Indeed, popular religiosity exists on the margin of the official church and frequently prescinds from the church's central religious acts. Popular religiosity is a force that could be transformed into a more ecclesial faith expression and it could even acquire a more social orientation. The post-Medellín church has accepted this as a challenge, but it is far from having touched the vast mass of ordinary Peruvians who live in the world of popular religiosity.

The "official" church has its own share of defects and limitations, some of which are inherited from the colonial past while others stem from the postindependence period. As seen in chapter 2, the priest shortage is an example of how different social, economic, and cultural factors combine to affect the church. Throughout the nineteenth century and even more acutely in the twentieth, the church found itself faced with a grave shortage of native-born priests. Given its overdependence on tradition and on Rome, the church lacked the necessary pastoral creativity and flexibility to face that crisis adequately. In this sense, the current dependence on foreign missionary personnel also reflects a weakness of the Peruvian church. To be sure, as seen in chapters 4 and 5, the foreign religious orders and congregations that came to Peru from Europe in the last century created the basic nuclei (schools and associations) from which a militant laity arose. Further, most contemporary foreign volunteers believe that their mission is to help the Peruvian church overcome its dependency and to produce its own clergy and lay leaders.

In Peru, as well as throughout the rest of Latin America, there are bishops, priests, and lay groups that did not fully understand or absorb the spirit of the councils of Medellín and Puebla. They are the "conservatives" of the Peruvian church. In some dioceses the bishops discourage lay participation and marginalize priests and religious who have tried to implement the reforms of the council or to live the spirit of Medellín. These groups exhibit a sectarian mentality that does not prepare them to live in an age of pluralism and dialogue. In the light of this situation, it should be obvious that the church's future development will be quite unequal; it will continue to mature in dioceses run by flexible and open-minded bishops and it will make much slower progress in dioceses run by conservatives. Although the conservative bishops and groups do not find much support for their way of thinking in official church documents, they will continue to be a force with which to contend.

As a consequence of the priest shortage and other factors, such as the prevalence of a closed mentality toward new thought currents and the lack of adequate formation programs in seminaries and centers for religious, the Peruvian church is not conspicuous for the intellectual level of its clergy or religious women. Nor does the official church have a notable presence in national universities or even in the private ones. As a result, the church has a very limited capacity to enter into serious dialogue with the world of science and culture. Liberation theology represented an important exception to this rule. Also, as a result of deficiencies in formation programs, many priests show little liturgical creativity and lack the ability to give a good sermon. Frequently, the laypersons who were trained in the catechetical schools and biblical courses display more enthusiasm and express their faith with greater conviction than many priests.

These shortcomings notwithstanding, the positive outweighs the negative in the church's evolution. Humanly speaking, there is no other institution in Peru that draws together so many people of such generosity and moral rectitude. Practicing Christians are also the principal source of hope in a country beset by poverty, violence, and endemic public corruption. For them the Vatican Council, Medellín, Puebla, the pope's visits (John Paul revisited Peru briefly in May 1988 on the occasion of a Bolivarian [in reference to the five countries liberated by Bolivar] eucharistic congress) served as sources of encouragement to redouble their efforts to "reevangelize" Peru, or to bring the first evangelization to perfection. During his 1985 visit the pope touched upon the themes of "nation" and "church." He exhorted the nation to devote its efforts to the task of creating a just and fraternal society, and he called upon the church to show by its example how to reach that promised land.

Notes

Chapter 1

1. Antonine Tibesar, "The Peruvian Church at the Time of Independence in the light of Vatican II," *Americas* 26 (April 1970): 349–50; see also Rubén Vargas Ugarte, S.J., *Historia de la Iglesia en el Perú*, vol. 5: 2–3.
2. Tibesar, "The Peruvian Church," 352–53; see also Paul Bentley Ganster, "A Social History of the Secular Clergy of Lima During the Middle of the Eighteenth Century" (Ph.D. diss., University of California, 1974).
3. Pedro de Leturia, *Relaciones entre la Santa Sede e Hispanoamérica* (Caracas: Sociedad Bolivariana de Venezuela, 1960), vol. 3: 209.
4. Tibesar, "The Peruvian Church," 350.
5. Jean Descola, *La Vida cotidiana en el Perú en tiempos de los españoles, 1750–1820* (Buenos Aires: Librería Hachette, 1962), 109, 205. See Las Heras's report in Leturia, vol. 3: 210–11.
6. Leturia, vol. 3: 173; Tibesar, "The Peruvian Church," 350.
7. Leturia, vol. 3: 168.
8. See Pablo Macerca, *Trabajos de historia* (Lima: Instituto Nacional de Cultura, 1977), vol. 3, and Nicholas P. Cushner, *Lords of the Land: Sugar, Wine and Jesuit Estates of Coastal Peru, 1600–1767* (Albany: State University of New York Press, 1980).
9. Tibesar, "The Peruvian Church," 350, n. 7; see also Avencio Villarejo, *Los Agustinos en el Perú y Bolivia* (Lima: Editorial Ausonia, 1965), 298–303, to appreciate the size of the properties of the Augustinians.
10. On the church and the Enlightenment in America, see John Tate Lanning, "The Church and the Enlightenment in the Universities," *Americas* 15 (April 1959): 333–49; Guillermo Lohman Villena, "The Church and Culture in Spanish America," *Americas* 14 (April 1958): 383–98.
11. Howard J. Wiarda (ed.), *Politics and Social Change in Latin America: The Distinct Tradition* (Amherst: The University of Massachusetts Press, 1974); see also Howard J. Wiarda, "Toward a Framework for the Study of Political Change in the Iberic-Tradition: The Corporative Model," *World Politics* 25 (January 1973): 206–35.
12. Lyle N. McAlister, "Social Structure and Social Change in New Spain," *Hispanic American Historical Review* 43 (1963): 364.
13. Emilio Harth-Terré, *Negros e indios* (Lima: Mejía Baca, 1973).
14. On these and other abuses see Jürgen Golte, *Repartos y rebeliones: Túpac Amaru y las contradicciones de la economía colonial* (Lima: Instituto de Estudios Peruanos, 1980), and Horst Pietschmann, "Burocracia y corrupción en Hispanoamérica colonial," *Nova Americana* 5 (1982): 1–37.
15. Alfred Stepan, *The State and Society: Peru in Contemporary Perspective* (Princeton: Princeton University Press, 1978).
16. José Ortega y Gasset, "El sentido del cambio político español," in *Obras*

completas (Madrid: Ediciones de *La Revista de Occidente*, 1969), vol. 11, "Escritos politicos," 317.

17. Jean Delumeau, *Catholicism between Luther and Voltaire: A New View of the Counter-Reformation* (Philadelphia: Westminister Press, 1977), 160, 166–68. First edition in French with the title *Le Catholicisme entre Luther et Voltaire* (Paris: Presses Universitaires de France, 1971).

18. See Juan Villegas, *Aplicación del Concilio de Trento en Hispanoamérica, 1564–1600: Provincia eclesiástica del Perú* (Montevideo: Instituto Teológico del Uruguay, 1975).

19. Jose Carlos Mariátegui, *Seven Interpretive Essays on Peruvian Reality* (Austin: University of Texas Press, 1971), 135–36.

20. On the Taki Onqoy cult, see Marco Curatola, "Mito y milenarismo en los Andes: del Taki Onqoy a Inkarrí. La visión de un pueblo invicto," *Allpanchis* 10 (1977): 65–92; Steve Stern, *Peru's Indian Peoples and the Challenge of Spanish Conquest: Huamanga to 1640* (Madison: University of Wisconsin Press, 1982), 51–71.

21. Víctor Andrés Belaunde, *La Realidad nacional*, 4th ed. (Lima: Banco Internacional del Perú, 1980), 92–93.

22. For a more complete discussion of this theme, see Manuel Marzal, *La Transformación religiosa peruana*, 2d ed. (Lima: Pontificia Universidad Católica, 1988).

23. Ivan Vallier, *Catholicism, Social Control, and Modernization in Latin America* (Englewood Cliffs, N.J.: Prentice-Hall, 1970), 27–28.

24. Mary A. Y. Gallagher, "Imperial Reform and the Struggle for Regional Self-Determination: Bishops, Intendants and Creole Elites in Arequipa, Peru (1748–1816)" (Ph.D. diss., City University of New York, 1978), 85–110.

25. Antonine Tibesar, "The Lima Pastors, 1750–1820: Their Origins and Studies as Taken from Their Autobiographies," *Americas* 38 (July 1971): 49–50.

26. Pablo Macera, *Trabajos de historia* (Lima: Instituto Nacional de Cultura, 1977), vol. 3, "Sexo y coloniaje," 297–352.

27. Ivan Vallier, *Catholicism, Social Control and Modernization*, 72. Although some of Vallier's fundamental ideas have been incorporated into the outline presented here, the periodization as well as the nomenclature have been modified to fit the Peruvian model.

28. For a general view of republican legislation affecting the church, see J. Lloyd Mecham, *Church and State in Latin America*, 2d ed. (Chapel Hill: University of North Carolina Press, 1966), 160–78.

Chapter 2

1. Antonine Tibesar, "The Peruvian Church at the Time of Independence in the Light of Vatican II," *The Americas* 26 (April 1970): 349–50.

2. Secretariado del Episcopado Peruano, *Directorio eclesiástico del Perú, 1984* (Lima, 1984), 12.

3. Rubén Vargas Ugarte, *Historia de la Iglesia en el Perú* (Burgos, 1962), vol. 5: 3; Secretariado Nacional del Episcopado, *Iglesia en el Perú* 16 (March 1974), 7.

4. Secretariado Nacional del Episcopado, *Iglesia en el Perú* 19 (June 1974), 11; see also the study done by Augusto Beuzeville, "Estadística de la realidad

del clero en el Perú," *Libro anual: Facultad de Teología Pontificia y Civil* (1971) (Lima, 1971), 101–17.

5. Rubén Vargas Ugarte, *Un gravísimo problema nacional* (Lima, 1948), 16.

6. *El Republicano*, May 22, 1847, in the Archdiocesan Archive of Lima, section "Censuses," file 9.

7. Vargas Ugarte, *Historia del Seminario de Santo Toribio de Lima (1591–1900)* (Lima, 1969), 84.

8. Vargas Ugarte, *Un gravísimo problema*, 14.

9. Paul Bentley Ganster, "A Social History of the Secular Clergy of Lima during the Middle of the Eighteenth Century" (Ph.D. diss., University of California, Los Angeles, 1974); Antonine Tibesar, "The Lima Pastors, 1750–1820: Their Origins and Studies as Taken from Their Autobiographies," *The Americas* 28 (July 1971): 39–56.

10. Manuel A. Fuentes, *Estadística general de Lima* (Lima, 1858), 413.

11. Ministerio de Fomento, *Censo de Lima 1908* (Lima, 1915), vol. 2: 920–21.

12. Manuel Lorenzo de Vidaurre, *Plan del Perú* (Philadelphia, 1823), 98.

13. Antonine Tibesar, "The *Alternativa*: A Study in Spanish-Creole Relations in Seventeenth-Century Peru," *The Americas* 11 (January 1955): 229–83.

14. Mariano Paz Soldán, *Historia del Perú independiente* (Le Havre, 1874), vol. 2: 106.

15. R. M. Taurel, *Colección de obras selectas del clero contemporáneo del Perú* (Paris, 1855), vol. 1: xii; see also the study on this topic by Antonine Tibesar, "The Suppression of the Religious Orders in Peru, 1826–1830," *The Americas* 39 (October 1982): 205–39.

16. Tibesar, "The Suppression of the Religious Orders," 233.

17. *El Redactor eclesiástico*, Lima, February 4, 1845, 4.

18. Manuel J. Bustamante de la Fuente, *La Monja Gutiérrez y la Arequipa de ayer y hoy* (Lima, 1971).

19. William Bennet Stevenson, *A Historical and Descriptive Narrative of Twenty Year's Residence in South America* (London: Hurst, Robinson and Co., 1825), vol. 1: 251.

20. See Fr. Juan de la Cruz, *Monografía del Covento de las Rdas Madres Carmelitas Descalzas de Trujillo, 1724–1924* (Trujillo, 1924), 57–58.

21. Manuel A. Fuentes, *Estadísticas general de Lima*, 467.

22. Pedro José Rada y Gamio, *El arzobispo Goyeneche: Apuntes para la historia del Perú* (Rome: Imprenta Políglota Vaticana, 1917), 237–41.

23. Tibesar, "The Peruvian Church at the Time of Independence" *The Americas*.

24. Jorge Basadre, "Para la historia de las ideas en el Perú: un esquema histórico sobre el catolicismo ultramontano, liberal y social y democratismo cristiano," *Scientia et Praxis* (Lima, University of Lima, November 1976): 54.

25. On the life of Valdivia, see M. A. Cateriano, *Ojeada sobre la vida de Monseñor Juan Gualberto Valdivia, Deán de Arequipa* (Arequipa, 1884), and Bishop José Dammert's comments, "Acerca de una interpretación histórica," *Histórica* 6 (July 1982): 113.

26. Luis Lituma, "La Iglesia peruana en el siglo XX," in José Pareja Paz-Soldán, ed., *Visión del Perú en el siglo XX* (Lima: Ediciones Librería Studium, 1963), vol. 2: 489.

27. Manuel Tovar, *Obras* (Lima, 1904–1907), vol. 2: 230–31.

28. Lituma, 487.
29. Ambrosio Huerta, "Informe que el Illmo. S. D. D. Juan A. Huerta, obispo de Puno dirije al Illmo. S. D. D. José Sebastián Goyeneche, dignísimo Arzobispo de Lima, sobre reducción de los derechos de matrimonios y abolición cuartas funerales," in *Obras de Huerta*, vol. 1: 9.
30. José Ezequiel Moreyra, "Carta del Obispo de Ayacucho, Ezequiel Moreyra al Arzobispo Goyeneche sobre el proyecto de supresión de primicias y derechos parroquiales" (Ayacucho, 1867), in *Iglesia en el Perú* 38, Vargas Ugarte Collection, 38.
31. Episcopado peruano, *Mensaje del episcopado peruano* (Lima, 1891), 8.
32. Moreyra, "Carta del Obispo de Ayacucho" 26.
33. Estéban Pérez, "Visita de la Provincia de Yauyos, 1903," Archdiocesan Archive of Lima, section "Visits," file 25.
34. Estéban Pérez, Ibid., 6.
35. Valentín Ampuero, "Informe de la visita pastoral del Obispo Valentín Ampuero (Puno) al Supremo Gobierno," (Puno, 1913), AAL (Archdiocesan Archive of Lima), section "Visits," file 25, 7.
36. "Un sacerdote cuzqueño," *El clero del Cuzco durante la administración del Ilto. y Rdmo. Señor Obispo D. D. Juan Antonio Falcón* (Cuzco, 1904), in *Iglesia en el Perú* 8, Vargas Ugarte Collection, 16.
37. Manuel Tovar, *Obras*, vol. 3: 170.
38. Conrado Oquillas, *Historia del Colegio Seminario de S. Carlos y S. Marcelo* (Trujillo, 1925–1928), vol. 2: 127.
39. Ibid., 278.
40. Ibid., 305–6.
41. Oquillas, vol. 3: 81.
42. Ibid., 81.
43. *Memoria que presenta el Ministro de Justicia, Culto, Instrucción y Beneficencia al Congreso ordinario de 1890* (Lima, 1890), 66–67. The data on priests ordained for the archdiocese of Trujillo were supplied by Father José Oñate, S.J., of the archdiocesan curia of Trujillo, 1985.
44. José Dammert Bellido, "Acerca de una interpretación histórica," 112.
45. AAT (Archdiocesan Archive of Trujillo), section "Correspondence, 1918–1920."
46. On this question, see L. Lopétegui, "El Papa Gregorio XIII y la ordenación de mestizos hispano-incaicos," in *Miscellánea Histórica Pontificiae* (Rome, 1943), vol. 2: 181–203.
47. Rubén Vargas Ugarte, *Historia del Seminario de Santo Toribio de Lima (1591–1900)*, 57.
48. Moreyra, 28–29.
49. Ampuero, "Informe de la visita pastoral del Obispo Valentín Ampuero," 6–7.
50. "Un sacerdote cuzqueño," *El clero del Cuzco*, 16.
51. Pedro Pablo Drinot y Piérola, *Carta pastoral que el Obispo de Huánuco Mon. Pedro Pablo Drinot y Piérola dirige al clero y fieles* (Lima, 1907), 23–24.
52. Ruben Vargas Ugarte, *Un gravísimo problema nacional* (1948), 10; in the second edition of 1967, 10.
53. Vargas Ugarte (1948), 22; edition of 1967, 31.
54. José María Alvarez Romero, "Un sacerdote indígena peruano el Doctor Joseph Joaquín de Avalo Chauca, canónigo y profesor universitario," *Mercurio Peruano* (November–December, 1964): 57–67.
56. José Dammert Bellido, "Observaciones al esquema de *Sacerdotio Mi-*

Notes 369

nisteriali enviado por la Secretaría del Sínodo de los obispos" (Cajamarca, April 4, 1971), 14.

57. AAT, section "Visits," file 4.

58. Manuel A. Fuentes, *Estadística general de Lima*, 47.

59. Ministerio de Fomento, *Censo de la Provincia de Lima 1908* (Lima: Imprenta de la Opinión Nacional, 1915), vol. 1: 127.

60. Marfil Francke, "Situación actual de la mujer peruana y perspectivas para el desarrollo," *Cuadernos CNP* (National Council for Population), 2 (December, 1983), 4.

61. Ricardo Beltrán y Rózpide, "Memorial de Don Francisco de Toledo" in *Colección de las memorias o relaciones que escribieron los virreyes del Perú* (Madrid, 1921), 75.

62. Arzobispado de Lima, *Informe de pastoral y sociología, Misión Conciliar, 1967, Lima* (Lima, 1967), 40.

63. Iván Illich, "The Seamy Side of Charity," *America* (January 21, 1967), 88–91.

Chapter 3

1. Carta pastoral que el Illmo. y Revm. Señor Arzobispo de Berito y Administrador Apostólico de Huánuco dirige al clero y fieles de la diócesis con motivo del Jubileo Universal concedido por Nuestro Santísimo Padre León XIII (Huánuco, 1879), 1.

2. *El Amigo del Clero*, February 15, 1915, 91.

3. Manuel Lorenzo de Vidaurre, *Proyecto de un código penal* (Boston: Hiram Tupper, 1828), 147.

4. Not translated into English; confer bibliography.

5. Francisco Javier Mariátegui, *Anotaciones a la "Historia Independiente" de Don Mariano Felipe Paz Soldán* (Lima, 1925), 16.

6. Jorge Basadre, *Historia de la República del Perú* (Lima: Editorial Universitaria, 1969), 5: 141.

7. *El Católico* (Lima), May 12, 1855, 30.

8. Instituto Libertador Ramón Castilla, *Archivo Castilla*, vol. 5: *Epistolario*, 157–64.

9. Basadre, 3: 227.

10. *Anales de la Sociedad Católico-Peruana* (Lima, 1868), vol. 1: 42.

11. Ibid., 51–55.

12. *Anales de la Sociedad Católico-Peruana* (Puno, 1868), vol. 1: 7.

13. *Anales . . .* (Lima, 1868), vol. 1: 5.

14. Javier Prado y Ugarteche, *Estado social del Perú durante la dominación española* (Lima, 1941), 112.

15. Ibid., 196–205.

16. Jorge Basadre, *Perú: Problema y posibilidad,* 2d ed. (Lima: Banco Internacional del Perú, 1978), 161–70.

17. Adriana González Prada, *Mi Manuel* (Lima: Editorial Cultura Antártica, 1947), 135.

18. For examples of racism in González Prada, see Bruno Podestá, *Pensamiento político de González Prada* (Lima: Instituto Nacional de Cultura, 1975), 188, 194.

19. Luis Alberto Sánchez, *Balance y liquidación del novecientos*, 4th ed. (Lima: Editorial Universo, 1973), 178.

20. *El Comercio*, May 26, 1923, 3.

21. *Diccionario enciclopédico de la Masonería* (Habana, 1889?), vol. 3: *República del Perú*, 364–65; see also Alejandro Alayza y Paz Soldán, *Breve historia de la Francmasonería peruana y del pacto celebrado entre la Gran Logia del Perú y el Supremo Consejo del Grado 33 del Rito escosés* (Lima, n.d.).

22. Armando Nieto, S.J., *Historia del Colegio de la Inmaculada* (Lima, 1978), vol. 1: 74–75.

23. Manuel González Prada, *Horas de Lucha* (Lima: Fondo de Cultura Popular, 1964), 42.

24. Manuel Tovar, *Obras* (Lima, 1904–1907), vol. 2: 319–27.

25. Jorge Basadre, among others, considered Piérola a "prepopulist." See *Elecciones y centralismo en el Perú* (Lima: Universidad del Pacífico, 1980), 56. For a biography of Piérola, see Alberto Ulloa, *Don Nicolás de Piérola*, 2d. ed. (Lima: Editorial Minerva, 1981).

26. *Hombres y cosas de la Revolución de 1894–95* (Lima, 1901), 60.

27. Manuel A. Fuentes, *Guía histórico-descriptiva administrativa, judicial y de domicilio de Lima*, 2d. ed. (Lima, 1861), 242–43.

28. Cited in Armando Nieto, S.J., *Historia del Colegio de la Inmaculada*, 28.

29. Elvira García y García, *La Mujer peruana a través de los siglos* (Lima, 1925), vol. 1: 59–61.

30. Ibid., 51–52.

31. AAT (Archdiocesan Archive of Trujillo), "Confraternities," file 15, "year 1912."

32. See Armando Nieto, *Historia del Colegio de la Inmaculada*, chap. 7.

33. *Revista Católica*, vol. 40, October 2, 1886, 296; October 16, 305–20.

34. *Discurso pronunciado por el Sr. D. Carlos M. Elías, Presidente de la Unión Católica del Perú, en la sesión inaugural del Consejo Central Provincial el 5 de agosto de 1888* (courtesy of Fr. Enrique Bartra, S.J., Lima).

35. Rubén Vargas Ugarte, S.J., *Historia de la Ilustre Congregación de seglares de N. S. de la O* (Lima: Milla Batres, 1973).

36. *Revista Católica*, vol. 17, July 6, 1889, 7–8.

37. See Fernando López de Romaña, *Datos biográficos de Edmundo López de Romaña* (1973).

38. *Revista Católica*, vol. 40., November 27, 1886, 466–67, 509.

39. Ibid., October 23, 1886, 326–27.

40. *El Deber*, September 23, 1919, 2.

41. AAC (Archdiocesan Archive of Cuzco), section "Republic," C–14: 1, 10.

42. AAT, section "Visits," file 4, "García Irigoyen, 1916."

43. *El Amigo del Clero*, July 1938, 55–57.

44. *Revista Católica*, vol. 13, July 28, 1887, 99.

45. *Revista Católica*, vol. 23, November 26, 1892, 359.

46. *El Deber*, October 27, 1919, 2.

47. AAT, "Confraternities," file 15.

48. AAT, "Confraternities," file 15, "Unión Católica de Señoras," 77.

49. AAT, "Confraternities," file 15, "Year 1912."

50. AAT, Ibid., "Year 1916."

51. AAT, "Confraternities," file 14.

52. AAT, Libro de "Visitas pastorales," file 4, *Boletín eclesiástico de Trujillo*, August 25, 1926, 242.

53. AAT, "Confraternities," file 15.

54. *Revista Católica*, vol. 21, August 1, 1891, 1–23.

55. Jorge Basadre, "Para la historia de las ideas en el Perú . . .," *Scientia et Praxis*, 11 (1976), 61.
56. Sra. Jesús I. de Piérola, *Primer Congreso Católico del Perú, 1896* (Lima, 1897), 73.
57. Ibid., 77.
58. Ibid., 309.
59. Ibid., 314–15.
60. Ibid., 311.
61. *La Colmena* (Arequipa), April 17, 1921, 5–8.
62. Ibid., 13.
63. *El Deber*, May 7, 1919, 2.
64. *La Colmena*, April 17, 1921, 18.
65. AAC, 14: 1, 12.
66. *La Unión* (Lima), August 12, 1915, 1
67. Manuel Vicente Villarán, *Estudios sobre la educación nacional* (Lima, 1922), 12.
68. AAC, 80: 1, 5.
69. AAC, 65: 1, 6.
70. AAC, 80: 1, 5.
71. AAA (Archdiocesan Archive of Arequipa), file 281.
72. AAC, 80: 1, 5.
73. *Boletín eclesiástico de la diócesis de Cajamarca*, year 4, December 1, 1915, 815.
74. *La Unión*, August 12, 1915, 1.
75. AAC, 80: 2, 33.
76. *Carta pastoral que el Obispo de Huánuco Mons Pedro Pablo Drinot y Piérola dirige al clero y fieles* (Lima, 1907), 14.
77. Emilio Romero, *3 Ciudades* (Lima: Imprenta Torres Aguirre, 1929).
78. *La Crónica* (Lima), April 10, 1917, 12–13.
79. See also Rubén Vargas Ugarte, S.J., *Historia del Santo Cristo de los Milagros*, 3d. ed. (Lima, 1966); José Luis Idígoras, "La más grande procesión del mundo," *Revista Teológica Limense*, vol. 12: 1, 67–104; Jeffrey Klaiber, S.J., "El Señor de los Milagros: Fe y Liberación," *Debate* 11 (November 1981), 70–75.
80. AAA, file 286, "Huerta."
81. AAT, "Confraternities," file 14.
82. Cipriano Laos, *Lima, la Ciudad de los Reyes (El Libro Peruano), 1928–1929* (Lima: Editorial Perú, n.d.), 265.
83. On Anglo-Saxon Protestantism in Peru, see the theses of Wenceslao Oscar Bahamonde, "The Establishment of Evangelical Christianity in Peru (1822–1900)" (Hartford, Connecticut: Hartford Seminary, 1952) and of María Elvira Romero, "El Protestantismo anglo-sajón en el Perú, 1822–1915" (Lima: Universidad Católica, 1974).
84. Bahamonde, 123.
85. Dan Chapin Hazen, "The Awakening of Puno: Government Policy and the Indian Problem in Southern Peru, 1900–1955" (Ph.D. diss., Yale University, 1974), 112.
86. Luis Valcárcel, *Tempestad en los Andes* (Lima: Editorial Universo, 1972), 85, 88–91, 123–24; Manuel González Prada, *Propaganda y ataque* (Buenos Aires: Ediciones Imán, 1939), 118.
87. AAC, 80: 2, 33.

88. Hazen, 38–39, 115.
89. AAC, C–44: 44.
90. On Mackay, see the comments by Luis Alberto Sánchez in *Leader*, annual magazine of Saint Andrew's School, Lima, December, 1972, 49–53.
91. *El Amigo del Clero*, October 6, 1929, 1505–9.
92. *El Amigo del Clero*, September 1, 1919, 276.
93. J. Lloyd Mecham, *Church and State in Latin America*, 2d ed. (Chapel Hill, NC: University of North Carolina Press, 1966), 174; Bahamonde, 175.
94. On Asiatic immigration to Peru, see Watt Stewart, *Chinese Bondage in Peru: A History of the Chinese Coolie in Peru, 1849–1874* (Durham, North Carolina: Duke University, 1951); Clinton Harvey Gardiner, *The Japanese and Peru, 1873–1973* (Alberquerque, NM: University of New Mexico Press, 1975); Amelia Morimoto, *Los inmigrantes japoneses en el Perú* (Lima: Universidad Nacional Agraria, 1979).
95. Manuel Tovar, *Obras*, vol. 2: 361–63.
96. AAT, "Padrones," file 8.
97. *El Deber*, November 25, 1919, 2.
98. Wenceslao Fernández Moro, O.P., *Cincuenta años en la selva amazónica* (Madrid, 1952), 276.
99. Urbain-Marie Yonekawa, O.F.M., *Lumière nippone au Perou* (Québec: Aux Editions Franciscaines, 1959), vol. 1: 146.
100. Ismael Portal, *Lima religiosa (1535–1924)* (Lima, 1924), 383–87.
101. Yonekawa, vol. 1, 1–5.
102. José Pareja Paz-Soldán, *Visión del Perú en el siglo XX* (Lima: Ediciones Librería Studium, 1963), vol. 2: 488.
103. Rubén Vargas Ugarte, S.J., *Un gravísimo problema nacional*, 2d. ed. (Lima, 1966), 29.
104. Felipe A. de Piérola, *Anales de la Iglesia de Puno* (Puno, 1865), 65.
105. *La Unión* (Lima), September 11, 1915, 1.
106. Roberto MacLean y Estenós, *Sociología del Perú* (México, D.F.: Universidad Nacional Autónoma de México, 1959), 76.
107. Rubén Vargas Ugarte, S.J., "Situación jurídica de la Compañía de Jesús en el Perú" (Archive of the Society of Jesus, Lima), 21–22.
108. *La Unión* (Lima), October 3, 1915, 2.
109. *El Amigo del Clero*, February 24, 1929, 1013–16.
110. Fausto Linares Málaga, *Monseñor Lissón y sus derechos al Arzobispado de Lima* (Lima, 1933), 28.
111. *El Amigo del Clero*, September 14, 1930, 571–73.

Chapter 4

1. Jesús Jordán Rodríguez, *Pueblos y Parroquias del Perú* (Lima, 1950), vol. 1: 119.
2. Secretariado del Episcopado Peruano, *Directorio eclesiástico del Perú, 1984*, 12.
3. Secretaría del Episcopado Peruano, *Iglesia en el Perú* (October 1978), 8.
4. *Reforma de Regulares promovida por el Ilustrísimo Señor D. D. José Sebastián de Goyeneche y Barreda, Arzobispo de Lima* (Lima, Vargas Ugarte Collection, *Iglesia en el Perú*, no. 18, 11).
5. "Exposición del R. P. Juan Manuel Arias sobre los sucesos ocurridos en el Convento de Nuestra Señora de las Mercedes en Lima, Callao, 1871" (Lima, Vargas Ugarte Collection, *Iglesia en el Perú*, no. 19, 14).

Notes 373

6. *Reglas y estatutos para las Hermanas de la Tercera Orden de San Francisco que viven en Congregación en el venerable Beaterio de Viterbo de Lima.* Lima, *1879* (Vargas Ugarte Collection, *Iglesia en el Perú*, no 19).
7. Avencio Villarejo, *Los Agustinos en el Perú y Bolivia (1548–1965)* (Lima, 1965), 364–65.
8. *La Rosa del Perú*, May 30, 1887, 347.
9. *Provincia franciscana de los Doce Apóstoles del Perú, sus conventos y personal, año 1942* (Lima, 1942).
10. Odoricus Sáiz, O.F.M., *De Ruina ac restauratione in peruvia collegiorum franciscalium propagandae Fidei Saec. XIX, 1824–1860* (Lima, 1972), 122.
11. Rafael María Taurel, *Colección de obras selectas del clero contemporáneo del Perú.* (París, 1855), vol. 1: 206.
12. Ibid., 284–85.
13. Odorico Sáiz, O.F.M., and Julián Heras, O.F.M., *La Provincia misionera de San Francisco Solano del Perú*, 2d ed. (Madrid, 1977), 17–18.
14. Fernando Domínguez, O.F.M., *El Colegio Franciscano de Propaganda Fide de Moquegua (1775–1825)* (Madrid, 1955).
15. Luis Arroyo, O.F.M., *La Recoleta de Arequipa* (Lima, 1951), 175.
16. Ibid., 199.
17. Enrique D. Tovar y R., *El Apóstol de Ica, Fr. José Ramón Rojas (El Padre Guatemala)* (Lima, 1943).
18. Pedro Gual, O.F.M., *Curso de misiones apostólicas, doctrinas y sermones* (Barcelona, 1884), vol. 1: 261–62. See also the study by Julián Heras, O.F.M., *Los Franciscanos y las misiones populares en el Perú* (Madrid: Editorial Cisneros, 1983).
19. Francisco de A. Quintana, O.F.M., *Tercera Orden Franciscana: Album del Congreso Terciario-franciscano celebrado en Ocopa en los días 31 de julio al 5 de agosto de 1936* (Lima, 1936); Francisco Cabré, O.F.M., *Crónica del Primer Congreso Nacional de Terciarios franciscanos, Lima 3–7 octubre de 1945* (Lima, 1946), 592; Odorico Sáiz, O.F.M., *Provincia misionera de S. Francisco Solano del Perú*, 29.
20. AAT (Archdiocesan Archive of Trujillo), section "Visits 20," file 4.
21. Luis Arroyo, *Comisarios generales del Perú* (Madrid, 1950), 562–68.
22. *Provincia franciscana de los Doce Apóstoles del Perú: sus conventos y personal, año 1942* (Lima, 1942).
23. *Memoria que presenta el Ministro de Justicia, Culto, Instrucción y Beneficencia al Congreso Ordinario de 1890* (Lima, 1890), 46–47.
24. Ibid., 60.
25. Arroyo, *La Recoleta de Arequipa*, 427.
26. Odorico Sáiz and Julián Heras, O.F.M., *Provincia misionera de S. Francisco Solano*, 46–47.
27. José Amich, O.F.M., *Historia de las misiones del Convento de Santa Rosa de Ocopa* (Lima: Editorial Milla Batres, 1975), 235; *Memoria que presenta el Ministro de Justicia . . . al Congreso Ordinario de 1890* (Lima, 1890), 60–61.
28. Antonine Tibesar, O.F.M., "The Suppression of the Religious Orders in Peru, 1826–1830," *The Americas* 29 (October 1982): 238–39.
29. R. M. Taurel, *Obras selectas del clero contemporáneo del Perú* (París, 1855), vol. 1: 13.
30. Rubén Vargas Ugarte, S.J., *Historia de la Iglesia en el Perú* (Burgos, 1962), vol. 5: 244.
31. Jorge Basadre, *Historia de la Republica del Perú*, 6th ed. (Lima: Editorial Universitaria, 1970), vol. 2: 95.

32. Manuel Fuentes, *Estadística general de Lima* (Lima: Tipografía Nacional de M. N. Corpancho, 1858), 288–91.
33. Alberto Tauro, ed., *Viajeros en el Perú republicano* (Lima: U.N.M. San Marcos, 1967), 85.
34. Manuel Fuentes, *Estadística general de Lima*, 91.
35. Ibid., 79.
36. Ibid., 80, 85, 92.
37. Many of these facts are taken from a summary made especially for the author by Sister Vicente Perea, secretary to the Visitor General of the Peruvian Province, March 22, 1983. See also the pamphlet, *125 años en el Perú: Hijas de la Caridad y Padres Vicentinos* (Lima, 1983).
38. Urbain-Marie Yonekama, O.F.M., *Lumière Nippone au Perou* (Québec: Aux Éditions franciscaines, 1959), vol. 1: 3–5.
39. Carlos Enrique Paz-Soldán, *Vida y obras de Sor Rosa Larrabure* (Lima: Imprenta de San Marcos, 1963).
40. *Homenaje de la Sociedad Francesa de Beneficencia a sus fundadores, benefactores, presidentes y colaboradores en el primer centenario de su fundación* (Lima, 1960).
41. *Anales de las religiosas de Nuestra Señora de la Caridad del Buen Pastor de Angers en Lima, 1871–1900* (Lima: Imprenta "El Lucero," 1903), 11–12.
42. Ibid., "El Año 1878."
43. *Crónica, casas y Provincia Santa Rosa de Lima* (historical album in the center house of the religious of Santa Ana, San Miguel, Lima).
44. Gaetan Bernoville, *Las Hermanas de San José de Tarbes* (Trujillo, Perú, 1962), 114–16; 206–08.
45. José Villa Cerri, "Clérigos Regulares Ministros de los Enfermos, Religiosos Camilos, celebrando el IV Centenario," *Conferencia de Religiosos del Perú, Boletín Especial* 52 (1982): 7–16.
46. Eustasio Estéban, O.S.A., *La Sierva de Dios, Madre Rafaela de la Pasión Veintemilla* (Lima: Sanmartí y Cía, 1938).
47. Personal interview with Mother María de la Pasión Castelló, Barranco (Lima), March 8, 1983.
48. Félix Vernet, *Dom Gréa (1828–1917)* (Paris, 1937), 136–37.
49. *Un glorioso centenario (1848–1949): la Congregación Claretiana en el Perú* (Lima, 1949).
50. Teresa Alvarez Calderón y María Candamo, *Teresa de la Cruz Candamo*, ed. José de la Puente Candamo (Lima, 1969).
51. Secretariado Latinoamericano M.S.C., *M.S.C. en Latinoamérica*, 12–16.
52. Avencio Villarejo, *Los Agustinos en el Perú y Bolivia (1548–1965)*, 387.
53. Dionisio Ortiz, O.F.M., *Monografía del Vicariato de San Ramón (Chanchamayo)* (Lima, 1979), 102.
54. Personal interview with Mother Josefa Merino of the Franciscan Missionaries of Mary, Lima, January 6, 1983.
55. Personal interview with Mother Juana Eifertinger, cofounder of the Franciscans of Bamberg in Peru, Lima, March 5, 1983.
56. Wenceslao Fernández Moro, O.P., *Cincuenta años en la selva amazónica* (Madrid, 1952), 3–4. On the Dominicans, see Father José María Arévalo, O.P., *Los Dominicos en el Perú* (Lima: Editorial San Antonio, 1970).
57. Carlos Lizárraga, *En las Fuentes del Amazonas: Mons. Jáuregui, Obispo Misionero* (Bilbao, 1981), 43–44.

58. Personal interview with Father Clemente Sobrado, Passionist priest, Lima, February 13, 1983.
59. Villarejo, 387.
60. Fernández Moro, O.P., 95.

Chapter 5

1. Manuel González Prada, *Horas de lucha* (Lima: Fondo de Cultura Económica, Ediciones "Futuro," 1964), 162.
2. Armando Nieto Vélez, S.J., "El derecho a la educación y la legislación peruana en el siglo XIX" (Lima: Bachelor's thesis, Pontificia Universidad Católica, 1956), 106 and passim.
3. The *colegio* in Latin America usually includes both primary and secondary education, the equivalent of grade and high school in the United States system.
4. In 1970 approximately 8 percent of the national student body were students in Catholic schools. In 1982 this percentage dropped to 7.22%. See "Informe sobre la educación católica en el Perú" (Lima, August, 1972) and "Informe sobre el estudio estadístico de los centros educativos de la Iglesia" (Lima, January 20, 1983). These reports can be found in the National Office of Catholic Education in Lima.
5. Manuel González Prada, *Propaganda y ataque* (Buenos Aires: Ediciones Imán, 1939), 85.
6. Luis Alberto Sánchez, *Testimonio personal* (Lima: Ediciones Villasán, 1969), vol. 1: 90.
7. Manuel González Prada, *Horas de lucha*, 163.
8. See Armando Nieto, S.J., "El Derecho a la educación. . . ."
9. For the beginnings of Catholic education in republican Peru, see the thesis by Margarita María Recavarren, "Los Primeros cincuenta años de la Escuela Normal de Mujeres y su rol en el panorama educativo nacional" (Lima: Universidad Nacional Mayor de San Marcos, 1974).
10. Víctor Andrés Belaunde, *Trayectoria y destino: Memorias* (Lima: Ediciones Ediventas, 1967), vol. 1, "El Colegio del Padre Duhamel," 179–91.
11. On San Carlos, see Rubén Vargas Ugarte, S.J., *El Real Convictorio carolino y sus dos luminares* (Lima: Carlos Milla Batres, 1970) and Oscar Barrenechea y Raygada, *Bartolomé Herrera, educador y diplomático peruano (1808–1864)* (Buenos Aires, 1940).
12. Rubén Vargas Ugarte, S.J., *Historia del Seminario de Santo Toribio de Lima (1591–1900)* (Lima, 1969), 62.
13. Ibid., 49.
14. *Exámenes anuales del Seminario Conciliar de Santo Toribio* (Lima: Tipografía La Sociedad, 1880), 45.
15. *El Amigo del Clero*, September 21, 1905, 765–66.
16. *El Amigo del Clero*, May 24, 1928, 386–87.
17. Alejandro Málaga Medina, *Arequipa: Estudios históricos* (Arequipa, 1981), 129–33.
18. *El Deber* (Arequipa), October 23, 1940, 28.
19. Conrado Oquillas, *Historia del Colegio Seminario de S. Carlos y S. Marcelo* (Trujillo: Imprenta Colegio Seminario, 1925–28), vol. 2: 59.
20. *Un glorioso centenario, 1849–1949: la Congregación claretiana en el Perú* (Lima, 1949), 35.

21. Eleuterio Alarcón Bejarano, O.M., "Los Conventos mercedarios del Perú y la legislación canónico-civil en siglo XIX," *Analecta Mercedaria* vol. 1 (1982): 173.

22. Avencio Villarejo, *Los Agustinos en el Perú y Bolivia (1548–1965)* (Lima: Edición "Ausonia," 1965), 371–78.

23. *Colegio de los SS.CC. Belén: Conmemoración del primero centenario de su fundación, 1848–1948* (Lima, 1950).

24. On the Jesuits' return to Peru, see Rubén Vargas Ugarte, S.J., "Situación jurídica de la Compañía de Jesús en el Perú," *Derecho* (Pontificia Universidad Católica), no. 13 (1953): 5–39. See also César Pacheco Vélez, "Trayectoria histórica de los Jesuitas en el Perú," *Mercurio Peruano*, no. 473 (1968): 253–85.

25. Armando Nieto Vélez, S.J., *Historia del Colegio de la Inmaculada* (Lima, 1978), vol. 1, chap. 3, "La Fundación."

26. Margarita María Recavarren, "Los Primeros cincuenta años de la Escuela Normal...," 168.

27. Interview with Sister Shona García, directress of the Teachers Normal School of Monterrico, December 9, 1982.

28. Recavarren, 63.

29. See the pamphlet, *Madre Clara del Corazón de María* (Lima: Imprenta-Editorial "San Antonio," 1962).

30. "Los Salesianos están por cumplir 75 años en el Perú" (Typewritten summary, archives of the Salesian congregation, Lima).

31. *El Deber* (Arequipa), July 21, 1931, 6.

32. Interview with Father Juan Pedro Perucchi, secretary to the Inspector General of the Salesians, December 17, 1982.

33. "Los SS.CC. en América Latina," manuscript in the archives of the parish of La Recoleta, Lima.

34. *Almanaque de conmemoración para las bodas de oro, 1893–1943*.

35. Eugenio Valentín, S.D.B., *Madre Teresa del Sagrado Corazón (1856–1950)* (Burgos, 1978).

36. Data taken from the archives of the Teaching Dominicans, Colegio Santa Rosa, Lima.

37. Data taken from "La Obra marista en el Perú," typewritten pages in the archive of the Marist brothers, Lima; see also the album *150 Aniversario: Maristas, 1817–1967* (Lima, 1967); and personal interview with the provincial of the Marists, Brother Eduardo Palomino, December 4, 1982.

38. *Signo* (Magazine of the Consortium of Catholic Educational Centers), Lima (June 1976), 7.

39. Personal interview with Brother Noé Zevallos, former provincial of the Brothers of La Salle in Peru, Lima, December 10, 1982.

40. Servants of the Immaculate Heart of Mary, *Forty Years in Peru, 1922–1962* (Lima, n.d.).

41. Personal interview with Sister Thomas Eugene, I.H.M., directress of Villa María Academy, January 15, 1983.

42. *La Barca de Santa Ursula, 1936–1961* (commemorative album).

43. Data taken from a summary written by Sister Amabilis Geimer, O.P., superior of the Dominicans of Saint Mary Magdalene in Peru, Chosica, February 12, 1984.

44. Personal interviews with Father Oscar Alzamora, S.M., December 7, 1982, and Brother George Lytle, provincial of the Marianists in Peru, July 8, 1983.

45. *Fides* (Lima), October 15, 1949, 5.
46. National Office of Catholic Education, "Informe sobre el estudio estadístico de los centros educativos de la Iglesia," January 20, 1983.
47. Cipriano Laos, *Lima, La ciudad de los virreyes (el libro peruano), 1928–1929* (Paris: Editorial Perú, 1927), 324.
48. Luis Alayza y Paz Soldán, *Mi País* (Lima, 1960), vol. 1: 45–56.
49. Luis Alberto Sánchez, *Testimonio personal*, vol. 1: 102.
50. Raúl González, "Los Primeros años de Armando Villanueva," *Caballo Rojo* (Sunday supplement of *Diario Marka*), November 28, 1982, 5.
51. Pablo Macera, *Trabajos de historia* (Lima: Instituto Nacional de Cultura, 1977), vol. 1: xxvii–xxviii.
52. Cipriano Laos, 319.
53. Ibid.
54. Ibid., 324.

Chapter 6

1. Thomas Ford, *Man and Land in Peru* (Gainesville: University of Florida Press, 1955), 11.
2. Ibid.
3. Instituto Nacional de Estadísticas, *Estimaciones y proyecciones de población* (Lima, April 1983), 65–66.
4. Ibid., 25.
5. Antonio Gramsci, *Selections from the Prison Notebooks of Antonio Gramsci*, trans. and ed. by Quintin Hoare and Geoffrey Nowell Smith (London: Lawrence and Wishart, 1971), 396–97.
6. Manuel González Prada, *Grafitos* (Paris: Tipografía Louis Bellenand et Fils, 1937), 182.
7. George Foster, "Peasant Society and the Image of the Limited Good," *American Anthropologist* 67 (April 1965): 293–315.
8. José Carlos Mariátegui, *Seven Interpretive Essays on Peruvian Reality*, trans. Marjory Urquidi (Austin: University of Texas Press, 1971), 135.
9. Víctor Andrés Belaunde, *La Realidad nacional*, 4th ed. (Lima: Banco Internacional, 1980), 86–93.
10. Claudio Véliz, "Latitudinarian Religious Centralism," *The Centralist Tradition of Latin America* (Princeton, New Jersey: Princeton University Press, 1980), 189–217.
11. Antonine Tibesar, "Raphael María Taurel, Papal Consul General in Lima, Peru, in 1853: Report on Conditions in Peru," *Revista interamericana de bibliografía* (April 1981), 57–58.
12. Un sacerdote cuzqueño, *El Clero del Cuzco durante la administración de lltmo. y Rdmo. Señor Obispo D.D. Juan Antonio Falcón* (Cusco, 1904), 16.
13. R. P. Fray Jesús Jordán Rodríguez, *Pueblos y parroquias del Perú* (Lima, 1950), vol. 1: 119.
14. AAL, section "Visits," file 22.
15. On the economic resources of the colonial clergy, see the doctoral dissertation of Paul Bently Ganster, "A Social History of the Secular Clergy of Lima during the Middle Decades of the Eighteenth-Century" (Los Angeles: University of California, 1974), 145–51.
16. Francisco García Calderón, *Diccionario de la legislación peruana*, 2d ed. (Lima, 1879), vol. 1: 759–61.
17. "Pastoral Colectiva" in *El Amigo del Clero* (July 1905), 415.

18. "Visita a la Parroquia de Pueblo Nuevo, Provincia de Pacasmayo, 9–5–1916." AAT, section "Visits," file 4.
19. "Primera visita pastoral practicada por el Excmo. Mons. Juan G. Guevara, 4–11–1941." AAT. section "Visits," file 5.
20. "Extracto del arancel eclesiástico mandado reimprimir de orden de S. S. I. El Arzobispo Mi Señor para que perciban los curas con arreglo a El, los derechos parroquiales. Lima, 1837." Vargas Ugarte Collection, *Iglesia en el Perú*, no. 39.
21. AAT, section "Visits XV," file 4.
22. "Visita Pastoral a Ica, 25–1–1904." AAL, section "Visits," file 25.
23. "Informe que el Ilmo. S. D. D. Juan A. Huerta, Obispo de Puno, dirige a Ilmo. S. D. D. José Sebastián de Goyeneche . . . sobre reducción de los derechos de matrimonios y abolición de cuartas funerales." Lima, 1869. Huerta, *Obras*, vol. 1.
24. Thomas Ford, *Man and Land in Peru*, 78–80. See also the references to the properties of the Bethlemites and the Augustinians in Luis Miguel Glave and María Isabel Remy, *Estructura agraria y vida rural en una región andina: Ollantaytambo entre los siglos XVI y XIX* (Cusco: Centro de Estudios Rurales Andinos "Bartolomé de las Casas," 1983).
25. "Razón de las tierras pertenecientes a las iglesias de Faray, Pisac, y S. Salvador. 3 de agosto de 1855. José Casimiro Cabañay." AAC, CLXII, 1, 5.
26. "Carta Pastoral que dirige el Ilustrísimo Sr. Obispo de Puno a sus amados Párrocos" (May 30, 1866, 4). Huerta, *Obras*, vol. 2.
27. "Visita parroquial de la Doctrina de Santa Magdalena de Cao que corre al cuidado del Párroco de Chocope. 19 de julio de 1902." AAT, section "Visits," file 4.
28. "El Párroco de la Doctrina de Paruro, al Obispo." June 2, 1901. AAC, XVII, 1, 13.
29. "Visita pastoral a Huaraz, 1848." AAL, section "Visits," file 21.
30. "Informe de la visita pastoral del Obispo Valentín Ampuero al Supremo Gobierno." AAL, section "Visits," file 25.
31. "Relación de la visita pastoral practicada por el R. P. Fray Deogracias de Ondonégui a las provincias de Otuzco, Santiago de Chuco, Pataz y Huamachuco, en los años 1924 y 1925." AAT, section "Visits," file 5.
32. "Memoria que el Vicario Capitular presenta al Iltmo. y Rmo. Mons. Obispo del Cuzco, Dr. Pedro Pascual Farfán, 1918." AAC, CXXXIX, 1, 14, 5–6.
33. *El Obispo de Huánuco: su vindicación contra la prensa periódica (1895)*, 127. Vargas Ugarte Collection, *Iglesia en el Perú*, no. 44.
34. On colonial clerical concubinage, see Antonine Tibesar, O.F.M., "The Peruvian Church at the Time of Independence in the Light of Vatican II," *The Americas* 26 (April 1970), 370–73.
35. "Memoria que el Vicario Capitular presenta. . . ." AAC, CXXXIX, 1, 14, 7.
36. "Expediente sobre la causa seguida por Manuel Atauchi, Indígena tributario de Colquepata, contra el Pbro. Pedro Mercado, por abusos y maltratos," Cuzco, February 25, 1826. Lima, National Library, Research Room, Manuscript D 10577.
37. AAC, XXXIII, 1, 17.
38. AAC, XXXIII, 1, 4.
39. Antonine Tibesar, O.F.M., "Raphael María Taurel, Papal Consul

General in Lima, Peru, in 1853: Report on Conditions in Peru," *Revista interamericana de bibliografía* (April 1981), 57.
  40. AAC, LXIX, 2, 18.
  41. Angel Menéndez Rua, *Paso a la civilización* (Quillabamba, 1948), 87.
  42. Ibid., 97.
  43. AAT, section "Confraternities 1935–1941," file 18.
  44. "Visita pastoral a las parroquias de las provincias de Otuzco, Santiago de Chuco, Pataz y Huamachuco, 1926." AAT, in *Boletín eclesiástico*, 135–36, section "Visits," file 4.
  45. "Informe de la visita pastoral del Obispo Valentín Ampuero al Supremo Gobierno." AAL, section "Visits," file 25.
  46. AAL, section "Pastoral Visits," file 21.
  47. Vargas Ugarte Collection, *Iglesia en el Perú*, no. 4.
  48. "Informe. . . del Obispo Valentín Ampuero." AAL, section "Visitas," file 25, 2–3.
  49. *Constituciones del Primer Sínodo diocesano punense*, in Huerta, *Obras*, vol. 3: 72–73.
  50. Ibid., 38.
  51. Ibid., 85.
  52. *Primer Congreso Interdiocesano de Acción Social* (Cusco, 1922), 41.
  53. Ibid, 128, 186.
  54. Ibid., 347.
  55. Ibid., "Acuerdos," 36.
  56. *Constitutiones Synodi*, Appendix 2, "De los indios," 72.
  57. *Primer Congreso Interdiocesano de Acción Social*, "Acuerdos," 62–72.
  58. *Constitutiones IV Synodi diocesis cuzcuencis*, 45, 49.
  59. AAC, C-XXXIII, 1, 16.
  60. On Farfán as president of the Indian Patronage, see the thesis by Laura Hurtado Galván, "Cusco, Iglesia y Sociedad: El Obispo Pedro Pascual Farfán de los Godos (1918–1933) en el debate indigenista" (Lima: Universidad Católica, 1982).
  61. *Constitutiones IV Synodi*, 51.
  62. Ibid., 53.
  63. *Primer Congreso Interdiocesano*, "Acuerdos," 64.
  64. On the religious factor in these uprisings, see chap. 3, "Holy Week in Huaraz, 1885," in Jeffrey Klaiber, S.J., *Religion and Revolution in Peru, 1824–1976* (Notre Dame, Indiana: University of Notre Dame Press, 1977).
  65. *Constituciones del Primer Sínodo diocesano punense*, in Huerta, *Obras*, vol. 3: 77.
  66. Huerta, *Obras*, vol. 2: 21–24.
  67. *El Perú Católico* (Lima), October 24, 1867, 1.
  68. Olivas Escudero, *Obras de Monseñor Dr. Fidel Olivas Escudero, Obispo de Ayacucho* (Lima: Imprenta Comercial de Horacio La Rosa, 1911), vol. 2: 274.
  69. *El Comercio*, December 24, 1896, 1.
  70. *El Comercio*, June 26, 1895, 2.
  71. "Parte elevado a la subprefectura de la provincia de Chucuito por el comisario de policía de la frontera del Perú con Bolivia, informándole sobre los sucesos de Ilave. Ilave, abril 10 de 1897." National Library, Research Room, Manuscript D 4551.
  72. Ibid.
  73. On the European background of the confraternities, see Manuel

Marzal, *La Transformación religiosa peruana* (Lima: Universidad Católica, 1988), 403–19; Olinda Celestino and Albert Meyers, *Las Cofradías en el Perú: Región central* (Frankfurt/Main: Vervuert, 1981).

74. Rafael Varón, "Cofradías de indios y poder local en el Perú colonial: Huaraz, siglo XVII," *Allpanchis*, 17 (no. 20, 1982): 127–42.

75. Celestino and Meyers, 109, 111, 125–27.

76. Gustavo Benza, "Las Tierras de los Santos de las comunidades indígenas cusqueñas y los cambios sociales en la región, 1890–1965" (Bachelor's thesis, Universidad Católica, Lima 1983), 2–4.

77. Richard Adams, *A Community in the Andes: Problems and Progress in Muiquiyauyo* (Seattle, Washington: University of Washington Press, 1959), 52–53.

78. Celestino and Meyers, 234–35.

79. See Gustavo Benza, "La Tierra de los Santos. . . ."

80. Celestino and Meyers, 215.

81. Adams, 73–74.

82. Paul L. Doughty, "The Interrelationship of Power, Respect, Affection and Rectitude in Vicos," *The American Behavioral Scientist* 8 (March 1965), 17.

83. Adams, 77.

84. José Uriel García, *El Nuevo indio* (Lima: Editorial Universo, 1973), 165–69.

85. "Visitas pastorales del Ilmo. y Rvdmo. Mons. Don Carlos García Irigoyen Obispo de Trujillo desde el año 1910 al año 1926." AAT, section "Visits," file 4.

86. On this demographic decline, see the various studies of the Cornell-Vicos project: Hernán Castillo et al. *Chaquicocha: Community in Progress* (Ithaca: Cornell University, 1964), report 5, 12–13; Paul L. Doughty and Luis Negrón, *Pararín: A Break with the Past*, report 6 (1964), 11–14.

87. Consejo Nacional de la Universidad Peruana, *Huamanga, una larga historia* (Lima, 1974), 210–12, fn 4.

Chapter 7

1. *El Amigo del Clero*, July 20, 1905, 422.
2. Ibid., August 15, 1912, 473.
3. Ibid., July 1, 1923, 295.
4. Pedro Drinot y Piérola, *La Libertad de cultos y la Acción Social Católica en el Perú* (Huánuco, 1915), 27.
5. *El Amigo del Clero*, May 10, 1038–42; May 18, 1929, 1049–69.
6. *Verdades* (Lima), January 10, 1931, 4.
7. *El Amigo del Clero*, May, 1935, 48.
8. See the *Anuario eclesiástico de la Arquidiócesis de Lima para el año 1916 . . . para el año 1935*, both published under the direction of Belisario A. Philipps.
9. See César Arróspide, "El movimiento católico seglar en los años 20," *La Revista de la Universidad Católica*, n.s. 5 (August 1979): 5–24. Also, personal interview with César Arróspide, November 20, 1981.
10. Archdiocesan Archive of Cuzco, L–2, 32.
11. For the Fides Center see the bulletin *Fides*, February 1, 1950, 1; September 1, 1951; May, 1952, 1 (in Bartolomé de las Casas Documentation Center, Lima). Also, personal interview with Gerardo Alarco, November 25, 1981.

12. On Amelio Placencia see *Verdades*, February 25. Also, personal interview with Ernesto Alayza Grundy, June 11, 1982.
13. Personal interview with Father Eduardo Suárez Jimena, June 26, 1982.
14. *El Deber* (Arequipa), July 13, 1931, 3.
15. Archdiocesan Archive of Trujillo, section "Visits," file 4, "Visitas 1912."
16. AAT, "Confraternities 1920–1926," file 16.
17. Ibid.
18. "Circular urgiendo la organización de centros parroquiales," July 2, 1929. Private collection of Vega Centeno, Lima.
19. AAT, "Confraternities, 1927–34."
20. AAT, "Confraternities, 1935–1941," file 18.
21. *El Deber*, October 31, 1931, 7.
22. *El Amigo del Clero*, November 7, 1931, 226–55.
23. *El Deber*, January 13, 1931, 7.
24. *El Comercio*, January 19, 1931, 3.
25. *El Deber*, July 20, 1931, 1.
26. *Verdades*, February 7, 1931, 2.
27. *Verdades*, January 31, 1931, 1, 5.
28. *Verdades*, January 24, 1931, 2.
29. *Verdades*, October 25, 1931, 4.
30. *La Crónica*, June 2, 1931, 13.
31. *El Deber*, September 1, 1931, 3.
32. *Patria*, September 17, 1931, 5.
33. "Actas del Comité Popular Cusco creado por la Acción Social Católica para intervenir en actividades políticas y conseguir la elección de representantes ante la Asamblea Nacional Constituyente." AAC, file 53, 1, 12.
34. AAC, file C, 18, 1, 19.
35. See Alberto Flores Galindo, *Arequipa en el sur andino, siglos XVIII–XX* (Lima: Editorial Horizonte, 1977); Baltazar Caravedo, "Poder central y descentralización: Perú, 1931," *Apuntes* 9 (1979): 111–29; José Luis Rénique, "Los descentralistas arequipeños en la crisis del 30," *Allpanchis* 12 (1979): 51–78.
36. *El Deber*, January 9, 1931, 3.
37. Víctor Andrés Belaunde, *Trayectoria y destino: memorias completas* (Lima: Ediciones de Ediventas, 1967), vol. 2: 787.
38. Belaunde, *La Realidad nacional*, 4th ed. (Lima: Banco Internacional del Perú, 1980), 216.
39. *El Deber*, August 3, 1931, 3.
40. *El Deber*, July 22, 1931, 3.
41. *El Deber*, August 3, 1931, 3.
42. *Patria*, September 9, 1931, 2.
43. *El Deber*, September 5, 1931, 1.
44. *El Deber*, September 18, 1931, 1.
45. *Patria*, September 22, 1931, 1.
46. Jorge Basadre, *Historia de la República del Perú* (Lima: Editorial Universitaria, 1970), vol. 14: 168.
47. AAC, file C, 48, 1, 2.
48. *El Amigo del Clero*, February, 1935, 84–85.
49. "Carta al Señor Presidente de la Junta de Defensa Social de Lima," September 26, 1932. AAC, file C, 48, 1, 19.

50. Letter to Mariano Holguín, September 13, 1935, Riva-Agüero Institute, Riva-Agüero Archive, section "Letters."
51. José de la Riva-Agüero, *Obras completas, Escritos políticos* (Lima: Publicaciones del Instituto Riva-Agüero, 1975), vol. 11, 265–66.
52. Víctor Andrés Belaunde, *Memorias completas*, vol. 2, 1050.
53. José de la Riva-Agüero, *Por la verdad, la tradición y la patria* (Lima, 1937), 373–78.
54. Jorge Dintilhac, *Cómo nació y se desarrolló la Universidad Católica del Perú: 30 años de vida (1917–1946)*, 5.
56. "Breve historia de la Universidad Católica," *El Estandarte católico*, Ayacucho, 1934, 12
57. Dintilhac, 23.
58. *El Estandarte católico*, 12.
59. *Segundo Congreso Iberoamericano de Estudiantes Católicos* (Lima, 1941), 182.
60. *El Amigo del Clero*, July and August 1937, 19.
61. *El Amigo del Clero*, June 1936, 58–59.
62. Ibid., 60.
63. Jeffrey Klaiber, S.J., *Religion and Revolution in Peru, 1824–1976* (Notre Dame: University of Notre Dame Press, 1977), 230, n. 72.
64. *El Amigo del Clero*, year 44 (October–November–December 1935), 24–25.
65. Ibid, 147.
66. *El Amigo del Clero*, year 45, no. 1345 (January 1936), 7.
67. Ibid.
68. Acción Católica de la Juventud Femenina, *Memoria* (Lima, 1936), Benvenutto Library, University of El Pacífico, Lima.
69. *Verdades*, October 23, 1937, 3–6.
70. *Primer Congreso Nacional de Acción Católica* (Lima, 1958), 264.
71. Jorge Alayza Grundy, "Memoria de la Junta Nacional de la Acción Católica correspondiente al período 1958–1959," Bartolomé de las Casas Documentation Center, Lima.
72. "Acción Católica, Cusco," AAC, 20, 1, 5.
73. "Nómina de la Junta Directiva del Centro de Oficinistas de la Juventud Femenina de la Acción Católica Peruana, Trujillo." AAT, "Confraternities 1942–1946," file 19.
74. These reflections by César Arróspide can be found in his typewritten manuscript, "Apuntes sobre el apostolado laico en el Perú en las primeras décadas del siglo" (April 1977), Bartolomé de las Casas, Lima. Also, personal interview with César Arróspide, November 20, 1981.
75. Fernando Stiglich, *Relaciones Estado-Iglesia en el Perú* (Lima, 1959), 86–87.
76. *La Rosa del Perú*, May 1931, 188.
77. AAT, "Confraternities 1927–34," file 17.
78. *La Colmena* (Arequipa), November 28, 1931, 3.
79. *Crónica del Segundo Congreso Eucarístico Nacional* (Arequipa, 1941), 416.
80. Jorge Alayza Grundy, "Anexo a la Memoria de la Junta Nacional por el año 1959," 9.
81. *Verdades*, June 24, 1939, 4.
82. César Arróspide, "El movimiento católico seglar en los años 20," *Revista de la Universidad Católica*, 22.

83. César Arróspide, "Apuntes sobre el apostolado laico en el Perú...," 20.
84. César Arróspide, "La Crisis cultural," *V Semana Interamericana de Acción Católica*. Bartolomé de las Casas Documentation Center, Lima.

Chapter 8

1. On the Christian Democratic parties in Latin America, see Harry Kantor, "Catholic Political Parties and Mass Politics in Latin America," in Donald Eugene Smith, ed., *Religion and Political Modernization* (New Haven: Yale University Press, 1974), 202–23.
2. See Virginia Forrester, "Christian Democracy in Peru" (Ph.D. diss., Columbia University, 1970), and Jaime Rey de Castro, ed., *Testimonio de una generación: los Social Cristianos* (Lima: Universidad del Pacífico, 1985).
3. Ibid., 168–69.
4. See the prologue of Louis-Joseph Lebret to his work, *Dinámica concreta del desarrollo* (Barcelona: Editorial Herder, 1966).
5. *Verdades*, October 18, 1959.
6. Forrester, 181–82.
7. Ibid., 184.
8. *El Deber*, October 8, 1955, 4; Héctor Cornejo Chávez, *Socialcristianismo y revolución peruana* (Lima: Ediciones Andinas, 1975, 133).
9. Personal interview with Héctor Cornejo Chávez, Lima, September 6, 1976.
10. William J. McIntire, "U.S. Labor Policy," in Daniel Sharp, ed. *U.S. Foreign Policy and Peru* (Austin, Texas: University of Texas Press, 1972), 294–95.
11. Adela Pardo Gámez de Belaunde, *Arequipa, su pasado, presente y futuro* (Lima: Imprenta Litográfica del Perú, 1967), 130–32. See also the bibliographical notes on Landázuri in *Iglesia en el Perú*, no. 30 (June 1975): 6; and no. 84 (June 1980): 1–2.
12. José Matos Mar, *Desborde popular y crisis del Estado*, 2d ed. (Lima: Instituto de Estudios Peruanos, 1985), 71–72.
13. *Iglesia en el Perú*, no. 30 (June 1975): 6.
14. *Verdades*, August 4, 1956; *El Amigo del Clero*, October–November 1957, 270–77.
15. *Boletín del Arzobispado de Lima*, November 1978, 66–67.
16. *El Amigo del Clero*, July–August 1958, 189–190.
17. Secretaría General del Episcopado del Perú, *Primera Semana Social del Perú: exigencias sociales del catolicismo en el Perú* (Lima, 1959), 185.
18. *El Comercio*, April 17, 1983, 6.
19. *El Amigo del Clero*, January 1957, 359–65.
20. SENATI, *Memoria y balance, 1965* (Lima, 1965), 23.
21. *Primera Semana Social del Perú*, 259; the letter convoking the Social Week can also be found in *El Amigo del Clero*, January–February 1958, 8–21.
22. *Primera Semana Social del Perú*, 183–84.
23. See *El Amigo del Clero*, June–July–August 1961, 563–79, and *Segunda Semana Social del Perú: La Propiedad*, published by the Permanent Committee of the Social Weeks (Lima, 1962).
24. On the church's agrarian reform in Cuzco, see Gustavo Benza, "Las Tierras de los Santos de las comunidades indígenas cusqueñas y los cambios sociales en la región, 1890–1965" (Bachelor's thesis, Pontificia Universidad Católica, 1983), 71–81.

25. See the two works of Salomón Bolo, *Cristianismo y liberación nacional* (Lima, 1962) and *Cristianismo y marxismo: ¿son conmpatibles?* In the first he approves of communism and in the second he rejects it.
26. Pontificia Universidad Católica, *Política: deber cristiano* (Lima: Ediciones Librería Studium, 1963), 113–15, 119.
27. *El Amigo del Clero*, January 1963, 14–19.
28. Arzobispado de Lima, *Informe de pastoral y sociología: Misión Conciliar de Lima* (Lima, 1967), 40.
29. *El Amigo del Clero*, May–June 1967, 285–89.
30. *Iglesia en el Perú*, no. 30 (June 1975): 6.
31. See James N. Steidel, "Renewal in the Latin American Church: A Study of the Peruvian Dioceses of Cajamarca and Ica" (Ph.D. diss., University of Southern California, 1975), 223–59.
32. *Boletín del Arzobispado de Lima*, June 1979, 107–8.
33. *Primera Asamblea Plenaria de Cursillistas* (November l, 1964), Bartolomé de las Casas Documentation Center, Lima, document no. 199.
34. See the *Anuario eclesiástico del Perú* for the years 1947, 1959, 1969 and the *Directorio eclesiástico del Perú, 1984*.
35. Gerald M. Costello, *Mission to Latin America* (Maryknoll, New York: Orbis Books, 1979), 46.
36. Ibid., 55.
37. These data can be deduced by examining the *Directorio eclesiástico del Perú, 1984*. See also the study by Augusto Beuzeville, "Estadística de la realidad del clero en el Perú," in *Libro anual de la Facultad de Teología Pontificia y Civil* (Lima, 1971), 116.
38. Centro de Animación Misionera, *Misioneros combonianos, 40 años en el Perú, 1938–1978* (Lima, 1978). Also, personal interview with Father Romeo Ballán, director of *Misión sin fronteras*, April 2, 1985.
39. Robert Kearns, *Maryknoll Fathers in Peru*, vol. 1 (1943–53), 11–12.
40. On Bishop Fedders, see *Iglesia en el Perú*, no. 10 (April 1973), 14.
41. Kearns, *Maryknoll Fathers in Peru*, vol. 3 (1960–64): 124–33; vol. 4 (1965–77): 579–86.
42. William J. McIntire, "Maryknoll and Peruvian Education," *Catholic Mind* (November 1972), 50.
43. Kearns, vol. 4: 34–35.
44. Personal interview with Father Michael Fitzgerald, one of the founders of the Columbans in Peru, Lima, December 17, 1982.
45. Costello, 36–37.
46. Personal interview with Father Jerry Pashby, Lima, December 16, 1982.
47. Personal interview with Father Joseph Martin, one of the founders of the St. James Society in Peru, Lima, December 4, 1982.
48. *Crónica de los Carmelitas del Perú, llamados de la Antigua Observancia* (Lima, 1974).
49. Steidel, 270.
50. *America* (New York), January 21, 1967, and reproduced in Costello, 283–89. For a critical analysis of the North American missionaries in Peru, see Dan C. McCurry, "U.S. Church-Financed Missions in Peru," in Daniel Sharp, ed., *U.S. Foreign Policy and Peru*, 393–96.
51. Kearns, vol. 4 (1965–77): 1074. See also the study done by IBEAS (Bolivian Institute of Studies and Social Action): Jaime Ponce and Daniel Roach, *Los Maryknoll en el Perú: estudio de opiniones y actitudes* (1968).

52. Kearns, vol. 4: 1216.
53. *Oiga*, May 23, 1969, 41.

Chapter 9

1. *Latin America Press*, October 18, 1972, 1.
2. For an overall view of the changes in the Latin American church, see Enrique Dussel, *A History of the Church in Latin America: Colonialism to Liberation (1492–1979)* (Grand Rapids, Michigan: Eerdmans, 1981); Penny Lernoux, *Cry of the People* (New York: Penguin Books, 1982); Edward Cleary, *Crisis and Change: The Church in Latin America Today* (Maryknoll, New York: Orbis Books, 1985).
3. General Secretariat of CELAM, *The Church in the Present-Day Transformation of Latin America in the Light of the Council*, vol. 2: *Conclusions*, 2d ed. (Washington, D.C.: Division for Latin America, USCC, 1973): 59.
4. Lernoux, 42; Cleary, 43, 47.
5. Juan Luis Segundo, Ricardo Cetrulo, Juan José Rossi, and Dora M. Mastiari, *Iglesia latinoamericana ¿protesta o profecía?* (Avellaneda, Argentina: Ediciones Búsqueda, 1969), 287–99.
6. For the history of ONIS, see Michael G. Macaulay, "Ideological Change and Internal Cleavages in the Peruvian Church: Change, Status Quo and the Priest; The Case of ONIS" (Ph.D. diss., University of Notre Dame, 1972), and Fernando Montes, "How the ONIS Movement Began and Grew," *LADOC* 45 (Washington, D.C., February, 1974).
7. The principal publications of ONIS can be found in Bartolomé de las Casas Documentation Center, Lima.
8. Macaulay, 72.
9. Segundo, Centrulo, and Rossi, *Iglesia latinoamericana*, 301–6.
10. Ibid., 307–11.
11. "Conclusiones de la XXXVI Asamblea General del Episcopado Peruano," in Secretaría General del Episcopado Peruano, *Documentos del Episcopado, 1968–1977* (Lima: Editorial Apostolado de la Prensa, 1977), 7.
12. "Base doctrinal y orgánica de la Comisión Episcopal de Acción Social" (Lima: Comisión Episcopal de Acción Social), 3–4.
13. Jorge Fernández Maldonado, "Fuerzas Armadas, cristianismo y revolución en el Perú," *Participación*, August, 1979, 9–10.
14. For exhaustive treatments of the church and the military, see Thomas J. Maloney, "Church and Peruvian Revolution: Resource Exchange in an Authoritarian Setting" (Ph.D. diss., University of Texas at Austin, 1978), and James Agut, "The Peruvian Revolution and Catholic Corporatism: Armed Forces Rule since 1968" (Ph.D. diss., University of Miami, 1975). For briefer studies, see Jeffrey Klaiber, S.J., "The Church and the Military," in *Religion and Revolution in Peru, 1824–1976* (Notre Dame: University of Notre Dame Press, 1977); Carlos Alberto Astiz, "The Catholic Church in the Peruvian Political System," in David Chaplin, ed., *Peruvian Nationalism: A Corporatist Revolution* (New Brunswick, New Jersey: Transaction, Inc., 1976); George W. Grayson, "The Church and the Military in Peru: From Reaction to Revolution," in Donald Eugene Smith, ed., *Religion and Political Modernization* (New Haven: Yale University Press, 1974).
15. See Luna Victoria's works, *El problema indígena y la tenencia de tierras en el Perú* (Trujillo: Departamento de Investigaciones Científicas y Divulgación Cultural, 1964); *Ciencia y práctica de la revolución, manual para dirigentes polí-*

ticos (Lima: Editorial Studium, 1966); and *Por una democracia socialista en el Perú* (Lima: Ediciones Agape, 1978). In this last work he fully supports the reformist military.

16. Maloney, "Church and Peruvian Revolution," 157.
17. See Alfred Stepan, *The State and Society: Peru in Comparative Perspective* (Princeton, New Jersey: Princeton University Press, 1978).
18. In his encyclical *Libertas* (1888), Leo XIII criticizes liberalism but he also recognizes democracy itself as a valid form of government for Christians. In his "Motu Propio" on Catholic Action (*Fin Dalla Prima Nostra Encíclica*, 1903), Pius X praises the concept of "Christian Democracy."
19. *Expreso*, October 11, 1968, 1.
20. "Declaración del Episcopado del Perú sobre la ley de Reforma Agraria" (July 18, 1969), in *Documentos del Episcopado*, 28–31.
21. Comisión Episcopal de Acción Social, *Propiedad social, Cuadernos de documentación*, no. 4.
22. *Latin America Press*, March 17, 1969, 1–3.
23. Oficina Nacional de Educación Católica, "Centros educacionales dirigidos por religiosos: estudio de su distribución por diócesis" (1971), 11.
24. On the educational reform see the chapter by Robert S. Drysdale and Robert G. Meyers, "Continuity and Change: Peruvian Education," in Abraham F. Lowenthal, ed., *The Peruvian Experiment. Continuity and Change under Military Rule* (Princeton, New Jersey: Princeton University Press, 1975).
25. "Mensaje del Episcopado peruano con ocasión del II Congreso Nacional de Educadores Católicos (September 20, 1970)," in *Documentos del Episcopado*, 92.
26. *El Comercio*, May 24, 1973, 11.
27. "Sobre la justicia en el mundo" (August 14, 1971), in *Documentos del Episcopado*, 143–44.
28. Ibid., 151.
29. Ibid., 146.
30. Ibid., 151.
31. See the edition of *La Justicia en el mundo* published by CEAS in *Cuadernos de documentación*, no. 1, 35 (no date).
32. "Evangelización, algunas líneas pastorales," in *Documentos del Episcopado*, 189.
33. Ibid., 205.
34. Ibid.
35. Segundo, Cetrulo, and Rossi, *Iglesia latinoamericana*, 314–22.
36. *Noticias Aliadas*, February 19, 1969, 6; March 26 & 29, 1969, 2. Segundo, Cetrulo, and Rossi, *Iglesia latinoamericana*, 323–26.
37. *Noticias Aliadas*, April 23, 1969, 4.
38. See Carboni's letter and other related documents in the documentation center of MIEC (Movimiento Internacional de Estudiantes Católicos), Lima.
39. *Latin America Press*, April 29, 1969, 1–3; May 9, 1–3.
40. *Caretas*, May 13, 1971, 20–22.
41. *Latin America Press*, June 2, 1972, 1–7. 1972.
42. *El Comercio*, June 14, 1969, 1; June 15, 1969, 3.
43. See Henry Dietz, *Poverty and Problem-Solving under Military Rule: The Urban Poor in Lima, Peru* (Austin: University of Texas Press, 1980).
44. Klaiber, *Religion and Revolution in Peru*, 186–91.

45. *Oiga*, February 5, 1971, 14–16, 38.
46. CEAS, *Justicia, un clamor en la selva, Cuadernos de documentación*, no. 2 (no date).
47. *Oiga*, September 29, 1972, 14–16.
48. *Latin America Press*, February 18, 1972, 8–9.
49. Maloney, "Church and Peruvian Revolution," 322.
50. "Declaración del Episcopado peruano sobre el estatuto de prensa" (August 1974), in *Documentos del Episcopado*, 261–64.
51. CEAS, *Participación popular, una visión cristiana* (December 4, 1975), *Cuadernos de documentación*, no. 6.
52. Maloney, 391. See also Mary H. Mooney and Walter C. Soderlund, "Clerical Attitudes Toward Political Development in Peru," *The Journal of Developing Areas* 12 (October 1977): 17–30.

Chapter 10

1. See especially the episcopal document *Reflexiones de la fe sobre el momento actual*, October 1976.
2. Personal interview with Father Gutiérrez, Lima, March 21, 1983. See also the interview by Mario Campos in *La República*, April 20, 1984, 13–21.
3. For a study of the evolution of Father Gutiérrez's ideas, see Roberto Oliveros, *Liberación y teología: génesis y crecimiento de una reflexión, 1966–1976*, 2d ed. (Lima: C.E.P., 1980), and Miguel Manzanera, *Teología y salvación en la obra de Gustavo Gutiérrez* (Bilbao: Universidad de Deusto, 1978).
4. In Peru just as there is a "school" of liberation theology, so too there is a "school" of opposition. One of the most balanced critics of Father Gutiérrez's works is the Jesuit José Luis Idígoras, especially in his article "Reflexiones sobre la teología en el Perú," *Revista de la Universidad Católica*, new ser., 7 (June 1980): 45–80; see also the works of two other Jesuits, Francisco Interdonato, *Teología latinoamericana, ¿teología de la liberación?* (Bogotá: Ediciones Paulinas, 1978), and Ricardo Durand Florez, *Observaciones a teología de la liberación* (Callao, 1985).
5. For one view of the influence of liberation theology, see "Teología de la liberación: diez años caminando con el pueblo pobre," *Páginas*, December 1981.
6. These data are taken from the records of the Theology Department of the Catholic University; see also *Informative quincenal* (published by C.E.P.) January 14, 1983, 5, March 3, 3. In 1983 a second session of the course was opened in August. Hence the "summer" course is no longer strictly for the "summer."
7. Records of the Theology Department, Catholic University.
8. For more facts on the conservative groups, see *Marka* (Lima), November 13, 1975, 11–13; September 13, 1979, 20–21, 27–28; *Oiga*, October 19, 1981, 43; *La República*, January 11, 1985, 8.
9. An excellent summary of the Puebla conference is found in Penny Lernoux, *Cry of the People* (New York: Penguin Books, 1982), 413–44.
10. Consejo Episcopal Latinoamericano, "La Evangelización en el presente y en el futuro de América Latina," *Documento de consulta a las conferencias episcopales* (November 1977), paragraph 86.
11. Lernoux, 423.

12. See José Luis Idígoras, "La Liberación en Puebla," *Revista teológica limense* 13:2, 315–44.
13. See Gustavo Gutiérrez's criticism of the *Documento de consulta* in *The Power of the Poor in History* (Maryknoll, New York: Orbis Books, 1983), 111–24.
14. *Aporte de la Conferencia Episcopal peruana al Documento de Consulta para la Tercera Conferencia General del Episcopado latinoamericano* (May 1978), 5.
15. Ibid., 56–58.
16. The most complete summary of the EMO-Calama affair is found in Alfredo Garland, *Como lobos rapaces: Perú, ¿una Iglesia infiltrada?* (Lima: Servicio de Análisis Pastoral e Informativo, 1978), 201–30.
17. For the Chimbote incident, see *Caballo Rojo* (Sunday supplement of *Marka*), June 17, 1981, 5; *La Prensa*, May 31, 1981, 20; *Ojo* (Lima), May 27, 2; *CEP: Informativo quincenal*, June 6, 2.
18. See the article in *Oiga*, "Teología de la liberación: cronología de un cuestionamiento," October 8, 1984, 21, 70, and Bishop Durand's defense of the bishops' right to judge liberation theology, *El Comercio*, October 29, 1984, 2. *La República* assumed the defense of liberation theology in numerous articles: April 22, 1984, 10–11; June 10, 10; September 4, 7–11; September 9, 6–7, 14–15; September 16, 7, 26; September 23, 4; September 28, 11; October 2, 8; October 3, 8; October 5, 4; October 6, 10–11.
19. *Latin America Press*, September 27, pp. 1–8; November 1, 1–2, 1984.
20. *ICLA Boletín* (Lima), September 1984, 7; *CEP Informativo quincenal*, September 14, 1984, 9.
21. *La República*, February 3, 1985, 4; *Misión sin Fronteras* (Lima), March 1985, 12.
22. José Matos Mar, *Desborde popular y crisis de Estado*, 2d ed. (Lima: I.E.P., 1985), 71.
23. Personal interview with Father Carlos Pozzo, S.J., September 1, 1982; see also *Iglesia en el Perú*, no. 85, July 1980, 7–8.
24. José Tamayo Herrera, *Historia del indigenismo cuzqueño, siglos XVI-XX* (Lima: Instituto Nacional de Cultura, 1980), 317–21.
25. See Father Lassegue's *Guía del investigador en el Archivo Arzobispal del Cuzco* (Lima: Fondo del Libro del Banco Industrial del Perú, 1981).
26. Cecilia Tovar, ed., *Dos obispos del Sur Andino: Luis Vallejos y Luis Dalle: en el corazón de su pueblo* (Lima: C.E.P., 1982), 209–26.
27. *CEP Informativo quincenal*, August 22, 1980, 1–2.
28. *CEP Informativo quincenal*, November 9, 1984, 5.
29. See Cecilia Tovar, cited above.
30. See *Iglesia en el Perú*, no. 28, April 1975, 7–8.
31. "Integración silenciosa de 600 hombres," *Las obras misionales pontificias* (Lima, 1974); see also *Anuario eclesiástico del Perú, 1974*.
32. "Las comunidades nativas y la Asamblea Constituyente" (document composed by CIPA), *Shupihui* 8, 30.
33. José María Guallart, S.J., *Fronteras vivas* (Lima: CAAAP, 1981); Aurelio Chumap Lucía and Manuel García Rendueles, S.J., *Duik Muun: Universo mítico de los Aguaranas*, 2 vols. (Lima: CAAAP, 1979); James Regan, S.J., *Hacia la tierra sin mal*, 2 vols. (Iquitos: CETA, 1983).
34. For the summer language institutes in Latin America, see David Stoll, *Fishers of Men or Founders of Empire: The Wycliffe Bible Translators in Latin America* (London: Zed Press, 1982).

35. Personal interview with Father Luis Fernando Crespo, Moderator of UNEC in Lima, May 12, 1982.
36. *CEP Informativo quincenal*, November 22, 1985, 4; *La República*, November 15, 1985, 27.
37. Personal interview with Father Robert Dolan, S.J., National Moderator of the Christian Life Communities, December 12, 1985.
38. *CEP Informativo quincenal*, May 10, 1985, 5; interview with Father Juan Dumont, National Moderator of the Teaching Teams, March 11, 1986.
39. See Giorgio Zevini, SDB, "La Iniciación cristiana de adultos en las comunidades neocatecumenales," *Concilium* 142 (February 1979): 240–48.
40. Personal interview with Father Miguel Girón, S.J., one of the founders of the Neocatechumenate movement in Peru, February 11, 1986.
41. Personal interview with Father Michael La Fay, Carmelite, December 19, 1985.
42. Data provided by Father Edward Schmidt, S.J., National Moderator of Marriage Encounter, March 19, 1986; see also *Boletín del Arzobispado de Lima*, July 1979, 130–32.
43. Personal interview with Señor Juan Beltrán, permanent deacon and teacher in the Program for Deepening Christian Commitment, December 18, 1985.
44. *Boletín del Arzobispado de Lima*, July 1979, 129–30.
45. On existing confraternities in Lima, see Olinda Celestino and Albert Meyers, *Las Cofradías en el Perú: Región Central* (Frankfurt, 1981), 249, and appendix, graph 40; see also Anthony de la Cruz Espinosa, "Las Cofradías de los negros de Lima: una institución colonial en evolución" (Bachelor's thesis, Universidad Católica, Lima, 1985).
46. Luis Germán Echevarría, "La Hermandad de Caballeros de San Martín de Porras y San Juan Macías, O.P., del Convento de Santo Domingo de Lima" (Bachelor's thesis, Instituto Superior Pedagógico Champagnat, Lima), 82.
47. *Directorio eclesiástico del Perú, 1984*, 12.
48. Isidoro Alonso, Ginés Garrido, Mons. Dammert Bellido, and Julio Tumiri, *La Iglesia en Perú y Bolivia* (Freiburg/Bogotá: Federación Internacional de los Institutos Católicos de Investigaciones Sociales, 1961), 75–78.
49. On Sister Joan Sawyer, see the *Boletín del Arzobispado de Lima* 6, January 1984, 8–11.
50. Personal interview with Sister Teresa Avalos, superior of the Sisters of Saint Joseph of Carondolet, December 4, 1985.
51. Personal interview with Father José Ridruejo, S.J., December 9, 1985.
52. ISET, *Líneas teológico-pastorales de planes de estudios* (Lima, 1986), 25–27.
53. Federación de Centros Educativos Católicos, "Memoria de la Junta Directiva, 27 de diciembre a 11 de junio de 1977," 4–5.
54. Bishop Ricardo Durand Florez, "Informe de la Comisión Episcopal de Educación a la Asamblea Episcopal, 18 de enero de 1976," 2 (in the National Office of Catholic Education).
55. General Juan Mendoza, *Nuevo potencial para la educación peruana* (Lima, 1956), 102.
56. Oficina Nacional de Educación Católica, "Informe sobre el estudio estadístico de los centros educativos de la Iglesia" (Lima, 1982), 2.
57. *El Amigo del Clero*, March 1963, 154–55.

58. Mendoza, *Nuevo potencial* . . ., 229.
59. ONDEC, "Centros educacionales dirigidos por religiosos; estudio de su distribución por diócesis" (Lima, 1971), 11.
60. Ibid., 1–2.
61. Ministerio de Educación, *Reglamento de centros educativos parroquiales* (Lima, 1977), 1.
62. *El Comercio*, December 20, 1975, 2.
63. *El Comercio*, May 24, 1973, 11.
64. *Boletín del Consorcio de los Centros Educativos de la Iglesia*, October 1975, 6.
65. "Informe de la Comisión Episcopal de Educación sobre la actual huelga magisterial, 10 de julio de 1979" (File "Huelga Magisterial 1979," ONDEC, Lima).
66. *Boletín de la Federación de Centros Educativos Católicos*, July–September 1980, 11–12, 16–30.
67. Pontificia Universidad Católica, *Decreto Ley No. 17437 sobre el régimen de la Universidad peruana: opinión de la Universidad Católica* (Lima, 1969).
68. Comisión de Reorganización Universitaria, *Informe a la comunidad universitaria* (Arequipa, November 30, 1973).
69. Pontificia Universidad Católica del Perú, *Plan de desarrollo y funcionamiento 1985–1986* (Lima, 1985), 14.
70. This church-state agreement may be found in the *Directorio eclesiástico del Perú, 1984*, 13–15.
71. On the participation of the church in the constitutional assembly of 1978–79, see José Dammert Bellido, "Iglesia y Estado," *Revista teológica limense* 14:2 (May–August 1980): 131–35; José Luis Idígoras, S.J., "Iglesia y Estado en la Constitución peruana (1979)" (Lima: Pastoral Center, Catholic University); Rosa Luisa Rubio de Hernández, "Acerca de las relaciones entre la Iglesia y el Estado peruano: presentación y documentos," *Revista de la Universidad Católica*, new ser., 7, 109–15.
72. For an analysis of the sociopolitical factors affecting church-state relations during this period, see Catalina Romero de Iguíñiz, "Cambios en la relación Iglesia-Sociedad en el Perú: 1958–1978," *Revista Debates en Sociología* (Catholic University of Peru) 7: 115–41.
73. See *La República*, April 22, 1984, 28–29; *El Observador Nacional*, April 23, 1984, 5.
74. *Páginas* 39, August 1981, 4–5.
75. *CEP Informativo quincenal*, February 4, 1983, 4.
76. *Boletín del Arzobispado de Lima*, April 1984, 60.
77. *La República*, October 3, 1984, 3; October 5, 6.
78. Luis Peirano, ed., *Educación y comunicación popular en el Perú* (Lima: DESCO, 1985), 36–39.
79. Oficina Nacional de Estadística y Censos, *Censos nacionales VII de población de vivienda* (Lima, 1972), 1:134–50; *Censos nacionales VIII de población, III de vivienda* (Lima, 1981), 1:171–76.
80. For the Adventists, see Gabriel Escobar, *Adventistas: organización social y cultural del sur del Perú* (México: Instituto Indigenista Interamericano, 1967); George Primov, "Aymara-Quechua Relations in Puno," in K. Ishwaran, ed., *Class and Ethnicity in Peru* (Leiden: E. J. Brill, 1974), 57–59.
81. Santiago Aquilino Huamán, *La Primera historia del movimiento pentecostal en el Perú* (Lima, 1982), 112. See also Yolanda Rodríguez González, "Una

aproximación al estudio del protestantismo en el Perú" (Bachelor's thesis, Catholic University, Lima, 1984); and Manuel Marzal, *Los caminos religiosos de los inmigrantes en la Gran Lima* (Lima: Pontificia Universidad Católica, 1988).

82. See, for example, Christian Lalive d'Epinay, *Haven of the Masses: A Study of the Pentecostal Movement in Chile* (London: Lutterworth Press, 1969).

83. On the Old Testament character of popular religiosity in Peru and Latin America, see Manuel Marzal, S.J., "La Religiosidad popular en el Perú," *Iglesia en el Perú*, no. 4 (April 1972), 16; José Luis Idígoras, S.J., "Religiosidad popular y marxismo 'popular,' " *Revista teológica limense* 10:3 (1976): 289–313.

84. On the Israelites, see *La República*, April 24, 1984, 15–17;

85. Concilio Nacional Evangélico del Perú, *Directorio Evangélico: Lima, Callao y Balnearios* (Lima: PROMIES, 1986), 104.

86. For the non-Christian sects, see José María Cabreras, S.J., *Las Nuevas sectas en el Perú* (Lima, 1983); *El Comercio* Sunday supplement, February 20, 27, and March 6, 1983.

Bibliography and Sources

Preliminary Note

The following bibliography refers principally to the postindependence church. Nevertheless, for the benefit of the reader who wishes to know more about the church in the rest of Latin America as well as the colonial period in Peru, we shall include here a brief orientation. For their solid scholarship the church histories of Zubillaga for the northern hemisphere (1965) and that of Antonio Egaña for the southern hemisphere (1966) are helpful guides. However, these two works represent a traditional historiography and do not include newer points of view that take social and ideological factors more into account. In this sense, the reader would be advised to consult the church history of Enrique Dussel (1981), which was written in the light of Medellín and liberation theology. The history by Hans-Jürgen Prien (1985) has the same general orientation as Dussel's, but unlike Dussel's, it gives more attention to the church in Brazil and to Protestantism. Penny Lernoux (1982) and Edward Cleary (1985) give good global overviews of the changes in the Latin American church since Vatican II. See also the brief account by Fredrick Pike (1984). Brian Smith (1975) traces the evolution of thought in the contemporary Latin American church, and Ivan Vallier (1971) analyzes the church's evolution from a sociological perspective. The classic treatment of church-state relations in Latin America is that of Mecham (2d ed., 1966). All of these works contain ample bibliographies that will help the student pursue many other areas and subareas not touched upon here.

The basic building blocks for Peruvian church history are the five volumes of Rubén Vargas Ugarte, which cover the sixteenth to the nineteenth centuries (1962). For a briefer overview of Peruvian church history, see the chapters by Armando Nieto in the eleventh volume of the Mejía Baca collection on Peruvian history (1980). The works by Rubén Vargas represent a classical and apologetic church history and do not sufficiently analyze social, economic, and ideological factors in history. To appreciate the importance of these factors, the reader should refer to Marzal's work on the religious transformation of Peru in the sixteenth century (2d ed., 1988) and Duviol's study of the anti-idolatry campaigns (1971). On the church and the economy, see Cushner (1980) and Macera (1977, vol. 3) on the Jesuit haciendas. The educational work of the Jesuits is covered in the works of Luis Martín (1968) and Sánchez López (1974). On the colonial religious orders, see Tibesar (1968) on the Franciscans, Villarejo (1965) on the Augustinians, and Gallagher (1978) on the Convent of Santa Catalina in Arequipa. The missionary work of the Franciscans is covered by Tibesar (1981) and Heras (1983). See Noé Zevallos for the figure of Toribio Rodríguez de Mendoza and Enrique Bartra (1982) on the Third Lima Council. The Archdiocesan Committee on the

Bicentennial of Tupac Amaru has published two volumes on Tupac Amaru and the Church (1983). See also the work of Celestino and Meyers on the confraternities (1981). An excellent instrument for any researcher is the *Research Guide to Andean History* by John TePaske, ed. (Duke University Press, 1981), which contains a description of church archives in the Andean republics.

For the church in the independence period, see Nieto (1960; 1980), Klaiber (1980), and Aparicio Vega (1974). The last volume of Vargas Ugarte covers the church in the nineteenth century. For more on the different intellectual currents in that century, see Pike (1967) and Basadre (1976). Luis Lituma gives a general view of the church in the twentieth century before the Council (in Pareja Paz-Soldán, 1963). Catalina Romero covers the changing relations between church and society from the decade of the fifties until the seventies. Luis Pásara analyzes internal tensions in the post-Medellín church (1986). For a fuller view of popular religiosity in Peru, see Marzal (1971, 1977), Garr (1972), Irarrázaval (1978), González and Ronzelen (1983), and Regan (1983). See also the excellent study of Stephen Judd (1987) on the southern Andean church.

Books, Pamphlets, and Articles

Adams, Richard. *A Community in the Andes: Problems and Progress in Muquiyauyo.* Seattle, Washington: University of Washington Press, 1959.

Agut, James R. "The Peruvian Revolution and Catholic Corporatism: Armed Forces Rule since 1968." Ph.D. diss., University of Miami, 1975.

Alarcón Bejarano, Eleuterio. "Los conventos mercedarios del Perú y la legislación canónico-civil en el siglo XIX." *Analecta Mercedaria*. Rome. Vol. 1 (1982): 127–77.

Alayza Grundy, Jorge. "Memoria de la Junta Nacional de la Acción Católica correspondiente al período 1958–1959." Lima: Bartolomé de las Casas Documentation Center.

Alayza y Paz Soldán, Alejandro. *Breve historia de la Francmasonería peruana y del pacto celebrado entre la Gran Logia del Perú y el Supremo Consejo del Grado 33 del Rito escosés.* Lima, n.d.

Alonso, Isidoro, Ginés Garrido, José Dammert Bellido, and Julio Tumiri. *La Iglesia en Perú y Bolivia.* Freiburg/Bogotá: Federación Internacional de los Institutos Católicos de Investigaciones Sociales, 1961.

Alvarez Calderón, Teresa, and María Candamo. *Teresa de la Cruz Candamo.* Edited by José de la Puente Candamo. Lima, 1969.

Alvarez Romero, José María. "Un sacerdote indígena peruano el doctor Joseph Joaquín de Avalo Chauca, canónigo y profesor universitario." *Mercurio peruano*, November–December 1964, 57–67.

Alzamora Castro, Víctor. *Mi hospital.* Lima, 1963.

Amich, José. *Historia de las misiones del Convento de Santa Rosa de Ocopa.* Edited by Julián Heras. Lima: Editorial Milla Batres, 1975.

Anales de la Iglesia de Puno, 1865.

Anales de la Sociedad Católico-Peruana. 2 vols. Lima, 1868.

Anales de la Sociedad Católico-Peruana. Arequipa, 1868.

Anuario eclesiástico de la Arquidiócesis de Lima para el año 1916 . . . para el año 1935. Lima.

Anuario eclesiástico del Perú. Lima, 1947, 1959, 1969, 1974.

Bibliography

Aparicio Vega, Manuel Jesús. *El clero patriota en la revolución de 1814.* Cuzco, 1974.
Aquilino Huamán, Santiago. *La primera historia del movimiento pentecostal en el Perú.* Lima, 1982.
Arévalo, José María. *Los Dominicos en el Perú.* Lima, 1970.
Arróspide de la Flor, César. "Apuntes sobre el apostolado laico en el Perú en las primeras décadas del siglo." Lima, 1977.
———. "La crisis cultural." *V Semana Interamericana de Acción Católica.* Lima, Bartolomé de las Casas.
———. "El movimiento católico seglar en los años 20." *La Revista de la Universidad Católica.* N.s. Vol. 5 (August 1979): 5–24.
———. "Perú." In *El catolicismo contemporáneo en Hispanoamérica,* edited by Richard Pattee, pp. 377–403. Buenos Aires: Editorial Fides, 1951.
Arroyo, Luis. *La Recoleta de Arequipa.* Lima, 1951.
Arzobispado de Lima. *Informe de pastoral y sociología. Misión Conciliar, 1967.* Lima, 1967.
Astiz, Carlos A. "The Catholic Church in the Peruvian Political System." In *Peruvian Nationalism: A Corporatist Revolution,* edited by David Chaplin. New Brunswick, New Jersey: Transaction, Inc., 1976.
———. *Pressure Groups and Power Elites in Peruvian Politics.* Ithaca, New York: Cornell University Press, 1969.
Bahamonde, Wenceslao Oscar. "The Establishment of Evangelical Christianity in Peru (1822–1900)." Ph.D. diss., Hartford, Connecticut: Hartford Seminary, 1952.
Barrenechea y Raygada, Oscar. *Bartolomé Herrera, educador y diplomático peruano (1808–1864).* Buenos Aires, 1940.
Bartra, Enrique. *Tercer Concilio Limense 1582–1583.* Lima: Facultad de Teología Pontificia y Civil, 1982.
———. "Trayectoria histórica de la Facultad de Teología de Lima." In *Libro anual, Facultad de Teología Pontificia y Civil.* Lima, 1971.
Basadre, Jorge. *Elecciones y centralismo en el Perú.* Lima: Universidad del Pacífico, 1980.
———. *Historia de la República del Perú.* 16 vols. Lima: Editorial Universitaria, 1968–1970.
———. "Para la historia de las ideas en el Perú: un esquema histórico sobre el catolicismo ultramontano, liberal y social y democratismo cristiano." *Scientia et Praxis* (Universidad de Lima) 11 (1976): 52–65.
———. *Perú: problema y posibilidad.* 2d ed. Lima: Banco Internacional del Perú, 1978.
Belaunde, Víctor Andrés. *La realidad nacional.* 4th ed. Lima: Banco Internacional, 1980.
———. *Trayectoria y destino: memorias.* 2 vols. Lima: Ediciones Ediventas, 1967.
Beltrán y Rózpide, Ricardo, ed.. *Colección de las memorias o relaciones que escribieron los virreyes del Perú.* Madrid, 1921.
Benza, Gustavo. "Las tierras de los Santos de las comunidades indígenas cusqueñas y los cambios sociales en la región, 1890–1965." Bachelor's thesis. Lima: Universidad Católica, 1983.
Bernoville, Caetan. *Las Hermanas de San José de Tarbes.* Trujillo, Peru, 1962.
Beuzeville, Augusto. "Estadística de la realidad del clero en el Perú." *Libro anual: Facultad de Teología Pontificia y Civil (1971).* Lima, 1971.

Bolo, Salomón. *Cristianismo y liberación nacional.* Lima, 1973.
——. *Cristianismo y marxismo: ¿son compatibles?* Lima, 1973.
Brady, Patrick. "Peru, Revolution, Church, Salvation." *Furrow* 23 (March 1972): 140–52.
Bustamante de la Fuente, Manuel J. *La monja Gutiérrez y la Arequipa de ayer y hoy.* Lima, 1971.
Cabré, Francisco. *Crónica del Primer Congreso Nacional de Terciarios Franciscanos, Lima 3–7 octubre de 1945.* Lima, 1946.
Cabreras, José María. *Las nuevas sectas en el Perú.* Lima, 1983.
Caravedo, Baltazar. "Poder central y descentralización: Perú, 1931." *Apuntes* (Universidad del Pacífico) vol. 9 (1979): 111–29.
Castillo, Hernán, et al. *Chaquicocha: Community in Progress.* Ithaca, New York: Cornell University Press. Series "Socio-Economic Development of Andean Communities." Report No. 5, 1964.
Cateriano, M. A. *Ojeada sobre la vida de Monseñor Juan Gaulberto Valdivia, Deán de Arequipa.* Arequipa, 1884.
Celestino, Olinda, and Albert Meyers. *Las cofradías en el Perú: región central.* Frankfurt/Main: Vervuert, 1981.
Centro de Animación Misionera. *Misioneros combonianos, 40 años en el Perú 1938–1978.* Lima, 1978.
Centro de Estudios de Historia Eclesiástica del Perú. *Monografía de la diócesis de Trujillo.* 3 vols. Trujillo, 1930.
Cleary, Edward L. *Crisis and Change: The Church in Latin America Today.* Maryknoll, New York: Orbis Books, 1985.
(Colegio de la Recoleta). *Almanaque de conmemoración para las bodas de oro, 1893–1943.* Lima, n.d.
Comisión Episcopal de Acción Social (CEAS). *La Justicia en el mundo.* In *Cuadernos de documentación.* Vol. 1. Lima, n.d.
——. *Justicia, un clamor en la selva.* In *Cuadernos de documentación.* Vol. 2.
——. *Participación popular, una visión cristiana.* In *Cuadernos de documentación.* Vol. 6.
——. *Propiedad social.* In *Cuadernos de documentación.* Vol. 4.
Comisión de Reorganización Universitaria. *Informe a la comunidad universitaria.* Arequipa, 1983.
Comité Arquidiocesano del Bicentenario de Túpac Amaru. *Tupac Amaru y la Iglesia. Antología.* Lima: Banco de los Andes Edubanco, 1983.
Concilio Nacional Evangélico del Perú. *Directorio Evangélico: Lima, Callao y Balnearios.* Lima: PROMIES, 1986.
Consejo Episcopal Latinoamericano. *La Evangelización en el presente y en el futuro de América Latina. Documento de consulta a las conferencias episcopales.* Medellín, 1977.
Consejo Nacional de la Universidad Peruana. *Huamanga, una larga historia.* Lima, 1974.
Cornejo Chávez, Héctor. *Socialcristianismo y revolución peruana.* Lima: Ediciones Andinas, 1975.
Costello, Gerald. *Mission to Latin America.* Maryknoll, New York: Orbis Books, 1979.
Crónica del Segundo Congreso Eucarístico Nacional. Arequipa, 1941.
Crónica de los Carmelitas del Perú, llamados de la Antigua Observancia. Lima, 1974.
Curatola, Marco. "Mito y milenarismo en los Andes: del Taki Onqoy a Inkarrí. La visión de un pueblo invicto." *Allpanchis* 10 (1977): 65–92.

Cushner, Nicholas. *Lords of the Land: Sugar, Wine and Jesuit Estates of Coastal Peru, 1600–1767*. Albany, New York: State University of New York Press, 1980.
Dammert Bellido, José. "Acerca de una interpretación histórica." *Histórica* 6 (July 1982): 109–15.
———. "Iglesia y Estado." *Revista Teológica Limense* (Faculty of Theology, Lima) 14, No. 2 (May–August 1980): 131–35.
———. "Luna Pizarro Arzobispo de Lima." *Revista Teológica Limense* 15, No. 2 (May–August 1981): 151–59.
———. "Observaciones al esquema de *Sacerdotio Ministeriali* enviado por la Secretaría del Sínodo de los Obispos." Cajamarca. April 4, 1971. Mimeographed pages (1–21).
Descola, Jean. *La vida cotidiana en el Perú en tiempos de los españoles, 1710–1820*. Buenos Aires: Librería Hachette, 1962.
Delumeau, Jean. *Catholicism Between Luther and Voltaire: A New View of the Counter-Reformation*. Philadelphia: Westminster Press, 1977.
Dietz, Henry A. *Poverty and Problem-Solving under Military Rule: The Urban Poor in Lima, Peru*. Austin: University of Texas, 1980.
Dintilhac, Jorge. *Cómo nació y se desarrolló la Universidad Católica del Perú: 30 años de vida (1917–1946)*. Lima, 1946.
Directorio del Episcopado Peruano, 1984. Lima: Secretaría del Episcopado Peruano, 1984.
Domínguez, Fernando. *El Colegio Franciscano de Propaganda Fide de Moquegua (1775–1825)*. Madrid, 1955.
Doughty, Paul L. "The Interrelationship of Power, Respect, Affection and Rectitude in Vicos." *American Behavioral Scientist* 8 (March 1965): 13–17
———, and Luis Negrón. *Pararín: A Break with the Past*. Cornell University. Series "Socio-Economic Development of Andean Communities." Report no. 6 (1964): 11–14.
Drinot y Piérola, Pedro. *La libertad de cultos y la Acción Social Católica en el Perú*. Huánuco, 1915.
Durand Florez, Ricardo. *Observaciones a teología de la liberación; La fuerza histórica de los pobres*. Callao, 1985.
Dussel, Enrique D. *A History of the Church in Latin America: Colonialism to Liberation (1492–1979)*. Translated and revised by Alan Neely. Grand Rapids, Michigan: Wm. B. Eerdmans Pub. Company, 1981.
Duviols, Pierre. *La lutte contre les religions autochtones dans le Pérou colonial*. Lima: Institut Français d'Etudes Andines, 1971.
Echevarría, Luis Germán. "La Hermandad de San Martín de Porres y San Juan Macías, O.P., del Convento de Santo Domingo de Lima." Bachelor's thesis. Lima: Instituto Superior Pedagógico Marcelino Champagnat, 1985.
Egaña, Antonio de. *Historia de la Iglesia en la América española desde el descubrimiento hasta comienzos del siglo XIX: Hemisferio Sur*. Madrid: Biblioteca de Autores Cristianos, 1966.
Episcopado peruano. *Aporte de la Conferencia Episcopal peruana al Documento de consulta para la Tercera Conferencia General del Episcopado latinoamericano*. Lima, May, 1978.
———. *Mensaje del Episcopado peruano*. Lima, 1891.
Escobar, Gabriel. *Adventistas: organización social y cultural del sur del Perú*. Mexico: Instituto Indigenista Interamericano, 1967.
Esteban, Eustasio. *La Sierva de Dios, Madre Rafaela de la Pasión Veintemilla*. Lima: Sanmartí y Cía., 1938.

Fernández Maldonado, Jorge. "Fuerzas Armadas, cristianismo y revolución en el Perú." *Participación* (August 1973): 4–13.
Flores Galindo, Alberto. *Arequipa en el sur andino, siglos XVIII–XX.* Lima: Editorial Horizonte, 1977.
Ford, Thomas. *Man and Land in Peru.* Gainesville, Florida: University of Florida Press, 1955.
Forrester, Virginia. "Christian Democracy in Peru." Ph.D. diss., New York: Columbia University, 1970.
Foster, George. "Peasant Society and the Image of Limited Good." *American Anthropologist* 67 (April 1965): 293–315.
("Franciscanas Nacionales"). *Madre Clara del Corazón de María.* Lima: Imprenta-Editorial "San Antonio," 1962.
Francke, Marfil. "Situación actual de la mujer peruana y perspectivas para el desarrollo." *Cuadernos CNP* (Consejo Nacional de Población) 2 (December 1983).
Fuentes, Manuel A. *Estadística general de Lima.* Lima, 1858.
———. *Guía histórico-descriptiva administrativa, judicial y de domicilio de Lima.* 2d ed. Lima, 1861.
Gallagher, Mary A. Y. "Imperial Reform and the Struggle for Regional Self-Determination: Bishops, Intendants and Creole Elites in Arequipa, Peru (1784–1816)." Ph.D. diss., New York: City University of New York, 1978.
Ganster, Paul Bentley. "A Social History of the Secular Clergy of Lima during the Middle Decades of the Eighteenth Century." Ph.D. diss., Los Angeles: University of California, 1974.
Garaycoa Hawkins, Hugo. *Primeras relaciones entre la Santa Sede y el Perú.* Roma: Pontificia Universidad Lateranense, 1964.
García Calderón, Francisco. *Diccionario de la legislación peruana.* 2 vols. 2d ed. Lima, 1879.
García y García, Elvira. *La mujer peruana a través de los siglos.* 2 vols. Lima, 1925.
García Jordán, Pilar. "¿Poder eclesiástico frente a poder civil? Algunas reflexiones sobre la Iglesia peruana ante la formación del Estado moderno (1808–1860)." *Boletín Americanista* (Barcelona) 34 (1984): 45–74.
García Rendueles, Manuel, and Aurelio Chumap Lucía. *Duik Múun: universo mítico de los Aguarunas.* 2 vols. Lima: CAAAP, 1979.
Gardiner, Clinton Harvey. *The Japanese and Peru. 1873–1973.* Albuquerque: University of New Mexico Press, 1975.
Garr, Thomas M. *Cristianismo y religión quechua en la prelatura de Ayaviri.* Arequipa: Editorial Miranda, 1972.
General Secretariat of CELAM. *The Church in the Present-Day Transformation of Latin America in the Light of the Council.* 2 vols. Washington, D.C.: Latin American Bureau, United States Catholic Conference, 1970.
Glave, Luis Miguel, and María Isabel Remy. *Estructura agraria y vida rural en una región andina: Ollantaytambo entre los siglos XVI y XIX.* Cuzco: Centro de Estudios Rurales Andinos "Bartolomé de las Casas," 1983.
Golte, Jürgen. *Repartos y rebeliones: Túpac Amaru y las contradicciones de la economía colonial.* Lima: Instituto de Estudios Peruanos, 1980.
González, José Luis, and Teresa María Van Ronzenlen. *Religiosidad popular en el Perú.* Lima: Centro de Estudios y Publicaciones, 1983.
González Prada, Adriana. *Mi Manuel.* Lima: Editorial Cultura Antártica, 1947.

González Prada, Manuel. *Horas de lucha.* Lima: Fondo de Cultura Económica-Ediciones "Futuro," 1964.
———. *Grafitos.* Paris: Tipografía de Louis Bellenand et Fils, 1937.
———. *Propaganda y ataque.* Buenos Aires: Ediciones Imán, 1939.
Gramsci, Antonio. *Selections from the Prison Notebooks of Antonio Gramsci.* Edited and translated by Quintin Hoare and Geoffrey Nowell Smith. London: Lawrence and Wishart, 1971.
Grayson, George W. "The Church and Military in Peru: From Reaction to Revolution." In *Religion and Political Modernization,* edited by Donald Eugene Smith, 303–24. New Haven and London: Yale University Press, 1974.
Gual, Pedro. *Curso de misiones apostólicas, doctrinas y sermones.* 2 vols. Barcelona, 1884.
Guallart, José María. *Fronteras vivas.* Lima: CAAAP, 1981.
Gustavo Gutiérrez. *On Job: God-Talk and the Suffering of the Innocent.* Maryknoll, New York: Orbis Books, 1986.
———. *The Power of the Poor in History.* Maryknoll: Orbis Books, 1983.
———. *A Theology of Liberation. History, Politics and Salvation.* 2d ed. Maryknoll: Orbis Books, 1988.
———. *We Drink From Our Own Wells: The Spiritual Journey of a People.* Maryknoll: Orbis Books, 1984.
Hammett, Brian R. *Revolución y contrarrevolución en México y en Perú: Liberalismo, realeza y separatismo, 1800–1824.* Mexico: Fondo de Cultura Económica, 1978.
Harth-Terré, Emilio. *Negros e indios.* Lima: Mejía Baca, 1973.
Hazen, Dan Chapin. "The Awakening of Puno: Government Policy and the Indian Problem in Southern Peru, 1900–1955." Ph.D. diss., Yale University, 1974.
Heras, Julián. *Los Franciscanos y las misiones populares en el Perú.* Madrid: Editorial Cisneros, 1983.
(Hermanos Maristas). *150 Aniversario: Maristas, 1817–1967.* Lima, 1967.
Herrera, Bartolomé. *Escritos y discursos.* Prologue by Jorge Guillermo Leguía. Lima: Librería Francesa y Científica and Casa Editorial E. Rosay. Vol. 1, 1929. Vol. 2, 1934.
Hombres y cosas: la revolución de 1894–95. Lima, 1901.
Homenaje de la Sociedad Francesa de Beneficencia a sus fundadores, benefactores, presidentes y colaboradores en el primer centenario de su fundación. Lima, 1960.
Huerta, Ambrosio. *Obras de Huerta.* 3 vols. Vargas Ugarte Collection.
Hurtado Galván, Laura. "Cusco, Iglesia y Sociedad: el Obispo Pedro Pascual Farfán de los Godos (1918–1933) en el debate indigenista." Bachelor's thesis. Lima: Universidad Católica, 1982.
Idígoras, José Luis. "Iglesia y Estado en la constitución peruana (1979)." Lima: Centro de Asesoría Pastoral de la Universidad Católicaz, n.d.
———. "La liberación en Puebla." *Revista Teológica Limense* 13, No. 3: 315–44.
———. "La más grande procesión del mundo." *Revista Teológica Limense* 12, No. 1: 67–104.
———. "Reflexión sobre la teología en el Perú." *Revista de la Universidad Católica.* N.s. Vol. 7 (June 1980): 45–80.
———. "Religiosidad popular y marxismo popular." *Revista Teológica Limense* 10, No. 3 (1976): 289–313.

Illich, Ivan. "The Seamy Side of Charity." *America*. January 21, 1967. Pp. 88–91.
Instituto Libertador Ramón Castilla. *Archivo Castilla*. Vol. 5: *Epistolario*. Pp. 157–64.
Instituto Nacional de Estadísticas. *Estimaciones y proyecciones de población*. Lima, April, 1983.
Interdonato, Francisco. *Teología latinoamericana: ¿teología de la liberación?* Bogotá: Ediciones Paulinas, 1978.
Irarrázabal, Diego. *Religión del pobre y liberación en Chimbote*. Lima: Centro de Estudios y Publicaciones, 1978.
Jordán Rodríguez, Jesús. *Pueblos y parroquias del Perú*. 2 vols. Lima, 1950.
Judd, Stephen P. "The Emergent Andean Church: Inculturation and Liberation in Southern Peru, 1968–1986." Ph.D. diss., Berkeley, California: Graduate Theological Union, 1987.
Kantor, Harry. "Catholic Political Parties and Mass Politics in Latin America." In *Religion and Political Modernization*, edited by Donald Eugene Smith, pp. 202–23. New Haven: Yale University Press, 1974.
Kearns, Robert. *Maryknoll Fathers in Peru*. 4 vols. Published privately.
Klaiber, Jeffrey. "Arequipa Católica: La Roma de América." *Debate* 17: 30–33.
———. "The Battle over Private Education in Peru, 1968–1980: An Aspect of the Internal Struggle in the Catholic Church." *Americas* 43, No. 2 (October 1986): 137–58.
———. "The Catholic Lay Movement in Peru, 1867–1959." *Americas* 40, No. 2 (October 1983): 149–70.
———. *Independencia, Iglesia y clases populares*. Lima: Universidad del Pacífico, 1980.
———. "La Escasez de sacerdotes en el Perú: una interpretación histórica." *Histórica* 1 (July 1981): 1–19.
———. "Los Partidos católicos del Perú." *Histórica* 7, No. 2 (December 1983): 157–77.
———. *Religion and Revolution in Peru, 1824–1976*. Notre Dame, Indiana: University of Notre Dame Press, 1977.
———. "El Señor de los Milagros: fe y liberación." *Debate* 11 (November 1981): 70–75.
La Cruz, Juan de. *Monografía del Convento de las Rdas. Madres Carmelitas Descalzas de Trujillo, 1724–1924*. Trujillo, 1924.
La Cruz Espinoza, Anthony de. "Las cofradías de los negros de Lima: una institución colonial en evolución." Bachelor's thesis, Lima: Universidad Católica, 1985.
Lalive d'Epinay, Christian. *Haven of the Masses: A Study of the Pentecostal Movement in Chile*. London: Lutterworth Press, 1969.
Lanning, John Tate. "The Church and the Enlightenment in the Universities." *Americas* 15 (April 1959): 333–49.
Laos, Cipriano. *Lima, la ciudad de los Reyes (El Libro Peruano), 1928–1929*. Lima: Editorial Peru, n.d.
Lassegue, Juan Bautista. *Guía del investigador en el Archivo Arzobispal del Cuzco*. Lima: Fondo del Libro del Banco Industrial del Perú, 1981.
Lebret, Louis-Joseph. *Dinámica concreta del desarrollo*. Barcelona: Editorial Herder, 1966.
Leguía, Jorge Guillermo. *Estudios históricos. Hombres e ideas*. Santiago de Chile: Ediciones Ercilla, 1939.

Lernoux, Penny. *Cry of the People*. New York: Penguin Books, 1982.
Leturia, Pedro de. *Relaciones entre la Santa Sede e Hispanoamérica*. 2 vols. Caracas: Sociedad Bolivariana de Venezuela, 1959–1960.
Lizárraga, Carlos. *En las fuentes del Amazonas: Mons. Jáuregui, obispo, misionero*. Bilbao, 1981.
Linares Málaga, Fausto. *Monseñor Lisson y sus derechos al arzobispado de Lima*. Lima, 1933.
Lituma, Luis. "La Iglesia católica en el Perú en el siglo XX." In *Vision del Peru en el siglo XX*, edited by José Pareja Paz-Soldán. Vol. 2: 473–523. Lima: Ediciones Librería Studium, 1963.
Lohmann Villena, Guillermo. "The Church and Culture in Spanish America." *The Americas* 4 (April 1958): 383–98.
Lopétegui, León. "El Papa Gregorio XIII y la ordenación de mestizos hispano-incaicos." *Miscellánea Historiae Pontificiae* 2: 181–203. Roma, 1943.
———, and Felix Zubillaga; Antonio de Egaña. *Historia de la Iglesia en la América española desde el descubrimiento hasta comienzos del siglo XX. México, América Central, Antillas*. Madrid: Biblioteca de Autores Cristianos, 1965.
López de Romaña, Fernando. *Datos biográficos de Edmundo López de Romaña*. 1973.
Lowenthal, Abraham F.(ed.). *The Peruvian Experiment. Continuity and Change under Military Rule*. Princeton, New Jersey: Princeton University Press, 1975.
Luna Pizarro, Francisco Javier de. *Escritos políticos*. Prologue by Alberto Tauro. Lima: Universidad de San Marcos, 1959.
Luna Victoria, Romeo. *Ciencia y práctica de la revolución. Manual para dirigentes políticos*. Lima: Editorial Studium, 1966.
———. *Por una democracia socialista en el Perú*. Lima: Ediciones Agape, 1978.
———. *El Problema indígena y la tenencia de tierras en el Perú*. Trujillo, 1964.
McAlister, Lyle N. "Social Structure and Social Change in New Spain." *Hispanic American Historical Review* 43, No. 3 (August 1963): 349–70.
Macaulay, Michael G. "Ideological Change and Internal Cleavages in the Peruvian Church: Change, Status Quo and the Priest: The Case of ONIS." Ph.D. diss., University of Notre Dame, 1972.
McCurry, Dan C. "U.S. Church Financed Missions in Peru." In *U.S. Foreign Policy and Peru*, edited by Daniel A. Sharp, 379–415. Austin: University of Texas, 1972.
Macera, Pablo. *Trabajos de historia*. 4 vols. Lima: Instituto Nacional de Cultura, 1977.
McIntire, William J. "Maryknoll and Peruvian Education." *Catholic Mind*. November 1972. Pp. 48–54.
———. "U.S. Labor Policy." In *U.S. Foreign Policy and Peru*, edited by Daniel A. Sharp, 289–336. Austin: University of Texas, 1972.
MacKay, John. *Christianity on the Frontier*. New York: MacMillan, 1950.
———. *The Other Spanish Christ*. London: The Student Christian Movement Press, 1932.
Mac-Lean y Estenós, Roberto. *Sociología del Perú*. Mexico: Universidad Nacional Autónoma de México, 1959.
(Madres del Buen Pastor). *Anales de las religiosas de Nuestra Señora de la Caridad del Buen Pastor de Angers en Lima, 1871–1900*. Lima, 1903.
(Madres de Santa Ana). *Crónica, casas y Provincia Santa Rosa de Lima*. Lima, n.d.

(Madres Ursulinas). *La Barca de Santa Ursula, 1936–1961*. Lima, n.d.
Málaga Medina, Alejandro. *Arequipa: estudios históricos*. Arequipa, 1981.
Maloney, Thomas J. "The Catholic Church and the Peruvian Revolution: Resource Exchange in an Authoritarian Setting." Ph.D. diss., Austin: University of Texas, 1978.
Manzanera, Miguel. *Teología y salvación en la obra de Gustavo Gutiérrez*. Bilbao: Universidad de Deusto, 1978.
Mariátegui, Francisco Javier. *Anotaciones a la Historia Independiente de don Mariano Felipe Paz Soldán*. Lima, 1925.
Mariátegui, José Carlos. *Seven Interpretive Essays on Peruvian Reality*. Austin: University of Texas Press, 1971.
Martín, Luis. *The Intellectual Conquest of Peru: The Jesuit College of San Pablo, 1568–1767*. New York: Fordham University Press, 1968.
———. *The Kingdom of the Sun: A Short History of Peru*. New York: Charles Scribner's Sons, 1974.
Marzal, Manuel. *Los Caminos religiosos de los inmigrantes en la Gran Lima*. Lima: Universidad Católica, 1988.
———. *Estudios sobre religión campesina*. Lima: Universidad Católica, 1977.
———. *El Mundo religioso de Urcos*. Cuzco: Instituto de Pastoral Andina, 1971.
———. "La Religiosidad popular en el Perú." *Iglesia en el Perú* (April 1972): 1–6.
———. *La Transformación religiosa peruana*. 2d ed. Lima: Universidad Católica, 1988.
Matos Mar, José. *Desborde popular y crisis de Estado*. 2d ed. Lima: Instituto de Estudios Peruanos, 1985.
Mecham, J. Lloyd. *Church and State in Latin America: A History of Politico-Ecclesiastical Relations*. 2d ed. Chapel Hill, North Carolina: University of North Carolina, 1966.
Mendoza, Juan. *Nuevo potencial para la educación peruana*. Lima, 1956.
Menéndez Rua, Angel. *Paso a la civilización*. Quillabamba, 1948.
Ministerio de Educación. *Reglamento de centros educativos parroquiales*. Lima, 1977.
Ministerio de Fomento. *Censo de Lima, 1908*. 2 vols. Lima, 1915.
(Ministerio de Justicia). *Memoria que presenta el Ministro de Justicia, Culto, Instrucción y Beneficencia al Congreso ordinario de 1890*. Lima, 1890.
Montes, Fernando. "How the ONIS Movement Began and Grew." *LADOC* 45. Washington, D.C., February, 1974.
Mooney, Mary H., and Walter C. Soderlund. "Clerical Attitudes toward Political Development in Peru." *The Journal of Developing Areas* 12, No. 1 (October 1977): 17–30.
Moreyra, José Ezequiel. "Carta del obispo de Ayacucho, Ezequiel Moreyra al Arzobispo Goyeneche sobre el proyecto de supresión de primicias y derechos parroquiales." Ayacucho, 1867. Vargas Ugarte Collection.
Morimoto, Amelia. *Los Inmigrantes japoneses en el Perú*. Lima: Universidad Nacional Agraria, 1979.
Nieto Vélez, Armando. *Contribución a la historia del fidelismo en el Perú, 1808–1810*. Lima, 1960.
———. "El Derecho a la educación y la legislación peruana en el siglo XIX." Bachelor's thesis. Lima: Universidad Católica, 1956.
———. *Historia del Colegio de la Inmaculada*. Vol. 1. Lima, 1978.

———. "La Iglesia Católica en el Perú." In *Historia del Perú*, edited by Juan Mejia Baca. Vol. 11: *Procesos e instituciones*. Lima, 1980.
———. "Notas sobre la actitud de los obispos frente a la independencia peruana." *Boletín del Instituto Riva-Agüero* 8: 363–73.
Las Obras misionales pontificias. Lima, 1974.
Oficina Nacional de Educación Católica (ONDEC). *Centros educacionales dirigidos por religiosos: estudio de su distribución por diócesis*. Lima, 1971.
———. *Informe sobre el estudio estadístico de los centros educativos de la Iglesia*. Lima, 1982.
Oficina Nacional de Estadística y Censos. *Censos nacionales VII de población II de vivienda*. 2 vols. Lima, 1972.
———. *Censos nacionales VII de población III de vivienda*. 2 vols. Lima, 1981.
Olivas Escudero, Fidel. *Obras de Monseñor Dr. Fidel Olivas Escudero, obispo de Ayacucho*. 6 vols. Lima: Imprenta Comercial de Horacio La Rosa, 1911.
Oliveros, Roberto. *Liberación y teología: génesis y crecimiento de una reflexión, 1966–1976*. 2d ed. Lima: Centro de Estudios y Publicaciones, 1980.
Oquillas, Conrado. *Historia del Colegio Seminario de San Carlos y San Marcelo*. 3 vols. Trujillo, 1925–1928.
Ortega y Gasset, José. *Obras completas*. Vol. 11: *Escritos políticos*. Madrid: Ediciones de la Revista de Occident, 1969.
Ortiz, Dionisio. *Monografía del Vicariato de San Ramón (Chanchamayo)*. Lima, 1979.
———. *Pucallpa y el Ucayali ayer y hoy*. Vol. 1: *1557–1943*. Lima: Editorial Apostolado de la Prensa, 1984.
Pacheco Vélez, César. "Trayectoria histórica de los Jesuitas en el Perú." *Mercurio peruano* 473 (1968): 253–85.
Pardo Gámez de Belaunde, Adela. *Arequipa, su pasado, presente y futuro*. Lima: Imprenta Litográfica del Perú, 1967.
Pareja Paz-Soldán, José. (ed.). *Visión del Perú en el siglo XX*. 2 vols. Lima: Ediciones Librería Studium, 1963.
Pásara, Luis. *Radicalización y conflicto en la Iglesia peruana*. Lima: Ediciones El Virrey, 1986.
Paz-Soldán, Carlos Enrique. *Vida y obras de Sor Rosa Larrabure*. Lima: Imprenta de San Marcos, 1963.
Paz-Soldán, Mariano. *Historia del Perú independiente*. Le Havre, 1874.
Peirano, Luis (ed.). *Educación y comunicación popular en el Perú*. Lima: DESCO, 1985.
Pietschmann, Horst. "Burocracia y corrupción en Hispanoamérica colonial." *Nova Americana* 5 (1982): 1–37.
Pike, Fredrick B. "Catholic Church and Modernization in Peru and Chile." *Journal of Inter-American Affairs* 20 (1966): 272–88.
———. "Heresy, Real and Alleged in Peru: An Aspect of the Conservative-Liberal Struggle, 1830–1875." *Hispanic American Historical Review* 47 February 1967): 50–74.
———. "La Iglesia en Latinoamérica. De la Independencia a nuestros días." In *Nueva historia de la Iglesia*, edited by L. J. Rogier, R. Aubert, M. D. Knowles. Vol. 5: *La Iglesia en el mundo moderno*. Madrid: Ediciones Cristiandad, 1984.
———. *The Modern History of Peru*. New York: Frederick A. Praeger, 1967.
———. "The Modernized Church in Peru." *Review of Politics* 26 (July 1964): 307–18.

---. "Religion, Collectivism, and Intrahistory: The Peruvian Ideal of Dependence." *Journal of Latin American Studies* 10, part 2 (November 1978): 239–62.

---. "South America's Multifaceted Catholicism: Glimpses of Twentieth-Century Argentina, Chile and Peru." In *The Church and Social Change in Latin America*, edited by Henry Landsberger. Notre Dame: University of Notre Dame Press, 1970.

Podestá, Bruno. *Pensamiento político de González Prada.* Lima: Instituto Nacional de Cultura, 1975.

Ponce, Jaime, and Daniel Roach. *Los Maryknoll en el Perú: estudio de opiniones y actitudes.* La Paz: Instituto Boliviano de Estudios y Acción Social, 1968.

Pontificia Universidad Católica. *Decreto Ley no. 17437 sobre régimen de la Universidad Peruana: opinión de la Universidad Católica.* Lima, 1969.

---. *Plan de desarrollo y funcionamiento, 1985–1986.* Lima, 1985.

---. *Política: deber cristiano.* Lima: Ediciones Librería Studium, 1963.

Portal, Ismael. *Lima religiosa (1525–1924).* Lima, 1924.

Prado y Ugarteche, Javier. *Estado social del Perú durante la dominación española.* Lima, 1941.

Prien, Hans-Jürgen. *La Historia del cristianismo en América Latina.* Salamanca: Ediciones Sígueme, 1985. 1st ed. in German in 1978.

Primer Congreso Católico del Perú, 1896. Published by Sra. Jesús Iturbide de Piérola. Lima, 1897.

Primer Congreso Interdiocesano de Acción Social. Cuzco, 1922.

Primer Congreso Nacional de Acción Católica. Lima, 1958.

Primov, George. "Aymara-Quechua Relations in Puno." In *Class and Ethnicity in Peru*, edited by K. Ishwaran. Leiden: E. J. Brill, 1974.

Provincia franciscana de los Doce Apóstoles del Perú, sus conventos y personal, año 1942. Lima, 1942.

Quintana, Francisco de A. *Tercera Orden Franciscana: Album del Congreso Terciario-Franciscano celebrado en Ocopa en los días 31 de julio al 5 de agosto de 1936.* Lima, 1936.

Rada y Gamio, Pedro José. *El Arzobispo Goyeneche: Apuntes para la historia del Perú.* Roma: Imprenta Políglota Vaticana, 1917.

Recavarren, Margarita María. "Los primeros cincuenta años de la Escuela Normal de Mujeres y su rol en el panorama educativo nacional." Bachelor's thesis, Lima: Universidad de San Marcos, 1974.

Regan, Jaime. *Hacia la tierra sin mal.* 2 vols. Iquitos: CETA, 1983.

Rénique, José Luis. "Los descentralistas arequipeños en la crisis del 30." *Allpanchis* 12 (1979): 51–78.

"República del Perú." *Diccionario encyclopédico de la masonería* 3 (1889): 364–65.

Rey de Castro López de Romaña, Jaime (ed.). *Testimonio de una generación: los social cristianos.* Lima: Universidad del Pacífico, 1985.

Riva-Agüero, José de la. *Obras completas.* Vol. 11: *Escritos políticos.* Lima: Publicaciones del Instituto Riva-Agüero, 1975.

---. *Por la verdad, la tradición y la patria.* Lima, 1937.

Rodríguez González, Yolanda. "Una aproximación al estudio del protestantismo en el Perú." Bachelor's thesis. Lima: Universidad Católica, 1984.

Romero de Iguíñiz, Catalina. "Cambios en la relación Iglesia-sociedad en el Perú: 1958–1978." *Revista Debates en Sociología* (Universidad Católica). Vol. 7: 115–41.

Romero, Emilio. *3 Ciudades del Perú*. Lima: Imprenta Torres Aguirre, 1929.
Romero San Martín, María Elvira. "El Protestantismo anglo-sajón en el Perú, 1822–1915." Bachelor's thesis. Lima: Universidad Católica, 1974.
Rubio, David A. "The Present State of Catholicism in Peru." *Catholic Historical Review* 36, No. 2 (July 1940): 67–182.
Rubio de Hernández, Rosa Luisa. "Acerca de las relaciones entre la Iglesia y el Estado peruano: presentación y documentos." *Revista de la Universidad Católica*. N.s. No. 7 (June 1980): 109–35.
Sáiz, Odorico. *De Ruina ac restauratione in peruvia collegiorum franciscalium Propagandae Fidei Saec. XIX, 1824–1860*. Lima, 1972.
———, and Julián Heras. *La Provincia Misionera de San Francisco Solano del Perú*. 2d ed. Madrid, 1977.
Salazar Bondy, Augusto. *Historia de las ideas en el Perú contemporáneo*. 2 vols. Lima: Francisco Moncloa, 1965.
Sánchez, Luis Alberto. *Balance y liquidación del novecientos*. 4th ed. Lima: Editorial Universo, 1973.
———. *Testimonio personal*. 4 vols. Lima: Ediciones Villarán, 1969. Vol. 4: Mosca Azul, 1976.
Sánchez Arjona, Rodrigo. *La Religiosidad popular católica en el Perú*. Lima, 1981.
Sánchez López, Zoila Luz. "Importancia de la labor educativa realizada por los Jesuitas en el período colonial." Bachelor's thesis. Lima: Universidad de San Marcos, 1974.
Santa Teresa, Basilio de. *El Monasterio del Carmen de la Ciudad de los Reyes (1643–1943)*. Lima, 1943.
Secretaría General del Episcopado del Perú. *Documentos del Episcopado, 1968–1977*. Lima: Editorial Apostolado de la Prensa, 1977.
———. *Primera Semana Social del Perú: exigencias sociales del catolicismo en el Perú*. Lima, 1959.
Secretariado Latinoamericano MSC. *MSC en Latinoamérica*. Lima: Misioneros del Sagrado Corazón, 1978.
Segunda Semana Social del Perú: la propiedad. Lima: Comité Permanente de las Semanas Sociales del Perú, 1962.
Segundo, Juan Luis, Ricardo Cetrulo, Juan José Rossi, and Dora Mastieri. *Iglesia latinoamericana, ¿protesta o profecía?* Avellaneda, Argentina: Ediciones Búsqueda, 1969.
Segundo Congreso Iberoamericano de Estudiantes Católicos. Lima, 1941.
(Seminario Santo Toribio). *Exámenes anuales del Seminario Conciliar de Santo Toribio*. Lima, 1880.
Servants of the Immaculate Heart of Mary. *Forty Years in Peru, 1922–1962*. Lima, n.d.
Smith, Brian. "Religion and Social Change: Classical Theories and New Formulations in the Context of Recent Developments in Latin America." *Latin American Research Review* 10 (Summer 1975): 3–34.
Sparks Miró-Quesada, María Consuelo. "The Role of the Clergy during the Struggle for Independence in Peru." Ph.D. diss., University of Pittsburgh, 1972.
Stanger, Francis Merriman. "Church and State in Peru." *Hispanic American Historical Review* 8 (August 1927): 410–37.
Steidel, James Norval. "Renewal in the Latin American Church: A Study of the Peruvian Dioceses of Cajamarca and Ica." Ph.D. diss., Los Angeles: University of Southern California, 1975.

Stepan, Alfred. *The State and Society: Peru in Comparative Perspective.* Princeton, New Jersey: Princeton University Press, 1978.
Stern, Steve. *Peru's Indian Peoples and the Challenge of Spanish Conquest: Huamanga to 1640.* Madison: University of Wisconsin Press, 1982.
Stevenson, William Benet. *A Historical and Descriptive Narration of Twenty Year's Residence in South America.* 2 vols. London: Hurst, Robinson and Co., 1825.
Steward, Watt. *Chinese Bondage in Peru: A History of the Chinese Coolie in Peru, 1849–1874.* Durham, North Carolina: Duke University Press, 1951.
Stiglich, Fernando. *Relaciones Estado-Iglesia en el Perú.* Lima, 1959.
Stoll, David. *Fishers of Men or Founders of Empire? The Wycliffe Bible Translators in Latin America.* London: Zed Press, 1982.
Tamayo Herrera, José. *Historia del indigenismo cuzqueño, siglos XVI–XX.* Lima: Instituto Nacional de Cultura, 1980.
Taurel, Raphael María. *Colección de obras del clero contemporáneo del Perú.* 2 vols. Paris, 1853.
Tauro, Alberto (ed.). *Viajeros en el Perú republicano.* Lima: Universidad de San Marcos, 1967.
Tibesar, Antonine. "The *Alternativa*: A Study in Spanish-Creole Relations in Seventeenth-Century Peru." *Americas* 11 (January 1955): 229–83.
———. "Introducción: La conquista del Perú y su frontera oriental." In Manuel Biedma, O.F.M., *La Conquista franciscana del Alto Ucayali.* Lima: Editorial Milla Batres, 1981.
———. "The Lima Pastors, 1750–1820: Their Origins and Studies as Taken from their Autobiographies." *Americas* 28 (July 1971): 39–56.
———. "The Peruvian Church at the Time of Independence in the Light of Vatican II." *Americas* 26 (April 1970): 349–75.
———. "Raphael María Taurel, Papal Consul General in Lima, Peru, in 1853. Report on Conditions in Peru." *Revista Interamericana de Bibliografía.* (April 1981): 36–69.
———. "The Suppression of the Religious Orders in Peru, 1826–1830, or The King Versus the Peruvian Friars: The King Won." *Americas* 39 (October 1982): 205–39.
Tovar, Cecilia, (ed.). *Dos obispos del Sur Andino: Luis Vallejos y Luis Dalle: en el corazón de su pueblo.* Lima: Centro de Estudios y Publicaciones, 1982.
Tovar y R., Enrique D. *El Apóstol de Ica, Fr. José Ramón Rojas (el Padre Guatemala).* Lima, 1943.
Tovar, Manuel. *Obras.* Lima, 1904–1907. 2 vols.
Ulloa, Alberto. *Don Nicolás de Piérola.* 2d ed. Lima: Editorial Minerva, 1981.
Un glorioso centenario: breve reseña histórica de la actuación de los Misioneros Hijos del Inmaculado Corazón de María en el Perú, con motivo del primero centenario de la congregación claretiana, 1849–1949. Lima, 1949.
Un sacerdote cuzqueño. *El Clero del Cuzco durante la administración del Iltmo. y Rdmo. Señor Obispo D.D. Juan Antonio Falcón.* Cusco, 1904. Vargas Ugarte Collection.
Uriel García, José. *El Nuevo indio.* Lima: Editorial Universo, 1970.
Valcárcel, Luis. *Tempestad en los Andes.* Lima: Editorial Universo, 1972.
Valentín, Eugenio. *Madre Teresa del Sagrado Corazón (1856–1950).* Burgos, 1978.
Vallier, Ivan. *Catholicism, Social Control, and Modernization in Latin America.* Englewood Cliffs, N.J.: Prentice-Hall, Inc., 1970.

Bibliography 407

Vargas, Isaías. *La Democracia auténtica*. Cuzco, 1947.
Vargas Ugarte, Rubén. *El Episcopado en los tiempos de la emancipación sudamericana*. 2d ed. Lima, 1962.
———. *Historia de la Iglesia en el Perú*. 5 vols. Burgos, 1962.
———. *Historia de la Ilustre Congregación de seglares de N.S. de la O*. Lima: Milla Batres, 1973.
———. *Historia del Santo Cristo de los Milagros*. 3d ed. Lima, 1966.
———. *Historia del Seminario de Santo Toribio de Lima (1591–1900)*. Lima, 1969.
———. *El Real Convictorio Carolino y sus dos luminares*. Lima: Milla Batres, 1970.
———. "Situación jurídica de la Compañía de Jesús en el Perú." Lima, Archives of the Society of Jesus, n.d.
———. *Un gravísimo problema nacional*. Lima, 1948. 2d ed. in 1966.
Varón, Rafael. "Cofradías de indios y poder local en el Perú colonial: Huaraz, siglo XVII." *Allpanchis* 17, No. 20 (1982): 127–42.
Véliz, Claudio. *The Centralist Tradition of Latin America*. Princeton, New Jersey: Princeton University Press, 1980.
Vernet, Féliz. *Dom Gréa (1828–1917)*. Paris, 1937.
Vicente Hondarza: vivir y morir por los pobres. Lima: Centro de Estudios y Publicaciones, 1984.
Vidaurre, Manuel Lorenzo de. *Plan del Perú*. Philadelphia, 1823.
———. *Proyecto de un código penal*. Boston: Hiram Tupper, 1828.
Vigil, Francisco de Paula Gonzalez. *Defensa de la autoridad de los gobiernos y de los obispos contra las pretensiones de la Curia romana*. 6 vols. Lima: Imprenta Jose Huidobro Molina, 1848–1849.
Villa Cerri, José. "Clérigos Regulares, Ministros de los Enfermos, Religiosos Camilos, celebrando el IV centenario." *Conferencia de Religiosos del Perú, Boletín especial*. 52 (1982): 7–16.
Villarán, Manuel Vicente. *Estudios sobre la educación nacional*. Lima, 1922.
Villarejo, Avencio. *Los Agustinos en el Perú y Bolivia, 1548–1965*. Lima, 1965.
Villegas, Juan. *Aplicación del Concilio de Trento en hispanoamérica, 1564–1600: Provincia eclesiástica del Perú*. Montevideo: Instituto Teológico del Uruguay, 1975.
(The Vincentians). *125 años en el Perú: Hijas de la Caridad y Padres Vicentinos*. Lima, 1983.
Wiarda, Howard J.(ed.). *Politics and Social Change in Latin America: The Distinct Tradition*. Amherst: The University of Massachusetts Press, 1974.
———. "Toward a Framework For the Study of Political Change in the Iberic-Latin Tradition: The Corporative Model." *World Politics* 25, No. 2 (January 1973): 206–35.
Yonekawa, Urbain-Marie. *Lumière nippone au Perou*. 2 vols. Quebec: Aux Editions Franciscaines, 1959.
Zevallos, Noé. *Toribio Rodríguez de Mendoza*. Lima: Editorial Bruño, n.d.
Zevini, Giorgio. "La Iniciación cristiana de adultos en las comunidades neocatecumenales." *Concilium* 42 (February 1979): 240–48.

Index

Abreu, Manuel, 210
Adventists, 21, 94–95, 355–56 *See* Protestantism
Alarco, Gerardo, 210–12, 214, 220, 231–32, 235, 237–38, 240, 242, 304
Alayza Grundy, Ernesto, 170, 210–12, 231–32, 235, 237, 244, 251
Alayza Grundy, Jorge, 236–37, 257
Alayza, Ernesto, 282
Alayza y Paz Soldán, Luis, 150, 168
Albacete, Juan, 210, 235
Alfaro, Eloy, 124, 155
Allison, Cargín, 210, 214, 220, 242
Allpanchis, 323
Alternativa, 12, 42
Althaus, Miguel de, 281
Alvarez, Ricardo, 327
Alvarez Calderón, Carlos, 246, 274, 293
Alvarez Calderón, Jorge, 246, 260, 274, 279–80, 307, 331
Alvarez Calderón, María, 213
Alvarez Salas, Carmen, 154
Alzamora, Mario, 232
Alzamora, Oscar, 352
Amat y Junient, 17
Amat y León, Carlos, 281
Amazónic Center of Applied Pastoral Anthropology (CAAAP), 326–28
Ames, Rolando, 281–82
Amézaga, Carlos, 73
Amézaga, Juana, 76
Amézaga, Mariano, 76
Ampuero, Valentín, 49, 53, 94, 123, 186, 192–93
anarchists, 20, 59, 172, 191
Andean Pastoral Institute, 313, 322–24, 355
Antoncich, Ricardo, 246, 274, 281–82, 307, 315
APRA (Aprista Party), 24–25, 73, 137, 159, 168, 172, 191, 207–8, 214–16, 218, 220–23, 225, 227–28, 233–34, 241–42, 246, 249, 252, 258–59, 283–84, 353
Araoz, María R., 238, 255, 266
Araraz, Josefina, 230
Arce, Mariano José de, 62, 74, 143, 224

Arenas y Loayza, Carlos, 81, 159, 170, 210, 214–21, 231
Arguedas, José María, 306
Ariz, Javier, 314
Armendáriz, José Pérez de, 1
Arróspide, César, 210–11, 214, 220, 232, 235–39, 243–44, 246, 249, 257, 281, 304
Arrupe, Pedro, 350
Artola, Armando, 33, 293–95, 320
Ascondo, Pablo, 111
Asiatics, 96–97, 173–75
Association of Mary Immaculate, 311
Atusparia, 200–201
Augustinian Daughters of the Most Holy Savior, 120–21
Augustinians, 43, 103, 105, 129, 131–33, 139–40, 145, 166–67, 272, 325–28, 378
Avalo Chauca, José, 55
Avalos, Teresa, 341
Ayala, Plácido, 169, 211
Ayllón, José Jesús, 69

Baella, Alfonso, 212, 242
Baldo, Luis, 124, 292
Ballivián, José, 146
Ballón, Manuel, 69
Balta, José, 117, 148
Bambarén, Carolina, 77
Bambarén, Celso, 77
Bambarén, Luis, 33, 151, 248, 254, 276, 282, 294–96, 314, 316, 320–21
Bandini, Manuel T., 39, 66, 83, 141, 158
Bartolomé de las Casas Center (Lima), xi, 306, 355
Bartolomé de las Casas Center for Rural Andean Studies, 323–24
Bartra, Enrique, 288, 314–15, 370
Basadre, Jorge, 359–60
Bastos, Eduardo, 345
"Beata de Humay," 91
Bedoya Reyes, Luis, 212, 243, 248–51
Belaúnde, Fernando, 29, 212, 223, 251, 258, 353–54, 359
Belaúnde, Javier, 249–50

409

410 Index

Belaúnde, Mariano, 78–79, 83, 89, 223
Belaunde, Rafael, 74, 212–13, 218, 221, 223
Belaunde, Víctor Andrés, 24, 72, 74, 89, 99, 109, 123, 137, 140, 150, 168, 177, 208, 210–11, 215, 218–29, 231–33, 235
Bellido de Dammert, Rebeca, 213, 237–38
Benavides, Oscar, 122, 221, 235, 243
Benedictines, 271–72, 320
Benvenutto, Pedro, 231
Bernales, Enrique, 281
Berroa, Vitalino, 88, 265
Bethlemites, 112–13, 378
Beuzeville, Augusto, 321, 354
Bielich, Ismael, 157, 170, 210, 236–37
Boff, Leonardo, 303
Bolaños, Jorge, 238, 250
Bolívar, Simón, 42, 45, 136
Bolo, Salomón, 259
Borda, Armando, 330
Bottaro, José María, 110
Boulard, Fernando, 260
Bourbons, 6–7, 12, 42
Breña, Guido, 352
Brotherhood of Workers, 331
Burke, James, 271
Bustamante, Juan, 199
Bustamante y Barreda, Manuel, 78
Bustamante de la Fuente, Manuel, 220–21
Bustamante y Rivero, José Luis, 74, 79, 148, 150, 157, 209–10, 220, 249–50, 254
Busto, Jorge del, 232, 249

Cabré, Francisco, 85, 111, 213
Cabrejos, Héctor Miguel, 111
Cáceres, Andrés, 78, 83, 149, 153
Cáceres, Róger, 250
Caldera, Rafael, 232, 248
Calderón, Jesús, 322
Camacho, Augusto, 241, 257
Camacho, Enrique, 274, 333
Cámara, Helder, 253, 278, 313
Camillians (Fathers of a Good Death, Ministers of the Sick), 43, 112, 120, 126, 133, 162
Caminada, Juan, 315
Candamo de Puente, Virginia, 213
Canonesses of the Cross, 126–27, 231
Canons Regulars, 124, 126
Cantuarias, Teresa, 148
Capestany, Esther, 314, 341
Cappa, Ricardo, 77, 149
Carassa, Francisco and Virginia, 114

Carboni, Rómulo, 264, 273, 293, 340
Cárdenas, Héctor de, 329–30
Cardijn, Joseph, 241
Cáritas, 28, 33, 255, 267
Carmelites, 121–22, 126, 133, 161–62, 270–71, 323, 332
Carpenter, José María, 89
Carrera, Ermelinda, 111, 154
Casaroli, Agostino, 263
Casimir, Cipriano, 124, 126
Casós, Fernando, 144
Castañeda y Coello, Rosa Mercedes de, 157–58
Castelló, María de la Pasión, 122
Castilla, Ramón, 7, 19–20, 47, 63–64, 66, 97, 136, 147, 174
Catechetical School, 334
catechumenate, 36, 329, 331–32
Catholic Action, 11, 22, 24–26, 28, 33, 35, 93, 100–111, 123, 148, 159, 168, 170, 208–213, 217–18, 233, 235–44, 246–47, 250–51, 257–58, 261–62, 304, 331, 351, 361
Catholic Congress, 74, 80, 82–84, 121, 208
Catholic parties, 85–88, 101, 213–22, 229
Catholic press, 69–70, 79, 81, 85, 88–89, 199, 214, 238, 242, 265, 267, 274, 323, 354–55
Catholic Society, 65, 70
Catholic Union, 74, 76, 77–81, 83–84, 86–87, 93–94, 126, 156, 208–10, 214, 235–37
Catholic University of Peru, 22, 24, 157, 160, 164, 195, 218, 221, 225, 27, 229–32, 237, 294, 304–8, 311, 332, 348–52, 355
Catholic Youth Students (JEC), 240, 250
CEAS (See Episcopal Commission of Social Action)
CELADEC (Latin American Evangelical Commission For Christian Education), 355, 357
CELAM (Permanent Council of the Latin American Bishops), 245, 253–54, 259–60, 277–79, 311–12, 314, 317
CEP (Centro de Estudios y Publicaciones), xi, 306, 355
CETA (Center for Theological Studies of the Amazon), 326–27, 355
Chapi, Our Lady of, 16, 91, 203
charismatic renewal, 36, 301–2, 329–33
Charún, Guillermo, 45, 64, 65

Index

Chávez, Juan, 96
Chávez de la Rosa, Pedro José, 13, 43
Chesterton, Gilbert Keith, 25, 211
Chirinos Soto, Enrique, 250
Choice, 36, 328, 333–34
"Christian democracy," 28, 214–16, 222, 285
Christian Democratic Party, 26, 28, 170, 209, 212, 222, 239–40, 243, 248–52, 258, 283–85 *See* Christian democracy
Christian Family Movement, 28, 236, 262, 344
Christian Life Community (CLC), 328–30
Christian Teaching Teams, 331
Christian Worker's Movement, 307, 331 *See* Circle for Catholic Workers, Young Christian Workers
Church-State relations, colonial times, 12–14; Republic, 19–20, 23, 47, 97–99, 153, 213–14; Velasco, 30–31, 283–90, 292, 294–98; post-Velasco, 34, 300, 314, 344–45, 348–49, 353–354 *See* Catholic parties
Cicognani, Cayetano, 97, 100
Cipriani, Juan Luis, 310
CIRCA (Catholic Circles), 321–22
Circle for Catholic Workers, 84–85, 195, 209, 233, 241
Cisneros, Beatriz, 148, 231
Cisneros, Manuel, 70
Claretians, 124–25, 133, 144, 166
Columbans, 27, 265, 268–69, 320, 339
Comblin, Joseph, 303
Comboni Fathers, 265–66, 355
El Comercio, 72–73, 99, 199, 214, 222, 250, 288, 297, 344
Communion and Liberation, 330
Conciliar Mission of Lima, 57, 260, 320
Conference of Religious, 245, 314, 340–41
Confraternities, 16, 183, 191, 202–6, 215–16, 335 *See* Lord of Miracles
Congar, Ives, 26
Considine, John, 264
Consortium of Catholic Schools, 288, 342–47
Constantín, Carlos María, 159
Cornejo, Mariano, 153
Cornejo, Mario, 293
Cornejo Chávez, Héctor, 170, 243, 246, 249–51, 297
Cornejo Polar, Jorge, 238
Correa Elías, Javier, 170, 210, 237, 249
Corso, José María, 218–19
Corvacho, Moisés, 217

Cox, Harvey, 27
Crespo, Luis Fernando, 279, 306, 329
Cuadros, Jorge, 330, 341
Cubero, Carmen, 341
Cushing, Richard, 27, 263–64, 269
Cussiánovich, Alejandro, 274, 280, 293
Cursillos de Cristiandad, 28, 262, 281, 283, 303, 328–29

Dalle, Luis, 322, 324
Dam, Christian, 73
Dammert Bellido, José, 28, 51, 56, 170, 231, 237–38, 244, 246–47, 254–55, 257–58, 260–61, 278, 296, 304, 352–53
Danielou, Jean, 26
Daughters of Charity, 112, 114–17, 123, 126, 133–34, 155
Daughters of Mary, 93
Daughters of Saint Anne, 118–19, 167
El Deber, 89, 214, 216, 218, 223, 242, 354
De la Cruz Sardinas, Alfonso, 154
De la Torre, Zoila Victoria, 80
Delgado, César, 282
Delgado, Santiago, 258
Delrán, Guido, 323
de Lubac, Henri, 26, 304
Del Valle, Teodoro, 46, 59, 65, 69–70, 148, 155
Denegri Luna, Félix, 232
Deustua, Alejandro, 153
diaconate, permanent, 329, 334
Díaz-Mateos, Manuel, 307
Diharce, Carlos, 327
Dintilhac, Jorge, 85, 210, 225, 227, 230–31, 350
Dolan, Robert, 330
Dominicans, 43, 89, 96, 103, 105 131–34, 139–40, 145, 156, 158, 161–63, 208, 241, 260, 325–28, 333, 335, 341, 350, 354–55
Dormier, Cleonisa du, 147
Drinot y Piérola, Pedro Pablo, 53, 90, 209–10
Dugenne de Cebrián, Rosina, 213, 238
Duhamel, Hipólito, 123, 140, 143, 168, 223
Dumont, Juan, 331
Durand, Ricardo, 151, 278, 288, 314, 316, 323, 345
Dussel, Enrique, 303

Echegaray, Enrique, 237
Echegaray, Hugo, 306, 330
Echenique, José Rufino, 19, 66, 74, 136
Eguiguren, Luis Antonio, 150

Elías, Carlos, 78, 83, 170
Elías, Domingo, 141
Elorza, Martín, 132
EMO-Callao, 315–16
Episcopal Commission of Social Action (CEAS), 282, 286, 289, 296, 354
Espinoza, Antonio, 212
Espinoza, Oscar, 282
Estéban, Eustacio, 105, 121, 145
eucharistic congress, 104, 197, 234–35, 241
Ezequiel Moreyra, José, 48–49, 53, 69

Faculty of Theology, 311, 348, 341, 348
Faith and Solidary Action, 281
Falcón, Juan Antonio, 69
Farfán, Pedro Pascual, 24, 86–87, 99, 121, 161–62, 188–90, 194–98, 207, 211, 217, 221, 233–35
Fedders, Edward, 266, 323
Fernández Castañeda, José Luis, 341
Fernández Maldonado, Jorge, 283, 296
Ferrero Rabagliati, Raúl, 157, 231–32
Ferrero, Rómulo, 257
Fe y Alegría schools, 122, 127, 150, 321, 347
Fides Center, 211–12, 214, 238, 242
Figari, Luis Fernando, 311
Fitzgerald, Michael, 384
Franciscans, 9, 42–43, 46, 56, 69, 89, 97, 103, 105–112, 122, 129–34, 140, 163, 167, 201, 233, 252, 303, 325–27
Franciscans of the Immaculate Conception, 122
Franciscans ("National") of the Immaculate Conception, 154, 165
Franciscan Missionaries of Mary, 130, 133, 341
Franciscan Sisters of Christian Charity, 163
Franco, Francisco, 25, 232, 285, 310
Frasnelli, Dante, 271
Frei, Eduardo, 232, 248
Freire, Paulo, 32, 287
Fuentes, Manuel A., 57, 76, 113–14

Gago, José María, 106
Gallicanism, 42–43
Gálvez, José, 141
Gálvez, Pedro, 66–67, 141
Gamarra, Agustín, 63, 66
Gandolfo, Carlos, 248–49, 281
Garatea, Gastón, 279, 341
Garaycoa, Hugo, 314, 352
García, Joaquín, 326–27
García, Melchor, 149

García Irigoyen, Carlos, 81, 126, 181, 186–87, 205–6
García Naranjo, Pedro Manuel, 39, 124–25
Garrity, Thomas, 267, 334
Gazcón, Dominga, 96
Giesecke, Albert, 195
Gobert, Nicolás, 341
Golconda, 280
Gómez, Evaristo, 78, 141
González, Bernardino, 111
González, Julio, 294
González de la Rosa, Manuel, 69
González Prada, Manuel, 21, 62, 71–73, 75–76, 82, 94, 136, 138–39, 176, 191, 359
Good Shepherd Sisters, 117–18, 134, 138–39, 155, 167
Goyeneche, José Sebastián, 1, 19, 45, 48, 63–64, 74, 105, 117, 233
Goyeneche, Marquise of, 127
Granda, José María, 330
Gremillion, Joseph, 278
Griffith, Harold, 274, 279
Gros, Francoise, 97, 116
Grotons, Milagro, 122
Gual, Pedro, 46, 69, 105, 107–9, 157
Guallart, José María, 150, 327
Guerrero, Vicente, 260
Guevara, "Che", 29
Guevara, Juan Gualberto, 27, 89, 181, 212, 218, 224, 245, 252, 268
Guillén, Juan José, 123
Gutiérrez, Armando, 239
Gutiérrez, Dominga, 43
Gutiérrez, Gustavo, 32, 238, 240, 246–47, 274, 278–79, 293, 303–7, 313, 315, 318–19, 329, 332, 351

Haby, Gerald, 311
Handmaids of the Sacred Heart, 127
Hansen, Theo, 315
Haya de la Torre, Víctor Raúl, 73, 80, 85, 87, 95, 100–101, 137, 144, 195, 207–8, 216, 220, 223, 258 See APRA
Hayes, Nevin, 271, 323
Hernáez, Javier, 76, 148
Herrera, Bartolomé, 19–20, 45–46, 55, 64–69, 101, 136, 138, 140–41, 147, 208, 224, 227, 230
Herrera, Gonzálo, 88, 214, 220
Herrera, Rodrigo, 81
Herrera, Salvador, 112, 162, 266
Hinojosa, Erasmo, 89,
Hispanism, 25, 66, 228–29, 232 See Riva-Agüero

Index 413

Holguín, Mariano, 24, 84–87, 99, 111, 207, 218, 221, 233, 235
Hooij, Rafael, 255
Hornedo, Antonio, 151
Huerta, José, 69
Huerta, Juan Ambrosio, 39, 46, 48, 65, 69, 74, 92–93, 98, 194, 198–99, 224
Hugues, Juan, 323
Huidobro, Emilio, 88

Idígoras, José Luis, 274, 356
Illich, Ivan, 58, 273–74, 287, 305
Iluminato de la Riva Liguri, 255–56
Immaculate Heart of Mary sisters, 160–61, 163–66, 342
Inmaculada, Colegio de la, 77, 137–38, 149–50, 157, 164, 166, 168, 169–170, 210, 295
Inquisition, 2, 10–12, 17
Institute of Rural Education, 261
Institute of Aymara Studies, 323
Izuzquiza, Santiago, 334

Jara y Ureta, José María de la, 81, 220
Jaro, Benito, 127, 213
Jáuregui, Atanasio, 132
Jaworski, Helan, 282
Jesuits, 2, 7, 9, 12, 22, 42, 47, 77–80, 92–93, 103, 125–27, 133, 137–43, 146–52, 156–59, 166–69, 223, 235, 283, 304, 307, 320–21, 325–330, 333, 341–42, 350, 355–56 *See* Inmaculada, Colegio de la
Jiménez Borja, José, 145, 232
John XXIII, 26–27, 244, 246, 259, 263, 269, 272, 276–77, 282
John Paul II, 312–13, 318, 357, 359–60, 363
Judge, Catalina, 341
Jurgens, Carlos María, 124, 258, 292
"Justice in the World," 289–90

Kaiser, Federico, 128
Kearns, Robert, 266–67
Kenard, Frank, 269
Kennedy, John, 245, 269, 272
Koenigsknecht, Albert, 322, 324–25
Kühner, Antonio, 265

La Cruz Calienes, Juan, 111
La Cruz Candamo, Teresa, 124, 126–27
La Fay, Michael, 332
Landázuri Ricketts, Juan, 27, 110–11, 240, 245, 247–48, 252–55, 259, 278, 283, 285, 293, 295, 305, 309, 314, 346, 352, 354

Larrabure, Rosa, 116
Larraín, Manuel, 239, 253, 278
La Salle, Brothers of, 158–60, 167–68, 231, 341
Las Heras, Bartolomé, 1
Lassegue, Juan Bautista, 323
Lastarria, José Victorino, 113–14
Lauri, Lorenzo, 126
Lawler, John, 266
Lazo, Benito, 126
LeBon, Gustave, 71
Lebret, Louis-Joseph, 28, 208, 248–49
Lecocq, Francisco Javier, 159
Legion of Mary, 281, 334–35
Leguía, Augusto B., 22–24, 81, 88, 99–101, 160, 196, 206–7, 217, 224, 229, 243
Leguía, Jorge Guillermo, 95
Leo XIII, 68, 82, 84, 106, 158, 222, 257, 284–85, 325
León, Lorenzo, 314
Leonardo, Ennio, 333
León Bueno, José, 211
Leuridan, Juan, 330
Liberation theology, 31–32, 36–37, 237, 277, 280–82, 286, 289–90, 301, 303–9, 312-13, 317–19, 329, 345, 351, 355, 363
Lira, Guillermo, 221
Lissón, Emilio, 23, 88, 95, 100–101, 123, 142–43, 160, 207, 230, 233
Little Sisters of Jesus, 339
Lituma, Luis, 231–32
Llanque, Domingo, 324
Loayza, José Jorge, 83
López de Romaña, Alberto, 72, 213, 219
López de Romaña, Alejandro, 72, 79, 89, 137
López de Romaña, Alfredo and Roberto, 72, 78, 213, 219
López de Romaña, Juan Manuel, 72, 78–79, 137
López de Romaña, Mariano, 72, 108
López Trujillo, Alfonso, 311–14, 317
Lord of Miracles, 10, 16, 91–92, 335
Lorente, Sebastián, 141
Lorscheider, Aloisio, 254, 312–13
Losada y Puga, Cristóbal, 236–37
Loyola Weinart, Sister, 162, 169
Luis, Plácido, 159
Lulli, Antonio, 212, 242
Luna Pizarro, Javier de, 19, 39–40, 43, 46, 62–63, 65, 68–69, 74, 107, 142, 147, 188, 193, 223
Luna Victoria, Romeo, 151, 246–47, 274, 279, 283, 286, 288, 297

Macauley, Neil, 332
McCarthy, William, 267
McClellan, Daniel, 255–56, 266–68, 293
Macera, Pablo, 168
McGrath, Marcos, 254, 278
MacGregor, Felipe, 150–51, 160, 232, 247, 256–57, 304, 343, 350–51
Mackay, John, 95
McNabb, John, 272
Maguiña, Alejandrino, 83
Maloney, Thomas, 298
Marianists, 161, 163–64, 166–67, 311, 349
Mariátegui, Francisco Javier, 63, 73
Mariátegui, José Carlos, 10, 92, 177, 225–27
Marina, Manuel, 87
Marists, 158–60, 166–67, 283, 304, 330, 348
Maritain, Jacques, 25, 208, 211, 248
Marmanillo, Teófilo, 217
marriage encounter, 36, 301–2, 328, 333–24
Martin, Joe, 269–70
Martínez, Luis, 333, 351
Martínez de Compañón, 13
Maryknoll, Fathers and Sisters of, 27, 56, 209, 255, 264–70, 274, 320, 323, 334, 339, 354–55
Marzal, Manuel, 356
Masiá, José María, 107–8
Masonry, 21–22, 45, 59, 73, 77, 83, 98, 108, 139, 148–49
Medellín, 30, 34–35, 139, 237–38, 253–54, 259, 261, 263, 268–69, 273–75, 278–82, 287, 289–92, 298, 300–303, 307, 309–15, 322, 324, 329, 340, 345, 353, 358, 361–63
Melgar, Mariano, 143
Mendoza, Alcides, 314
Mendoza Rodríguez, Juan, 343
Mercado Jarrín, Edgardo, 283
Mercedarians, 43, 103, 105, 121, 140, 144
Metz, Johannes, 27
Metzinger, Luciano, 254, 278, 314, 323, 353
Miccheli, Lorenzo, 322
Michenfelder, Joseph, 267
Mimbela, Pablo Sixto, 121
Miró Quesada, Aurelio, 150
Mission of Lima, 254–55, 260, 320
Missionaries of the Sacred Heart, 122, 128–29
Moltmann, Jürgen, 27
Montagne Markholz, Ernesto, 122
Montagne Sanchez, Ernesto, 283
Morales Basadre, Ricardo, 247, 286, 287–88
Morales Bermúdez, Francisco, 34, 137, 150, 283, 300, 345
Moreno, José Ignacio, 64
Moreyra, José Ezequiel, 48–49, 53, 69
Morris, William, 163, 349–50
Moscoso y Peralta, Manuel, 1, 13
MOSICP (Christian Union Movement), 252
Mussolini, 216

Nardini, Vicente, 105, 145
National Office of Catholic Education (ONDEC), 238, 245, 342–47
Navarete, José Francisco, 140
Noriega, Alfredo, 151, 321, 352
Noriega, Mariano, 241
Noriega, Pedro José, 219

Oblates of Immaculate Mary, 271, 332
Ocopa, Santa Rosa de, 42, 44, 46, 106–7, 109–10, 112, 154, 252
Odría, Manuel, 209, 243, 249, 250, 258, 343
Olivas Escudero, Fidel, 60, 87–88, 154, 200–201
Onda Azul, 266, 354–55
Ondonégui, Deogracias, 186–87
ONIS (National Office of Social Information), 279–80, 286, 291–93, 296–97, 305, 307, 347
Opus Dei, 31, 271, 310, 349–50
Oquillas, Conrado, 50–51, 125, 213
Orbegozo, Ignacio, 271, 310, 314
Orbegozo, Luis J., 19, 106
Ortega y Gasset, 5, 7
Osores, Arturo, 220
Our Lady of the O, 16, 78, 83, 149

Pacheco, Fernando, 79
Paget, Hermasia, 147
Palencia, Angel, 330
Palma, Ricardo, 77
Pando Egúsquiza, César, 259
Papal Volunteers (PAVLA), 272
Pardo, José, 22, 72, 99, 173, 230
Pardo, Manuel, 66, 72, 118, 141, 148, 151–53, 173
Pardo, Mariana Barreda de, 78, 173
Pardo, Petronila Lavalle de, 72, 117
Pardo y Aliaga, Felipe, 147, 173
Pareja Paz-Soldán, José, 211, 231
Pashby, Jerry, 270
Pasquel, José Manuel, 186
Passionists, 132–33, 167, 325–28

Index 415

Pastor, Alfredo, 279, 329
Paul VI, 259, 276–78
Pax Romana, 240, 252
Paz Soldán, José Gregorio, 98, 136–37, 148
Paz Soldán, Mariano, 42
Pease, Franklin, 343
Pelach, Enrique, 271, 310
Penzotti, Francisco, 21, 93–94
Pérez, Estéban, 49
Pérez Araníbar, Augusto, 220
Pérez del Pozo, Roberto, 211, 237
Pérez Godoy, Ricardo, 145, 258
Pérez Palacios, Matilde, 148
Pérez Silva, Federico, 123
Perón, Juan Domingo, 7
Perroud, Pedro, 124
Peruvian Association of Missionaries, 267
Peruvian Catholic Society, 65, 70
Pezet, Juan Antonio, 147
Picher, Eduardo, 212, 238, 278, 304, 314
Piérola, Eva María de, 83
Piérola, Felipe Amadeo, 74
Piérola, Jesús Iturbide de, 74, 83
Piérola, Nicolás de, 20, 22, 69, 73–75, 83, 99, 120, 217
Pierre, Abbé, 255–57
Pineda, José, 96–97
Pironio, Eduardo, 254, 278
Pius IX, 20, 46, 63, 68, 105
Pius X, 285
Pius XI, 209–210, 242
Pius XII, 27, 242, 244, 257, 263
Placencia, Amelio, 123, 212, 236, 241
Polar, Mario, 250–51
Popular Christian Party, 212, 251
popular religiosity, 89–93, 177–79, 202–6, 227, 361–62 *See* confraternities, Lord of Miracles
Popular Union, 213–21, 238, 242
Porras Barrenechea, Raúl, 95, 137, 211
Portal, Ismael, 81
Pozzo, Carlos, 321
Prado, Javier, 21, 71, 150, 153
Prado, Mariano Ignacio, 149
Prado Pérez-Rosas, Manuel, 150, 314
Prado Ugarteche, Manuel, 137, 150
Prevost, Gustavo, 327
Proaño, Leonidas, 278, 313
Program for Deepening Christian Commitment, 334
Protestantism, 8–10, 20–22, 43, 59, 68, 83, 85, 93–95, 140, 159, 161, 166, 195, 204, 236, 242, 305, 355–58
Puebla, 35, 139, 237–38, 253–54, 279, 299, 300–301, 311–315, 317, 358, 361–363
Puerta, Angel de la, 212
Puirredón (Puyrredón), Ismael, 56, 184
Pulgar, Javier, 231

Quadragesimo Anno, 216
Quinn, Albano, 271, 322
Quiroz, Francisco, 143
"Quollur Rit'i," 91, 203

Rada y Gamio, Pedro José, 81, 83
Radio Santa Rosa, 330, 354–55
Rahner, Karl, 26, 305
Ramírez del Villar, Roberto, 250–51
Ratzinger, Joseph, 318
Razquin, María Teresa, 341
Recavarren, Margarita, 341
Recharte, Angélica, 128
recurzo de fuerza, 42
Redemptorists, 109, 124, 133–34, 255
regalism, 42–43
Regan, James, 327
Renault, Ferminie, 117
Rendueles, Manuel, 327
Reparation, Sisters of the, 157–58
Rerum Novarum, 23, 81–85, 194, 197, 208, 215, 284
Rey de Castro, Alberto, 219–220
Rey de Castro, Jaime, 250–51
Richter Prada, Federico, 112
Richter Prada, Pedro, 283
Ridruejo, José, 340
Riva-Agüero, José de la, 24, 25, 72, 109, 137, 157, 208, 211, 221–24, 228–31, 235
Roca, José Antonio, 69, 74, 117
Rodríguez, Alberto, 351
Rodríguez Ballón, Leonardo, 110–11
Rodríguez de Mendoza, Toribio, 13, 40, 141
Rojas, José Ramón, 108
Romero, Emilio, 90–91
Rubio, Marcial, 282
Ruggere, Pedro, 334
Ruiz, Ambrosio, 234
Ruiz, Samuel, 278
Rumi Maqui, 195

Sacred Heart, Missionaries of the, 122, 128–29, 161
Sacred Heart, Sisters of the, 93, 149, 151–54, 164–69, 213, 341, 348
Sacred Hearts, Fathers of the, 137, 139, 156–57, 165–67, 210, 228, 230, 323, 341–42, 352

Sacred Hearts, Sisters of the, 137–38, 145–48, 156–57, 165–67, 213
Saint James Society, 264–65, 269–70, 320
Saint John of God, Religious of, 112–13
Saint Joseph of Carondolet Sisters, 340–341
Saint Joseph of Cluny Sisters, 116–17, 119, 133, 139, 166–67
Saint Joseph of Tarbes Sisters, 119–20, 133
Saint Martin of Porres (or Porras), 16, 55, 91
Saint Rose of Lima, 91, 233
Saíz, Odorico, 111
Salat, Rudy, 240
Salazar Bondy, Augusto, 287
Sales Arrieta, Francisco de, 111, 146
Sales Soto, Francisco, 78, 80, 157
Salesians, 83, 118, 130, 138–39, 155–56, 164, 166–67, 280, 347, 354
Samanez Ocampo, David, 217, 229
San Antonio Abad, 65, 195
San Carlos, 65–66, 140–41, 143
San Carlos y San Marcelo, 50–52, 55, 125, 137, 143–44
Sánchez, Luis Alberto, 95, 137–38, 168, 360
Sánchez, Vicente, 211
Sánchez Carrión, José Faustino, 144
Sánchez Cerro, Luis Miguel, 48, 101, 207, 213, 215–18, 220–21, 225, 229, 231, 233
Sánchez Moreno, Luis, 271, 310
Sánchez Rangel, Hipólito, 111
San Jerónimo, Seminary of, 65, 123, 140, 143
San Marcos University, 21, 55, 65, 72, 95, 100–101, 121, 140–41, 153, 211, 224–25, 228–31, 233, 238, 304, 330–31
Sanmartí, Primitivo, 70, 78, 88
San Martín, José de, 140
San Román, Jesús, 327
Santa Catalina, 13, 43
Santa María Catholic University, 163, 340, 349–50
Santo Toribio, Seminary of, 19, 39–40, 49–50, 55, 64, 74, 100, 124–25, 142–43, 160, 209–10, 237–38, 348 *See* Faculty of Theology
Santos García, Brother, 169
Saravia, Hugo, 352
Sarita Colonia, 91
Sawyer, Joan, 339
Schillebeeckx, Edward, 26, 305
Schmidt, Edward, 389

Schmitz, Germán, 128, 248, 279, 295, 314, 321, 334
SENATI, 256
Seoane, Edgardo, 212, 238
"Siempre," 329–30
Sisters of Mercy of Mother Theresa, 339
social weeks, 243–44, 251, 257–58
Sodalitium Christianae Vitae, 311, 319, 329
Solano, Francisco, 69
Southern Andean church, 322–25
Stevenson, William B., 43
Stiglich, Fernando, 212, 240, 249
Stiglich, Germán, 212, 237
Suárez, Eduardo, 212
Summer Language Institute, 328
Superior Institute of Theological Studies (ISET), 307, 340–42
SUTEP, 346–47

Tabini, Alejandro, 256
Taki Onqoy, 10
Taurel, Rafael María, 189
Tezza, Luis, 120, 126
Theresians, 164, 348
Thomson, James, 93, 140
Tola Pasquel, José, 352
Toledo, Francisco de, 57
Toribio de Mogrovejo, 103
Torres, Camilo, 29
Touvier, Juan Marcelo, 123
Tovar, Manuel, 39, 49, 50, 55, 69, 74, 83, 96, 142–43, 230
Trent, Council of, 8–9, 26, 302
Tubino, Fidel, 278, 350
Túpac Amaru, 6, 196

Uchcu Pedro, 200–201
Ugarte Pérez, Juan Antonio, 310
Ulloa, Manuel, 150
UNEC (National Union of Catholic Students), 212, 236, 238–41, 258, 281, 305–8, 328–330
Unfried, Lorenzo, 265
UNIFE (Women's University of the Sacred Heart), 154, 349–50
University of El Pacífico, 256, 349–50
University of San Martín de Porres, 330, 349–50
Uriarte, Buenaventura, 111
Uriel García, José, 205
Urraca, Father, 91
Ursulines, 161–62, 165–67, 341–42

Valcárcel, Luis, 94, 217
Valdivia, Juan Gualberto, 46, 62, 74, 223–24

Index

Vallebuona, Emilio, 346
Vallejos Santoni, Luis, 237–38, 246, 322, 324, 329
Vallier, Ivan, x, 13, 18, 24
Vankann, Pedro, 162
Vannutelli, Serafín, 105
Varela y Valle, Felipe, 78, 83
Vargas, Augusto, 151
Vargas, Fernando, 151, 311, 314
Vargas, Getulio, 7
Vargas, Isaías, 194–95, 197
Vargas Ugarte, Rubén, 39, 53–54, 98, 150, 231–32, 234, 350
Vasco de Quiroga, 103
Vásquez, Pablo, 330
Vatican I, 65, 98, 107, 148
Vatican II, 3, 11, 26–27, 30, 33–35, 68, 116, 119, 122, 127, 132, 139, 160–61, 170, 209, 239–40, 246–48, 259–63, 267–68, 273–74, 277, 282, 285, 291, 299, 301–2, 309–11, 319, 324, 328–29, 335–40, 342, 353, 358
Vega Centeno, Emilio, 217
Vega Centeno, Hernando, 89, 194
Vega Centeno, Máximo, 238
Vega Christie, David, 210–11, 232, 237, 248
Veintemilla, Rafaela, 120–21
Vekemans, Roger, 311
Velaochaga, Jorge, 170, 231
Velaochaga, Luis, 279
Velasco Alvarado, Juan, 7, 30–31, 34–35, 151, 246, 250–51, 275–78, 283, 285–86, 295–99, 300, 345
Vidaurre, Manuel Lorenzo de, 41, 61
Vigil, Francisco de Paula González, 40, 46, 62–63, 73, 143
Villanueva, Armando, 159, 168
Villanueva, Gastón, 327
Villarán, Manuel Vicente, 221
Vinatea, Abraham, 79, 89
Vincentians, 100, 114–17, 122–23, 125, 133, 137, 143, 155, 160, 166, 223
Vivanco, Manuel Ignacio de, 64

Wagner de Reyna, Alberto, 211, 232
Walsh, James, 266
Wicht, Juan Julio, 288
Wiese, Carlos, 153
Wiese, María, 148
Winternitz, Adolfo, 351
Wood, Thomas, 94
Work of Hispanic Priestly Cooperation (OCSHA), 271

YMCA, 95, 211
Yonekawa, Calixte G., 97
Yonekawa, Urbain-Marie, 97
Young Christian Workers (JOC), 236, 241, 257, 281, 307–8, 328

Zegarra, Felipe, 306
Zevallos, Noé, 341–42
Zubieta, Ramón, 96, 131, 134

The Catholic Church in Peru, 1821–1985
was composed in 10.5/12 Baskerville by
World Composition Services, Inc., Sterling,
Virginia; printed and bound by Braun-Brumfield,
Inc., Ann Arbor, Michigan; and designed and
produced by Kachergis Book Design,
Pittsboro, North Carolina.